iPad® and iPhone®
Tips and Tricks

SIXTH EDITION

Jason R. Rich

800 East 96th Street,
Indianapolis, Indiana 46240 USA

iPAD® AND iPHONE® TIPS AND TRICKS, SIXTH EDITION

ISBN-13: 978-0-7897-5679-4 | ISBN-10: 0-7897-5679-X

Library of Congress Control Number: 2016955014

1   16

TRADEMARKS

WARNING AND DISCLAIMER

SPECIAL SALES

EDITOR-IN-CHIEF
Greg Wiegand

SENIOR ACQUISITIONS EDITOR
Laura Norman

DEVELOPMENT EDITOR
Wordsmithery, LLC

MANAGING EDITOR
Sandra Schroeder

SENIOR PROJECT EDITOR
Tonya Simpson

INDEXER
Valerie Perry

PROOFREADER
Elizabeth Campbell

TECHNICAL EDITOR
Paul Sihvonen-Binder

EDITORIAL ASSISTANT
Cindy Teeters

COVER DESIGNER
Chuti Prasertsith

COMPOSITOR
Maureen Forys, Happenstance Type-O-Rama

CONTENTS AT A GLANCE

TABLE OF CONTENTS

ABOUT THE AUTHOR

Jason R. Rich (www.jasonrich.com) is an accomplished author, journalist, and photographer, as well as an avid iPhone, iPad, Apple Watch, Apple TV, and Mac user. In addition to having written the five previous editions of this book, some of his recently published books for Que Publishing include *My Digital Photography for Seniors, My Digital Entertainment for Seniors,* and *My Digital Travel for Seniors.*

Jason's photography (www.jasonrich.photography) continues to appear with his articles in major daily newspapers, national magazines, and online, as well as in his various books. He also works with professional actors, models, and recording artists to develop their portfolios and take their headshots. Jason also continues to pursue travel and animal photography.

Through his work as an enrichment lecturer, he often offers workshops and classes about digital photography, the Internet, and consumer technology aboard cruise ships operated by Royal Caribbean, Princess Cruise Lines, Norwegian Cruise Lines, and Celebrity Cruise Lines, as well as through adult education programs in the New England area. Please follow Jason R. Rich on Twitter (@JasonRich7) and Instagram (@JasonRich7).

DEDICATION

This book is dedicated to my family and friends, including my niece, Natalie, my nephew, Parker, and my Yorkshire Terrier, Rusty, who is always by my side as I'm writing.

ACKNOWLEDGMENTS

Thanks once again to Laura Norman, Cindy Teeters, and Greg Wiegand at Que for inviting me to work on this project, and for their ongoing support. Thanks also to Charlotte Kughen, and Paul Sihvonen-Binder, who were instrumental during the book's editing and layout process. I'd also like to thank everyone else who worked on the editing, design, layout, marketing, printing, and distribution of this book for their hard work and dedication.

WE WANT TO HEAR FROM YOU!

As the reader of this book, *you* are our most important critic and commentator. We value your opinion and want to know what we're doing right, what we could do better, what areas you'd like to see us publish in, and any other words of wisdom you're willing to pass our way.

We welcome your comments. You can email or write to let us know what you did or didn't like about this book—as well as what we can do to make our books better.

Please note that we cannot help you with technical problems related to the topic of this book.

When you write, please be sure to include this book's title and author as well as your name and email address. We will carefully review your comments and share them with the author and editors who worked on the book.

Email: feedback@quepublishing.com

Mail: Que Publishing
           ATTN: Reader Feedback
           800 East 96th Street
           Indianapolis, IN 46240 USA

READER SERVICES

Register your copy of *iPad and iPhone Tips and Tricks* at quepublishing.com for convenient access to downloads, updates, and corrections as they become available. To start the registration process, go to quepublishing.com/register and log in or create an account*. Enter the product ISBN, 9780789756794, and click Submit. When the process is complete, you will find any available bonus content under Registered Products.

* Be sure to check the box that you would like to hear from us to receive exclusive discounts on future editions of this product.

Introduction

Time never stands still, and neither does the evolution of smartphone and tablet technology. In late 2016, Apple once again introduced a major update to its iOS operating system and also released new iPhone and iPad mobile devices—each offering a plethora of features and functions not available in older models.

With each new edition of the iOS operating system, Apple focuses on enhancing the overall user experience, making it possible for the iPhone or iPad to more easily integrate into someone's day-to-day life, while serving as an even more powerful communications, productivity, and organizational tool.

As you're about to discover, iOS 10 is no exception, especially when it's used with one of the latest iPhone or iPad models, such as the iPhone 7 or iPhone 7 Plus.

This all-new, sixth edition of *iPad and iPhone Tips and Tricks* quickly gets you up to speed on using iOS 10 by uncovering the most important functionality that this operating system

has to offer, while acclimating you to the newest functions of the latest iPhone and iPad models.

However, if you haven't yet upgraded to one of these new devices, you can still take full advantage of what iOS 10 has to offer, as long as you're using a compatible smartphone or tablet that was released by Apple in the past few years.

> **NOTE** In addition to the iPhone and iPad models released in late 2016 (and beyond), the iOS 10 operating system is compatible with the iPhone 5, iPhone 5c, iPhone 5s, iPhone SE, iPhone 6, iPhone 6 Plus, iPhone 6s, and iPhone 6s Plus, as well as the iPod touch (6th generation). It's also compatible with the following iPad models: the iPad mini 2, iPad mini 3, iPad mini 4, iPad 4th generation, iPad Air, iPad Air 2, iPad Pro (9.7-inch), and iPad Pro (12.9-inch).
>
> Keep in mind that although iOS 10 runs on these devices, not all of the new features and functions are compatible with all iPhone and iPad models.

> **TIP** If you purchased a new iPhone, iPad, or iPod touch after September 16, 2016, iOS 10 came preinstalled on your mobile device, but you might still need to upgrade to a more recent version of iOS 10 (such as iOS 10.1 or later).

For those who are new to using an iPhone or iPad and have recently migrated from another smartphone or tablet (such as an Android device), this edition of *iPad and iPhone Tips and Tricks* teaches you what you need to know to become proficient using iOS 10 on your new smartphone or tablet.

> **TIP** If you're making the switch from an Android mobile device to an iPhone or iPad, be sure to take advantage of Apple's Move to iOS app for Android. This free app, which is available from the Google Play Store, helps you easily transfer all your important data from your old Android smartphone or tablet to your new iOS mobile device.

With the introduction of iOS 10, Apple has implemented hundreds of new features and functions and improved upon what was offered by iOS 9. For example, the Music and Maps apps have been redesigned, and the Photos app now makes it even easier to find, organize, view, edit, enhance, print, and share your digital photos. You'll also discover a handful of awesome new tools in the Messages app that make communicating with your contacts even more enjoyable.

When it comes to home automation, iOS 10's new Home app makes it more efficient to manage the compatible lights, locks, thermostat, home security, and major appliances in your home. As always, Siri enables you to control your iPhone or iPad using voice commands.

iOS 10 **WHAT'S NEW** When it comes to screen size, iPhone and iPad users have more of a choice than ever before. Depending on which model iPhone you choose, it will have a 4", 4.7", or 5.5" (diagonal) display. The latest iPad, iPad Pro, and iPad mini models offer a 7.9", 9.7", or 12.9" (diagonal) display.

Regardless of which smartphone or tablet model you select, all the latest devices run iOS 10. However, the appearance and layout of screens and menus in apps automatically adapt and vary based on the device you're using. For example, Figure I.1 shows the Music app running on an iPad mini 4 (with a 7.9" display), whereas Figure I.2 shows the same iOS 10 edition of the Music app running on an iPhone 6s (with 4.7" display).

Thus, as you're looking at screenshots throughout this book, keep in mind that what you see on your device's screen will vary slightly if you're using a different model iPhone or iPad than what was used to create the screenshot.

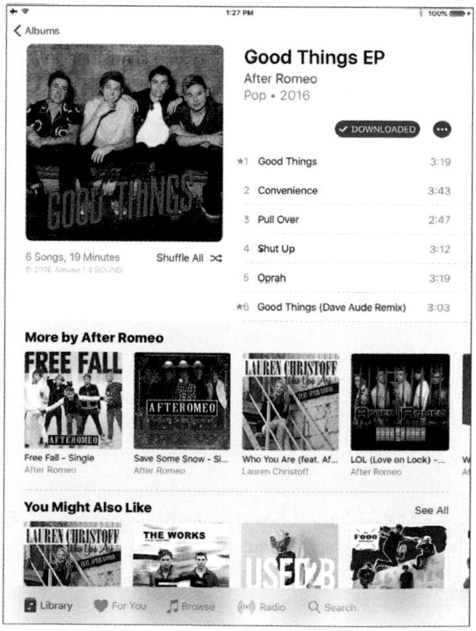

Figure I.1
The Music app running on an iPad mini 4.

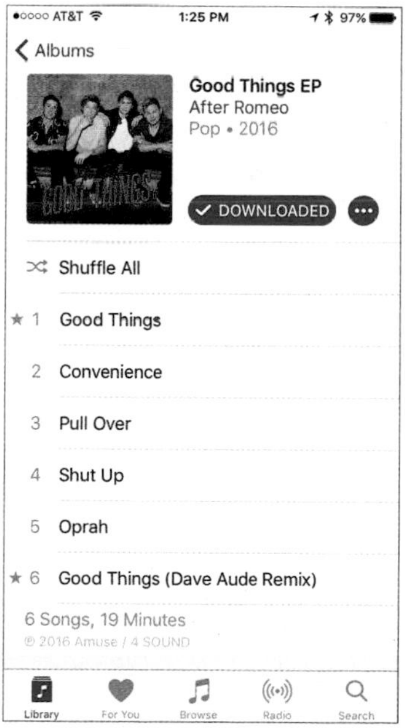

Figure I.2
The Music app running on an iPhone 6s.

For iPad Pro users, iOS 10 has improved and expanded what's possible using the optional Apple Pencil (when used with compatible apps), and on the latest iPhone models there have been enhancements to the device's 3D touch capabilities that make it faster and easier to access apps, commands, features, and functions from the Home screen and within compatible apps.

(iOS 10) **WHAT'S NEW** Although the iPhone 7 and iPhone 7 Plus offer faster processors and higher internal storage capacity options (32GB, 128GB, or 256GB), along with a bunch of other new features, what's missing is a headphone jack. Both new iPhone models come with Apple EarPods that utilize a Lightning connector (which plugs in to the Lightning port located on the bottom of the latest iPhones). However, these new phones also come with a Lightning-to-3.5mm headphone jack adapter, enabling you to use your favorite headphones or earpods with the iPhone 7 or iPhone 7 Plus.

Alternatively, the new and optional AirPods ($159.00) are higher-end wireless earpods for listening to audio from any model iPhone or iPad. A wide range of wireless (Bluetooth) headphones are also available from Beats by Dr. Dre and many other manufacturers, as are headphones and earpods with a Lightning connector (instead of a 3.5mm headphone jack).

Not only has iOS 10 introduced awesome improvements to the operating system itself, but many of the core apps that come preinstalled with iOS 10—such as Contacts, Calendar, Reminders, Notes, Safari, Mail, and Messages—have some impressive and useful new features. Plus, you'll discover how to use the new or redesigned apps that come bundled with iOS 10, like Home, News, and Music.

Of course, features introduced with iOS 9 continue to be improved upon. For example, using the Continuity and Handoff features, you can begin using one application on your iPhone and then pick up exactly where you left off on your iPad or Mac (or vice versa). In addition, it's possible to answer incoming calls made to your iPhone from your iPad, Apple Watch, or Mac, as long as your smartphone is nearby and wirelessly linked with your other computers and devices.

For iPad users, the Split Screen, Slide Over, and Picture in Picture features have also been enhanced, and they now work with even more apps. These features allow you to truly multitask while using your tablet because it's possible to simultaneously work with two apps, or watch video content while using another app.

If you're a veteran iPhone or iPad user, when you upgrade from iOS 9 to iOS 10, you'll discover that the graphical interface is pretty similar to what you're already accustomed to, although improvements and tweaks have been made.

> **NOTE** Throughout this book, *iOS mobile device* refers to any Apple iPhone, iPad, or Apple mobile device that's running the iOS 10 operating system.
>
> Unless a specific iPhone or iPad model is mentioned (such as iPhone 6s or iPhone 7), the term *iPhone* refers to all iPhone models capable of running iOS 10. Likewise, unless a specific iPad model is described (such as iPad Pro or iPad mini 4), the term *iPad* refers to all iPad models that are capable of running Apple's latest mobile device operating system.
>
> If you plan to continue using iOS 9 with your iOS mobile device, pick up a copy of *iPad and iPhone Tips and Tricks*, Fifth Edition, which focuses on the older version of Apple's mobile device operating system.

Many app icons (on the Home screen) have a new look, and the locations of on-screen icons and menu options have been revised. The Lock Screen, Notifications screen, Spotlight Search screen, and Command Center menu have also been redesigned and offer faster access to useful information and popular functions. How to use each of these tools is described later in the book.

If you're a first-time iPhone or iPad user, congratulations! Now is the perfect time to introduce yourself to these mobile devices or switch from another smartphone or tablet to what Apple has to offer. Not only can you expect an exciting experience as you begin using your new iPhone or iPad hardware that's running the iOS 10 operating system, but you have the opportunity to access the App Store to use any of the more than 2 million third-party apps that can greatly expand the capabilities of these mobile devices.

> **NOTE** Chapter 10, "Improve Your Health and Manage Your Wealth Using Your iPhone," explains how Apple Pay offers a secure way to use your iPhone (and in some cases your iPad) to make purchases from the iTunes Store, your favorite retail stores, and/or online stores by taking advantage of the Touch ID sensor that's built in to Apple's more recently released smartphones and tablets. Among other things, the Touch ID sensor enables you to scan your fingerprint to securely confirm debit or credit card purchases.
>
> This past year, not only have hundreds of new banks and credit unions begun supporting Apple Pay, but thousands of additional retail and online merchants now accept it. In fact, you probably have seen the Apple Pay logo displayed near the checkout counter at many of your favorite retail stores, and these sightings will become even more frequent in 2017 and beyond.
>
> To view a list of Apple Pay participating banks in the United States, Europe, Canada, and Asia-Pacific countries, visit https://support.apple.com/en-us/HT204916.

In addition, Apple Pay supports the Discover and American Express (Amex) credit cards, as well as store credit cards from participating merchants. You can use the Wallet app (which comes preinstalled on the latest iPhone models) to manage retail store reward cards, so when you adopt the Wallet app into your life, you can dramatically slim down your traditional wallet.

In a nutshell, iOS 10 has become better at integrating the technological capabilities of the iPhone or iPad with apps and the Internet to put a vast amount of personalized information at your fingertips, exactly when and where you need it. This includes content such as breaking news stories, your personal schedule, important emails, incoming text/instant messages, and your personal financial information from your bank(s) and credit card issuers. Plus, these mobile devices make it more efficient to stay in contact with people via phone calls, video calls, emails, text/instant messages, and/or social media.

DISCOVER WHAT'S NEW IN iOS 10

Let's take a quick look at some of the major new features and enhancements made to iOS 10. You'll learn strategies for best utilizing the majority of these features later in the book. But first, here's a rundown of what's new and noteworthy about iOS 10:

- **3D Touch**—When used with a compatible iPhone, accessing popular app-specific features from the Home screen is now easier than ever. 3D Touch functionality now works with more preinstalled apps and third-party apps than before.

- **Apple Pay**—In addition to allowing you to use your debit or credit card to make iTunes purchases or retail purchases, the feature now works with an ever-growing selection of online shopping websites, making it easier to approve and pay for purchases using the Touch ID sensor that's built in to compatible iPhones and iPads.

> **NOTE** If your iOS mobile device gets lost or stolen, simply use the Find My iPhone feature to lock down the device. If you have Apple Pay activated, your stored credit/debit card details can't be used by an iPhone thief because their fingerprint will not be recognized by the device's Touch ID sensor. Because Apple Pay does not retain your actual credit/debit card numbers, there's no need to contact your bank to cancel the cards and have them reissued.

■ **Bedtime**—Built in to the Clock app, this new feature helps you manage your sleep schedule by offering a recurring wake-up alarm and corresponding reminders when it's time to go to sleep.

WHAT'S NEW Exclusively offered with the iPhone 7 Plus are two 12-megapixel rear-facing cameras. When using the Camera app, for example, you can now instantly switch between the front- and either one of the rear-facing cameras to take the perfect shot. The rear-facing cameras include one with a wide-angle lens and another with a telephoto lens. This allows for a 2x optional zoom or up to 10x digital zoom. (The iPhone 7 and older iPhone models do not have an optional zoom, and have a digital zoom only up to 5x.)

Both the iPhone 7 and iPhone 7 Plus also include the new Quad-LED True Tone flash, optical image stabilization, body and face detection, and a collection of other digital photography features that enable you to take awesome eye-catching photos, indoors or outdoors, and in a wide range of lighting situations. These are the most powerful cameras ever built into any iPhone.

■ **Control Center**—In addition to offering quick access to some of the iPhone's and iPad's most popular tools, features, and functions, the newly redesigned Control Center gives you access to the new Night Shift mode, as well as a separate window (referred to as a *card*) offering Music and Video app controls.

■ **Home**—Many home automation devices, such as light bulbs, thermostats, door locks, home security cameras, and some major appliances, can now be controlled from an iOS mobile device (via the Internet). However, until now, each device needed to be operated using its own proprietary app. Thanks to the new Home app, all home automation devices that are HomeKit compatible can be controlled using this single app and/or Siri (which comes preinstalled with iOS 10).

■ **Maps**—Once again, the Maps app has been redesigned to offer a broader range of information, in addition to even more accurate navigational directions. Maps now integrates with the OpenTable app, so you can make restaurant reservations while looking up a restaurant from within the Maps app. It's also possible to request a ride from Uber or Lyft when you look up an address or seek out directions between two locations from within the Maps app. In addition to more accurate walking or driving directions, mass transit directions are available in a growing number of cities around the world. Using the turn-by-turn directions, it's easy to find points of interest (such as a gas station or restaurant) along the way, plus you get a realistic time of arrival to your destination based on the route you're taking, traffic conditions, and your current travel speed.

- **Messages**—This app still allows you to send/receive text messages, but it now also offers several additional (and in some cases more fun) ways to communicate. For example, it's now possible to include large (animated) stickers in your messages, convey information graphically using a larger collection of emojis, plus emphasize important messages with awesome-looking full-screen effects, such as animated fireworks, balloons, or confetti (as shown in Figure I.3). Using your finger (or the Apple Pencil on a compatible iPad), it's also possible to handwrite or annotate messages rather than type them.

Figure I.3

Add animated stickers, emojis, animated backgrounds, and a wide range of other content to your text messages in the Messages app.

- **Music**—The iOS 10 edition of the Music app has been redesigned, giving users easier access to the Apple Music service, Apple's streaming radio stations, and their personal collections of digital music.

NOTE As mentioned in Chapter 15, "Get Acquainted with the Music, Videos, and iTunes Store Apps," the Apple Music service requires a monthly subscription fee of $9.99 for a personal account or $14.99 for a family account, but a free, three-month trial subscription is offered to everyone. This is an online-based service, so your mobile device requires cellular or Wi-Fi Internet access to use it.

- **News**—The iOS 10 edition of the News app has been redesigned to make it easier to access only the articles and breaking news headlines that are of direct interest to you. In addition to enhanced personalization options, the app enables users to subscribe to specific publications and access breaking news notifications with ease.

- **Notification Center**—The new layout of the Notification Center makes it easier to customize and organize what information is displayed. This includes app-specific alerts, alarms, and notifications, recently used apps, access to news headlines, and control over customizable app-specific widgets.

> ### ☑ TIP
>
> To access the Notification Center window, regardless of which app you're working with or what you're doing on your iOS mobile device, simply swipe your finger from the top of the screen in a downward direction. To begin customizing how Notification Center functions on your device, launch Settings and then tap the Notifications option listed in the main Settings menu.
>
> You can access additional customization options by launching Notification Center, tapping the Today tab, and then scrolling to the bottom of the screen. Tap the Edit button to determine what information should appear in this screen, and to rearrange the order in which information is displayed.

- **Photos**—In addition to helping you view, organize, edit, enhance, print, and share digital photos, the updated Photos app enables you to create Memories and group together specific selections of photos and videos to present them in a special way. You can also better organize images using facial, object, and/or scene recognition, which is now built in to the app. It's also possible to edit Live photos (captured using the Live mode that's built in to the Camera app and that's accessible from newer iOS mobile devices).

- **Siri**—Siri now works with more preinstalled iPhone and iPad apps, features, and functions, and it makes better use of the Internet to obtain answers to a broader range of questions. For the first time, third-party app developers can also integrate Siri into apps, so you'll be able to issue voice commands when using those Siri-compatible apps.

- **Split Screen in Safari**—In addition to being able to run two apps side by side on compatible iPads, it's now possible to display two Safari web browser windows simultaneously on the tablet's screen, so you can view two websites at once. To do this, open one web page in Safari. Tap the + icon, and then open a second web browser tab. Place your finger on one of the open browser tabs (displayed near the top of the screen) and drag it to the right or left edge of the screen. Split-screen mode activates and displays two open browser windows (see Figure I.4).

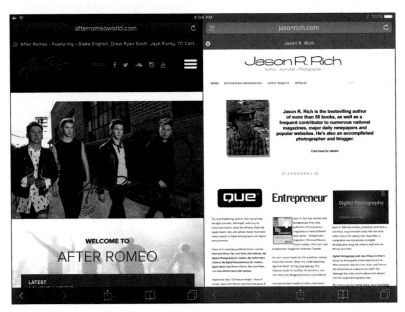

Figure I.4

View and navigate two separate web pages simultaneously when using the iOS 10 version of Safari with a compatible iPad.

> **TIP** After you launch most apps, they continue running in the background if you simply press the Home button to exit out of them to return to the Home screen. You can shut down an app from the app switcher. If an app was running before you turned off your device, however, it automatically reopens in the background when you restart the device.

What you'll soon discover is that with iOS 10, Apple has worked hard to make it easier to truly personalize and customize your iPhone or iPad, while giving you faster and more convenient access to content that's stored in your mobile device or that's available via the Internet. In addition, apps integrate better with one another, as well as with iCloud and other popular online (cloud-based) services. Thus, your most important data, documents, photos, files, content, and information are more readily available to you and can seamlessly sync between all of your iOS mobile devices and computers that are linked to the same online account(s). For example, if you snap a photo on your iPhone, within seconds the photo syncs with and is available on your iPad or Mac, as long as the device has Internet access and is linked to the same iCloud account.

Likewise, if you create a contact entry using the Contacts app, add an appointment to your schedule using the Calendar app, compose a note using the Notes app, or create a to-do list using the Reminders app on one of your mobile devices, that content almost immediately syncs and becomes accessible from all of your other mobile devices and computers, as well as iCloud.com.

How to do this will be explained later, but for now, understand that iOS 10 helps you better create, organize, manage, view, share, print, and sync all of your important information and content, so it's always available when and where it's needed. Meanwhile, your iPhone and/or iPad will also help you communicate more effectively and efficiently in even more ways than ever before.

WHAT'S NEW Real-time collaboration tools have been incorporated into the iOS 10 edition of the Notes app, as well as the iWork for iOS apps (Pages, Numbers, and Keynote). Now, in addition to just sharing app-specific files with other people, you can invite others to collaborate with you by tapping the Collaboration icon in the app and choosing the person with whom you'd like to collaborate. Then, as edits or additions are made to a file that is utilizing the collaboration tools, everyone you're collaborating with will immediately see all file updates, regardless of which collaborator makes them. All of your other app content, however, remains private.

The collaboration tools work with the Notes, Pages, Numbers, and Keynote apps that run on the iPhone, iPad, Mac, and iCloud.com, so from the Notes app on your iPad, for example, you can collaborate with someone else using the Notes app on a Mac.

WHAT THIS BOOK OFFERS

This all-new, sixth edition of *iPad and iPhone Tips and Tricks* helps you quickly discover all the important new features and functions of iOS 10 and shows you how to begin fully utilizing this operating system and its bundled apps so that you can transform your smartphone or tablet into the most versatile, useful, and fun-to-use tool possible.

Each chapter of this book focuses on using various aspects of iOS 10 or the apps that come preinstalled with it. You also discover strategies for finding and installing optional third-party apps from the App Store, plus learn all about how to experience various types of content—from music, TV shows, and movies to eBooks and audiobooks. The book also shows you how to best organize, view, and share your digital photos.

In terms of using your iPhone or iPad as a powerful communications tool, the book introduces you to strategies for efficiently making and receiving calls, sending and receiving text messages, participating in FaceTime calls (video calling), and participating on the online social networking services (like Facebook, Twitter, and Instagram), while simultaneously making full use of iOS 10's latest features. The book also explores how to take full control of and customize your phone or tablet using the tools and features available from Settings, Control Center, and Notification Center.

iPad and iPhone Tips and Tricks, Sixth Edition uncovers tricks for utilizing iCloud with your iOS mobile device, and explains how to use the most popular apps that come bundled with the iOS 10 operating system (including Contacts, Calendar, Reminders, Notes, Mail, Messages, Safari, Camera, Photos, Home, Maps, Music, Videos, Wallet, iCloud Drive, News, FaceTime, and iTunes Store), as well as popular apps released by Apple and third parties that enhance the capabilities of your device, including YouTube, Facebook, and Twitter. You also read about how to manage your health using the iPhone's Health app and how to use Apple Pay.

ATTENTION, PLEASE...

Throughout the book, look for What's New, Tip, Note, Caution, and More Info boxes that convey useful tidbits of information relevant to the chapter you're reading. In some chapters, you'll also discover Quick Tips sections, which quickly outline how to perform a series of common tasks related to the iOS 10 features, functions, or app(s) that are being discussed.

The What's New boxes, for example, highlight new features or functionality introduced in iOS 10, while the More Info boxes provide website URLs or list additional resources that you can use to obtain more information about a particular topic.

IN THIS CHAPTER

- How to turn on and off your iPhone or iPad
- How to upgrade from iOS 9 to iOS 10
- How to interact with your mobile device
- How to keep your iPhone or iPad secure

1

GET ACQUAINTED WITH YOUR iPHONE OR iPAD

The various iPhone and iPad models are similar in some ways, but in other ways they're different. For example, some new iPad Pro models have a built-in camera flash, have a Touch ID sensor built in to the Home button, and support the Apple Pencil accessory, whereas older iPad models do not. All iOS mobile devices run the same iOS operating system and come with a comprehensive collection of preinstalled apps.

Thanks to the iCloud online service, which offers functionality that's integrated into iOS 10 and many of the apps you'll be using, keeping all of your information, data, and content synchronized between all your computers and iOS mobile devices has become a straightforward process, which is covered in Chapter 6, "Use iCloud and the iCloud Drive App."

Before you begin creating, managing, and using data and content, however, it's important to develop a basic understanding of how you'll be interacting with your iPhone or iPad using taps, swipes, and pinch-figure gestures; the device's virtual keyboard; and your voice.

Especially if you're a new iPhone or iPad user, this chapter will help you quickly become familiar with the basic operation of your smartphone or tablet.

CHARGING IT UP, AND GETTING READY TO GO

Your iPhone or iPad comes with a built-in battery that has about a 10-hour battery life, depending on how the device is used throughout the day. To ensure your smartphone or tablet will be ready to use whenever you need it, get into the habit of keeping its battery charged.

You have several options for charging the iPhone or iPad's battery:

■ Use the white USB cable that came with your iOS mobile device to connect your iPhone or iPad to your computer.

■ Connect a power adapter to the USB end of the white cable that came with your device, and then plug in the power adapter to an electrical outlet. Plug in the Lightning connector end of the cable to the bottom of your iPhone or iPad.

■ Connect an optional external battery pack to your iPhone and/or iPad, either directly to its Lightning port or using the white USB cable that came with the device.

■ Invest in an optional car charger that's compatible with your iPhone or iPad, so you can recharge the battery and use the mobile device while you're driving, without consuming battery power.

Displayed in the top-right corner of the screen is the device's battery life indicator (shown in Figure 1.1). When this icon is a solid green color, the battery is fully charged. As the battery depletes, the battery icon becomes white.

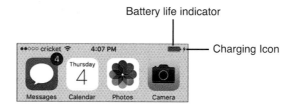

Battery life indicator

Charging Icon

Figure 1.1

The battery life indicator is almost always displayed in the top-right corner of the screen.

> **NOTE** When a lightning bolt icon (refer to Figure 1.1) appears to the right of the battery life indicator, the device is connected to an external power source and is charging. You can continue using your iPhone or iPad while it's charging.

If the battery drains before you plug it into an external power source, your iPhone or iPad automatically shuts down (powers off) and is not functional again until it's plugged in to charge. However, no information or content is lost if the phone turns off due to a dead battery.

> **TIP** In addition to the battery icon, you can have the percentage of battery power remaining display to the immediate left of the battery icon (shown in Figure 1.2). Launch Settings, tap the Battery option, and then turn on the virtual switch associated with the Battery Percentage option.
>
> When your iPhone or iPad's battery is running low but you don't immediately have a way to recharge it, extend the life of the battery by turning on Low Power mode. To turn on this feature, launch Settings, tap the Battery option, and then turn on the virtual switch associated with Low Power mode (shown in Figure 1.3).
>
> As soon as you turn on the Low Power Mode feature, certain features and functions that typically consume a lot of battery power are deactivated, allowing you to extend the life of the battery and continue to use your device a bit longer.

Percentage of
Battery Life
Remaining

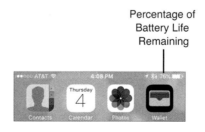

Figure 1.2

Display the percentage of battery power remaining on your iPhone or iPad's display.

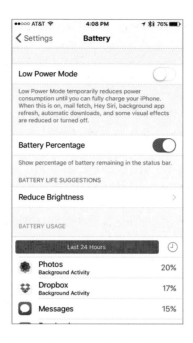

Figure 1.3

Adjust the battery percentage display and the device's Low Power mode from this Battery sub-menu within Settings.

TURNING OFF OR PUTTING TO SLEEP THE iPHONE OR iPAD

Your iOS mobile device can be turned on, turned off, placed into Sleep mode, or placed into Airplane mode.

■ **Turned on**—When your phone or tablet is turned on, it can run apps and perform all the tasks it was designed to do. The touchscreen is active, as is its capability to communicate. To turn on the iPhone or iPad when it is powered off, press and hold the Sleep/Wake button for about 5 seconds, until the Apple logo appears on the screen. Release the Sleep/Wake button, and then wait about 15 seconds while the device boots up. When the Lock screen appears, you're ready to begin using the iPhone or iPad.

> ⌇ **NOTE** Depending on which iPhone or iPad model you're using, the Sleep/Wake button is either on the very top of the device (on the right) or on the right side of the device (near the top).

- **Turned off**—When your iPhone or iPad is turned off and powered down, it is not capable of any form of communication, and all apps that were running are shut down. The device is dormant. To turn off your phone or tablet, press and hold the Sleep/Wake button for about 5 seconds, until the Slide to Power Off banner appears on the screen. Swipe your finger along this red-and-white banner from left to right. The device shuts down.

- **Sleep mode**—To place your iPhone or iPad into Sleep mode, press and release the Sleep/Wake button once. To wake up the device, press the Sleep/Wake button or the Home button. In Sleep mode, your device's screen is turned off but the phone or tablet can still connect to the Internet, receive incoming calls (iPhone) or text messages, retrieve emails, and run apps in the background. Notification Center also remains fully operational, so you can be alerted of preset alarms. Sleep mode offers a way to conserve battery life when you're not actively using your phone or tablet.

> **NOTE** By default, your iPhone or iPad goes into Sleep mode and Auto-Lock after 5 minutes. To adjust this time interval or turn off the Auto-Lock feature, launch Settings, tap the Display & Brightness option, and then tap the Auto-Lock feature. Your options include the ability to activate Auto-Lock after 2, 5, 10, or 15 minutes, or never.

> **TIP** Another way to place an iPad into Sleep mode is to place an optional Apple Smart Cover (or compatible cover) or Apple Smart Keyboard (which doubles as a Smart Cover) over the screen (the iPad Cover Lock/Unlock option must be turned on from the General menu in Settings). In Sleep mode, an iPad "wakes up" for an incoming call (when used with iOS 10's Continuity feature), a FaceTime call, or an incoming text message.

- **Airplane mode**—This mode enables your device to remain fully functional, except it can't communicate in any way using a cellular (3G/4G/LTE) connection. The iPhone cannot make or receive calls, and neither the iPhone nor iPad can send or receive text/instant messages via a cellular network. Apps that do not require Internet access continue to function normally. So, if you're aboard an airplane, you can switch to Airplane mode and continue reading an eBook, playing a game, word processing, watching a movie that you've downloaded from the iTunes Store, or working with a wide range of other apps. After switching into Airplane mode, it is possible to turn Wi-Fi

Internet access back on, yet keep the cellular connection turned off. This is useful if you're traveling abroad, for example, and don't want to incur international cellular roaming charges, or if you're aboard an airplane that offers Wi-Fi service.

> **☑ TIP** To turn on/off Airplane mode, launch Settings, and from the main Settings menu, tap the virtual switch for Airplane mode. Alternatively, launch Control Center (by placing your finger at the bottom of the screen and swiping upward), and then tap the Airplane mode icon.
>
> Once the device is in Airplane mode, keep in mind that from Control Center it's possible to quickly reenable Wi-Fi, if needed, by tapping the Wi-Fi icon.

It's also possible to place an iPhone or iPad into Do Not Disturb mode. This mode automatically routes incoming calls directly to voicemail. You can customize the Do Not Disturb feature to allow certain people that you preselect to reach you, when you otherwise want to be left alone.

> **☑ TIP** To activate and customize the Do Not Disturb feature, launch Settings and tap the Do Not Disturb option. From the Do Not Disturb menu, turn on the Manual or Scheduled virtual switch, based on how you have this feature set up.
>
> To later turn on or off the feature, access the Control Center and tap the crescent moon–shaped icon.
>
> When turned on, a moon icon is displayed on the iPhone or iPad's status bar, and all calls and alerts are silenced. You can turn on or off this feature at any time, or you can preschedule specific times you want Do Not Disturb to be activated, such as between 11:00 p.m. and 7:00 a.m. on weekdays. From the Do Not Disturb menu in Settings, you can also determine whether certain callers are allowed to reach you when the phone is in Do Not Disturb mode.
>
> If you set the Alarm Clock feature in your iPhone or iPad via the Clock app or using Siri, this feature continues to work, even with Do Not Disturb turned on.

When your iPhone is turned off, all incoming calls are forwarded directly to voicemail, and it is not possible to initiate an outgoing call. Likewise, incoming text messages, FaceTime calls, and other communications from the outside world cannot be accepted when an iPhone or iPad is turned off. Instead, when you turn on the device, notifications for these missed messages are displayed in the Notification

Center, in their respective apps, and potentially on the Lock screen, depending on how you set up Notification Center.

---

iOS 10 WHAT'S NEW It's now possible to wake up a compatible iPhone using the new Raise to Wake feature. When this feature is turned on, you automatically wake up an iPhone that's in Sleep mode simply by lifting the device.

To turn on this feature, launch Settings, tap the Display & Brightness option, and then turn on the virtual switch associated with the Raise to Wake feature (see Figure 1.4).

Meanwhile, the Night Shift feature automatically adjusts the display of your iPhone or iPad to make it easier on your eyes to view during nighttime hours. To turn on and customize this option, go to the Display & Brightness menu, and tap the Night Shift option to customize this new feature. When it's been activated, you can manually turn on or off the Night Shift feature from the redesigned Control Center (see Figure 1.5).

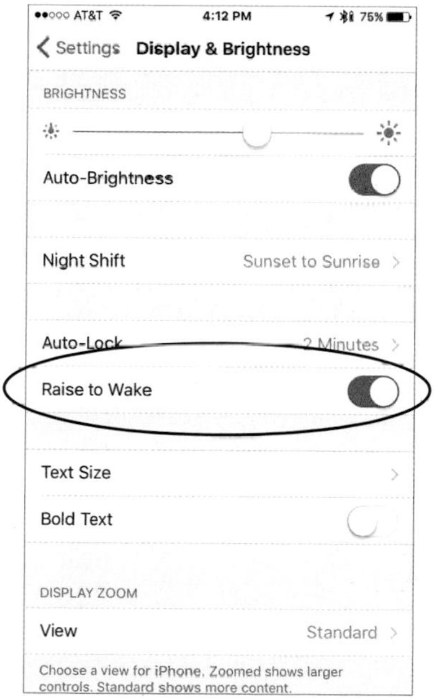

Figure 1.4
You can find the Display & Brightness menu within Settings on an iPhone.

Figure 1.5
Turn on or off the Night Shift feature from within Control Center.

UPGRADING FROM iOS 9 TO iOS 10

Anyone who purchased an iPhone, iPad, or iPod touch before September 1, 2016 needs to upgrade to iOS 10. The easiest way to do this is to use your mobile device to access any Wi-Fi hotspot or wireless home network to establish a high-speed Internet connection. Then, from the device's Home screen, launch Settings.

> **☑ TIP** Before upgrading your iOS mobile device from iOS 9 to iOS 10, be sure to create a backup of your iPhone or iPad using the iTunes Sync Backup feature or the iCloud Backup feature. After you install the iOS 10 operating system, all your apps, data, and personalized device settings will automatically be fully restored.

Next, tap the General option from the main Settings menu, and then tap the Software Update option. If your device is running iOS 9.3.3, for example, a message appears indicating that an operating system upgrade is available. Follow the onscreen prompts to download and install the latest version of iOS 10 for free.

The upgrade process takes between 20 and 30 minutes, depending on which iPhone or iPad model you're using, its internal storage capacity, the Internet connection speed, and how much information is currently stored on your device.

> **✓ TIP** Every few months, Apple updates the iOS to add new features to your iPhone or iPad. When a free iOS update is available, a message appears on your device's screen and a Badge icon appears in the Settings app icon on your Home screen. iOS updates typically add new features and functions, fix bugs, and improve device performance. Thus, it's a good strategy to ensure your devices are running the most current version of iOS, and if you use both an iPhone and iPad, that they both have the same version of iOS installed.

INTERACTING WITH YOUR iPHONE OR iPAD

If you're a veteran iPhone or iPad user, you already know that Apple's iOS mobile operating system enables you to interact with your mobile device using its touchscreen. Data entry, for example, is typically done using the virtual keyboard displayed on screen when it's needed. Based on the type of information you're entering and the app you're using, the keyboard's layout adapts automatically.

> **(iOS 10) WHAT'S NEW** In addition to interacting with your iOS mobile device using the touchscreen, the capabilities of Siri have been improved with iOS 10, allowing you to better control your iPhone or iPad and your favorite apps using voice commands.
>
> Plus, the Spotlight Search feature built in to iOS 10 has been dramatically improved, so it's now faster and easier to find information stored in your mobile device and simultaneously retrieve information from the Internet, when applicable.

When not using the virtual keyboard, much of your interaction with the iPhone or iPad is done using a series of taps, swipes, and other finger gestures on the Multi-Touch display.

WHAT'S NEW iPad Pro users have the opportunity to interact with their tablets using an optional pen-shaped stylus, called Apple Pencil, which enables users to write or draw directly on the tablet's screen with extreme accuracy.

TOUCHSCREEN TECHNIQUES

To navigate your way around iOS 10 on your iPhone or iPad, you need to learn a series of basic taps and finger gestures.

WHAT'S NEW The iPhone 6s and iPhone 6s Plus (as well as all newer iPhone models, including the iPhone 7 and iPhone 7 Plus) offer the 3D Touch feature, which introduces two touchscreen gestures, called Peek and Pop.

When accessing the Home screen or using a growing number of compatible apps, if you press and hold your finger firmly on an icon or item, you can get a quick glimpse of what tapping or holding down your finger would reveal. Then, if you want to access that content, press a bit harder on the screen to "pop" into it.

For example, if you're using the Mail app and looking at your Inbox, which displays a listing of incoming messages, you can gently hold your finger on a message to preview it ("peek"), and then if you want to open the message and work with it, press your finger down a bit harder to "pop" it open.

This also works on the Home screen. Many apps offer quick access to the most common features of the app by pressing firmly on its icon. For example, if you hold your finger on the Camera app icon, a menu that enables you to quickly take a selfie, record a video, record a slow-mo video, or take a photo (shown in Figure 1.6) is displayed.

As you learn more about iOS 10's features throughout this book, you'll also discover how to best utilize them by executing the necessary taps, swipes, pinches, and other finger gestures.

Figure 1.6

The Peek feature on the iPhone 6s. This menu appears when you press and hold your finger on the Home screen's Camera app icon.

As in previous editions of the iOS, when you turn on the device or wake it from Sleep mode, virtually all of your interaction with the smartphone or tablet is done though the following finger movements and taps on the device's highly sensitive Multi-Touch display:

- **Tap**—Tapping an icon, button, or link that's displayed on your device's screen serves the same purpose as clicking the mouse when you use your main computer.

- **Hold**—Instead of a quick tap, in some cases it is necessary to press and hold your finger on an icon or onscreen command option. When a hold action is required, place your finger on the appropriate icon or command option, and hold it there with a slight pressure. There's never a need to press down hard on the smartphone or tablet's screen. (Hold works with all iOS mobile devices running iOS 10, and is different from the Peek and Pop gestures that are exclusive to the iPhone 6s, iPhone 6s Plus, iPhone 7, and iPhone 7 Plus.)

- **Swipe**—A swipe refers to quickly moving your finger along the screen from right to left, left to right, top to bottom, or bottom to top, in order to scroll left, right, up, or down, depending on which app you're using.

■ **Pinch**—Using your thumb and index finger, perform a pinch motion on the touchscreen to zoom out when using certain apps. Or "unpinch" (by moving your fingers apart quickly) to zoom in on what you're viewing on screen when using many apps.

> **☑ TIP** Another way to zoom in or out when looking at the device's screen is to double-tap the area of the screen on which you want to zoom. This works when you're surfing the Web in Safari or looking at photos using the Photos app, as well as in most other apps that support the zoom in/out feature. To zoom out again, double-tap the screen a second time.

■ **Pull-down**—Quickly swipe your finger down from the very top of the iPhone or iPad's screen. This causes the Notification Center to appear. You can hold the device in portrait or landscape mode for this to work. As you'll discover in Chapter 2, "Customize Your iPhone or iPad," the appearance of Notification Center and the information you can access from it has been enhanced in iOS 10.

> **☑ TIP** The pull-down gesture is also used to access iOS 10's enhanced Spotlight Search feature. Use a pull-down gesture that starts in the *middle* of the iPhone or iPad's Home screen to access the improved Spotlight Search feature.
>
> One use of Spotlight Search is to quickly find any information that's stored in your mobile device, such as a Contacts entry, Calendar event, or content in an email message.
>
> Enter a keyword or search phrase into the Search field, tap the Search key on the virtual keyboard, and then tap one of the search result listings to access the related data or content by automatically launching whichever app it relates to.
>
> The Spotlight Search screen also showcases icons representing the last few apps you've used.
>
> When your iPhone or iPad has Internet access, Spotlight Search uses online resources automatically to give you access to additional information, including a local weather forecast, upcoming appointments, recently used apps, news headlines, relevant suggested websites, movie show times, local restaurants, and/or other content based on what you're searching for (shown in Figure 1.7).
>
> To view a more detailed Spotlight Search screen, from the Home screen, swipe your finger horizontally from left to right. Doing this displays the Search field, icons representing the last few apps you've used, and a listing of breaking news headlines. Any of these icons or listings are interactive, so you can tap them. Be sure to scroll down the screen, when applicable, to see everything.

Figure 1.7

From Spotlight Search, find content stored in your device, or perform a web search about anything by typing what you're looking for into the Search field at the top of the screen.

- **Swipe up**—At any time, you can swipe your finger in an upward direction to make the redesigned Control Center appear. From here, you can access a handful of functions, such as Airplane mode, Wi-Fi, Bluetooth, the Do Not Disturb feature, and the Screen Rotation lock, as well as screen brightness controls, Night Shift mode, and Music app controls. You can also utilize AirDrop and AirPlay/Bluetooth functions and access commonly used core apps, such as Clock, Calculator, and Camera. On the iPhone, you can quickly turn on/off the Flashlight function.

- **Five-finger pinch (iPad only)**—To exit any app and return to the Home screen, place all five fingers of one hand on the screen so that they're spread out, and then draw your fingers together, as if you're grabbing something. Be sure, however, that the Multitasking Gestures are turned on in the Settings app (found under the General heading).

> **✓ TIP** For iPad users, iOS 10 works with a two-finger gesture. It enables you to more accurately move the cursor around on the screen (in some apps), which is useful when editing text or highlighting text to select, copy, cut, and then paste, for example.
>
> To move the cursor on the screen, place two fingers next to each other over the cursor or text you want to highlight, and drag your fingers slowly around on the screen. The onscreen cursor follows your movement.

> **✓ TIP** Return to the Home screen anytime by pressing the Home button once, regardless of which app is being used. The Home button is the circular button located on the front (bottom center) of the device (below the screen) on the iPhone or iPad.

- **Multi-finger horizontal swipe (iPad only)**—When multiple apps are running simultaneously, swipe several fingers from left to right or from right to left on the screen to switch between the active app and the other apps that are currently running in the background (using the app switcher). Alternatively, iPad and iPhone users alike can access the app switcher to quickly switch between apps by quickly pressing the Home button twice.

> **✓ TIP** Apple continues to make navigating around your favorite apps with taps, finger gestures, and swipes easy. For example, on any screen where you're scrolling downward, such as when you're surfing the Web with Safari, you can simply tap the time that's displayed at the top center of the screen to quickly return to the top of the page or screen.
>
> Meanwhile, if you're typing something on your iPhone and don't like what you typed, instead of pressing and holding the Delete key to delete your text, simply shake the smartphone in your hand for a second or two to "undo" your typing. Be sure to turn on the Shake to Undo feature by launching Settings and tapping Accessibility.

> ## ☑ TIP
> You can also easily interact with the iPhone using just one hand. When using one of the more recently released iPhone models, double touch (use a gentle tap, as opposed to pressing) the Home button, and everything that's displayed on the screen shifts downward, so you can more easily reach it with your thumb. Plus, as you're reading emails, you can use your thumb (on the hand you're holding the iPhone with) to swipe left or right across an Inbox message listing to manage that incoming message.

🔍 MORE INFO: HOME BUTTON QUICK TIPS

Here's how to use some of the Home button's main functions when using iOS 10:

- **Activate Siri**—Press down and hold the Home button for 2 seconds from the Home screen or when using any app.

- **Access the app switcher**—From any app (or from the Home screen), quickly press the Home button twice. Press the Home button again (or select an app) to exit the app switcher.

- **Exit an app and return to the Home screen**—When using any app, press the Home button once to exit it and return to the Home screen. Keep in mind that in most cases this does not shut down the app; it continues running in the background.

- **Reboot the device (without deleting any of your apps or data)**—Press and hold the Home button simultaneously with the Sleep/Wake button for about 5 seconds, until the Apple logo appears on the screen. The Sleep/Wake button is located on the right side (near the top) of newer iPhones and on the top-right corner of older iPhones and all iPads.

- **Return to the main Home screen**—When viewing any of the Home screens on your mobile device, press the Home button once to return to the main Home screen.

- **Wake up the device from Sleep mode**—Press the Home button once when your iPhone or iPad is in Sleep mode. If the device is powered down, press and hold the Sleep/Wake button for several seconds instead.

Use the Touch ID that's built in to the Home button (available in the more recently released iOS mobile devices) to unlock the device or confirm a payment using Apple Pay, or when making a content purchase from the App Store, iTunes Store, iBook Store, or within a participating app. Touch ID can also be used to grant you access to certain apps that otherwise require a password, such as a banking or credit card app.

WHAT'S NEW   On the iPhone 7 and iPhone 7 Plus, the Home button (Touch ID sensor) has been redesigned. It now feels different when it's touched or pressed compared to older iPhone models. In Settings, it's now possible to customize how the button feels when you press it on the iPhone 7 or iPhone 7 Plus. To do this, launch Settings, tap the General option, and then tap the Home Button option. The 1, 2, and 3 circular icons are displayed; each represents a different feel for the Home button. Tap one at a time to experience the difference when you press the Home button, and then select the one you like best. Tap the Done option to save your selection.

On the iPhone 7 or iPhone 7 Plus, to reboot the device, press and hold the Sleep/Wake button with the volume down button located on the side of the smartphone.

USING THE VIRTUAL KEYBOARD

Whenever you need to enter data into your iPhone or iPad, you almost always use the virtual keyboard that pops up on the bottom portion of the screen when it's needed. The virtual keyboard resembles a typewriter or computer keyboard; however, certain onscreen keys have different purposes, depending on which app you're using.

For example, notice the large Search key on the right side of the keyboard when you access the Spotlight Search screen (refer to Figure 1.7). However, when you use the Microsoft Word app, the Search key becomes the Return key. When you surf the Web using Safari, the Search key becomes the Go key in certain situations, and other keys along the bottom row of the virtual keyboard change as well.

When you're using an app that involves numeric data entry, such as Numbers or Excel, the layout and design of the virtual keyboard can change dramatically.

Use these tips to more easily work with the virtual keyboard on your iPhone or iPad:

■ **Divide the virtual keyboard in half (iPad)**—Make it easier to type on the virtual keyboard with your two thumbs while holding the device. To split the keyboard, hold down the Hide Keyboard key, located in the lower-right corner of the virtual keyboard, and select the Split option. Alternatively, use the index fingers on your right and left hand simultaneously, place them in the center of the virtual keyboard when it's visible, and then move them apart.

■ **Unlock and move the virtual keyboard upward (iPad)**—Hold down the Hide Keyboard key (displayed in the lower-right corner of the keyboard).

You'll be given the opportunity to split or merge the keyboard, as well as unlock the keyboard.

- **Turn on/off the keyboard's key click sound**—Launch Settings, tap the Sounds option, and then from the Sounds menu, scroll down and turn on or off the virtual switch associated with Keyboard Clicks.

- **Adjust auto-capitalization, autocorrection, check spelling, enable caps lock, predictive, split keyboard (iPad only), and the keyboard short-cuts options**—Launch Settings, tap the General option, and then tap the Keyboard option to access the Keyboard menu. Turn on or off the virtual switch associated with each option.

- **Access alternative keys within the virtual keyboard**—When you press and hold down certain keys, it's possible to access alternative letters, characters, or symbols. For example, this works when you press and hold down the A, C, E, I, N, O, U, S, Y, or Z keys. When using Safari, press and hold down the period (.) for a second or two to access the .us, .org, .edu, .net, and .com extensions.

> ☑ **TIP** When using the virtual keyboard, to turn on Caps Lock, quickly double-tap the Shift key (it displays an upward-pointing arrow). Tap the key again to turn off Caps Lock as you're typing or doing data entry.

- **Make the virtual keyboard disappear**—You can often tap anywhere on the screen except on the virtual keyboard itself, or you can tap on the Hide Keyboard key (iPad only), which is always located in the lower-right corner of the keyboard.

- **Make the virtual keyboard appear**—If you need to enter data into your iPhone or iPad but the virtual keyboard doesn't appear automatically, simply tap an empty data field. An appropriately formatted virtual keyboard displays.

- **Make the keys on the virtual keyboard larger**—For some people, a larger keyboard makes it easier to type. Simply rotate the iPhone or iPad from portrait to landscape mode. Keep in mind that not all apps enable you to rotate the screen.

- **Access emoji/symbols keyboards**—Tap the smiley face key, located between the 123 and microphone key, to access alternative virtual keyboards that enable you to incorporate hundreds of different graphical emojis into your messages and documents. iOS 10 includes dozens of brand new emojis (shown in Figure 1.8).

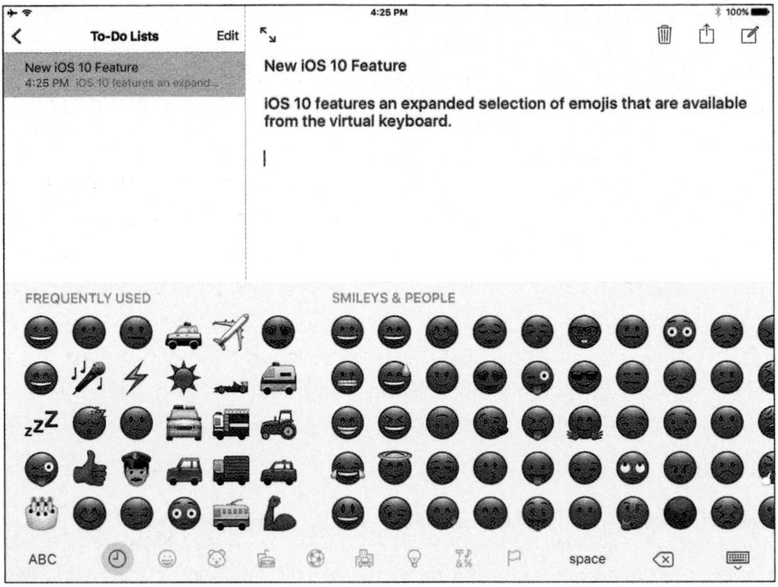

Figure 1.8
Shown here with the Notes app (iPad), it's possible to access iOS 10's expanded emoji keyboard.

■ **Create keyboard shortcuts**—If there's a sentence, paragraph, or phrase you need to enter repeatedly when using an app, it's possible to enter that text just once and save it as a keyboard shortcut. Then, instead of typing a whole sentence, you can simply type a three-letter code that you assign to that shortcut and the virtual keyboard inserts the complete sentence. To create your own keyboard shortcuts, follow these steps:

1. Launch Settings and tap the General option followed by the Keyboard option.
2. From the Keyboard menu, tap the Text Replacement option.
3. When the Text Replacement window appears, press the + icon to add a new shortcut.
4. Fill in the Phrase field with the complete sentence (or any text) you want to include, such as, "I am in a meeting and will call you back later."
5. In the Shortcut field, enter a three-letter combination to use as the keyboard shortcut, such as "IAM" (representing *In A Meeting*).
6. Now, anytime the virtual keyboard is displayed (when using any app), simply type *IAM* to input the sentence, "I am in a meeting and will call you back later."

TAKING ADVANTAGE OF THE iPAD'S DISPLAY OPTIONS

When you're using one of the newer iPad models, you can view multiple items at once on the screen. This is done using the Slide Over, Split View, and Picture in Picture features.

■ **Slide Over**—On the newer iPad models, when using any app, place your finger on the extreme right side of the tablet's screen and drag to the left. This activates the Slide Over feature. You can now launch and access a second app in the right margin of the screen (shown in Figure 1.9). To view a menu of compatible apps, swipe down on the bar icon displayed in the top center of the right margin window if a second app is already running. This feature enables you to do two things at once or quickly copy and paste (or in some cases, drag and drop) content between apps.

■ **Split View**—When using one of the newer iPad models, after you've opened a second app using the Slide Over option, place your finger on the horizontal app divider bar and drag it to the left to launch Split View mode. This enables both apps to run in equal-sized windows on the tablet's screen. Split View works better if you hold your iPad sideways in landscape mode (shown in Figure 1.10). By swiping the app divider bar left or right, it's possible to readjust the size of the two app windows.

Figure 1.9

Use the Slide Over option to access a second app while still using the first. Shown here are the Photos (left) and Safari web browser (right) apps.

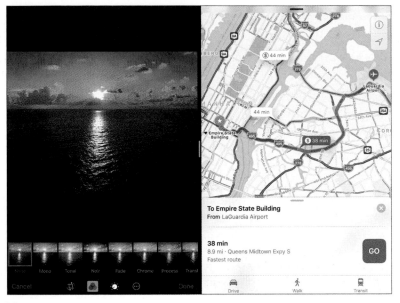

Figure 1.10

Run two apps at once, in equal-sized windows, on your iPad using the Split View mode. Here, the Photos app (left) and Maps app (right) are running simultaneously on an iPad mini 4.

■ **Picture in Picture**—When using compatible apps on your iPad that enable you to watch video, it's possible to display a small video window on your screen while using the majority of the screen to work with another app altogether. This feature is currently supported by the more recently released iPad models when used with the Videos app or another compatible app, such as Netflix, Hulu, Amazon Video, or YouTube.

TIP Depending on which app you're using, how to access the Picture in Picture feature varies. The Videos app displays a Picture in Picture icon located in the bottom-right corner of the screen.

When the tiny video window appears on your screen, place and hold your finger on the window to drag it around the screen and place it where you want. Use a reverse-pinch finger gesture to increase the window's size. Tap the video window again to make command icons appear that allow you to close the video window or pause the playback of the video.

USING AN EXTERNAL KEYBOARD OR STYLUS

If you expect to do a lot of data entry or word processing on your iOS mobile device, instead of using the virtual keyboard, you can purchase an optional external keyboard that connects to the smartphone or tablet using a wireless Bluetooth connection or the device's Lightning port.

> **NOTE** Two optional Apple Smart Keyboards ($149/$169) are available exclusively for the latest iPad Pro models. (Choose the keyboard designed for your tablet's screen size. The Smart Keyboard for the 12.9-inch iPad Pro is priced higher.) These two optional keyboards connect to the tablet using a proprietary Smart Connector that's built in to the newer iPad models and its keyboard accessory. When not in use, this keyboard serves as a Smart Cover for the tablet.
>
> The Apple Pencil stylus for the iPad Pro tablets ($99.00) enables you to handwrite or draw directly on the tablet's screen with extreme accuracy when using compatible apps, like Notes or Adobe Photoshop Sketch.

> **MORE INFO** For other iPad and iPhone models, Apple (http://store.apple.com), Brookstone (www.brookstone.com), Logitech (www.logitech.com), and Zagg (www.zagg.com) are a sampling of companies that offer compatible external keyboards. Some of these keyboards are built in to phone or tablet cases that also double as stands.

> **TIP** The Siri and Dictation features in iOS 10 have also been enhanced. Discover tips and strategies that focus on how to "communicate" with your iPhone or iPad using your voice in Chapter 3, "Say It and Make It So Using Siri."

SECURING YOUR iOS MOBILE DEVICE

If you're worried about other people being able to pick up your iPhone or iPad and access your confidential information or use it to access your favorite websites by signing in using your username, you can password protect your iOS mobile device. You turn on the Passcode Lock feature so that you must manually enter a four- or six-digit passcode (or a longer password) that you preselect to get past the device's Lock screen.

Alternatively, to unlock your compatible iPhone or iPad, place your finger on the Touch ID sensor that surrounds the Home button. This allows your smartphone or tablet to confirm your identity using your unique fingerprint, and your device auto-matically unlocks.

☑ **TIP** To customize the Touch ID sensor's functionality, plus initially scan and store your fingerprints (which you do only once), launch Settings and tap the Touch ID & Passcode option.

Based on how you want to be able to use the Touch ID sensor, turn on or off the virtual switches associated with the iPhone/iPad Unlock, Apple Pay, and/or iTunes & App Store options.

To add and store up to four different fingerprints in the device, from the Touch ID & Passcode menu, tap the Add a Fingerprint option and then follow the onscreen prompts.

📝 **NOTE** Older iOS mobile devices still use a four-digit passcode, but all newer iPhones and iPads initially require users to create a six-digit passcode. If you want to switch from a six-digit passcode to a four-digit passcode (or vice versa), or use a custom alphanumeric code or a custom numeric code, adjust this setting in the Touch ID & Passcode submenu in Settings. (On older devices, the option in Settings is simply called Passcode.)

Tap on the Touch ID & Passcode or Passcode option in Settings. When prompted, enter your current passcode, and then tap on the Change Passcode option. Enter your old passcode. When the Enter Your New Passcode screen is displayed, tap on Passcode Options (located just above the numeric keypad). From the menu, choose the type of new passcode/password you want to use, and then create it when prompted.

To turn on the Passcode Lock feature, launch Settings and tap the Touch ID & Passcode option. From the Touch ID & Passcode submenu, adjust the various vir-tual switches to turn on/off the passcode and/or Touch ID feature related to lock-ing/unlocking the iPhone or iPad itself, as well as utilizing Apple Pay and/or App and iTunes Store purchases.

When you activate the Passcode Lock or Touch ID feature, you are prompted to create and enter a passcode.

❗**CAUTION** When creating a passcode, do not use something obvious, like 123456, 654321, 111111, or your birthdate.

Also from the Touch ID & Passcode menu screen, it's possible to customize Passcode Lock functionality. For example, you can restrict certain iPhone/iPad features from being accessible from the Lock screen. Plus, by turning on the Erase Data option, you can set up the device to automatically delete its contents if some-one enters the wrong passcode 10 times in a row.

> **NOTE** Only the newer iPhone and iPad models have a Touch ID sensor built in to the Home button. This sensor enables the device to be unlocked using a fingerprint scan, as opposed to a passcode. This same Touch ID can be used to authorize Apple Pay purchases.

FINDING YOUR LOST OR STOLEN DEVICE

The Find My iPhone/iPad feature enables you to quickly pinpoint the exact location of your device if it gets lost or stolen, and then offers tools to help you lock down, erase, or retrieve your device. At the same time, if the device does get stolen, you can render the device absolutely useless unless someone knows your Apple ID and password.

For the Find My iPhone/iPad feature to work, however, you must turn on and acti-vate the feature (a one-time process). Then, to pinpoint the location of your phone or tablet, the device must be turned on and be able to connect to the Internet (that is, not be in Airplane mode).

To activate Find My IPhone/iPad, as soon as you install iOS 10 or anytime thereaf-ter, access Settings and tap the iCloud option from the main Settings menu. Then, from the iCloud menu, tap on the Find My iPhone/iPad option. When the Find My iPhone/iPad submenu screen is displayed, make sure the virtual switch associated with Find My iPhone/IPad feature is turned on.

> **TIP** Be sure to turn on the virtual switch associated with the Send Last Location option. To access this option, launch Settings, tap the iCloud option, select the Find My iPhone/iPad option, and then turn on the virtual switch associ-ated with Send Last Location.
>
> When you do this, anytime your smartphone or tablet's battery gets extremely low, the last thing it does before going dead is send the location of the device to Apple, so you can locate it via the iCloud.com website or the Find My iPhone app on another iOS mobile device or Mac.

Now, if you ever need to locate your iPhone or iPad, you have several options. Using a different iOS mobile device, use the free Find My iPhone app that comes preinstalled with iOS 10. Launch the app and sign in using your Apple ID and password. The location of all your Apple mobile device(s) and computer(s) that are linked to the same account are displayed on a detailed map.

Tap the virtual pushpin on the map, or any of the command buttons displayed at the bottom of the app's screen, to use online tools to help you locate, lock down, or erase your mobile device remotely.

Another way to locate your iOS mobile device is to use any computer's web browser and visit www.icloud.com/#find.

Sign in to the iCloud.com website using your Apple ID and password. The same tools for locating and protecting your iOS mobile device are made available to you online—from anywhere. You can also set up the Find My iPhone/iPad feature to work with iCloud's Family Sharing function, so you can use a family member's Apple equipment to pinpoint the location of your iPhone or iPad.

> **! CAUTION** Be sure you turn on Find My iPhone/iPad on your mobile device immediately. If this feature is not active, you will not be able to use the tools Apple offers to locate, lock down, or remotely erase your device if it later gets lost or stolen.
>
> Even if the device is not turned on or connected to the Internet when it's initially lost or stolen, the Find My iPhone/iPad feature can alert you the moment someone finds or tries to turn on your device.

MAINTAINING A BACKUP OF YOUR DEVICE

Using Apple's iCloud service, it is possible to set up your iPhone or iPad to automatically back itself up once per day, as long as you turn on the auto backup feature. For this feature to work, the device needs access to a Wi-Fi Internet connection. The device also must be locked and plugged in to an external power source to auto-initiate the backup process.

To set up the iCloud Backup feature, which needs to be done only once, follow these steps:

1. Launch Settings and tap the iCloud option.
2. Make sure Wi-Fi is turned on and your device can link to the wireless network in your home or office.

3. From the iCloud menu screen, tap the Backup option.

4. From the Backup menu screen, turn on the virtual switch that's associated with the iCloud Backup option.

> **TIP** You can initiate a manual backup of your device at any time. Access the Backup menu screen within Settings, and then tap the Back Up Now option (shown in Figure 1.11). You'll notice that the time and date of the last successful backup is displayed on this screen.

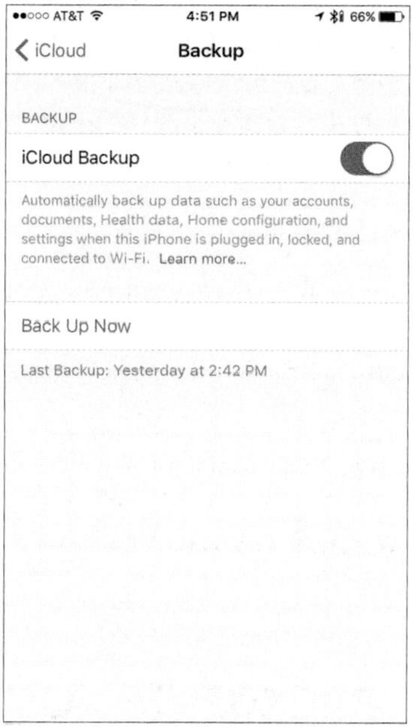

Figure 1.11

Initiate a backup of your iPhone or iPad anytime using the Back Up Now feature.

Later, if you need to reset your iPhone or iPad and erase its contents, or you need to replace your phone or tablet, you can easily restore your data using the last successful iCloud backup. When using this backup method, the backup files associated with your mobile device are stored "in the cloud" within your iCloud account. These backup files consume some of your allocated iCloud online storage space.

🔍 MORE INFO: Using iTunes Sync as a Backup Option

When it comes to syncing data between your primary computer(s) and other iOS mobile device(s), as well as maintaining a backup of your iPhone or iPad, you can connect your iOS mobile device(s) directly to your primary computer via the supplied USB cable and use the iTunes Sync process.

Because iOS 10 is fully integrated with iCloud, maintaining a backup of your device and syncing app-specific data, as well as transferring data, files, photos, and content between your Mac(s), PC(s), and other iOS mobile device(s), can be easily done using iCloud.

When you use iCloud Backup, your iPhone's or iPad's backup files are stored online "in the cloud," and not on your primary computer's hard drive. Because this is the more popular way to back up and sync data, it's the approach we'll focus on in this book.

To use the iTunes Sync process between your iPhone or iPad and a Mac or Windows-based PC, download and install the latest version of the iTunes software onto your computer. To do this, visit www.apple.com/itunes.

To learn more about using the iTunes Sync process to transfer, sync, and back up apps, data, content, and photos, visit www.apple.com/support/itunes.

2

CUSTOMIZE YOUR iPHONE OR iPAD

Thanks to iOS 10, the functionality of your iPhone or iPad is more customizable than ever. You can adjust many device and app-related options from within Settings, plus use Notification Center to help you manage alerts, alarms, notifications, and other informative content in one centralized location. Meanwhile, Control Center has been redesigned in iOS 10 to give you quicker access than ever before to a handful of commonly used features and functions, as well as additional control over the Music app.

This chapter focuses on personalizing and customizing your iOS mobile device and gets you acquainted with a selection of the most popular or useful options available from within Settings, Control Center, Notification Center, and Spotlight Search.

NOTE Depending on which model iPhone or iPad you're using, the options available from the main Settings menu (and all submenus within Settings) vary. Thus, if you read about an option that's not listed in the Settings menu or a Settings submenu on your own device(s), this typically means it's not available on the model iPhone or iPad you're using.

TIP To access Settings, simply tap the Settings app icon from the Home screen (shown in Figure 2.1).

Figure 2.1

To launch Settings, tap the Settings icon from the iPhone or iPad's Home screen.

After iOS 10 is installed on your iPhone or iPad, you'll definitely want to manually adjust some of the options in Settings, as opposed to relying entirely on their default settings. With iOS 10, there are a handful of adjustable options within Settings that were not available in older versions of the iOS.

> ☑ **TIP** As you install additional apps on your iPhone or iPad, if those apps enable you to customize specific features within the app, those customization options are often available to you from within Settings.

> ✐ **NOTE** To customize iCloud-related functions, including Family Sharing and iCloud Drive, launch Settings and tap the iCloud menu option. More about using iCloud with your iOS mobile device is covered in Chapter 6, "Use iCloud and the iCloud Drive App."

USING THE SETTINGS APP

After you launch Settings, the menus and submenus are displayed in a hierarchical structure. Under the main Settings heading are a handful of menu options related to various apps and functions offered by your iPhone or iPad (shown in Figure 2.2). When you tap many of these options, a submenu displays with additional related options.

> ☑ **TIP** To quickly find a feature/function you want to adjust while in Settings, use the Search option. To do this, first launch Settings. Place your finger near the middle of the screen, and then swipe down to display the Search field.
>
> Type a keyword associated with the feature/function you're looking for, such as "Wallpaper," "Handoff," or "Low Power Mode."
>
> For example, if you type "passcode" in the Search field, the search results include Change Passcode, Require Passcode, and Turn Passcode On/Off. Tap the option you want, and the Settings app accesses that feature/function so you can adjust it.

> ☑ **TIP** When a Settings option's virtual switch is positioned to the right and you see green, that option is turned on (shown in Figure 2.3). When the switch is positioned to the left, it's turned off. Tap the switch to toggle its setting on and off.
>
> When a right-pointing arrow (>) is displayed to the right of an option, this means that a submenu is available; tap the right-pointing arrow to open the submenu.

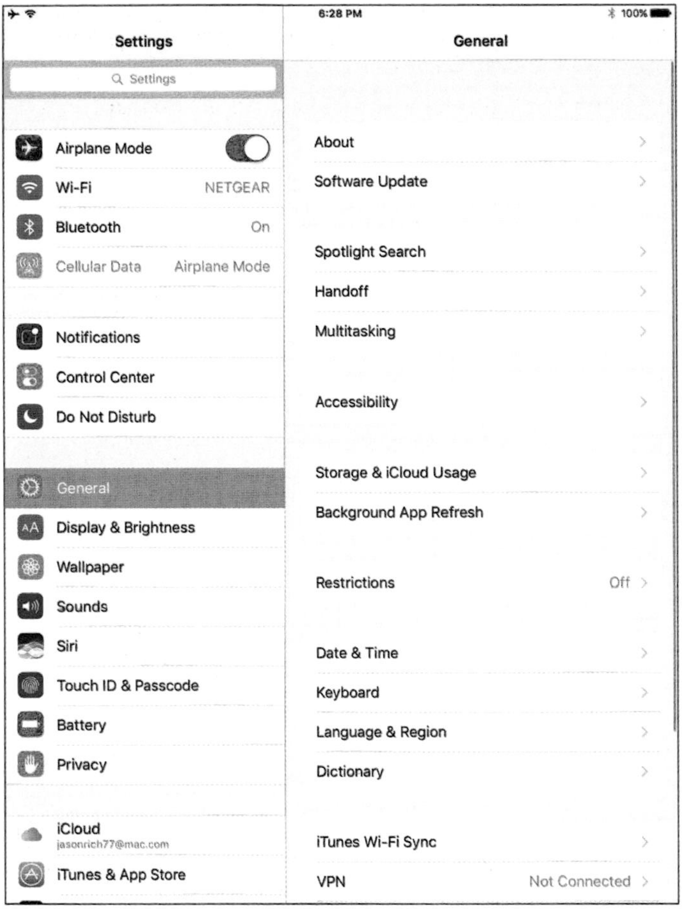

Figure 2.2

On the iPad, the left side of the screen shows the main Settings menu. To the right are available submenu options.

For example, if you tap the Wallpaper option, the submenus associated with customizing your device's Lock and Home screens appear. By tapping the Choose a New Wallpaper option (or one of the thumbnails displayed under the Wallpaper heading), additional submenu options are displayed.

As you work your way deeper into each submenu, a left-pointing arrow (<) icon appears near the upper-left corner of each submenu screen. It enables you to exit out of each Settings submenu and move a step back toward the main Settings menu. At any time, tap this left-pointing arrow icon to exit out of the submenu you're in (before or after you've made adjustments to the various option settings). If you opt to make adjustments, those changes are automatically saved when you exit out of the menu or submenu within Settings. If you exit out of a menu or sub-menu without making any changes, nothing is altered.

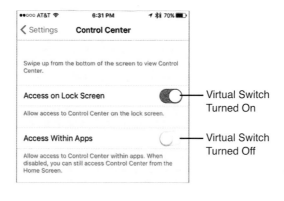

Figure 2.3

To turn on a feature, the switch should be positioned to the right and green should be showing.

Press the Home button once to exit out of Settings entirely (and, if applicable, save your changes).

COMMONLY USED OPTIONS AVAILABLE FROM THE MAIN SETTINGS MENU

The following is a list of the most commonly used options available from the Settings main menu. Remember, these options vary slightly, based on which model iPhone, iPad, or iPod touch you're using and the hardware configuration of that device.

AIRPLANE MODE (iPHONE/iPAD CELLULAR + WI-FI MODELS)

The Airplane mode option has no submenu; it simply offers one virtual on/off switch. When Airplane mode is turned on, a small airplane icon appears in the upper-left corner of the iPhone or iPad's screen.

Even while your device is in Airplane mode, you can still turn on Wi-Fi and/or Bluetooth, enabling the iOS device to access the Web via a Wi-Fi hotspot (to utilize the wireless web access available on some commercial aircrafts, for example), and also communicate with a Bluetooth-enabled wireless keyboard, external speaker(s), wireless headphones, a printer, and/or phone headset.

> **TIP** When you turn on Airplane mode, the Wi-Fi and Bluetooth features of your iPhone or iPad get turned off automatically. You can, however, turn them back on manually while still in Airplane mode. Do this from within Settings or Control Center.

In Figure 2.4, the iPhone is in Airplane mode; however, the smartphone is also connected to a Wi-Fi network. You can see the Wi-Fi signal strength icon displayed in the upper-left corner of the screen, near the Airplane Mode icon. In addition, this iPhone has Bluetooth turned on and a Bluetooth headset is linked to the phone. You can tell this from the Bluetooth icons displayed in the upper-right corner of the screen, next to the battery indicator icon and percentage meter.

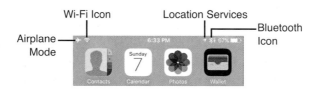

Figure 2.4

On this iPhone, Airplane mode is turned on but both Wi-Fi and Bluetooth have been reactivated.

The tiny arrow icon displayed to the left of the Bluetooth icon is the Location Services icon. When it's visible, the main Location Services (GPS) feature of your iPhone or iPad is turned on, and one or more apps are utilizing the feature to automatically determine the current location of your mobile device.

> **TIP** Turn on Airplane mode when plugging in your iPhone or iPad to speed up the charging process. Keep in mind, however, that this prohibits the device from receiving calls (they go straight to voicemail), and the iPhone or iPad does not receive incoming text messages, emails, or FaceTime calls until Airplane mode is turned off.

WI-FI (iPHONE/iPAD)

Located directly below the Airplane Mode option is the Wi-Fi option. When you tap this option, a submenu containing a virtual on/off switch is displayed. When it's turned on, a listing of available Wi-Fi networks (hotspots) is displayed directly below the Choose a Network heading.

TIP When you're reviewing a list of available Wi-Fi networks, look to the right side of each listing for a lock icon. This indicates that the Wi-Fi hotspot is password protected. Tap a hotspot that does not display a lock icon unless you possess the password for that network.

Also on the right side of each listing is the signal strength of each Wi-Fi hotspot in your immediate area. When given the option, choose a network with the strongest signal for the fastest web-surfing experience.

To choose any Wi-Fi hotspot listed, simply tap it. In a few seconds, a check mark appears to the left of your selected Wi-Fi hotspot and a Wi-Fi signal indicator appears in the upper-left corner of your device's screen, indicating that a Wi-Fi connection has been established.

If you select a Wi-Fi network that is password protected, you will see an Enter Password window when you tap that network. Using the device's virtual keyboard, enter the correct password to connect to the network you selected. You will often have to do this when connecting to a Wi-Fi hotspot offered in a hotel or at a private business, for example.

If you leave the Wi-Fi option turned on, your iPhone or iPad can automatically find and connect to an available Wi-Fi hotspot based on whether you have the Ask to Join Networks option turned on or off. When the Ask to Join Networks feature is turned off, your iPhone or iPad reconnects automatically to wireless networks and Wi-Fi hotspots that you have connected to previously, such as each time you return to your home or office.

NOTE If you attempt to access a public Wi-Fi hotspot—in an airport, library, or school, for example—you might be required to accept terms of a user agreement before Internet access is granted. In this case, your iOS device will say it's connected to a Wi-Fi hotspot, but until you launch Safari and accept the user agreement terms, your other apps, including Mail, will not be able to access the Internet.

! CAUTION The main drawback to using a Wi-Fi connection is that a Wi-Fi hotspot must be present, and you must stay within the signal radius of that hotspot to remain connected to the Internet. The signal of most Wi-Fi hotspots extends for only several hundred feet from the wireless access point (the Internet router). When you go beyond this signal radius, your Internet connection will be lost.

For example, if you want to fully utilize the Maps app for real-time, turn-by-turn navigation directions, a cellular data connection must be used. If you try using this feature with a Wi-Fi connection, as soon as you move out of the signal's radius, the Internet connection is dropped and your mobile device can't pinpoint your location or gather related information from the Internet.

NOTE There are several benefits to connecting to the Internet using a Wi-Fi connection as opposed to a cellular-based 3G/4G/LTE connection (If you're using an iPhone or iPad Cellular + Wi-Fi model), including the following:

- Wi-Fi connection is typically faster than a 3G/4G/LTE connection. (Although if you're within a 4G LTE coverage area, you might experience faster connectivity using it as opposed to Wi-Fi.)

- When connected to the Internet via Wi-Fi, you can send and receive as much data as you'd like without worrying about using up the monthly cellular data allocation from your cellular service provider. This is the best option when streaming content from the Internet, such as video or music programming from YouTube, Netflix, Hulu, Amazon Prime Video, Apple Music, Pandora, or Spotify.

- Using a Wi-Fi connection, you can download large files, such as movies and TV show episodes, from the iTunes Store directly onto your device. Use the iCloud Backup feature to create wireless backups of your iPhone or iPad that get stored in iCloud.

TIP By turning off the Ask to Join Networks option in the Wi-Fi submenu of Settings, your iOS mobile device automatically joins known Wi-Fi networks without first asking you for permission.

BLUETOOTH (iPHONE/iPAD)

Turn on Bluetooth functionality to use compatible Bluetooth devices, such as an Apple Watch, wireless headset, external keyboard, some printers, or wireless speakers/headphones with your iOS mobile device. Bluetooth is also needed to use AirDrop and certain iOS 10 Continuity features (including Handoff) that enable your iPhone or iPad to communicate with other iOS mobile devices and/or Macs.

In Figure 2.5, the Bluetooth menu screen in Settings shows that the Bluetooth feature of the phone is turned on and an Apple Watch, a Plantronics wireless headset (PLT_E500), a Polaroid Zip photo printer, and Powerbeats wireless headphones are currently linked to the device wirelessly via Bluetooth.

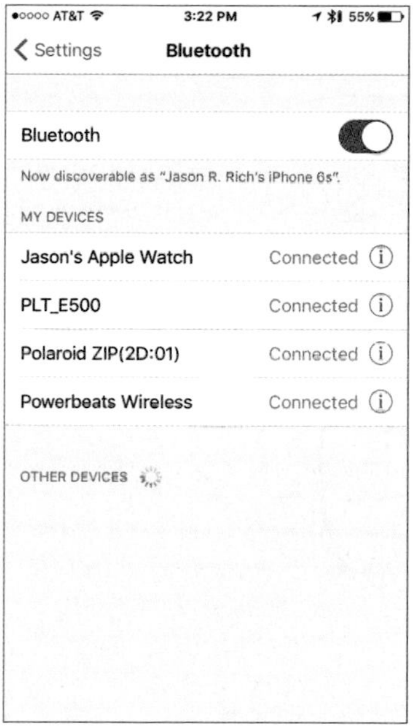

Figure 2.5

The Bluetooth menu screen within Settings (shown on an iPhone).

The rotating circle icon to the right of the Other Devices option means that your iOS mobile device is currently looking for Bluetooth devices to pair with and wirelessly connect to.

In Settings, tap Bluetooth, and then turn on the virtual switch in the submenu. The first time you use a particular Bluetooth device with your iOS mobile device, you will probably need to pair it. Follow the directions that came with the device or accessory to perform this initial setup task. Some Bluetooth 4.0 devices automatically pair with your iOS device. The pairing process should take less than one minute.

After an optional device has been paired once, as long as it's turned on and in close proximity to your iOS device and the iOS device has the Bluetooth feature turned on, the two devices will automatically establish a wireless connection and work together.

> **☑ TIP** If you're using your iPhone or iPad without having a Bluetooth device connected, and you do not want to use the Handoff feature built in to iOS 10, turn off the Bluetooth feature altogether. This helps extend the battery life of your iOS device.

> **✎ NOTE** Handoff enables your iPhone to forward calls to your iPad or Mac, so you can answer them on your tablet or computer. You can also initiate outgoing calls on your iPad (or Mac) that are ultimately routed through your iPhone when the Handoff feature is active on both your iPhone and iPad (and/or Mac).

CELLULAR (iPHONE) OR CELLULAR DATA (iPAD WITH CELLULAR + WI-FI)

When the Cellular Data option is turned on, your iOS mobile device can access the wireless data network from the cellular service provider to which you're subscribed. When this option is turned off, your device can access the Internet only via a Wi-Fi connection, assuming that a Wi-Fi hotspot is present.

Tap the Cellular Data option to turn on or off cellular data roaming. When turned on, Data Roaming enables your iPhone or iPad to connect to a cellular network outside the one you subscribe to through your wireless service provider. The capability to tap in to another wireless data network might be useful if you must connect to the Internet, there's no Wi-Fi hotspot present, and you're outside your own service provider's coverage area (such as when traveling abroad).

! CAUTION When your iPhone or iPad is permitted to roam (the Data Roaming option is turned on), you will incur hefty roaming charges, often as high as $20 per megabyte (MB). Refrain from using this feature unless you've prepurchased a cellular data roaming plan through your service provider, or be prepared to pay a fortune to access the Web.

Depending on your service provider, you might be able to transform your iOS device into a personal hotspot so other devices can connect wirelessly to the Internet via Wi-Fi using your iPhone or iPad's cellular data connection. If your provider allows, this option is available from the Cellular submenu of Settings. Tap the Personal Hotspot option, turn it on, and then set up a Wi-Fi password.

NOTE From the Cellular submenu, information about your call use (iPhone) and cellular data use (iPhone/IPad) Is displayed below the Call Time and Cellular Data Usage headings, respectively.

Also from the Cellular submenu within Settings, you can determine which apps and iPhone or iPad features can use your phone or tablet's cellular data network to connect to the Internet. Scroll down and set the virtual switch that's associated with each app or device feature to turn it on or off. When turned on, Internet access via a cellular data network and/or Wi-Fi is granted. When turned off, only Wi-Fi Internet access is granted.

NOTE To use iOS 10's Continuity and Handoff functions, your iPhone can establish a private wireless hotspot that can be used by your own iPad or Mac that is located within Bluetooth range. This enables you to answer incoming calls to your iPhone from your iPad or Mac. This feature is covered in Chapter 5, "Sync, Share, and Print Files Using AirDrop, AirPlay, AirPrint, and Handoff."

NOTIFICATIONS (iPHONE/iPAD)

This Settings option (shown in Figure 2.6) enables you to determine which apps function with Notification Center, plus it enables you to determine the other ways in which apps that generate alerts, alarms, or notifications notify you. This applies to preinstalled apps, as well as most other apps you install from the App Store.

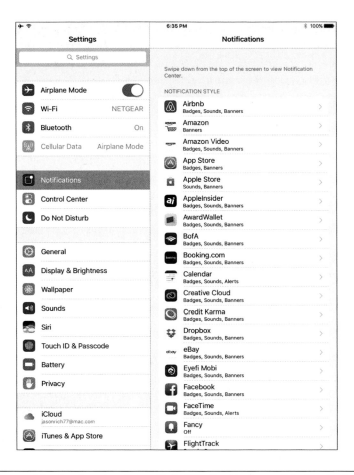

Figure 2.6
All apps that are capable of exchanging data with Notification Center are listed under the heading Notification Style.

> **NOTE** Widgets are associated with certain specific apps that get displayed in Notification Center and the Spotlight Search screen. When you use an app's widget, you can quickly manage or handle tasks associated with that app without manually launching the app. When looking at the main card (window) in Notification Center, scroll down and tap the Edit button to set up and configure available widgets. Not all apps have widgets associated with them.

When you tap the Notifications option in Settings, the Notification Style heading is displayed. Below it, you see a list of all apps currently installed on your iPhone or iPad that are compatible with Notification Center and that you can set up to automatically share data with Notification Center. Tap an app listing to customize how that app interacts with Notification Center. You must do this once for each app listed. Then, as you install additional apps onto your device from the App Store, return to this menu to adjust Notifications related to those apps as well.

> ## ☑ TIP   When you tap an app in the Notification Style list, the first option is labeled Allow Notifications. When turned on, this app shares information with Notification Center. When turned off, no alerts, alarms, or notifications will be generated by that app.
>
> When the Show in Notification Center option is turned on for an app (when applicable), it displays banners or alerts in Notification Center, and when the Show on Lock Screen option is turned on, those same banners and alerts are displayed on the device's Lock screen. The device is woken up from Sleep mode to display the app-related alert, alarm, or notification on the Lock screen, even when the device continues to be locked.
>
> When applicable, tap the Sounds option to customize the audible alert associated with the app. Tap the Badge App Icon option to display a badge on the app's icon on your Home screen when an alert, alarm, or notification is generated.

As you review each app listed under the Notification Style heading, tap it to reveal a secondary submenu pertaining specifically to that app.

Notifications can be viewed as banners or alerts on the Lock screen and within Notification Center, and/or as badges on the app icon (displayed on the Home screen).

Some apps have additional options. For example, the Calendar submenu under Notifications (shown in Figure 2.7) displays a submenu that enables you to separately customize alerts, alarms, and notifications related to Upcoming Events, Invitations, Invitee Responses, Shared Calendar Changes, Events Found in Apps (such as Mail), and Time to Leave. The submenu that appears for each of these options (shown in Figure 2.8) enables you to determine where related notifications are displayed and which alert style should be used.

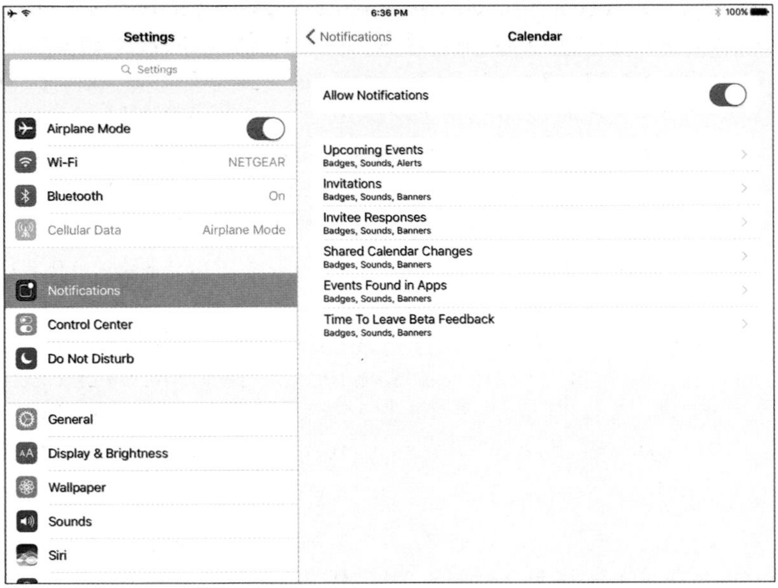

Figure 2.7

Depending on the app, there can be several levels of submenus that enable you to customize how each app exchanges information with Notification Center.

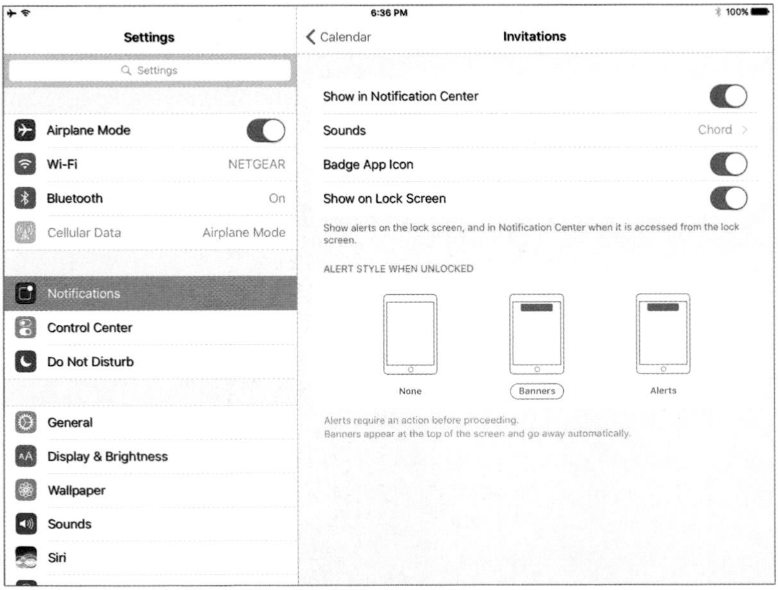

Figure 2.8

iOS 10 options give you control over what information is displayed by Notification Center, plus you can choose how, when, and where that information is displayed.

By selecting an alert style, you choose whether a banner or alert is displayed on the screen, even when you are using another app. If you choose Banners, a pop-up window appears at the top of the screen containing the alert-related information. It appears for a few seconds, and then automatically disappears.

If you choose the Alerts option, a pop-up window displays on the iPhone or iPad's screen until you tap or swipe it to dismiss or address the alarm. The Calendar app generates alerts by default if you set an alarm for an upcoming event.

If you select the None option, no app-specific banner or alert is displayed on the Lock and Home screens while you're using the iPhone or iPad. You can, however, have a custom sound played to get your attention; tap the Sounds option to turn this on.

By turning on the virtual switch associated with the Badge App Icon option (when applicable), the app you're customizing can display a badge on the Home screen along with its app icon. Some, but not all, apps can utilize Home screen badges.

> **NOTE** A badge (as shown in Figure 2.9) is a small red-and-white circle that can appear in the upper-right corner of an app icon on your device's Home screen. The badge contains a number that shows you that something relating to a specific app has changed. For example, a badge appears on your Mail app icon when you've received new incoming email messages, indicating how many unread messages you have waiting in your inbox.

Figure 2.9

On this iPhone's Home screen, the Bank of America (BofA), Twitterific, Facebook, and Mail apps display badges.

Remember, from the submenu associated with customizing app-specific Notification Center options, you can adjust the sounds generated if that app is capable of playing sounds with alerts, alarms, or notifications.

From the Calendar submenu in the Notification Center settings, tap the Upcoming Events option, for example, and then tap the Sounds option to access another submenu that enables you to choose a sound to be associated with event alarms. The default sound for this specific option is called Chord.

Turn on the virtual switch associated with Show in Notification Center if you want alerts related to that app to be displayed in Notification Center.

Determine whether notifications generated by a particular app should be displayed on the Lock screen when your device is otherwise in Sleep mode. When enabled, the phone or tablet is woken up automatically to display new notifications on the Lock screen for anyone to see, without the device first needing to be unlocked.

> **☑ TIP**   Use these quick tips to manage the Notification Center:
>
> ▪ Avoid getting bombarded by excessive notifications from apps that aren't too important to you by manually setting Notification Center to work only with apps that you deem important.
>
> ▪ At the very bottom of the Notification Center settings on the iPhone are two features: AMBER alerts and Emergency Alerts. When turned on, if the government issues an AMBER alert in your area or a message is broadcast over the Emergency Broadcast System, an alert appears on your device.
>
> ▪ To protect your privacy, consider setting up Notification Center to refrain from having alerts displayed on your Lock screen. To do this, tap each app under the Notifications Style heading, and turn off the Show on Lock Screen option.
>
> ▪ As you customize how Notification Center displays notifications, the options available to you vary by app. For example, for the Messages app, you can assign Notification Center to display message previews on the Lock and/or Home screens, plus repeat alerts between 0 and 10 times, at 2-minute intervals, to get your attention.

CONTROL CENTER (iPHONE/iPAD)

Control Center (shown in Figure 2.10 on an iPhone) grants you quick access to a handful of smartphone- or tablet-related functions and apps. Control Center has been redesigned in iOS 10. It now displays two cards, which you can switch between when Control Center is displayed.

Figure 2.10

The newly redesigned Control Center gives you quick access to a bunch of commonly used features and functions.

To display Control Center anytime, regardless of what you're doing on your iPhone or iPad, place your finger near the very bottom of the screen and swipe up. After Control Center opens, swipe right to left, or left to right, to switch between information cards. Each card displays different options.

From the Settings app, however, tap the Control Center option to choose whether to make Control Center accessible from the Lock screen and/or while using other apps.

When the Access on Lock Screen option is turned on, you can swipe your finger from the bottom of the screen up to display Control Center from the Lock screen. When the option is turned off, Control Center is accessible only after the device is unlocked. If Access Within Apps is turned off, you can access Control Center from the Home screen but not while you're using an app.

> **☑ TIP** If you play games that require a lot of onscreen tapping or swiping near the bottom of the screen, you might want to disable Control Center to keep it from opening accidently and disrupting your game. To do this, launch Settings, tap the Control Center option, and then turn off the virtual switch associated with the Access Within Apps option.

DO NOT DISTURB (iPHONE/iPAD)

This feature enables you to temporarily turn off your iPhone or iPad's capability to notify you about incoming calls or text messages, as well as app-specific alerts, alarms, or notifications just when the device is in Sleep mode (locked), or while the device is being used or in Sleep mode. From the Do Not Disturb menu option in Settings, it's possible to fully customize this feature.

At any time, you can manually turn on or off the Do Not Disturb feature by turning on or off the virtual switch that's labeled Manual (shown in Figure 2.11). This feature can also be manually turned on from the Control Center. Turn on the Scheduled switch to preset times when you want this mode to automatically activate—for example, between 11:00 p.m. and 7:00 a.m.

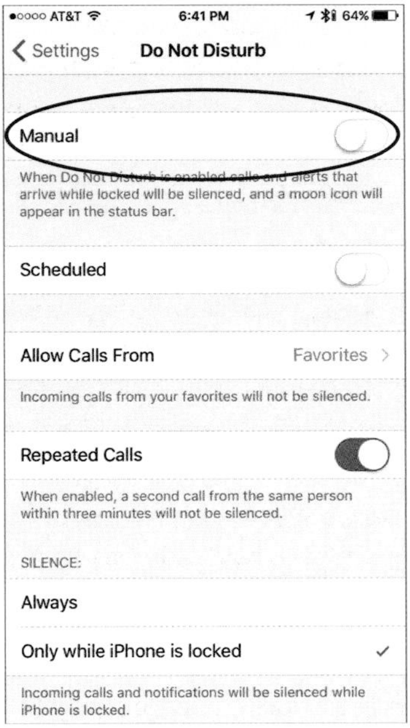

Figure 2.11

When you're in a meeting and you don't want to be bothered by your iPhone or iPad, you can manually turn on the Do Not Disturb feature from the Do Not Disturb submenu within Settings by turning on the Manual virtual switch.

GENERAL (iPHONE/iPAD)

When you tap the General option in the Settings app, various additional options become available. Unless otherwise noted, each option is available using an iPhone or iPad. Because many of these options remain consistent from iOS 9, only the most important or new options are discussed here.

- **About**—At the top of this screen is the Name field. Here, you can create a unique name for your mobile device, such as "Jason's iPad mini 4" or "Jason's iPhone 7." Naming your device is useful if you have multiple devices linked to the same iCloud/Apple ID account. The rest of this About screen includes details about your device, including what version of the iOS is installed, information pertaining to the cellular network to which it's connected (if applicable), and how its internal storage is utilized.

- **Software Update**—Use this option to update the iOS operating system via Wi-Fi, without having to connect your iPhone or iPad to your primary computer and use the now-antiquated iTunes sync procedure.

- **Spotlight Search**—Tap this option to determine which portions of your iPhone or iPad are searched when you use the Spotlight Search feature. When using one of the newer iOS mobile devices, turn on the Siri Suggestions option so that your iPhone or iPad can recommend apps, people, locations, and other content (based on recent use) before you type anything into the Spotlight Search field.

> ☑ **TIP** To access Spotlight Search from the Home screen, perform a swipe downward that originates from the center of the screen to make the Spotlight Search screen appear. If you swipe from the top of the screen you open the Notification Center, so be sure your swipe originates from the center. Separate Search fields also appear in some other apps.
>
> You can access a more robust Spotlight Search screen from the first card (page) of the Home or Lock screens by swiping horizontally from left to right.

> ✐ **NOTE** Turn on Location Services for Spotlight Search to show nearby businesses or points of interest as part of your search results. For example, if you enter "Chinese Food" in the Spotlight Search field, listings for local Chinese food restaurants are displayed. Tap one of the listings to launch the Maps app and learn more about it.
>
> To turn on Location Services related to Spotlight Search, launch Settings, tap the Privacy option, and tap the Location Services option. At the bottom of the Location Services screen, tap System Services and then make sure the switch for Safari & Spotlight Suggestions is on.

- **Handoff**—Handoff enables you to start performing a task on one iOS mobile device (or Mac) and continue it on another Mac or iOS mobile device linked to the same iCloud account.

- **CarPlay**—A growing number of popular car manufacturers are making their vehicles compatible with the iPhone via the CarPlay feature. When your iPhone is linked with your vehicle, you can activate Siri, control the Music app, or access other apps while driving simply by pressing the Siri button on your steering wheel or tapping various options displayed on your vehicle's infotainment center screen. Every car manufacturer interacts with CarPlay differently, so check the owner's manual for your car to determine what's possible. Tap the CarPlay option under the General menu in Settings to customize the feature and link your iPhone with your vehicle, if applicable.

> **NOTE** The Accessibility menu option displayed under the General menu of Settings gives you access to an extensive list of customization options that are designed for people with vision, hearing, or physical limitations.

- **Multitasking (iPad)**—The options available from the Multitasking submenu in Settings enable you to customize finger gestures used to navigate between apps when using the tablet.

- **Storage & iCloud Usage**—Tap this option to see how the storage capacity of your device and your iCloud account are being utilized. Tap the Manage Storage option under the Storage heading to view storage space consumed by individual apps installed on your iPhone or iPad and manage that content. Tap the Manage Storage option under the iCloud heading to see how your online ("cloud-based") storage space is being utilized and manage content. At the bottom of the iCloud Manage Storage screen, tap the Change Storage Plan option to purchase additional online storage space for your iCloud account.

- **Background App Refresh**—This enhanced feature enables you to control the capability of apps to automatically access the Internet to refresh app-specific content and/or Location Services data when the device has Internet access. Turning off this feature helps extend battery life and cuts down on your cellular data usage. You will, however, need to manually update apps each time you launch them. You can also turn on or off this feature on an app-by-app basis from within Settings.

- **Restrictions**—This feature provides a way to "childproof" your iPhone or iPad by enabling an authorized guest user (such as your child) to gain access exclusively to apps or content that you choose. To activate it, tap the Restrictions option, and then tap Enable Restrictions from the submenu. Set a passcode for the restrictions. You can then customize which apps are allowed, block the installation or deletion of apps, prevent in-app purchases, or set ratings limits for content.

> **! CAUTION** If you choose to use the Restrictions feature, be sure you remember the passcode you associate with it. If you forget the passcode, it might be necessary to erase your entire iOS device and reload everything from scratch. Do not give this passcode to your child or the person you're allowing to use your mobile device.

- **Keyboard**—You can make certain customizations from Settings that impact how your virtual keyboard responds as you're typing. It's possible to make supplemental keyboard layouts accessible and customize the Text Replacement feature, plus adjust settings, such as whether Auto-Capitalization, Auto-Correction, Check Spelling, and Dictation are turned on. You can add the popular emoji keyboard from the Keyboards option in the Keyboards submenu of Settings.

- **Reset** —Every so often, you might run in to a problem with your iPhone or iPad resulting in a system crash or the need to reset specific settings. For example, to restore your iPhone or iPad to its factory default settings and erase everything stored on it, tap the Reset option, and then tap the Erase All Content and Settings option. In general, you should refrain from using any of these settings unless you're instructed to do so by an Apple Genius or a technical support person. If you upgrade to a new iOS mobile device and want to return your old device to factory settings and erase all of your data and content so you can safely give away or sell the device, use the Erase All Content and Settings option in the Reset submenu of Settings.

> **! CAUTION** Before using any of the options found under the Settings Reset option, which could potentially erase important data from your iPhone or iPad, be sure to perform a manual iCloud backup or iTunes sync and create a reliable backup of your device's contents. See Chapter 6 for step-by-step directions on how to do this.

DISPLAY & BRIGHTNESS (iPHONE/iPAD)

The Display & Brightness options enable you to control the brightness of your iPhone or iPad's screen, plus customize the default text size and type style. In general, you should leave the virtual switch for the Auto-Brightness feature turned on, and then use the Brightness slider only when you manually need to adjust the screen to accommodate a specific lighting situation.

Drag the white dot on the Auto-Brightness slider to the right to make the screen brighter or to the left to make it darker.

When the Auto-Brightness virtual switch is turned on, your device takes into account the surrounding lighting where you're using your iPhone or iPad, and then adjusts the screen's brightness accordingly. This can also be set from the Control Center. In addition, some apps, such as iBooks, have their own Brightness sliders built in to the app.

(iOS 10) WHAT'S NEW From the Display & Brightness menu in Settings, it's possible to activate and customize the new Night Shift screen viewing feature. When turned on, this feature adjusts the onscreen colors and brightness that are displayed to make viewing the screen less strenuous on your eyes when you're using the iPhone or iPad at night or in a low-light area.

If you often use your iPhone or iPad at night, while lying in bed before you go to sleep, for example, be sure to turn on the Night Shift feature.

The customization options offered within Settings enable you to auto-schedule the Night Shift feature to turn on at sunset and turn off at sunrise, or you can set the specific times this feature will automatically turn itself on/off nightly by tapping the From/To option.

Use the Color Temperature slider to manually adjust the warmth of the color palette used when the feature is turned on. Most people find the default mid setting on the slider to be suitable.

After the feature is activated from within Settings, you can manually toggle it on or off from Control Center or from the Night Shift menu within Settings.

WALLPAPER (iPHONE/iPAD)

The capability to choose a custom graphic to be used as the wallpaper behind your device's Lock and Home screen has its own option within Settings. From the main Settings menu, tap the Wallpaper option to adjust this.

> **NOTE**   Your iPhone or iPad has more than two dozen preinstalled wallpaper designs built in, plus you can use any digital images stored in the Photos app as your Lock screen or Home screen wallpaper. In Figure 2.12, you see a thumbnail graphic of an iPhone or iPad's Lock screen (left) and its Home screen (right).

Figure 2.12

Tap the Choose a New Wallpaper option to select a new graphic or photo to be used behind your Lock and/or Home screen as a wallpaper.

To change the wallpaper, tap the Choose a New Wallpaper option. Tap the Dynamic, Stills, or Live thumbnail to reveal iOS 10's built-in Wallpaper options, or select a photo from an album that's listed under the Photos heading.

> **TIP**   Live wallpapers (available for the latest iPhone models) animate when you place your finger on them as they're being displayed in the Lock or Home screen. They work better on the Lock screen where they're not covered with app icons.

Next, the graphic or image you select is displayed in full-screen mode. Based on the type of wallpaper you selected, a Still, Perspective, and Live tab may be displayed, along with a Cancel or Set button (shown in Figure 2.13).

Figure 2.13

Preview the selected wallpaper, and then tap Set to select it.

After making your selection, when you return to the iPhone or iPad's Lock screen or Home screen, you see your newly selected wallpaper graphic displayed.

Instead of choosing one of the preinstalled wallpaper graphics, you also have the option of using photos you've transferred to your iOS device and have stored in the Photos app, or photos you've shot using the Camera app.

To select one of your own photos to use as your Lock screen or Home screen wallpaper, tap the Wallpaper option in Settings, followed by the Choose a New Wallpaper option. Next, tap an Album thumbnail under the Photos heading.

When the thumbnails related to the contents of the image album you selected are displayed, tap the thumbnail that represents the image you want to use as your wallpaper. As soon as a preview screen is displayed, if necessary, use your finger to move the image around on the screen. You can also zoom in or out in some cases. When this is possible, the Perspective Zoom On/Off option is displayed in the lower-right corner of the preview screen.

Now, tap the Set option to save your selection. Figure 2.14 shows a custom Lock screen on an iPhone, and Figure 2.15 shows a custom Home screen on an iPad.

Figure 2.14

A newly selected Lock screen graphic, chosen from a photo stored on an iPhone (in the Photos app).

Figure 2.15

A still wallpaper selected from within Settings is now displayed as the Home screen wallpaper, behind the app icons (shown here on an iPad).

! CAUTION If the image you opt to use is not sized appropriately for both the portrait and landscape aspect ratio on the iOS mobile device's screen, the image can appear distorted or not fill the entire screen when you rotate your device.

SOUNDS (iPHONE/iPAD)

Tap this option to adjust the overall volume of the iPhone or iPad's built-in speaker (or the volume of the audio you hear through headphones), as well as to turn on or off various audible tones and alarms your phone or tablet generates.

From this menu, it's possible to assign specific audio tones, sounds, or ringtones to specific types of app-specific alerts and alarms, plus turn on or off the click noise associated with pressing keys on the iPhone or iPad's virtual keyboard.

It's also possible to turn on the Vibrate mode so that the iPhone handset shakes, instead of or in addition to playing a ringtone. You can control the ringer volume using an onscreen slider and adjust the custom ringtones and audio alerts associated with various features and functions of your iPhone. Your device has a built-in library of different audio alarms and alerts, as well as ringtones built in, plus you can download additional ringtones from the iTunes Store.

TIP In addition to customizing ringtones and the wallpaper, it's possible to customize the vibration patterns used by your device, such as when an incoming call is received. To do this, launch Settings, tap the Sounds option, and from under the Sounds and Vibration Patterns heading, tap any of the listed options, such as Ringtone or New Mail.

Next, tap the vibration option that's displayed at the top of the submenu for the option you selected. Choose one of the patterns from the Vibration submenu, or tap Create New Vibration to create your own pattern for the selected option.

TIP Manually adjust the ringer and speaker volume using the Volume Up and Volume Down buttons located on the left side of your iPhone or iPad.

You also can choose different vibration patterns to alert you to different things from the Sounds option in Settings. Volume controls are also accessible from the Control Center.

SIRI (iPHONE/iPAD)

The Siri feature enables you to communicate with and issue commands to your iPhone or iPad using your voice. With the Siri submenu in Settings (shown in Figure 2.16), you can fully customize this option.

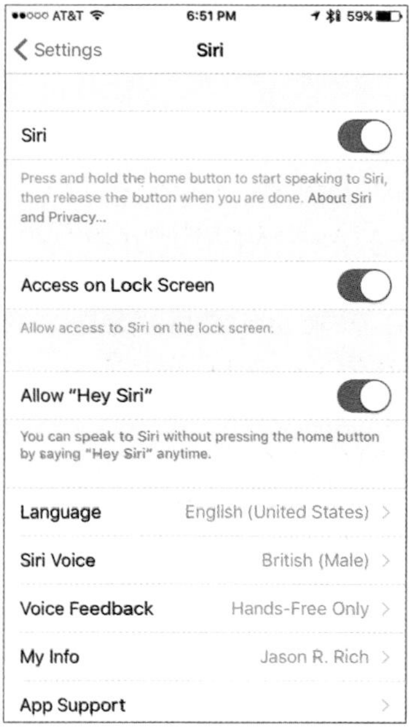

Figure 2.16

Customize Siri functionality from the Siri submenu in Settings.

To initially activate Siri, turn on the virtual switch associated with the Siri option. If you want Siri to be accessible from the device's Lock screen (while your device is locked), turn on the Access on Lock Screen option.

On many newer iPhone and iPad models, Siri can always be waiting for you to say, "Hey Siri," from anywhere nearby to activate the Siri feature and then issue a spoken command. Otherwise, it's necessary to press and hold the Home button for about two seconds to activate Siri.

From the Siri submenu within Settings, you can select the primary language Siri understands, choose between giving Siri a male or female voice, and select Siri's accent—American, Australian, or British.

> ☑ **TIP** Many of the newer iPhone and iPad models offer an always turned on "Hey Siri" feature that can be activated from within Settings. When this feature is on, instead of pressing and holding the Home button for 2 seconds to activate Siri (which can be done from any iOS mobile device), you simply need to say the words, "Hey Siri," followed by your verbal command or question.

To learn more about how to use Siri, see Chapter 3, "Say It and Make It So Using Siri."

TOUCH ID & PASSCODE (iPHONE/iPAD)

Determine whether your device's Touch ID (Home button sensor) can be used to identify your fingerprint to unlock the device and/or approve online purchases. Plus, turn on the Apple Pay option to activate Apple Pay on compatible devices. Tap the Add a Fingerprint option displayed as part of this menu to securely scan and store your fingerprint(s). These fingerprint scans cannot be accessed by Apple or third parties.

Scroll down on the Touch ID & Passcodes submenu to access options that enable you to decide which features, if any, will be accessible from the Lock screen (while the device is still locked).

For an added layer of protection against someone hacking into your iPhone or iPad, turn on the virtual switch associated with Erase Data. When turned on, if someone enters the wrong passcode 10 times in a row, the device automatically erases itself. As the device's primary user, you can later restore the device from an iCloud Backup or iTunes Sync Backup once you recover it.

> ☑ **NOTE** If your iPhone or iPad is equipped with a Touch ID sensor, options pertaining to setting up and using this fingerprint scanner feature are under the Touch ID & Passcode option in Settings. Devices not equipped with Touch ID, however, simply have a Passcode option available to them in Settings.

> ☑ **TIP** Consider storing the fingerprint for the thumb and index finger on both of your hands, so you can use Touch ID with any of those fingers based on how you're holding the device.

> **☑ TIP** Newer iPhone and iPad models require users to set up a six-digit passcode to unlock their device and set up Apple Pay. Older iPhone and iPad models require setting up a four-digit passcode. However, when initially creating the passcode, tap Passcode Options to select between creating a custom alphanumeric code, custom numeric code, four-digit numeric code, or six-digit numeric code.

BATTERY (iPHONE/iPAD)

This submenu enables you to display the battery life percentage remaining on your device in the top-right corner of the screen in addition to the Battery Status Bar. From this menu, you can also see how individual apps that are running on your iPhone or iPad are impacting the device's overall battery life. Tap the Last 24 Hours or Last 7 Days tab, and then view the apps listed below the Battery Usage heading if you're wondering why your iPhone or iPad's battery is draining too quickly. Shut down specific apps and keep them from running in the background when not in use to extend battery life.

From the Battery submenu screen, tap the clock icon to see information about how much time each app has been used.

> **⊙ WHAT'S NEW** If your iPhone or iPad's battery is running low but you can't immediately plug it in to an external power source, turn on the Low Power mode feature that's accessible from the Battery submenu in Settings. When this feature is turned on, all nonessential functions are turned off, allowing you to extend the battery life of your device a bit longer.
>
> Another way to extend the battery life of your iPhone or iPad is to tap the Reduce Brightness option on the Battery submenu. When you adjust the Brightness slider and make the screen dimmer, less battery power is used.

PRIVACY (IPHONE/IPAD)

This menu option in Settings gives you privacy control in terms of how information is shared between apps and shared with other people.

From this Settings submenu screen, it's possible to turn on/off the master Location Services (GPS) feature, plus separately control which apps have access to the device's Location Services feature. You're also able to control which apps can share data with certain preinstalled apps (including Contacts, Calendar, Reminders, and Photos).

Some apps and services, such as Maps, Home, or Find My iPhone (or Find My iPad), use Location Services to pinpoint your exact location. It's important to customize the Location Services options if you're concerned that certain apps can potentially share this information.

When the master virtual switch for Location Services option is turned on, your iPhone or iPad can fully utilize its GPS capabilities, in addition to crowd-sourced Wi-Fi hotspots and cell towers, to determine your exact location. When it's turned off, your device cannot determine (or broadcast) your location. However, some of your apps, like Maps, will not function properly.

> **✅ TIP** When the Location Services option is turned on and you snap a photo or shoot video using the Camera app, the exact location where that photo or video was shot is automatically recorded and saved. This feature is deactivated if you turn off the Location Services option. You can also leave the master Location Services feature for your device turned on but turn off this feature with specific apps, such as the Camera app.

> **✏️ NOTE** From the Privacy menu within Settings, determine which apps can share information with each other and with the public when you use Facebook, Twitter, Instagram, or other online social networking apps.

ICLOUD (iPHONE/iPAD)

Learn all about using iCloud with your iPhone or iPad in Chapter 6.

ITUNES & APP STORE (iPHONE/iPAD)

Choose which Apple ID account you want to associate with the iPhone or iPad you're using, and manage that account by tapping the Apple ID option displayed near the top of this menu.

From below the Automatic Downloads heading, determine whether the device you're using will automatically download content acquired from other computers or mobile devices that are linked to the same iCloud (Apple ID) account. This relates to Music, Apps, Books/Audiobooks, and App Updates acquired from the iTunes Store, iBook Store, and App Store.

It's also possible to turn on/off the Use Cellular Data option, which when turned on, enables your device to acquire various types of content using a cellular data connection (as opposed to just a Wi-Fi Internet connection).

WALLET & APPLE PAY (iPHONE/iPAD)

If you're using one of the more current iPhone or iPad models that has a Touch ID sensor built in to the Home screen, use the options available from the Wallet & Apple Pay submenu to initially set up the Apple Pay feature, as well as the Wallet app (on the iPhone).

This process involves linking one or more of your credit or debit cards to Apple Pay so that you can authorize purchases at retail stores, when shopping on the iTunes Store, while shopping on compatible websites, or while making purchases through certain third-party apps.

> **TIP** On compatible iPhones, to speed up making payments using Apple Pay in stores, turn on the Double-Click Home Button option. Then from the Lock screen, quickly press the Home button twice to launch the Wallet app and select the stored debit or credit card with which you want to pay. When this option is turned off, you must manually launch the Wallet app from the Home screen.

From under the Transaction Defaults heading, choose a default debit or credit card to use with Apple Pay transactions, plus store your default shipping address, email, and phone number. This speeds up the checkout process.

> **NOTE** The verification process for linking a credit, debit, or store credit card varies based on the card issuer. Follow the onscreen prompts.

If you're using an older model iPhone that does not have a Touch ID sensor, the Wallet app can still be used to manage store/company reward cards or membership cards that are set up to utilize Wallet functionality.

MAIL, CONTACTS, CALENDAR, NOTES, AND REMINDERS (iPHONE/iPAD)

If you use your iPhone or iPad to help manage your life, you probably rely heavily on the preinstalled Mail, Contacts, Calendar, Notes, and Reminders apps.

From Settings, it's possible to customize a handful of options pertaining to each of these apps. From the Mail option, for example, you must set up your existing email account(s) to work with your smartphone or tablet.

For information about how to use the Settings app to customize the Mail app-related settings, see Chapter 11, "Send and Receive Emails with the Mail App." You can find details about customizing the settings of the Contacts, Calendar, Reminders, and Notes apps in Chapter 14, "Use Calendar, Contacts, Reminders, and Notes."

TIP After tapping the Calendar option in Settings, one useful setting available from the Calendar submenu is Default Alert Times. Tapping this option reveals the Default Alert Times menu screen, from which you can automatically set advance alarms for birthdays, events, and all-day events stored in the Calendar app. You can set each of these options individually to alert you at 9:00 a.m. on the day of the event, one or two days prior, or one week before the event, based on your preference.

If you fill in the Birthday field as you create contact entries in the Contacts app, these dates can automatically be displayed in the Calendar app to remind you of birthdays. The advance warning of a birthday gives you ample time to send a card or a gift.

TIP From the Default Alert Times submenu screen, turn on the Time to Leave option if you want your device to determine how long it will take you to travel from your current location to the next event in the Calendar app based on distance and current traffic conditions. In addition to turning on this feature in Settings, the location of your event must be entered into the Location field for each event when using the Calendar app.

MORE APP-SPECIFIC OPTIONS WITHIN SETTINGS

As you scroll down on the main Settings menu on your iPhone or iPad, you'll see specific apps listed, including some of the core preinstalled apps, such as Messages, FaceTime, Maps, Compass (iPhone), Safari, News, Music, Videos, Photos & Camera, iBooks, Podcasts, and Game Center.

As you continue scrolling down, listings for Twitter, Facebook, Flickr, and Vimeo lead to submenus that offer the capability to fully customize integration with these online social networking services with many of the apps you'll soon be using.

USER-INSTALLED APPS

By further scrolling toward the bottom of the Settings menu, you'll discover a listing of other individual apps that you have installed on your iPhone or iPad and that have user-adjustable options or settings available. Tap one app listing at a time to modify these settings. Remember, as you install new apps in the future, additional app listings will be added to this section of the Settings menu, and you can modify them accordingly.

WORKING WITH CONTROL CENTER

At any time, regardless of what you're doing on your iPhone or iPad, it's possible to access Control Center. To do this, simply place your finger near the bottom of the screen and swipe up. This causes Control Center to appear.

On the iPhone, several circular icons appear on the main card of Control Center, near the top of the window. Each icon enables you to control a frequently used feature (refer to Figure 2.10). From left to right, the icons include the following:

- **Airplane Mode**—Quickly turn on/off Airplane mode on your iPhone or iPad by tapping on this icon.
- **Wi-Fi**—Turn Wi-Fi on or off with a single tap, without having to access Settings.
- **Bluetooth**—Turn Bluetooth on or off so that your iPhone or iPad can link to Bluetooth devices it has already been paired with.
- **Do Not Disturb**—Manually turn on/off the Do Not Disturb feature after you've customized this option in Settings.
- **Rotation Lock**—Normally, when you rotate your iPhone or iPad sideways, the screen automatically switches from portrait to landscape mode. To prevent this from happening when the phone or tablet is rotated, turn on the Rotation Lock feature by tapping on its icon.

> **! CAUTION** Turning on the Rotation Lock could prevent you from accessing certain app-specific features or views, depending on which app you're using. For example, turning on Rotation Lock prevents you from using the Week view in the Calendar app.

Also displayed with these icons is the screen brightness slider, and below that are the button controls for AirPlay, AirDrop, and Night Shift. Tap AirDrop to quickly activate this feature and determine which content or data you want to wirelessly share with nearby iPhone, iPad, or Mac users. Tap the AirPlay button to select where AirPlay-compatible apps will direct content. Tap Night Shift to manually turn on or off this feature.

> **☑ TIP**　When AirDrop is turned on, your iPhone or iPad is discoverable by any iPhone, iPad, or Mac user that's in your immediate vicinity that also has the AirDrop feature turned on (or just by people included in your Contacts database). You can then wirelessly transfer data from certain apps, such as Contacts and Photos. To protect your privacy when out in public, consider keeping this feature turned off unless you specifically want to use it.

Displayed along the bottom of the Control Center window on the iPhone are four additional icons. Tap the flashlight icon to turn on the iPhone's flash so that it serves as a bright flashlight. (This feature is also available on the newest iPad models that have a built-in flash on the back of the device.)

Tap the Timer icon to set and manage timers (that is, access the World Clock, Alarm Clock, Bedtime, Stopwatch, and Timer features). Tap the Calculator icon to launch the Calculator app quickly. Finally, tapping the Camera icon offers yet another way to quickly launch the Camera app and begin snapping photos.

Control Center on the iPad is similar to that of the iPhone; however, as you can see from Figure 2.17, the layout of the options is slightly different.

Figure 2.17

The Control Center is shown here on an iPad.

(iOS 10) WHAT'S NEW   Control Center now features a second card (window), which you can access by swiping your finger from right to left across the main Control Center window (shown in Figure 2.18 on an iPhone). This secondary card enables you to control the Music app (or other apps that utilize audio, such as iBooks or Audible, for listening to audiobooks).

From this secondary card, you can play, pause, fast forward, or rewind audio; use the volume slider to adjust the speaker/headphones volume; and select and control audio-related devices (such as Bluetooth wireless speakers or headphones) that are active and linked to the device you're using.

Figure 2.18
Control music or audio generated by the Music app, or another compatible app, such as Audible, from the Control Center's secondary card.

To close either Control Center window, tap anywhere near the top of the iPhone or iPad's screen, or place your finger on the Control Center window and swipe down.

ORGANIZING APPS IN FOLDERS

If you're like most iPhone and iPad users, you'll probably be loading a handful of third-party apps onto your device. After all, there are well over 2 million third-party apps to choose from. To make it easier to find your apps on the iPhone or iPad's Home screen, and to reduce onscreen clutter, you can place app icons in folders.

From the Home screen, tap and hold down any app icon until all the app icons begin shaking. Drag one app icon on top of another to automatically place both of those apps in a new folder.

You can organize your apps in folders based on categories, like Travel (shown in Figure 2.19), Games, or Productivity, or you can enter your own folder names and drag and drop the additional app icons into the folders you create. After your app icons are organized, simply press the Home button to save your folders and display them on your Home screen.

Figure 2.19
On this iPhone, a Travel folder has been created.

To open a folder, tap its icon. Tap any of the contained app icons to launch one of the apps. Figure 2.20 shows a Travel folder that contains several popular travel-related apps.

> **NOTE** You can create as many separate folders as you want to be displayed on your Home screens, plus there is no limit to how many apps you can place into each folder.

Figure 2.20

This Travel folder was created to organize the travel-related apps currently installed on this iPhone. Using folders helps to eliminate clutter on your Home screen.

If you later want to remove an app icon from a folder so that it appears as a stand-alone app icon on your Home screen, simply press and hold any of the folder icons until all the onscreen icons start to shake. The folder's contents are displayed.

While the app icons are shaking, simply drag the app icons, one at a time, back onto the Home screen. Each is then removed from the folder. Press the Home button to finalize this action.

MOVING APP ICONS AROUND ON THE HOME SCREEN

To move app icons around and reorganize them on the Home screen, press and hold down any app icon with your finger. When the app icons start to shake, you can use your finger to drag one app icon at a time around on the Home screen.

Your iPhone or iPad can extend the Home screen across multiple pages. (Switch pages by swiping your finger from left to right, or right to left when viewing the Home screen.)

To move an app icon to another Home screen page, while the icon is shaking, hold it down with your finger and slowly drag it to the extreme right or left, off the screen, so that it bounces onto another of the Home screen's pages.

When you switch pages, the row of up to four app icons displayed at the very bottom of the iPhone's screen (or up to six app icons on the iPad's screen) remains constant. Place your most frequently used apps in these positions so that they're always visible from the Home screen.

As the app icons are shaking on the Home screen, you can delete the icons that display a black-and-white X in the upper-left corner from your iPhone or iPad by pressing that X icon.

iOS10 WHAT'S NEW For the first time, iOS 10 enables users to manually delete most of the apps that come preinstalled on the iPhone and iPad, which means you can delete preinstalled apps that you opt not to use. (You can always reinstall deleted apps later.) However, certain apps, like Photos, Camera, Clock (iPhone), App Store, Settings, Wallet, Phone (iPhone), Safari, Messages, and Health (iPhone) still can't be deleted (but they can be moved around or placed in folders).

DISCOVERING WHAT'S POSSIBLE FROM THE LOCK SCREEN

The main Lock screen enables you to do more than just unlock your device or prevent unauthorized people from using it.

From within Settings, you can opt to turn off most functionality that displays app-specific Notifications content on the Lock screen, as well as access to the Spotlight Search screen and the ability to access Control Center (without first unlocking the device). You'd opt to turn off these functions to protect your privacy. Also, if you turn on Passcode Lock, strangers cannot pick up and use your phone or tablet or access any content from it.

The Lock screen automatically displays the current time and date and the wallpaper of your choice. You can also set it up so app-specific alerts or banners are displayed on the Lock screen when applicable, plus you can decide whether you want the ability to access Control Center directly from the Lock screen. These features can be customized from within Settings.

WHAT'S NEW While viewing the Lock screen, swipe your finger from left to right to access the secondary Lock screen, which is virtually identical to the Spotlight Search screen.

This Today screen displays information you configure from within Settings, such as the local weather forecast for your current location or upcoming appointments (scheduled using the Calendar app). You can also customize it to display a list of recently used apps, news headlines, information about upcoming destinations that utilize the Maps app, battery details, as well as access to app-specific widgets.

To choose which app-specific widgets are displayed, and then customize them, scroll down on the secondary Lock screen (or Spotlight Search screen) and tap the Edit button. After unlocking the device, you see the Add Widgets screen, which has a list of available widgets.

Currently activated widgets are listed first. To deactivate any of them, tap the – icon to the left of the listing. To change the display order of the widgets, place your finger on a widget listing's Move icon (to the right of its listing) and drag it up or down.

Scroll down on the Add Widgets screen to view a list of available widgets that are not yet active. They're displayed under the More Widgets heading. Tap the + icon associated with any of these widgets to activate it.

Tap Done to save your changes. It's also possible to control the information displayed on the Lock screen from within Settings. To do this, launch Settings, tap the Touch ID & Passcode option (or the Passcode option on older devices), and then scroll down to the Allow Access When Locked option. Turn on the virtual switches associated with the options you want accessible from the Lock screen, such as Today View and Notifications View.

TIP To unlock the Lock screen and access your Home screen, place your finger on the Home button to scan your fingerprint using the Touch ID sensor, and then press the Home button.

If you don't have the Touch ID sensor turned on, or if you're using an older device, press the Home button when viewing the Lock screen, and enter your passcode when the Enter Passcode screen is displayed.

When you have the Handoff feature turned on, if there was an app you were using on your Mac or another mobile device that's linked to the same iCloud account, a tiny icon for that app appears in the lower-left corner of the primary Lock screen. By tapping this icon, you can launch the app and pick up exactly where you left off. This works really well with Safari when surfing the Web, for example.

iOS 10 **WHAT'S NEW** To launch the Camera app from the Lock screen and quickly start taking photos, swipe your finger across the main Lock screen from right to left. There is no need to first unlock the device.

MANAGING YOUR CUSTOMIZED NOTIFICATION CENTER SCREEN

You can access iOS 10's redesigned Notification Center window/screen from the IPhone or iPad at any time by placing your finger near the top of the screen and swiping down.

NOTE Notification Center displays all alerts, alarms, and notifications generated by your device in one place.

The information displayed in Notification Center is now divided into two screens, which you can scroll between by swiping from right to left or from left to right. The first Notification Center screen (shown in Figure 2.21) displays a Search field at the top. From here, you can locate any information stored in your device or perform an Internet search.

The date is also displayed. Scroll down and tap the Edit icon at the bottom of the screen to customize what information is displayed, such as a weather forecast, stock information, upcoming Calendar events, upcoming reminders, or app-specific widgets.

The secondary Notification Center screen displays alerts, alarms, and notifications generated by your mobile device, and the apps you have set up to work with Notification Center (shown in Figure 2.22). It's important to customize what information is displayed on this screen by launching Settings, and then tapping the Notifications option.

From the Notifications menu in Settings, tap on each app listing to determine which apps will display content within Notification Center.

Figure 2.21

This Notification Center screen is customizable and can display a weather forecast, as well as content from other apps or app widgets.

Figure 2.22

This Notification Center screen displays alerts, alarms, and notifications generated by various apps running on your iPhone or iPad.

Any listing for an alert, alarm, or notification is interactive. You can tap or swipe the listing to launch the appropriate app and gain immediate access to the information that's related to what you're being alerted about.

All alerts, alarms, and notifications are displayed in chronological order, with the newest information displayed first.

To clear all notifications from Notification Center, tap the small X icon displayed to the right of the Recent, Yesterday, and/or a previous day's headings, and then tap Clear.

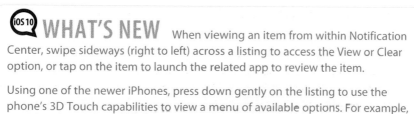

WHAT'S NEW When viewing an item from within Notification Center, swipe sideways (right to left) across a listing to access the View or Clear option, or tap on the item to launch the related app to review the item.

Using one of the newer iPhones, press down gently on the listing to use the phone's 3D Touch capabilities to view a menu of available options. For example, if you're looking at a message from the Mail app about a new incoming email, use the 3D Touch function to quickly preview the email, and then tap the Trash or Mark As Read option (shown in Figure 2.23). Press down on the preview to launch the Mail app and further read, respond to, or manage that message.

Figure 2.23

Press and hold a notification from the Mail app, for example, to preview the incoming message and quickly manage it without needing to launch the Mail app.

TIP When you first start using iOS 10, invest time to customize the Notifications options in Settings, as well as the appearance of the Spotlight Search and Lock screens. If you upgraded from iOS 9, some default settings have changed, and you'll want to ensure that only the information you deem important is presented to you using these redesigned features.

3

SAY IT AND MAKE IT SO USING SIRI

Siri is designed to be a virtual assistant that responds to commands, questions, and requests that you say, as opposed to type, into your mobile device. Siri has access to the content stored on your iPhone or iPad, as well as an ever-growing arsenal of Internet-based resources that you can use to quickly gather information or answers that you need within seconds after you verbally state your request.

WHAT'S NEW Because Siri functionality is primarily web-based and requires Internet access to use, it's continuously evolving. However, the big news related to iOS 10 is that third-party app developers can now integrate Siri functionality into their own apps, which will broaden the types of commands and questions Siri can respond to.

TIP Simply say, "Hey Siri," to activate Siri from most newer iPhones or iPads. Older devices must be plugged in to an external power source to activate Siri using the "Hey Siri" command. When you do this, the familiar, "What can I help you with?" screen appears, and you hear Siri's "ready" tone.

You can also press and hold down the Home button for 2 seconds to activate Siri at any time.

It's possible to deactivate the "Hey Siri" feature from the Siri menu within Settings. Simply turn off the virtual switch associated with the Allow "Hey Siri" option.

Even with ongoing improvements being made to Siri, it's important to realize that Siri does not understand everything, and this feature does have its limitations in terms of what it can do and which apps it works with. When you get accustomed to working with Siri, however, this feature can make you more efficient when using your iPhone or iPad.

MORE INFO The Hey-Siri.io website (https://hey-siri.io), which is operated independently from Apple, offers a frequently updated and comprehensive listing of ways iPhone and iPad users can interact with Siri. It focuses on the best ways to phrase questions, commands, and requests to achieve the desired outcome.

In addition to using cutting-edge voice recognition, Siri uses advanced artificial intelligence, so it doesn't just understand what you say, it interprets and comprehends what you mean and then translates your speech to text. And if you don't initially provide the information Siri needs to complete your request or command, you're prompted for more information.

> **✓ TIP** To get the most out of the Siri feature, turn on your iOS device's master Location Services functionality, and then make sure Location Services is set up to work with Siri. Launch Settings, tap the Privacy option, and then tap the Location Services option. Turn on the virtual switch that's associated with Location Services.

WHAT YOU SHOULD KNOW BEFORE USING SIRI

For Siri to operate, your phone or tablet must have access to the Internet via a cellular or Wi-Fi connection. Every time you make a request or issue a command to Siri, your iOS mobile device connects to Apple's data center. Thus, if you're using a cellular data connection, some of your monthly wireless data allocation gets used up (if a cellular data allocation, such as 5GB per month, is imposed by your wireless service provider).

> **✓ TIP** Because a Wi-Fi connection is typically significantly faster than a cellular data connection, Siri often responds faster to your requests and commands when you use a Wi-Fi connection.

You should also understand that heavy use of the Internet, especially when connected via a cellular data connection, depletes the battery life of the iPhone or iPad faster. So, if you constantly rely on Siri throughout the day, the battery life of your device will be shorter.

> **! CAUTION** If your iPhone or iPad is placed in Airplane mode (and Wi-Fi connectivity is turned off), Siri does not function. You'll receive a verbal message stating that Siri is unavailable.

CUSTOMIZING SIRI

To customize the Siri feature, launch Settings and tap the Siri option. From the Siri submenu (shown in Figure 3.1), there's a master switch for this feature. You can also turn on/off Siri's capability to function from the Lock screen (while your device is still locked), and turn on/off the "Hey Siri" function with the virtual switches labeled Access on Lock Screen and Allow "Hey Siri," respectively.

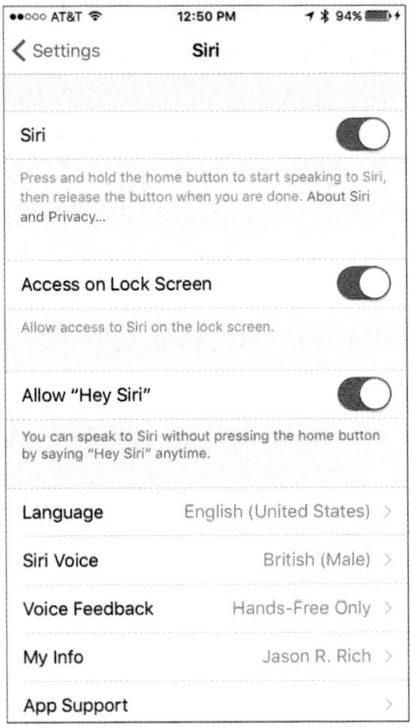

Figure 3.1

Be sure to customize Siri from within Settings. This needs to be done only once; however, you can alter these settings whenever you wish.

☑ **TIP**   The first time you turn on the "Hey Siri" feature, your iPhone or iPad asks you to speak several Siri-related commands so that the device can learn what your voice sounds like. Follow the onscreen prompt and say what's requested. This process takes less than one minute, and you need to do it only once.

Right from the start, Siri will probably understand most of what you say. However, as you begin using this feature often, you will become acquainted with the best and most efficient ways to communicate questions, commands, and requests to generate the desired response.

Toward the bottom of the Siri submenu in Settings are four customization options:

- **Language**—Tap this option to select your native language. If English is your native language, you can choose from eight options, including English (United States), English (United Kingdom), and English (Canada).

- **Siri Voice**—Tap this option to give Siri a male or female voice, as well as an American, Australian, or British accent. This option is based on user preference and is not related to the Language option previously selected.

- **Voice Feedback**—Determine when you want Siri to provide spoken feedback to your questions, commands, and requests. Options include Always On (meaning Siri always responds using its voice); Control with Ring Switch (meaning that Siri only responds verbally when the Ring Switch on the side of your iPhone is turned on, or when the Mute setting is turned off on the iPad); and Hands-Free Only (meaning that Siri only responds verbally when the "Hey Siri" feature is used or your mobile device is connected to Bluetooth speakers, a Bluetooth headset, or CarPlay).

- **My Info**—Select your own entry from the Contacts app so Siri knows who you are and has access to information about you, including your home and work addresses and who your relatives are. The more information you include in your personal Contacts entry, the more helpful Siri can be when it comes to responding to questions or commands, like, "How do I get home from here?" "How long will it take me to get to work today?" or "Call mom at home."

> **TIP** By default, Siri addresses you by your first name, based on the information in your own Contacts entry. However, you can activate Siri and say, "Siri, call me *[nickname]*." Siri remembers your request and addresses you by that name in the future.

HELPING SIRI GET TO KNOW YOU

The more information about yourself that you include in your personal entry in Contacts, the more useful Siri can be. For example, Siri uses information stored in the Related Name fields as you create or edit a contact in the Contacts app. By tapping this field, you can add a relationship title, such as mother, father, brother, or sister when creating or editing Contact app entries.

> **TIP** You can teach Siri which of your contacts are your relatives. Simply activate Siri and say, "*[name]* is my father," for example. Siri will remember these relationships in the future.

Then, when using Siri, if you say, "Call Mom at home," Siri knows exactly to whom you're referring. Otherwise, if you activate Siri and say, "Call my mom at home," the first time you use Siri for this task, Siri asks who your mother is.

As long as you have a Contact entry for your mother stored in the Contacts app, when you say your mother's real name, Siri links the appropriate contact and remembers this information. This applies to any nickname or title you have for other people, such as "wife," "son," "mother," "dad," or even "Uncle Jack."

ACTIVATING SIRI

If you want to use Siri, you first must activate it. There are multiple ways to do this:

- Use the "Hey Siri" function. This works when the device is in Sleep mode, but not when the iPhone or iPad is powered off altogether. On compatible iPhones and iPads, whatever you're doing, simply say the phrase, "Hey Siri" out loud, and Siri responds.
- Press and hold the Home button on your iPhone or iPad for 2 seconds.
- Press and hold the Call button on your wireless Bluetooth headset that is paired with your iPhone or iPad. This enables you to speak to Siri on your device from up to 30 feet away.
- If you're using Apple EarPods, press the middle button on the controls on the cable.
- Press the CarPlay button built in to the steering wheel or dashboard of your compatible car when your iPhone is linked with your vehicle.

When Siri is activated, the message "What can I help you with?" displays on the screen, along with a rainbow-colored, animated wave graphic (shown in Figure 3.2). On some iPhone and iPad models, you simultaneously hear Siri's activation tone. When not listening for spoken commands, a microphone icon replaces the animated wave graphic. Tap this microphone to activate or reactivate Siri.

Once activated, you have about 5 seconds to begin speaking before the feature deactivates. To reactivate it, simply tap the microphone icon or repeat one of the previously mentioned steps.

As soon as Siri is activated, speak your question, command, or request. For the most accurate results when using Siri, speak directly into the iPhone, iPad, or headset. Try to avoid being in areas with excessive background noise. Also, speak as clearly as possible so Siri can understand each word in your sentence.

Figure 3.2

When Siri is activated (shown here on the iPhone), the "What can I help you with?" message appears and you hear Siri's activation tone.

DISCOVERING HOW SIRI CAN HELP YOU

The great thing about Siri is that you don't have to think too much about how you phrase a command, question, or request. Siri automatically interprets what you say.

> ✓ **TIP** When you're in a quiet area, activate Siri and then speak. Stop speaking when you're finished, and Siri responds accordingly. However, if you're in a noisy area, Siri might have trouble determining when you've stopped speaking. To avoid this problem, press and hold the Home button as you speak to Siri. When you're finished speaking, release the Home button so Siri can process your request.

To get the most out of using Siri—with the least amount of frustration as a result of Siri not being able to comply with your requests—develop a basic understanding of which apps this feature works with and how Siri can be used with those apps. In general, Siri can be used with most of the apps that come preinstalled with iOS 10, plus Siri can find information on the Internet by performing web searches. You can use Dictation mode, however, in any app where the microphone key appears on the iPhone or iPad's virtual keyboard.

> **NOTE** Dictation mode offers an easy way to speak into your iPhone or iPad and have what you say translated into text and then inserted into the app you're using instead of typing.

The following sections provide a sampling of what Siri can be used for, as well as tips for how to use Siri effectively. Apple and third-party app developers are continuously working to upgrade Siri's capabilities, so you will likely discover additional functionality as you begin using Siri with various apps.

> **MORE INFO** For an up-to-date summary of Siri's capabilities and a sampling of how to phrase commands or requests to work with Siri's newest features, visit this page of Apple's website: www.apple.com/ios/siri.

Here are some quick tips on using Siri:

- Siri is one of the few features that work from the Lock screen. Thus, even if you have the Passcode Lock feature turned on, someone can potentially pick up your device and access your data using Siri without your permission. To keep this from happening, set up the Passcode feature on your device. Then turn off the Siri option in the Touch ID & Passcode submenu of Settings.

- Siri can be used to verbally launch any app. To do this, activate Siri and say, "Launch *[app name]*." If it's a game you want to play, simply say, "Play *[game name]*." Another option is to say, "Open *[app name]*."

- For more information about how Siri can be used, activate Siri and say, "What can you do?" Or after activating Siri, wait for the "What can I help you with?" message, and then swipe down on the screen. Tap the small question mark that's displayed in the bottom-left corner of the screen (see Figure 3.3). When you do this, the last question, command, or request you made using Siri is displayed.

> **TIP** Tap the Bluetooth icon displayed in the bottom-right corner of the screen (also shown in Figure 3.3) to switch between using your iPhone or iPad's built-in speaker, a Bluetooth headset/speaker, or CarPlay.

Figure 3.3
Tap the Info icon (which looks like a question mark) to discover the latest about what Siri can do.

iOS 10 WHAT'S NEW Siri is compatible with FaceTime, Messages, Reminders, Phone (iPhone), Calendar, Maps, Twitter, Facebook, Music (including the Apple Music service), Mail, Weather, Stocks (iPhone), Clock, Contacts, Notes, Settings, Safari, iTunes, iBooks, Photos, and Podcasts.

New to iOS 10, Siri now understands commands related to the Home, meaning that you can control home automation equipment that your iPhone or iPad is linked with, such as your lights, thermostat, door locks, or security cameras.

Siri also responds to requests or questions related to almost anything having to do with sports, movies, entertainment, restaurants, music, weather, locations, or stocks. Plus, Siri can look up information when you pose almost any type of question, or you can use it to verbally control almost any iPhone/iPad-related feature that's adjustable from within Settings or Control Center. For example, you can activate Siri and say, "Turn on Airplane mode" or "Turn off Do Not Disturb."

FINDING, DISPLAYING, OR USING INFORMATION RELATED TO YOUR CONTACTS

Every field in a Contact's entry is searchable and can be accessed by Siri. Or you can ask Siri to look up a specific contact for you and display that contact's Info screen.

Again, the more information you include in each entry stored in your Contacts database, the more helpful Siri can be. To have Siri look up and display information stored in Contacts, say something like the following:

- "Look up John Doe in Contacts."
- "What is John Doe's phone number?"
- "What is John Doe's home phone number?"
- "What is John Doe's work address?"
- "Where does John Doe live?"
- "Where does John Doe work?"

> ☑ **TIP** When Siri displays the Info screen for a Contact, it is interactive; therefore, you can tap a displayed phone number to initiate a call, or tap an email address to launch the Mail app to send email to that address. If you tap a regular address, the Maps app launches, and if you tap a website URL, Safari launches and opens that web page.

Siri can also use information stored in your Contacts database to comply with various other requests, such as

- **"Send John Doe a text message"**—This works if you have an iPhone-labeled phone number, iMessage username, or email address saved in John Doe's Contacts entry. It also works with the text messaging feature if you have a phone number in someone's Contacts entry that's associated with the "mobile" label.

- **"Send John Doe an email"**—This works if you have an email address saved in John Doe's Contacts entry.

- **"How do I get to John Doe's home?"**—This works if you have a home address saved in John Doe's Contacts entry. The Maps app launches, and directions from your current location are displayed.

- **"When is John Doe's birthday?"**—This works if you have a date saved in the Birthday field in John Doe's Contacts entry.

- **"What is John Doe's wife's name?"**—This works if you have a spouse's name saved in John Doe's Contacts entry.

INITIATING A CALL

Initiate a call by activating Siri and then saying, "Call *[name]* at home," or "Call *[name]* at work." This works if that person has a Contacts entry associated with their name, as well as a phone number labeled Home or Work, respectively.

You could also say, "Call *[name]*'s mobile phone," or "Call *[name]*'s iPhone." If you just use the command *call*, and that person has several phone numbers in their Contacts entry, Siri gives you the option to select which number you want to call.

Alternatively, if someone's contact information or phone number is not stored in your iPhone, you can say, "Call" or "Dial" followed by each digit of a phone number. Thus, you'd say, "Call 212 555 1212."

> ☑ **TIP** You can also ask Siri to look up a business phone number or address by saying, "Look up *[business name]* in *[city, state]*." Or, you could say, "Look up *[business type, such as a dry cleaner]* in *[city, state]*."

On the iPhone, when Siri finds the phone number you're looking for, Siri says, "Calling *[name]* at *[location]*," and then automatically initiates a call to that number by launching the Phone app. Siri also has the capability to initiate FaceTime video calls. Use a command, such as, "FaceTime with *[name]*."

> ☑ **TIP** On the iPhone or iPad, Siri works with FaceTime, so you can say, "FaceTime Natalie," or "Make a FaceTime call to Natalie" to initiate a video call. You can also use FaceTime to initiate an audio-only call by saying, "Make a FaceTime audio call to Natalie."

SETTING UP REMINDERS AND TO-DO ITEMS

If you constantly jot down reminders to yourself on scrap pieces of paper or sticky notes, or manually enter to-do items into the Reminders app, this is one Siri-related feature you'll truly appreciate.

To create a reminder (to be utilized by the Reminders app), complete with an alarm, simply activate Siri and say something like, "Remind me to pick up my dry cleaning tomorrow at 3 p.m." Siri then creates the to-do item, displays it on the screen for your approval, and then saves it in the Reminders app. At the appropriate time and day, an alarm sounds and the reminder message is displayed.

> ### ✅ TIP
> When creating a reminder using Siri, provide a specific date and time, such as "tomorrow at 3 p.m." or "Friday at 1 p.m." or "July 7th at noon." You can also include a location that Siri knows, such as "Home" or "Work." For example, you could say, "Remind me to feed the dog when I get home," or "Remind me to call Emily when I get to work."

READING OR SENDING TEXT MESSAGES

When you receive a new text message but can't look at the screen (such as when you're driving), activate Siri and say, "Read new text message." After Siri reads the incoming message, you're given the opportunity to reply to that message and dictate your response.

Using Siri with the Messages app, you can also compose and send a text/instant message to anyone in your Contacts database by saying something like, "Compose a text message to John Doe."

You are asked to select an email address or mobile phone number to use. To bypass this step, say, "Send a text message to John Doe's mobile phone," or "Send a text message to John Doe's iPhone." Then, Siri says, "What do you want to say to John Doe?" Dictate your text message.

When you're finished speaking, Siri says, "I updated your message. Ready to send it?" The transcribed message is displayed on the screen, along with Cancel and Send icons. You can tap an icon or speak your reply.

> ### ❗ CAUTION
> Any time you dictate a text message or email that will be sent to someone else, make sure that when Siri translates your spoken words into text that the transcription is correct; otherwise, you could wind up sending a message that makes no sense or that has a meaning you didn't intend.

CHECKING THE WEATHER OR YOUR INVESTMENTS

The Weather app can display an extended weather forecast for your immediate area or any city in the world, and the Stocks app can be used to track your investments. However, Siri has the capability to automatically access the Web and obtain weather information for any city, as well as stock-related information about any stock or mutual fund.

After activating Siri, ask a weather-related question, such as

- **"What is today's weather forecast?"**—Siri pinpoints your location and provides a current forecast.

- **"What is the weather forecast for New York City?"**—Of course, you can insert any city and state in your request.

- **"Is it going to rain tomorrow?"**—Siri accesses and interprets the weather forecast, and then vocalizes, as well as displays a response. Siri determines your current location before providing a forecast.

- **"Should I bring an umbrella to work?"**—Siri knows the location of your work and can access and then interpret the weather forecast to offer a vocalized and displayed response.

If you have stock-related questions, ask about specific stocks by saying something like

- "What is *[company name]*'s stock at?"
- "What is *[company name]*'s stock price?"
- "How is *[company name]*'s stock performing?"
- "Show me *[company name]*'s stock."

When you request stock information, you get a verbal response from Siri along with information about that stock displayed on the iPhone or iPad's screen, as you can see in Figure 3.4.

Figure 3.4

Siri can tell you how a specific stock is performing. Here, the command "Siri, show me Apple stock," was spoken.

FINDING INFORMATION ON THE WEB OR GETTING ANSWERS TO QUESTIONS

If you want to perform a web search, you can manually launch the Safari browser, and then use a keyboard to type what you're looking for in the Search field. Another option is to perform your web search by entering it into the Search field via your iPhone or iPad's Spotlight Search feature.

Siri can also be used to perform web searches, by saying something like

- "Look up the *[company]* website."
- "Access the website cnn.com."
- "Find *[topic]* on the Web."
- "Search the Web for *[topic]*."
- "Google information about *[topic]*."
- "Search Wikipedia for *[topic]*."
- "What is the definition of *[word]*?"

You also can ask almost any type of question, and Siri seeks out the appropriate answer from the Internet. A question might be, "What does the Canadian flag look like?" or "What is the population of New York City?"

> **NOTE** When you ask Siri a question that requires your iPhone or iPad to seek out the answer on the Internet, this is done through Apple using Wolfram Alpha. To learn more about the vast topics you can ask Siri about, from unit conversions to historical data, visit www.wolframalpha.com/examples.

SCHEDULING AND MANAGING MEETINGS AND EVENTS

Like many apps that come preinstalled with iOS 10, the Calendar app is fully compatible with Siri, which means it's possible to use Siri to create or modify appointments, meetings, or events by using your voice. To do this, some of the things you can say include

- "Set up a meeting at 10:30 a.m."
- "Set up a meeting with Drew at noon tomorrow."
- "Meet with Emily for lunch at 1:00 p.m."
- "Set up a meeting with Rusty about third-quarter sales projections at 4:00 p.m. on December 12th."

> ☑ **TIP**　You can use Siri to reschedule or cancel events stored in the Calendar app. For example, you could say, "Move my 2 p.m. meeting to 4:00 p.m.," or "Cancel my 6:00 p.m. dinner with Rusty."
>
> To obtain an overview of your schedule, ask a question like, "What does the rest of my day look like?," or "When is my next appointment?" You can learn about a specific event as well, by asking, "When is my next meeting with Kevin?" or "Where is my next meeting?"
>
> Siri can also tap the Calendar and Maps app simultaneously if you ask a question like, "How do I get to my next meeting?" This works if you've filled in the Location field when creating an event in the Calendar app.

SENDING EMAIL AND ACCESSING NEW (INCOMING) EMAIL

If you want to compose an email to someone, activate Siri and say, "Send an email to [name]." If that person's email address is listed in your Contacts database, Siri addresses a new message to that person. Siri then says, "What is the subject of your email?" Speak the subject line for your email. When you stop speaking, Siri says, "Okay, what would you like the email to say?" You can now dictate the body of your email message.

When you're finished speaking, Siri composes the message, displays it on the screen, and then says, "Here is your email to [name]. Ready to send it?" You can now respond "yes" to send the email message, or say "cancel" to abort the message. If the message isn't what you want to say, ask Siri to "Change the text to...."

Meanwhile, if you're expecting an incoming email from someone, you can activate Siri and say, "Any new email from [name]?" and not have to first manually launch the Mail app.

Siri also now has the capability to search through the subjects of your emails. So, you can activate Siri and say, "Do I have any emails about [subject]?"

SETTING AN ALARM OR TIMER

Siri can control the Clock app that comes preinstalled on your iOS device so that it serves as an alarm clock or timer. You can say something like, "Set an alarm for 7:30 a.m. tomorrow," "Wake me up tomorrow at 7:30 a.m." or "Set a recurring wakeup call for 7:30 a.m." to create a new alarm. Or, to set a 30-minute timer, say,

"Set a timer for 30 minutes." A countdown timer is displayed on the iPhone or iPad's screen, and an alarm sounds when the timer reaches zero.

You can also simply use "Hey Siri" and ask "What's today's date?," "What time is it?," or "How many days until Christmas?" if you're too busy to look at the iPhone or iPad's screen, such as when you're driving.

GETTING DIRECTIONS USING THE MAPS APP

Pretty much any feature you can use the Maps app for—whether it's to find the location or phone number for a business, obtain turn-by-turn directions between two addresses, access public transit information, or map out a specific address location—you can access using Siri.

To use Maps-related functions, say things like the following:

- "How do I get to [location]?"
- "Show [address]."
- "Directions to [contact name or location]."
- "Find a [business type, such as gas station] near [location]."
- "Find a [business or service name, such as Starbucks Coffee] near where I am."
- "Where is the closest [business type, such as post office]?"
- "Find a [cuisine type, such as Chinese] restaurant near me."
- "What time does [store name] close tonight?"
- "Where is a good barber?" (When you ask a question like this, Siri relies on Yelp! Reviews and other information to provide highly recommended businesses or restaurants.)

If Siri finds multiple businesses or locations that are directly related to your request, it asks you to select one, or all related matches are displayed on a detailed map.

CONTROLLING THE MUSIC

In the mood to hear a specific song that's stored on your iPhone or iPad or that's available via Apple Music (if you're a subscriber)? Maybe you want to begin playing a specific playlist, you want to hear all the music stored on your iOS device by a particular artist, or you want to play a specific album? Well, just ask Siri. You can control the Music app or the Apple Music service using your voice by saying things like the following:

- "Play [song title]."
- "Play [album title]."
- "Play [playlist title]."

- "Play [*artist's name*]."
- "Play [*music genre, such as* pop, rock, or blues]."

You can also issue specific commands, such as "Shuffle my [*title*] playlist," or speak commands, such as "Pause" or "Skip" as music is playing.

> **☑ TIP** If you subscribe to Apple Music and use the Music app, activate Siri and request to hear any of the songs in Apple's online music collection, which is comprised of more than 40 million songs and albums and is continuously expanding.
>
> You can request to play (stream) music by song title, album title, or artist. Start by activating Siri and saying, "Play [*song title*]," Play [*song title*] by [*artist name*]," or "Play [*album title*]." Without an Apple Music subscription, you're limited to hearing the digital music you own.

As you're listening to music on your mobile device, if you want to hear similar music, activate Siri and say, "Play more music like this," or if you want to hear music that's popular, say something like, "Siri, play the number one Country song right now."

When streaming music from Apple Music, to purchase a song or album, activate Siri and say, "Buy this song" or "Buy this album."

> **☑ TIP** If you are somewhere and hear a song being played and want to know the name of the song or who sings it, activate Siri and say, "What song is this?" or "Who sings this?" Siri listens for a few seconds and then provides information about the music that's playing.

DICTATING NOTES TO YOURSELF

Siri is compatible with the Notes app and enables you to create and dictate notes. To create a new note, activate Siri and begin a sentence by saying, "Note that I…." You can also say, "Note: [*sentence*]." What you dictate is saved as a new note in the Notes app.

> **✎ NOTE** When using the Siri or dictation feature, your iPhone or iPad can capture and process up to 30 seconds of your speech at a time.

ASKING SIRI ABOUT SPORTS, MOVIES, ENTERTAINMENT, AND RESTAURANTS

If you're looking for the latest scores related to your favorite professional or college team or sporting event, just ask Siri. It's also possible to ask sports-related questions and then have Siri quickly research the answers via the Internet. When it comes to sports, here are some sample questions or requests you can use with Siri:

- "Did the Yankees win their last game?"
- "What was the score of last night's Patriots game?"
- "What was the score the last time the Yankees and Red Sox played?"
- "Show me the baseball scores from last night."
- "When do the Dallas Cowboys play next?"
- "Who has the most home runs on the New York Mets?"
- "Show me the roster for the Patriots."
- "Are any of the Bruins players currently injured?"

When it comes to movies, Siri can also help you decide what to go see, determine where movies are playing, look up movie times, and provide details about almost any movie ever made. Here are some sample questions or requests you can use with Siri that relate to movies:

- "Where is [movie title] playing?"
- "What's playing at [movie theater]?"
- "Who directed the movie [movie title]?"
- "Show me the cast from [movie title]."
- "What's playing at the movies tonight?"
- "Find the closest movie theater."
- "Show me the reviews for [movie title]."
- "What movie won Best Picture in [year]?"
- "Buy two tickets to see [movie title] tonight at the [movie theater name]."

If you're looking to try out a new restaurant or want to learn more about a local dining establishment, Siri knows all about restaurants too. Plus, thanks to Yelp! and OpenTable integration, you can view detailed information about restaurants, make dining reservations, or read reviews.

Here are some examples of how you can use Siri when you want to know more about restaurants:

- "Where's the closest Japanese restaurant?
- "Find a good Italian restaurant in Boston."
- "Table for two at Palm Restaurant in Boston for 7 p.m."
- "Show me reviews for *[restaurant name]* in *[city]*."

Figure 3.5 shows the results for the question, "Siri, what's a good steak restaurant in Boston?" A series of listings based on Yelp! ratings was displayed. Tap a listing for more details about a particular restaurant (shown in Figure 3.6). When Siri locates restaurant information, thanks to Yelp!, details about that establishment, including its location, phone number, hours of operation, entree price range, and a star-based rating, are displayed.

> ✅ **TIP**   The detailed information Siri displays is interactive. For example, tap the phone number in a restaurant listing to initiate a call to that restaurant, or tap the listed address to launch the Maps app and get detailed directions.

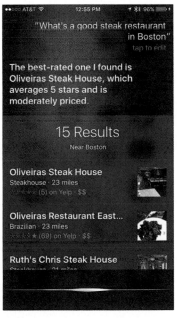

Figure 3.5
Activate Siri, and say, "Siri, what's a good restaurant in Boston?" Siri displays a list based on Yelp! ratings.

Figure 3.6
See more details about a restaurant from Siri's results.

☑ **TIP**   Here are some quick tips for using Siri:

- Siri is a mathematical genius. Simply say the mathematical calculation you need solved, and Siri presents the answer in seconds. For example, say, "What is 10 plus 10?," "What's the square root of 24?," or "What is 20 percent of 500?" This feature is particularly useful for helping you calculate the server's tip when you receive the check at a restaurant.

- When asking Siri to look up businesses, landmarks, popular destinations, or restaurants, in addition to just displaying a location on a map, Siri integrates with the Yelp! online service to provide much more detailed information about many businesses and restaurants.

- Send a tweet or update your Facebook status using your voice. Activate Siri and say something like, "Send a tweet that says, 'I am at Starbucks, come join me.'" To update your Facebook status, say something like, "Write on my wall, 'I just landed in New York City and I am leaving the airport now.'"

- When dictating a tweet, you can add the phrase, "Tweet with my location," to have Siri publish your current location with the outgoing tweet you're dictating.

- If you need to turn on or off certain iPhone or iPad features, activate Siri and say, "Turn on Wi-Fi" or "Turn off Bluetooth."

- When traveling overseas, use Siri to handle currency conversion calculations. For example, activate Siri and ask, "How many U.S. dollars is 500 pounds?"

- With the Photos app, you can activate Siri and say, "Show me my selfies," or "Show my photos from New York City." You can also be more specific and say something like, "Show my selfies from yesterday," or "Show selfies from my Florida vacation."

- Along with knowing about sports, TV shows, movies, restaurants, and music, Siri can quickly give you information about books. For example, activate Siri and say, "Show me books by Jason Rich" or "What are the best-selling books right now?"

USING DICTATION MODE

In many situations when the iPhone or iPad's virtual keyboard appears, a microphone key is located to the left of the spacebar. When you tap this microphone key, Dictation mode is activated (shown in Figure 3.7). An animated sound wave graphic displays on the screen as you speak.

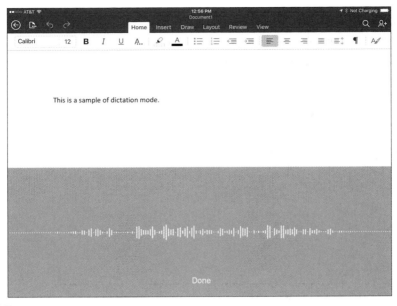

Figure 3.7
Use Dictation mode to enter text using your voice instead of typing on the virtual keyboard. It's shown here on an iPad running Microsoft Word.

You can now say whatever text you were going to manually type using the virtual keyboard. You can speak for up to 30 seconds at a time. When you're finished speaking, it's necessary to tap the Done key so that your device can translate your speech into text and insert it into the appropriate onscreen field.

For the fastest and most accurate results, speak one to three sentences at a time, and have your device connected to a Wi-Fi Internet connection.

> **☑ TIP** While using Dictation mode, you can easily add punctuation just by saying it. For example, you can say, "This is a sample dictation period," and Siri adds the period at the end of the sentence. You can also use words like "exclamation point," "open parenthesis," "close parenthesis," "open quotes," "close quotes," "comma," "semicolon," or "colon" as you dictate.

USING CARPLAY

Over the past few years, Apple has worked with most of the world's major car manufacturers to integrate the iPhone with the stereo system or infotainment system built in to many vehicles. This functionality varies depending on the make, model, and year of your car.

In some cases, if your vehicle is CarPlay compatible, there is a Lightning or USB port for your iPhone built in to the car. When you plug in your iPhone, your smartphone charges, plus it integrates directly with the car's in-dash infotainment system. This enables you to activate the iPhone's navigation capabilities via the Maps app, Siri functionality, and music capabilities by pressing the CarPlay button built in to your steering wheel or dashboard, for example.

In other cases, your device establishes a wireless Bluetooth connection with your car and enables you to play music that's stored on your iPhone via your car's stereo or that your iPhone streams from the Internet via Apple Music, Spotify, Pandora, or another compatible music streaming app. It's also possible to use the Phone feature to make and receive calls hands-free while you're driving.

Every vehicle manufacturer is implementing iPhone integration differently, and this functionality is only built in to 2013 or later model year vehicles. If you have an older car, you must use third-party accessories to link your iPhone to the vehicle.

Typically, when you use Siri, information that's requested is displayed on the iOS device's screen. CarPlay functionality, however, offers much of the same functionality as Siri but turns off the iPhone's screen altogether. Thus, Siri offers only verbal responses to a user's requests, commands, and questions.

This is a much safer solution for drivers who must pay attention to the road yet want to access content from their Internet-connected iOS mobile device to initiate calls, look up information, access email or text messages, or obtain turn-by-turn driving directions to a specific location.

> ☑ **TIP**   If you've invested in an Apple Watch, you also have full access to Siri from the watch when it is wirelessly paired to your iPhone. To activate Siri from the watch, press the Digital Crown for about two seconds until the Siri screen is displayed, and then start speaking into the watch.

4

FIND, BUY, AND USE THIRD-PARTY APPS

The collection of preinstalled apps that comes with iOS 10 enables you to use your iPhone or iPad for a wide range of popular tasks without first having to find and install additional apps. However, one of the things that has set the iPhone and iPad apart from the competition, and made these devices among the most sought-after and popular throughout much of the world, is the vast library of optional apps.

You can obtain all the apps currently available for your iOS device from Apple's online App Store. Then, as needed, iOS 10 can automatically update your apps to ensure you're always working with the most recently released version.

> 📝 **NOTE** Although some apps are tweaked to work exceptionally well on the latest iPhone or iPad models, all iPhone-specific apps can scale themselves automatically to accommodate the iPhone model you're using, whether it has a 4", 4.7", or 5.5" display. Likewise, apps for the iPad (as well as universal iPhone/iPad apps) automatically adapt to the screen size of the tablet you're using.

WORKING WITH THE APP STORE

There are two ways to access the App Store: directly from your iPhone or iPad (using the App Store app that comes preinstalled on your device) or using the iTunes software on your primary computer.

The App Store app is used exclusively for finding, purchasing (if applicable), downloading, and installing apps directly onto your device from the App Store. This option works when your mobile device has an Internet connection. Other apps, such as iTunes Store, are used to acquire various types of content (such as music, movies, and TV show episodes).

You use the iTunes software on your primary computer to access the App Store, as well as many other types of content. Anything you acquire is then transferred to your mobile device either using the iTunes Sync process or by downloading the apps and/or content from your iCloud account.

INSTALLING NEW APPS

If you're shopping for apps directly from your iPhone or iPad, tap the Price icon, followed by the Buy icon, to make a purchase. (Free apps display a Get icon in place of the Price icon.) You are asked to supply your Apple ID password (or place your finger on your device's Touch ID sensor—the Home button—to confirm the transaction). The app automatically downloads and installs itself on your device. After it is installed, its app icon appears on your iPhone or iPad's Home screen and is ready to use.

> ✅ **TIP** Instead of manually entering your Apple ID password to confirm an app purchase (or acquire a free app), if your iOS mobile device is equipped with a Touch ID sensor as part of its Home button, simply scan your fingerprint to approve the transaction. For this to work, the feature must be turned on once from within Settings. To do this, launch Settings, tap the Touch ID & Passcode option, enter your device's passcode, and then turn on the virtual switch associated with the iTunes & App Store option.

> **NOTE** When applicable, the tiny + icon in the top-left corner of a Buy or Get button indicates that the app is universal and will run on both the iPhone and iPad.

RESTORING OR REINSTALLING APPS YOU'VE ALREADY DOWNLOADED

If you have Family Sharing set up via iCloud (see Chapter 6, "Use iCloud and the iCloud Drive App"), it's possible to share apps you acquire with up to five other family members without having to repurchase that app. With or without Family Sharing, you're able to install an app you acquire from the App Store on all of your own iOS mobile devices that are linked to the same iCloud account, as long as the app is compatible with each device.

To download an app onto your iPad that you have already purchased or down-loaded onto another computer or device, tap the Purchased icon at the bottom of the screen in the App Store app. On the iPhone, tap the Updates icon, and then tap the Purchased option near the top of the Updates screen. All your app purchases to date are displayed.

> **NOTE** At the top of the Purchased screen on the iPhone or iPad, tap the All tab to view all of the apps you've purchased to date that are compatible with the device you're using. You also have the option to tap the Not on This iPhone/ Not on This iPad tab to view apps you've acquired in the past that are not currently installed on the device you're using.

When you see an iCloud icon rather than a Get or Price icon associated with an app description, you have already acquired the app, and it's available through your iCloud account. Tap the iCloud icon to download the app (without having to pay for it again) to the smartphone or tablet you're currently using. You can only install already purchased apps that are compatible with that iOS device.

> **TIP** From Settings, you have the option of having your iOS device auto-matically download and install any new (and compatible) apps, music, or eBooks purchased using your Apple ID on any other computer or device. To set this up, launch Settings, select the iTunes & App Store option, and then adjust the Automatic Downloads options, which include Music, Apps, Books & Audiobooks, and Updates. You also can decide whether this feature works with a cellular data Internet connec-tion or only when a Wi-Fi connection is available. To exclusively use a Wi-Fi connec-tion, turn off the virtual switch associated with the Use Cellular Data option.

FINDING APPS, MUSIC, AND MORE

If you're shopping for apps, music, movies, TV shows, podcasts, audiobooks, eBooks, ringtones, or other content from your primary computer, with the goal of transferring what you acquire to your iPhone or iPad later via the iTunes Sync process or via iCloud, use the latest version of the iTunes software on your Mac or PC computer.

From your Internet-connected iPhone or iPad, you can acquire and enjoy different types of content using a handful of different apps. Table 4.1 explains which app you should use to acquire and then enjoy various types of content on your iOS device.

Table 4.1 How to Acquire and Enjoy Various Types of Content on Your iPhone or iPad*

Content Type	Buy with App	Run with App
Apps	App Store	The app itself that you download and install
Digital editions of publications (including newspapers and magazines)	App Store	The digital publication's proprietary app or in some cases, the News app
Music	iTunes Store	Music
Movies	iTunes Store	Videos
TV Shows	iTunes Store	Videos
Podcasts	Podcasts	Podcasts
Audiobooks	iTunes (or the optional Audible app)	iBooks (or the optional Audible app)
eBooks*	iBooks (to access iBook Store)	iBooks
PDF files	Mail, iCloud, iTunes Sync	iBooks or another PDF reader app
iTunes U Personal Enrichment and Educational Content	iTunes U**	iTunes U
Ringtones (and Alert Tones)	iTunes Store	Phone, FaceTime, Messages (or other apps that generate audible alarms or ringtones)

* eBooks can also be purchased from Amazon.com and read using the free Kindle app, or purchased from BN.com and read using the free Nook app.

** The iTunes U app serves as a gateway to a vast selection of personal enrichment and educational courses, lectures, workshops, and information sessions that have been produced by leading educators, universities, and other philanthropic organizations. All iTunes U content is provided for free.

> **iOS 10 WHAT'S NEW** The Messages app now enables users to download and install optional animated Stickers and other content that can be embedded within text messages (to be sent via the iMessage service). To acquire this additional content, it's necessary to access a special area of the App Store via the Messages app.
>
> To do this, launch Messages and tap the Compose icon to begin writing a new message, or open an existing conversation. Tap the Menu (>) icon displayed to the immediate left of the compose message field. Tap the Media icon. Next, tap the Media Content icon displayed in the bottom-left corner of the screen. Tap the + Store icon. Tap the Featured tab to view all content and optional (third-party) Message-compatible apps, or tap the Categories tab, select Stickers, and then choose a Sticker category (such as Eating & Drinking or Gaming) to download and install a collection of animated Stickers that will then be accessible from within the Messages app as you're composing messages to be sent via iMessage. (Most Sticker collections are free.)

EVERYTHING YOU NEED TO KNOW ABOUT APPS

Apps are individual programs that you install onto your iPhone or iPad to give it additional functionality, just as you utilize different programs on your primary computer. For the iPhone or iPad, all apps are available from one central (online) location, called the App Store.

When you begin exploring the App Store, you'll discover right away that there are in excess of 2 million apps to choose from. They are divided into different categories to help make it easier and faster to find what you're looking for.

The App Store's main app categories include Games, Kids, Books, Business, Catalogs, Education, Entertainment, Finance, Food & Drink, Health & Fitness, Lifestyle, Magazines & Newspapers, Medical, Music, Navigation, News, Photo & Video, Productivity, Reference, Shopping, Social Networking, Sport, Travel, Utilities, and Weather.

UNDERSTANDING DEVICE COMPATIBILITY

In terms of compatibility, all iOS apps fall into one of these three categories:

■ **iPhone-specific**—These are apps designed exclusively for the various iPhone models that might not function properly on the iPad. Most iPhone-specific apps run on an iPad but do not take advantage of the tablet's larger screen.

- **iPad-specific**—These are apps designed exclusively for the iPad. They fully utilize the tablet's larger display and do not function on the iPhone or on other iOS devices. All iPad-specific apps do, however, function flawlessly on all iPad models.

- **Universal**—These are apps designed to work on all iOS mobile devices, including any model iPhone or iPad. These apps detect which device they're running on and automatically adapt.

> **☑ TIP** When reading the App Store description of any app, tap the Details tab and scroll down to the Information heading. Here, you can see a listing of which iOS mobile devices the app is compatible with. Look for the Compatibility listing under the Information heading (see Figure 4.1).

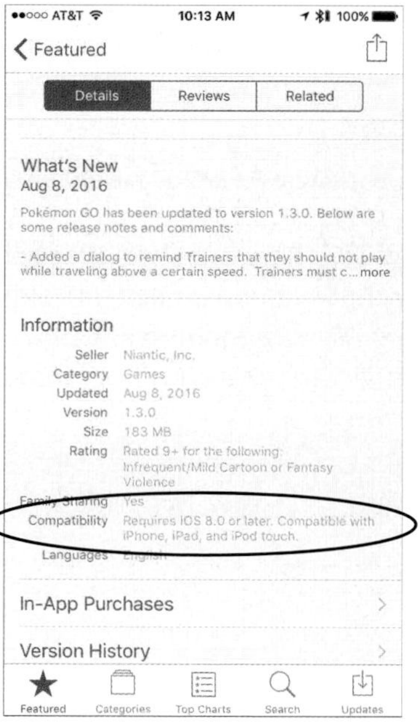

Figure 4.1

From an app's Description screen, you can see which iOS mobile devices the app is compatible with. Look for the Compatibility heading.

> ✓ **TIP** If you own two or more iOS devices, such as an iPhone and an iPad (or an iPod touch) and all the devices are linked to the same Apple ID (iCloud) account, you can purchase a universal (or iPhone-specific) app once, but then install it on all your iOS devices. This can be done through iTunes Sync or via iCloud after an app is initially purchased or downloaded.

When you're browsing the App Store from your iPhone, by default it displays all iPhone-specific apps followed by universal apps, but it does not display iPad apps. When you're browsing the App Store from your iPad, iPad-specific, universal, and iPhone-specific apps are all listed.

If you're shopping for apps using the iTunes software on your primary computer, click the iPhone or iPad tab near the top center of the iTunes screen (shown in Figure 4.2) to select which format apps you're looking for.

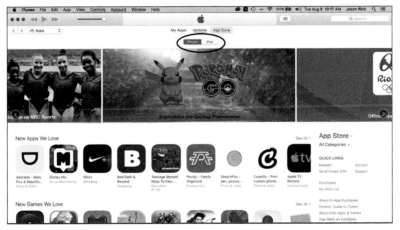

Figure 4.2
Click the appropriate tab to indicate which format apps you're looking for.

> ✓ **TIP** Because some app developers release the same app in both an iPhone-specific and an iPad-specific format, many iPad-specific apps have "HD" for High-Definition in their title, to help differentiate them from iPhone or universal apps. Some iPad-specific apps include the words "for iPad" in their title.

QUICK GUIDE TO APP PRICING

Regardless of whether you use the App Store app from your mobile device or visit the App Store using the iTunes software on your primary computer, you must set up an Apple ID account and have a major credit card or debit card linked to the account to make purchases.

> **TIP** If you don't have a major credit card or debit card that you want to link with your Apple ID account, you can purchase prepaid iTunes gift cards from Apple or most places that sell prepaid gift cards.
>
> To purchase prepaid iTunes gift cards online, visit www.apple.com/us/shop/gift-cards/itunes-electronic.
>
> iTunes gift cards are available in a variety of denominations and can be used to make app and other content purchases. They are distinct from Apple gift cards, which are only redeemable at Apple Stores or Apple.com.

The first time you access the App Store and attempt to make a purchase, you are prompted to enter your Apple ID account username and password or set up a new Apple ID account, which requires you to supply your name, address, email, and credit card information. For all subsequent online app purchases, you simply need to enter your Apple ID password (or place your finger on your device's Touch ID sensor), and the purchase is automatically billed to your credit or debit card or deducted from your iTunes gift card balance.

> **TIP** An Apple ID account can also be referred to as an iTunes Store account. To learn more about how an Apple ID account works or to manage your account, visit https://support.apple.com/apple-id. The same Apple ID you use to make purchases can also be used as your username when you're using FaceTime for video calling, Messages to access the iMessage service, or to access your iCloud account.

> **TIP** If you've forgotten your Apple ID username and/or password, using any Internet web browser, visit https://appleid.apple.com. Click the Forgot Apple ID or Password? option. Remember, even if you have multiple Apple computers and mobile devices, you need only one Apple ID account.

WHAT YOU NEED TO KNOW ABOUT APP PRICING

Some apps are free, but others need to be purchased, and/or require you to make in-app purchases to fully utilize them. The following is an overview of how app pricing works.

FREE APPS

Free apps cost nothing to download and install on your phone or tablet. Some programmers and developers release apps for free out of pure kindness to share their creations with the iPhone- and/or iPad-using public. These are fully functional apps.

There are also free apps that serve as demo versions of paid apps. In some cases, certain features or functions of the app are locked in the free version, but are later made available if you upgrade to the paid or premium version of the app.

A third category of free apps comprises fully functional apps that display ads as part of their content. In exchange for using the app, you must view ads. These ads typically offer the option to click special offers from within the app or learn more about a product or service being advertised.

> **NOTE** Many free apps that contain ads also have a paid app counterpart that's ad-free.

The final type of free app enables the user to make in-app purchases to add features or functionality to the app or unlock premium content. The core app, without the extra content, is free, however.

> **TIP** Some fully functional apps are free because they're designed to promote a specific company or work with a specific service. For example, to use the free HBOGo app, you must be a paid subscriber of the HBO premium cable channel.
>
> Likewise, to use the free Netflix app, you must be a paid subscriber to this streaming movie service. The AmEx app is useful only to people with an American Express card, but the free Target app is useful to anyone who shops at Target stores.
>
> The Chipotle app is also free and allows anyone to place a food order from their mobile device, pay for it using Apple Pay, and then have their order waiting for them for pickup at a predefined time.
>
> The Southwest Airlines app (or the app for any major airline) is also free. It can be used to make and manage airline reservations with that airline, check in for a flight, create and store digital boarding passes, and manage a frequent flier account.

PAID APPS

After you purchase an app, you own it and can use it as often as you'd like, usually without incurring additional fees (although in-app purchases might be possible). You simply pay a fee for the app upfront, which is often between $.99 and $9.99. Typically, future upgrades of the app are free of charge.

SUBSCRIPTION-BASED APPS

Each full-length digital edition of a magazine or newspaper requires its own proprietary app (also available from the App Store) to access and read that publication's content.

> **iOS 10** **WHAT'S NEW**   Many newspaper and magazine publishers also offer paid digital subscriptions for exclusive content through the newly redesigned News app, which you'll learn more about in Chapter 16, "Customize Your Reading Experience with iBooks and the Redesigned News App."

These apps are typically free, and then you pay a recurring subscription fee for content, which automatically gets downloaded into the app. Many digital editions of newspapers, such as the *New York Times* and the *Wall Street Journal*, utilize a subscription app model, as do hundreds of different magazines. Usually, the main content of the digital and printed version of a publication are identical; however, you can view the digital edition on your iPhone or iPad, plus take advantage of added interactive elements built in to the app.

If you're already a subscriber to the print version of a newspaper or magazine, some publishers offer the digital edition free, whereas others charge an extra fee to subscribe to the digital edition as well. Or you can subscribe to just the digital edition of a publication.

With some publications, you can download the free app for a specific newspaper or magazine and then purchase one issue at a time (including past issues) from within the app. There is no long-term subscription commitment, but individual issues of the publication still must be purchased and downloaded. Or you can purchase an ongoing (recurring) subscription, and new issues of that publication will automatically be downloaded to your iPhone or iPad as they become available.

WHAT'S NEW Through the News app, many leading publications offer content for free. You can fully customize what topics or publications you're interested in reading, and the News app presents all related content (potentially acquired from many sources) to you in an easy-to-read way.

Unless you acquire a paid subscription to a publication, when using the News app, you only have access to select articles and content, not the entire publication.

IN-APP PURCHASES

Some apps enable you to purchase additional content or add new features and functionality by making in-app purchases. The capability to make in-app purchases has become very popular and is being used by app developers in a variety of ways. If an app offers in-app purchases, they are listed under the In-App Purchases heading in the app description screen in the App Store.

! CAUTION The price you pay for an app does not translate directly to the quality or usefulness of that app. Some free or very inexpensive apps are extremely useful, are packed with features, and can really enhance your experience using your iPhone or iPad. However, there are also costly apps that are poorly designed, filled with bugs, or don't live up to expectations or to the description of the app offered by the app's developer or publisher. The price of an app is set by its developer.

Instead of using the price as the only determining factor if you're evaluating several apps that appear to offer similar functionality, be sure to read the app's customer reviews carefully, and pay attention to the average star-based rating the app has earned. These user reviews and ratings are much better indicators of an app's quality and usefulness than its price.

SHOPPING WITH THE APP STORE APP

From your iPhone or iPad's Home screen, access the App Store by tapping the blue-and-white App Store app icon. Your device must have access to the Internet via a cellular or Wi-Fi connection.

When you access the App Store app (shown in Figure 4.3 on the iPad), a handful of command icons at the top and bottom of the screen are used to navigate your way around the online-based store.

If you already know the name of the app you want to find, purchase, download, and install, tap the Search field, which is located near the upper-right corner of the screen in the iPad version. On the iPhone, tap the Search option displayed at the bottom of the App Store app's screen (as shown in Figure 4.4).

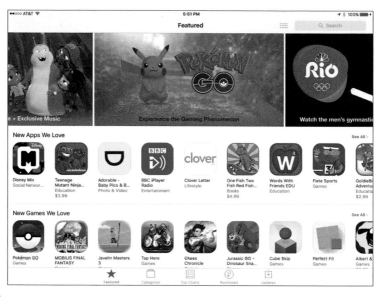

Figure 4.3

The main App Store app screen on the iPad. Find, purchase, download, and install apps directly from your tablet.

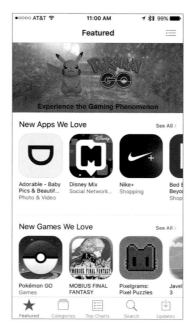

Figure 4.4

From your iPhone, tap the Search icon to search for any app in the App Store by name or keyword.

Using the virtual keyboard, enter the name of the app. Tap the Search key on the virtual keyboard to begin the search. You can also perform a search based on a keyword or phrase, such as "word processing," "to-do lists," "time management," or "photo editing."

In a few seconds, applicable results are displayed on the App Store screen in the form of app previews.

If you're shopping for apps from your iPad, as you browse the App Store, iPad-specific and universal apps are displayed if you tap the iPad Only option near the top of the screen in most areas in the App Store.

In Figure 4.5, in the Search field on an iPad I entered "Note Taking" to browse through various note-taking apps available from the App Store. The search results are displayed as app previews. Scroll down to view all search results. Use the filters at the top of the screen to narrow your search results.

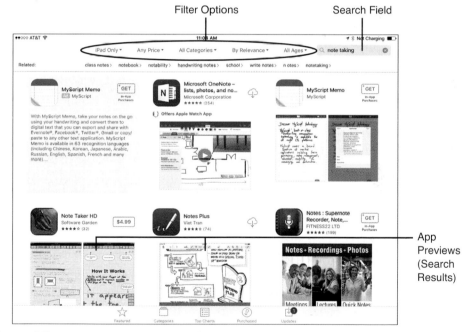

Figure 4.5

In the Search field, type the name of an app, or a keyword or search phrase that's related to the type of app you're looking for, to view related search results that are displayed as app previews.

> ☑ **TIP**   At the bottom center of the main App Store screen on the iPad are several command icons, labeled Featured, Categories, Top Charts, Purchased, and Updates. On the iPhone, the icons along the bottom of the screen are labeled Featured, Categories, Top Charts, Search, and Updates.
>
> If you don't know the exact name of an app you're looking for, these command icons will help you browse the App Store and discover apps that might be of interest to you.

THE FEATURED ICON

Tap the Featured icon near the bottom of the App Store screen to see a listing of what Apple considers "Featured" apps (refer to Figure 4.3 or Figure 4.4). These are divided into a handful of categories, such as New Apps We Love, New Games We Love, or Popular Apps. Flick your finger from right to left to scroll horizontally through the apps listed, or tap the See All option to the right of a category heading.

Near the top of the screen are large graphic banners that constantly change. These banners promote specific and popular apps, like Pokemon Go (also shown in Figure 4.3 and Figure 4.4) or app categories.

THE CATEGORIES ICON

Just like a bookstore, the App Store sorts its offerings by category, which makes it easier to browse through and find apps based on what you're looking for.

Tap the Categories icon, and then from the displayed categories listing, tap one that's of interest, such as Games, Business, Finance, News, or Photo & Video. Only apps that fall into your selected category are displayed (the Productivity category is shown in Figure 4.6 on an iPad). Keep in mind that some categories offer a menu of subcategories to help you narrow down your options.

For example, when you tap the Games category, 18 game subcategories—such as Action, Arcade, Board, Family, Puzzle, Role Playing, Strategy, and Trivia—are offered. Tap a subcategory to view applicable game apps.

THE TOP CHARTS ICON

When you tap the Top Charts command icon, located near the bottom center of the App Store app's screen, a listing of Paid, Free, and Top Grossing apps are displayed (shown in Figure 4.7). These charts are based on all app categories.

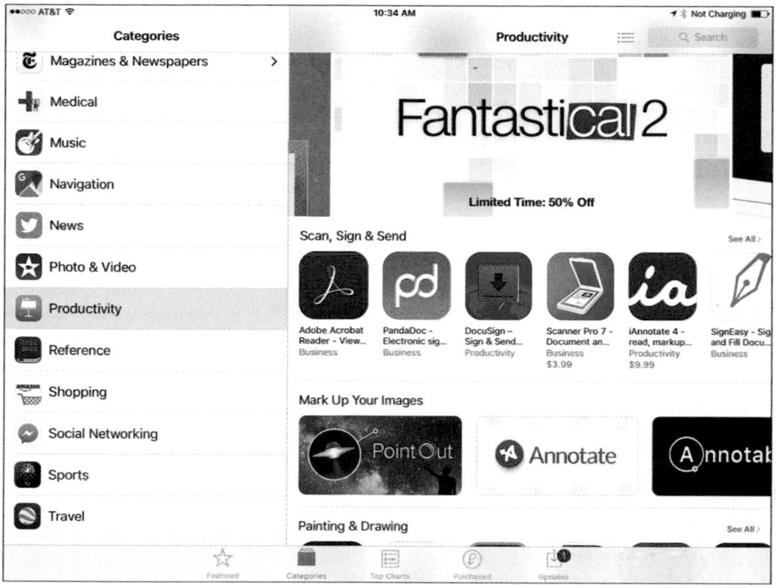

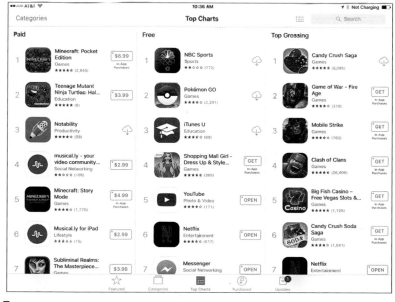

Figure 4.6

If you know the type of app you're looking for but don't have a specific app in mind, try browsing the App Store by category.

Figure 4.7

Discover the most popular apps available from the App Store by tapping the Top Charts icon.

To view charts related to a specific app category, such as Business or Games, first tap the Top Charts button, and then tap the Categories option and choose a specific category.

MANAGE YOUR ACCOUNT AND REDEEM iTUNES GIFT CARDS

When you scroll down to the very bottom of the Featured screen in the App Store, you see several Quick Links command buttons. Tap the Redeem button to redeem a prepaid iTunes gift card. Tap the Apple ID *[Your Apple ID Username]* button to manage your Apple ID account and update your credit card information. When the Apple ID window appears, tap the View Apple ID option. When prompted, enter your password.

Tap the Apple ID account button to manage your recurring paid subscriptions as well. When the Account Settings screen is displayed, scroll down to the Subscriptions heading and tap the Manage button. You can then modify or cancel your paid recurring subscriptions to digital newspapers or magazines, for example. If you don't have any active subscriptions, this option does not appear.

Tap the Send Gift option to send an iTunes gift card to someone else. Their gift will arrive via email, and they can redeem it almost instantly from the App Store, iTunes Store, or iBook Store.

FEATURES OF AN APP LISTING

As you browse the App Store, each screen is composed of many app listings (or more information-packed app previews). Each listing promotes a specific app and displays the app's title, graphic icon or logo, what category the app falls into, and its price.

Within app previews (refer to Figure 4.5), the app's title, its logo/graphic, the app's developer, its average star-based rating, how many ratings the app has received (the number in parentheses), the price icon, and a sample screenshot from the app itself are displayed.

THE APP'S DESCRIPTION PAGE

Before committing to a purchase, as you're looking at an app's listing or preview in the App Store, tap its title or graphic icon to view a detailed description. When you do this on the iPhone, the App Store screen is replaced with a detailed description of the app. On the iPad, a new app description window is displayed over the App Store screen.

An app description screen (shown in Figure 4.8) displays the app's title and logo near the top of the screen, along with its price icon (or Get icon if it's a free app), average star-based rating, and the number of ratings it has received.

You then see three command tabs, labeled Details, Reviews, and Related.

- Tap the Details tab to view a detailed description of the app.

- Tap the Reviews tab to view a ratings chart for that app, as well as detailed reviews written by your fellow iPhone and iPad users.

- Tap the Related tab to view similar apps that are available from the App Store.

Displayed immediately below the Details, Reviews, and Related tabs are sample screenshots from the app itself. In some cases, a promotional video for the app is also displayed.

Swipe your finger horizontally to scroll through the sample screenshots, or scroll down to view the Details, Reviews, or Related information, based on which command tab you've tapped.

Figure 4.8

An app's description screen tells you all about a specific app. This information can help you decide whether it's of interest to you or relevant to your needs.

WHAT'S OFFERED WHEN YOU TAP THE DETAILS TAB

Immediately below the sample screenshots from the app is a text-based description of the app that's been written by the app's developer. This is a sales tool designed to sell apps.

Below the description is information about new features that have been added to the app in the most recent version. Look for the What's New heading.

Displayed beneath the What's New heading, if applicable, is the Supports heading. Here, you can quickly determine whether the app is compatible with Apple's Game Center online service, for example. As you scroll down on this screen, the Information section offers more useful facts about the app.

Below the Information section, tap the In-App Purchases option, if this option is available, to discover what in-app purchases are available and their cost.

Tap the Version History option to see information about all revisions to the app that have been released since it was first introduced.

Tap the Developer Apps link to discover other apps available from the same developer or publisher. Tap the Developer Website option to access the website operated by the app developer or the app-specific website. When you do this, Safari automatically launches and then loads the applicable website.

WHAT'S OFFERED WHEN YOU TAP THE REVIEWS TAB

When you tap the Reviews tab, the App Store Ratings chart is displayed (shown in Figure 4.9). This graphically shows how many ratings the app has received, its overall average rating, and the total number of ratings. A top rating is five stars.

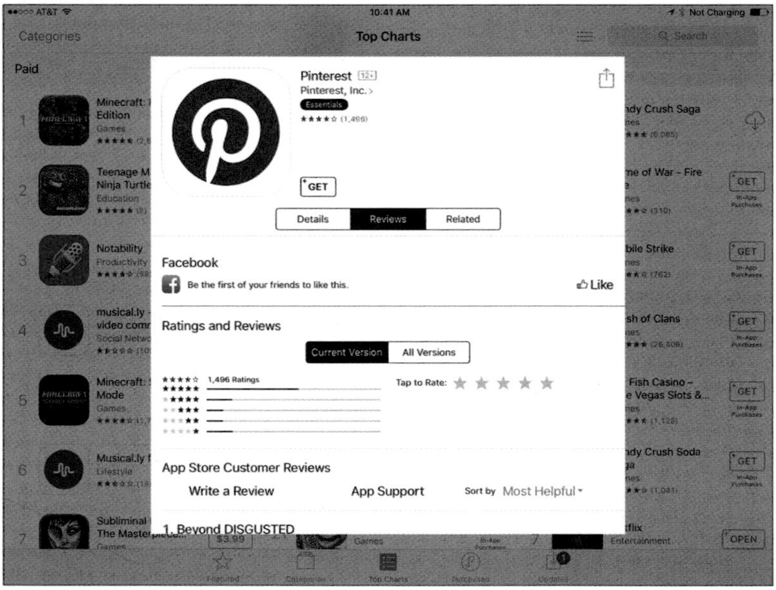

Figure 4.9

Every app description contains an average rating and a rating summary chart. Use it to quickly see what other users think about the app.

Below the App Store Ratings chart are reviews written by other App Store customers. Scroll down to read them.

> **✓ TIP** As you're looking at an app's Description screen, you can quickly share details about that app with others when you tap the Share icon near the top-right corner of the Description screen.

WHAT'S OFFERED WHEN YOU TAP THE RELATED TAB

These are listings for other apps, usually similar in functionality to the app you're looking at. On the iPhone, to exit an app's description page and continue browsing the App Store, tap the left-pointing arrow icon near the top-left corner of the screen. On the iPad, tap anywhere outside the app's description window.

> **✎ NOTE** If you opt to shop for apps using the iTunes software on your Mac or PC, you can transfer those apps to your iOS mobile device using the iTunes Sync process or download your purchases from iCloud by tapping on the Purchased option in the App Store app on your mobile device. It's also possible to set up the iTunes software to automatically download app updates and then transfer them to your iOS device(s) when they're synced.
>
> To learn more about using the iTunes software on your computer and the iTunes Sync process, visit www.apple.com/support/itunes.

QUICK TIPS FOR FINDING APPS

As you explore the App Store, it's easy to get overwhelmed by the sheer number of apps that are available for your iOS device. If you're a new iPhone or iPad user, spending time browsing the App Store introduces you to the many types of apps that are available and provides you with ideas about how your phone or tablet can be utilized in your personal or professional life.

However, you can save a lot of time searching for apps if you already know the app's exact title or you know what type of app you're looking for. In this case, enter either the app's exact title or a keyword description of the app in the App Store's Search field to see a list of relevant matches.

If you're looking for a word processing app, either enter the search phrase "Microsoft Word" into the App Store's Search field or enter the search phrase "word processor" to see a selection of word-processing apps.

If you're looking for vertical market apps with specialized functionality that caters to your industry or profession, enter that industry or profession (or keywords associated with it) in the Search field. For example, enter keywords like "medical imaging," "radiology," "plumbing," "telemarketing," or "sales."

As you're evaluating an app before downloading it, use these tips to help you determine whether it's worth installing on your phone or tablet:

- Figure out what types of features or functionality you want to add to your iPhone or iPad.

- Using the Search field, find apps designed to handle the tasks you have in mind. Chances are, you can easily find a handful of apps created by different developers that are designed to perform the same basic functionality. Pick which is the best based on the description, screenshots, and list of features each app offers.

- Check the customer reviews and ratings for the app. This useful tool quickly determines whether the app actually works as described in its description. Keep in mind that an app's description in the App Store is written by the app's developer and is designed to sell apps. The customer reviews and star-based ratings are created by fellow iPhone or iPad users who have tried out the app firsthand. If an app has only a few ratings or reviews and they're mixed, you might need to try out the app for yourself to determine whether it will be useful to you.

- If an app offers a free version, download and test that first before purchasing the premium version. You can always delete any app that you try out but don't wind up liking or needing.

KEEPING YOUR APPS UP TO DATE

Periodically, app developers release new versions of their apps. iOS 10 can automatically update your installed apps as long as your iPhone or iPad has access to the Internet.

To customize this auto-update option, launch Settings and tap the iTunes & App Store option. From the iTunes & App Stores submenu, make sure the virtual switch associated with the Updates option is turned on.

Next, scroll down to the Use Cellular Data option. Choose whether you want apps to update using a cellular data connection to the Internet. Keep in mind that some

apps that have a large file size associated with them require a Wi-Fi Internet connection to initially download or later update.

At any time, you can see which apps have been updated and read a summary
of what functionality or features have been added to the app update (as well as
which bugs have been fixed) by launching the App Store app and tapping the
Updates option.

If an app listed on the Updates screen has an Open button associated with it, the
app has been recently updated. The date of the update is listed in the heading.
Tap the app icon or its title to read about the update. Tap the Open button to
launch the app and use it on your iPhone or iPad.

From the Updates screen, if an Open button is not displayed, you might see a progress meter indicating the app is currently being updated and downloaded to your
device. If an update is available but has not yet been downloaded and installed, an
Update button, instead of an Open button, is displayed with that app.

As you're viewing the Updates screen, apps are listed in chronological order, based
on when they were updated. Pending updates, if any, are displayed near the top of
the screen (shown in Figure 4.10 on an iPhone).

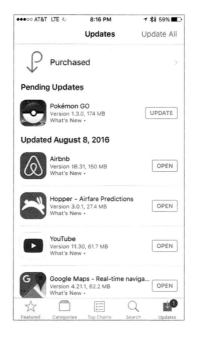

Figure 4.10

*iOS 10 can automatically download and install updates to apps. The Updates screen lists which
apps have been recently updated and what's new in those updates.*

MANAGING YOUR KIDS' APP ACQUISITIONS

As a parent, you're able to control what apps your child is allowed to purchase, install, and ultimately use on their iOS mobile device or yours. It's also possible to control their online spending when it comes to apps and in-app purchases in several different ways.

To determine which apps and content your child is allowed to use on an iOS mobile device, activate the Restrictions options. To do this, launch Settings on the device, tap the General option, and then tap the Restrictions option.

From the Restrictions submenu, tap Enable Restrictions, create a four-digit passcode, and then turn on the virtual switches associated with iTunes Store, Apple Music Connect, iBooks Store, Podcasts, News, Installing Apps, Deleting Apps, and In-App Purchases to limit what your child can do.

Under the Allowed Content heading, tap the Apps option and determine what apps your child is allowed to access, based on the App Ratings.

When you set up iCloud's Family Sharing, it's possible to set up your child's iOS mobile device so he or she needs to ask you for permission (via a text message to your iPhone or iPad) before acquiring any new apps or content. This feature also gives parents greater control over apps installed on a child's device.

> **NOTE** In addition to the apps that come preinstalled with iOS 10, Apple offers a handful of optional Made By Apple apps, such as Pages (similar to Microsoft Word), Numbers (similar to Microsoft Excel), Keynote (similar to Microsoft PowerPoint), iMovie (video editing), Apple Store (online shopping via the Apple.com Online Store or an Apple retail store), GarageBand (music composition and editing), and iTunes U (educational programming). These are available for free from the App Store.

IN THIS CHAPTER

- How to use AirDrop to share content with other nearby Mac, iPhone, and iPad users
- How to use your iPhone or iPad with AirPlay-compatible equipment
- How to print files wirelessly to a compatible AirPrint printer
- Discover iOS 10's Continuity and Handoff functionality

5

SYNC, SHARE, AND PRINT FILES USING AIRDROP, AIRPLAY, AIRPRINT, AND HANDOFF

When it comes to syncing and sharing files and data (including app-specific data), your iOS mobile device is equipped with several tools, including AirDrop, AirPlay, AirPrint, Continuity, and Handoff. These technologies are in addition to iCloud, which is covered in Chapter 6, "Use iCloud and the iCloud Drive App."

The AirDrop tool enables your iPhone or iPad to wirelessly transfer certain types of files (including photos) and app-specific data to other iPhones, iPads, and Macs that are in close proximity, and that also support the AirDrop function.

To turn on the AirDrop feature on your iPhone or iPad, launch Control Center by swiping your finger upward from the very bottom of the screen (shown in Figure 5.1). When the Control Center appears, tap the AirDrop option.

Figure 5.1

Tap the AirDrop button in Control Center to access the AirDrop menu (shown here on an iPad).

From the AirDrop menu (shown in Figure 5.2), choose whether you want to use AirDrop to communicate with any other nearby users (Everyone) or only with people in your Contacts database (Contacts Only). It's also possible to turn off the feature altogether by selecting the Receiving Off option.

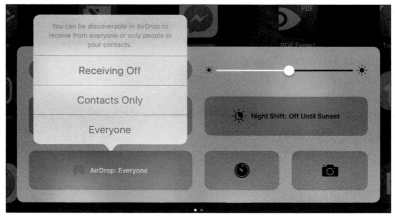

Figure 5.2

The AirDrop menu enables you to choose whether to utilize this feature with all nearby iPhone, iPad, and Mac users or only people who are in your Contacts database.

When it's turned on, use this feature to send content from the Share menu that's built in to compatible apps. For example, if you want to send a photo to another AirDrop user (or one of your other compatible Macs or mobile devices), launch Photos, view and select the photo(s) you want to send, and then tap the Share icon.

When the Share menu is displayed (shown in Figure 5.3 on an iPad), thumbnails representing people in close proximity and who have AirDrop turned on are displayed. Tap the intended recipient, and the selected photos are wirelessly sent. The recipient might need to tap the Accept button to accept the file transfer (shown in Figure 5.4).

AirDrop Icons

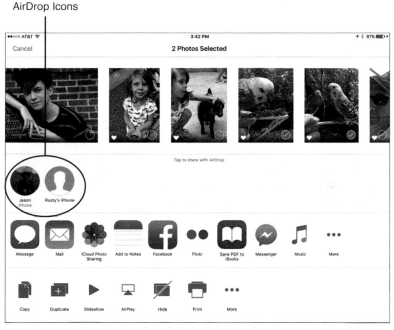

Figure 5.3

Select AirDrop from the Share menu of compatible apps to send app-specific content to other iOS mobile devices and Mac users.

NOTE AirDrop is available only when using iPhones and iPads released within the last few years that are running iOS 8, iOS 9, or iOS 10.

If you want to use AirDrop between an iOS mobile device and a Mac, the Mac must have been released in 2012 or later and be running OS X Yosemite, OS X El Capitan, or macOS Sierra.

TIP In addition to the Photos app, the AirDrop feature is supported by the Share menu found in other apps, including Contacts, Maps, Notes, Safari, iBooks, and iTunes Store.

Figure 5.4

Shown on an iPhone 5c, the recipient of files sent via AirDrop might need to accept what's being sent by tapping the Accept button.

After you receive content via AirDrop, to access that content, launch the relevant app. For example, to view, organize, or edit photos you receive, open the All Photos/Camera Roll album in the Photos app. If you receive a Contacts entry, it is automatically added to your Contacts database and is accessible from the Contacts app.

! CAUTION To avoid receiving unwanted content from strangers when you're in public places such as an airport or theater, consider turning on the AirDrop feature only when you need it. You can turn it off in Control Center. Alternatively, you can turn on AirDrop but set it up so only content from people with entries in your Contacts app's database will be received.

STREAMING CONTENT FROM YOUR iPHONE OR iPAD TO OTHER COMPATIBLE DEVICES USING AIRPLAY

AirPlay is a wireless feature that enables your mobile device to stream content such as photos, videos, or audio, to an AirPlay-compatible device, such as Apple TV, a Mac, or AirPlay-compatible speakers.

To use AirPlay, your iOS mobile device and the other AirPlay-compatible device must be connected to the same wireless home network (via Wi-Fi). Then, when you turn on the AirPlay feature, the two compatible devices automatically establish a wireless connection.

After the connection is made, an AirPlay icon appears in compatible apps, such as Music, Videos, and Photos, enabling you to transfer (stream) what you would otherwise see on your iPhone or iPad's screen, or what would be heard through the device's speaker, to another compatible device.

In addition to being able to stream photos and video (including iTunes Store TV show and movie purchases and rentals), you can use AirPlay to connect external speakers (without cables) to your iOS mobile device, and then stream music (from Apple Music, Pandora, or Spotify, for example) or other audio (such as audiobooks or podcasts) from your device to those compatible speakers.

When it's available, one of the easiest ways to turn AirPlay on or off is to access it from Control Center. Tap the AirPlay icon, and then choose where you want to stream the content.

In Figure 5.5, AirPlay is being turned on from Control Center and an AirPlay device (in this case, Apple TV) is being selected.

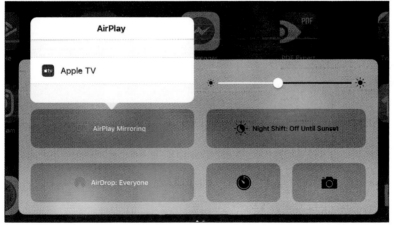

Figure 5.5

The AirPlay icon and menu in Control Center.

Figure 5.6 shows that an iPad is wirelessly connected to an Apple TV device to stream digital photos stored in the Photos app on the tablet, so that they can be viewed on the HD television set that's connected to the Apple TV device.

Figure 5.6
From Photos, tap the AirPlay icon and then select Apple TV (when available) to stream photos from the iPhone or iPad being used to an HD television set (with an Apple TV device connected).

✓ **TIP** It's possible to use AirPlay to present PowerPoint or Keynote digital slide presentations on a TV or monitor that has an Apple TV connected to it. What appears on the TV is exactly what's displayed on your smartphone or tablet.

🔍 **MORE INFO** AirPlay-compatible speakers are available from a handful of different companies, starting around $49.95. To learn more about AirPlay, visit https://support.apple.com/en-us/HT204289.

PRINTING FILES WIRELESSLY USING AN AIRPRINT-COMPATIBLE PRINTER

Another wireless feature offered by iOS 10 is AirPrint. It enables compatible apps to wirelessly send documents, data, or photos to be printed on an AirPrint-compatible laser, inkjet, or photo printer. For this feature to work, the iOS mobile device and the printer must be connected to the same wireless network.

> ## 🔍 MORE INFO   Dozens of different AirPrint-compatible printers are now available from companies such as Brother, HP, Canon, Lexmark, and Epson. To learn more about AirPrint-compatible printers, visit https://support.apple.com/en-us/HT201311.

After you've set up an AirPrint-compatible printer, use the Print feature that's built in to many apps, such as Pages, Notes, Safari, Maps, and Photos. The Print option is often found in the Share menu of these apps, although this can vary.

> ## (iOS 10) WHAT'S NEW   A growing selection of Bluetooth-compatible and wireless printers are also available for use with iOS mobile devices. For these printers, such as the Polaroid Zip Mobile Photo Printer, to work, you also need a free and proprietary app for the printer to print images stored in the Photos app. Read about this printer (and others like it) in Chapter 8, "Shoot, Edit, and Share Photos and Videos."

> ## ☑ TIP   If you're not using an AirPrint- or Bluetooth-compatible printer, it's possible to install specialized software on your Mac, such as handyPrint (www.netputing.com/handyprint) or Printopia (www.decisivetactics.com/products/printopia), to enable any printer to work with the AirPrint feature of your iPhone or iPad, as long as your Mac is turned on.

USING HANDOFF

Handoff is an iOS feature that works with many apps that come preinstalled with iOS 10, as well as the iWork for iOS apps. It's also compatible with a growing number of third-party apps. Basically, this feature enables you to begin a task on one of your Mac(s) or iOS mobile devices, and then pick up exactly where you left off on another Mac or iOS mobile device that's linked to the same iCloud account and is within Bluetooth range (about 33 feet).

> **NOTE** To use the Handoff feature between your iPhone and a Mac, the Mac must be running the latest version of OS X Yosemite, OS X El Capitan, or macOS Sierra.

To enable the Handoff feature on your mobile device, launch Settings, tap General, and then tap the Handoff option. Turn on the virtual switch associated with the Handoff option. You must do this on each of your iOS mobile devices. Also, make sure the device you're using is connected to the same wireless network as the device(s) with which you want to use these features, and make sure that Bluetooth is turned on.

When Handoff is turned on, start performing a compatible task on one of your Macs or iOS mobile devices. Then, to pick up what you were doing on a different iPhone or iPad, wake up the device. On the Lock screen, place your finger on the app icon displayed in the lower-left corner of the screen and swipe upward (shown in Figure 5.7). You can also access the app switcher. Apps available via Handoff are displayed at the bottom of the screen.

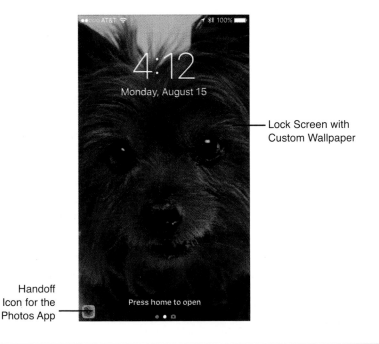

Lock Screen with Custom Wallpaper

Handoff Icon for the Photos App

Figure 5.7

When it's possible to take advantage of the Handoff feature, after you wake up your iPhone or iPad, swipe up on the Handoff app icon on the Lock screen.

> **NOTE** When you attempt to use the Handoff feature from the Lock screen, it is still necessary to unlock the iPhone or iPad you're currently using before accessing the app that you were using on your other computer or iOS mobile device.

> **NOTE** To pick up what you were previously doing while currently using a Mac, simply open the app you were previously using on your other Mac or iOS mobile device.

Handoff is one of iOS 10's Continuity features. Another Continuity feature, and one of the coolest if you're an iPhone user, is that when you receive an incoming call on your phone, when the Continuity/Handoff feature is also active on your iPad and/or Mac, you can answer that incoming call and engage in the phone conversation from one of these other devices.

Your iPhone continues to host the call, but the wireless connection between your iPhone and iPad (or iPhone and Mac) enables you to use the Mac or iPad's built-in microphone and speaker(s) as a speakerphone.

> **NOTE** For this aspect of the Handoff feature to work, your iPad or Mac must be linked to the same Wi-Fi network as your iPhone, plus both devices must be signed in to the same iCloud account and have Bluetooth turned on.

When an incoming call is displayed on your iPad or Mac's screen, tap or click the Answer icon to answer the call. If you want to initiate a call from your iPad or Mac (via your iPhone), tap or click a phone number in the Contacts, Calendar, Maps, or Safari apps, for example.

Another nice feature of Handoff is that you can send and receive SMS and MMS text messages via your cellular service provider's texting network (as opposed to Apple's Internet-based iMessage service) from your iPad or Mac(s). These incoming or outgoing messages use the Messages app running on your iPhone (with its cellular connection) as a conduit.

🔍 **MORE INFO**   To determine whether your iOS mobile device or Mac is compatible with iOS 10's Continuity, Handoff, Instant Hotspot, Phone Calling, and SMS features, visit this page of Apple's website: https://support.apple.com/en-us/HT204689.

To use the Personal Hotspot feature, which enables you to create a Wi-Fi hotspot (via your 3G/4G/LTE cellular data connection of your iPhone or iPad) for your other Wi-Fi–compatible mobile devices, this feature must be supported by your iPhone's cellular service provider and your service plan.

To activate the Personal Hotspot feature (if it's available from your iPhone or iPad), launch Settings and tap the Personal Hotspot option that's below the Cellular option in the main Settings menu.

From the Personal Hotspot menu, turn on the virtual switch associated with Personal Hotspot (shown in Figure 5.8), and then follow the onscreen directions. Tap the Wi-Fi Password option to create a custom password to access the personal Wi-Fi hotspot that's being created from your other Wi-Fi-compatible devices.

Figure 5.8

Assuming it's allowed by your cellular service provider and you're using a compatible iPhone or iPad, you can create a personal Wi-Fi hotspot from your mobile device.

IN THIS CHAPTER

- How to sync files, documents, photos, and data via iCloud
- Get acquainted with the iCloud Drive feature and the iCloud Drive mobile app
- Take advantage of iCloud's Family Sharing feature to share purchased content with up to five other family members

6

USE iCLOUD AND THE iCLOUD DRIVE APP

iCloud is Apple's cloud-based service, which has been designed from the ground up to work seamlessly with all iOS mobile devices and Macs. Functionality for using iCloud's various features and functions is built directly into the iOS 10 operating system, as well as the macOS Sierra operating system.

If you're an iPhone, iPad, and/or Mac user, setting up an iCloud account is essential for taking full advantage of the latest features and functions built in to your smartphone, tablet, and/ or computer.

> **☑ TIP** Regardless of how many separate Apple computers and mobile devices you own and use, you need only one iCloud account per person (not per device). Each of your Macs and iOS mobile devices should be linked to the same iCloud account to sync and access your app-specific data, photos, files, and content purchases.

Setting up an iCloud account continues to be free, but if you need to utilize more than the 5GB of online storage space that comes with each account, you must purchase additional online storage. The monthly fee structure for additional iCloud online storage space is shown in Table 6.1.

Table 6.1   iCloud Online Storage Space Fees*

iCloud Online Storage Space	Monthly Fee
5GB	Free
50GB	$0.99/£0.79
200GB	$2.99/£2.49
1TB	$9.99/£6.99
2TB	$19.99/£13.99

*Charges for the monthly fees are automatically billed to the debit or credit card linked to your Apple ID account as a recurring charge, once you acquire additional online storage space. For more information on pricing outside the U.S. and U.K., visit https://support.apple.com/en-us/HT201238.

> **! CAUTION** You can use the included 5GB of online storage space, plus any additional space you pay for, to store your app-specific data, backup files, photos, and personal files. In the past, online storage for your photos as part of iCloud's My Photo Stream and Shared Photo Streams was provided for free. This is no longer the case.
>
> Using iCloud Photo Library, which is managed from the Photos app on your iPhone, iPad, and/or Macs, photo storage now consumes some of your 5GB online storage allocation and any additional storage space you purchase (based on the size of your personal photo library). However, the additional online storage space required to store your iTunes Store, App Store, iBook Store, and other content purchases continues to be free.

MANAGING YOUR iCLOUD STORAGE SPACE

To see and manage how your iCloud online storage space is actually being allocated, launch Settings and tap the iCloud option. Then tap the Storage option.

From the Storage screen (shown in Figure 6.1 on an iPhone), you see how much online storage space is currently available, as well as how much is being consumed by photos, backups, documents, data, mail, and your other stored content.

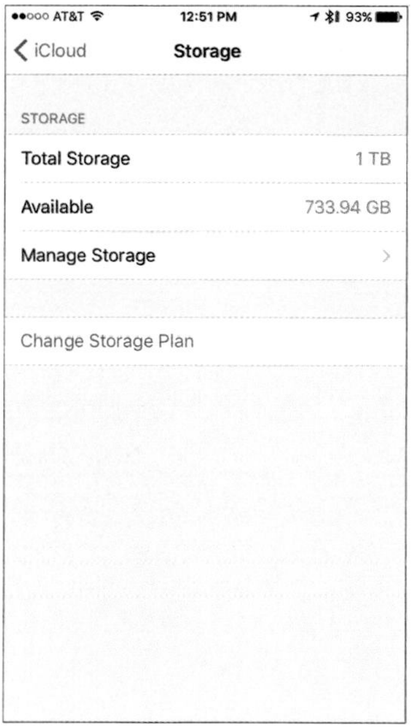

Figure 6.1

The Storage screen enables you to see how your iCloud account's online storage is currently being used. (The iCloud account shown here has been upgraded to have 1TB of online storage space.)

To conserve online storage space in your iCloud account, delete iCloud backup files for old devices, or backups that are redundant and no longer needed. To do this, launch Settings, tap the iCloud option, tap the Storage option, and then tap the Manage Storage option.

Under the Backups heading (shown in Figure 6.2 on an iPhone), tap any of your device-specific listings. Then, to delete that old or unwanted backup, tap the Delete Backup option.

Figure 6.2
To free up online storage space, consider deleting old or unwanted backup files. How this screen looks depends on how you're using your iCloud online storage space.

From below the Documents & Data heading, tap each app listed, one at a time, and delete any old or unwanted files, or delete all content from apps you no longer use. To do this, tap an app listing from the Manage Storage screen.

In some cases, you will only be able to see how much online storage space that app is using. To delete all content related to that app from your iCloud account, tap the Edit option, and then tap the Delete All option.

When you tap an app listing from the Manage Storage screen and a list of individual files is displayed, it's possible to delete one file at a time from your iCloud account. To do this, swipe from right to left across a file listing, and then tap the Delete button.

> ## MORE INFO Each iCloud account also includes a free @icloud.com email account, which you can use to send and receive email from any devices linked to your iCloud account. Once the account is set up, iCloud automatically keeps your email account synchronized via the Mail App.

> **NOTE** If you have an older Apple ID account that has an associated @mac.com or @me.com email address, its @icloud.com equivalent can automatically be used as the email address associated with your iCloud account.

ACCESSING CONTENT SAVED TO iCLOUD

By default, as soon as you establish your free iCloud account, anytime you acquire and download content from the iTunes Store, App Store, or iBook Store, a copy of that content is automatically saved in your iCloud account, and it's immediately available on all of your compatible computers and iOS mobile devices (including Apple TV) that are linked to that iCloud account. This includes all past purchases and downloads.

So, if you hear an awesome new song on the radio, you can immediately purchase and download it from the iTunes Store using your iPhone. As always, that song becomes available on your iPhone within a minute. Then, thanks to ICloud, you can access that same song from your computer(s), iPad, iPod touch, and/or Apple TV device without having to repurchase it. This feature also works with TV shows and movies purchased from the iTunes Store.

> **NOTE** Thanks to iCloud's Family Sharing feature, it's possible for up to six family members to have their own independent Apple ID/iCloud accounts but share some or all of their purchased content from the iTunes Store, App Store, and iBook Store. Family Sharing is covered later in this chapter. Another benefit to using iCloud is that syncing can be done from anywhere via the Internet, without using iTunes Sync or requiring a physical cable connection between your iOS mobile device and your primary computer.

Your Mac(s) and iOS mobile devices share many of the same apps, including Contacts, Calendar, Reminders, Notes, Photos, Safari, and Maps. Your personal data for each of these apps can easily be set up to sync between all of your computers and devices that are linked to the same iCloud account.

Once this feature is set up, it continues to work in the background. How to set up and use this feature is explained shortly.

NOTE The iTunes Sync process is still possible by installing the iTunes software onto your primary computer and then connecting your iOS mobile device using the supplied USB cable, but this process for backing up and syncing data is less convenient than using iCloud. (You can do the Wi-Fi iTunes Sync process without a cable as long as both devices are linked to the same wireless network.)

Because using the iTunes Sync process is considered an antiquated way to sync and back up data, this book focuses on using iCloud. If you're still interested in using iTunes Sync, however, visit Apple's website (https://support.apple.com/en-us/HT203977) for more information on how to use this feature.

If you ever opt to delete a content purchase from your iOS mobile device (such as an app, music, TV show episode, movie, eBook, or audiobook), for whatever reason, you always have the option of downloading and installing it again, for free, from iCloud.

TIP Depending on how you set up the iTunes Store, App Store, and iBook Store to work with iCloud, you can automatically have all your computers and iOS mobile devices download all new music, apps, and eBook content you purchase, or you can do it manually.

To adjust these Automatic Downloads settings, launch Settings, select the iTunes & App Store option, and then set the virtual switches associated with Music, Apps, and Books that are listed under the Automatic Downloads heading.

It's also possible to set up your iPhone or iPad to automatically update all your apps as new versions of previously installed apps are released. To do this, turn on the virtual switch associated with the Updates option listed below the Music, Apps, and Books options.

Due to their large file sizes, automatic downloads are not possible for TV show episodes or movies acquired from the iTunes Store. However, you can download these purchases manually onto all your computers and/or iOS mobile devices linked to the same iCloud account.

> ## NOTE
>
> Although your iTunes Store music purchases might represent a portion of your overall personal digital music library, chances are that library also includes CDs (which you have ripped into digital format), as well as online music purchases and downloads from other sources (such as Amazon.com).
>
> For an additional fee of $24.99 per year, you can upgrade your iCloud account by adding the iTunes Match services. This grants you full access to your entire personal digital music library (including non-iTunes Store purchases) from all of your computers and devices that are linked to the same iCloud account. To learn more about iTunes Match, visit www.apple.com/itunes/itunes-match.
>
> Alternatively, for $9.99 per month, you can sign up for the Apple Music service and have unlimited access to almost every song in the iTunes Store's digital music library (more than 40 million songs) via the Music app.

ACCESSING YOUR PURCHASED iTUNES STORES CONTENT FROM ANY DEVICE

If you do not have the Automatic Downloads option enabled, you can still manually load iTunes Store purchases onto your device by following these steps:

1. Make sure that your iOS device is connected to the Internet via a cellular data or Wi-Fi connection.

2. Launch the iTunes Store app on your device. If prompted, when the Apple ID Password window pops up on your screen, use the virtual keyboard to enter your Apple ID password. (You can also use your device's Touch ID to scan your fingerprint.)

3. On an iPhone, tap the More icon, and then tap the Purchased option. On an iPad tap the Purchase icon at the bottom of the screen. Then, tap the Music, Movies, or TV Shows option, based on the type of purchased content you want to access.

4. If you tapped Music, for example, a listing of music you have purchased (listed alphabetically by the artist/band's name) is displayed. Tap one listing to see what music is available from that artist (shown in Figure 6.3 on an iPad). If you chose Movies in step 3, you can directly select a movie. If you selected TV Shows, a list of TV series that you own episodes for is displayed. Tap a series name to view a listing of complete seasons or individual episodes you've previously purchased.

Figure 6.3

From the iTunes Store app, access and download your previous purchases by tapping the Purchased icon. Here, the Music option has been selected.

> **TIP** To see a listing of your most recently purchased content, tap a category (Music, Movies, or TV Shows, for example), and then tap the Recent Purchases option.

5. Tap the iCloud icons associated with specific listings, one at a time, to select content you want to (re)download onto the iPhone or iPad you're currently using. Or to download all the listed content, tap the Download All option at the top of the list. If you're looking at a listing of TV Shows, tap the main show listing to download all episodes you own. Otherwise, tap the iCloud icon that's associated with the specific episode(s) you want to download.

> **TIP** If you've acquired audiobooks, an additional tab is displayed alongside the Music, Movies, and TV Shows options for this content.

6. Within minutes (or faster, depending on the speed of your Internet connection), the content you selected to download is available to enjoy on the iOS mobile device you're currently using.

7. Exit the iTunes Store app by pressing the Home button, or use the App Switcher by quickly pressing the Home button twice.

8. Launch the Music or Videos app on your iOS mobile device to experience the newly downloaded (or redownloaded) content. To listen to audiobooks acquired from iBook Store, launch the iBooks app.

USING iCLOUD TO SYNC YOUR APP-SPECIFIC DATA, DOCUMENTS, AND FILES

Most cloud-based file-sharing services serve mainly as a place in cyberspace to remotely store files. However, you must manually transfer those files to and from the "cloud." This functionality is possible using the iCloud Drive feature. However, thanks to iCloud's integration with iOS 10, many of the core apps that come with the latest version of this mobile operating system, as well as a growing number of third-party apps, automatically keep data and files created or managed using those apps synchronized with other devices and computers linked to the same iCloud account.

From within Settings on your iPhone or iPad, turn on or off iCloud support for all compatible apps on your device. In terms of iOS 10's preinstalled apps, those compatible with iCloud data syncing include Contacts, Calendars, Reminders, Safari, Home, Notes, Photos, News, Wallet, and Mail (relating only to your free iCloud-related email account).

> **✓ TIP** iCloud Keychain can automatically store the usernames, passwords, and credit card information (for online purchases) related to all the websites you visit. Thus, you no longer need to manually sign in to websites when you revisit them, nor do you need to remember each username and password you associated with a website-related account.
>
> When this feature is turned on once on each of your iOS mobile devices and Macs, your iCloud Keychain database syncs automatically (and securely) with iCloud, and then all computers and iOS mobile devices linked to your iCloud account.

> 📝 **NOTE**   Bank- and personal finance–related websites purposely do not support the iCloud Keychain feature. When visiting sites that require added security, iCloud Keychain might be able to remember your username, but it cannot automatically remember your password.

> 🔍 **MORE INFO**   iCloud is fully compatible with Apple's optional iWork apps, which include Pages (word processing), Numbers (spreadsheet management), and Keynote (for digital slide presentations).
>
> Depending on which version of the Microsoft Office apps you're using (Word, Excel, PowerPoint, OneNote, and Outlook), some of these support iCloud, as well as Dropbox, and Microsoft's own OneDrive service (https://onedrive.live.com/about). Although Office 365 supports iCloud directly, with some other versions, you need to use the Save As option and then select iCloud as the file storage location.

When you turn on the iCloud functionality related to the Contacts app, for example, your iOS mobile device automatically syncs your Contacts app database with iCloud. Thus, if you add or update an entry on your iPhone, it automatically synchronizes with the Contacts app running on your other iOS devices, as well as the compatible contact management software that's running on your computers (such as the Contacts app or Microsoft Outlook on your Mac). This is also true if you delete a Contacts entry from one device. It is almost instantly deleted from all of your other computers and iOS mobile devices linked to the same iCloud account. (Keep in mind, there is no "undo" option related to this feature.)

As you surf the Web using Safari, when you turn on iCloud syncing functionality related to this app, all your Bookmarks and Bookmark Bar data, along with your Reading List information and open browser window/tabs data, are synced via iCloud.

To share your photos between iOS devices, your primary computer, and/or an Apple TV device, from the iCloud submenu in Settings, tap the Photos option to turn on the iCloud Photo Library feature.

CUSTOMIZING iCLOUD TO WORK WITH YOUR APPS

It's important to understand that the app-related synchronization feature offered by iCloud is different from iCloud Backup, which creates a complete backup of your iOS mobile device that is stored online as part of your iCloud account.

When you set up iCloud to work with a specific compatible app, that app automatically accesses the Internet, connects to your online-based iCloud account, and then uploads or downloads app-related files, documents, or data as needed. iCloud then shares (syncs) that app-specific data with your other computers and devices that are linked to the same iCloud account.

To customize which of your compatible apps use iCloud functionality, follow these steps:

1. Launch Settings from your iPhone's or iPad's Home screen.

2. Tap the iCloud option.

3. When the iCloud screen, which is also referred to as the iCloud Control Panel, appears (shown in Figure 6.4 on an iPhone and Figure 6.5 on an iPad), at the top of the screen, make sure the Apple ID–linked email address associated with your iCloud account is displayed next to the Account option. If it's not, use your existing Apple ID to create or access an iCloud account by tapping the Account option. It's imperative that all of your Macs and iOS mobile devices be linked to the same iCloud account.

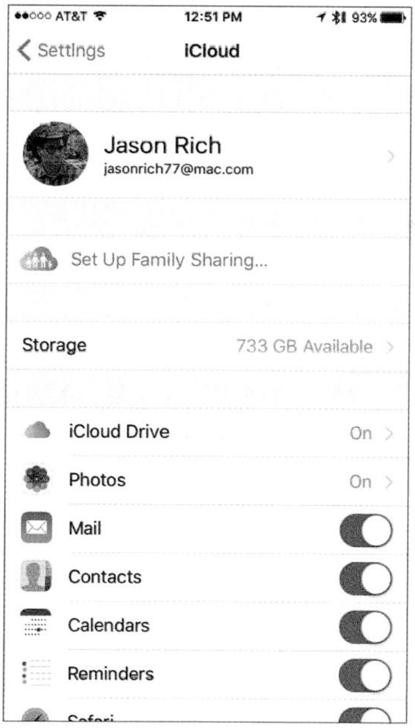

Figure 6.4

From your iPhone, turn iCloud functionality on or off for specific preinstalled Apple apps from the iCloud menu in Settings.

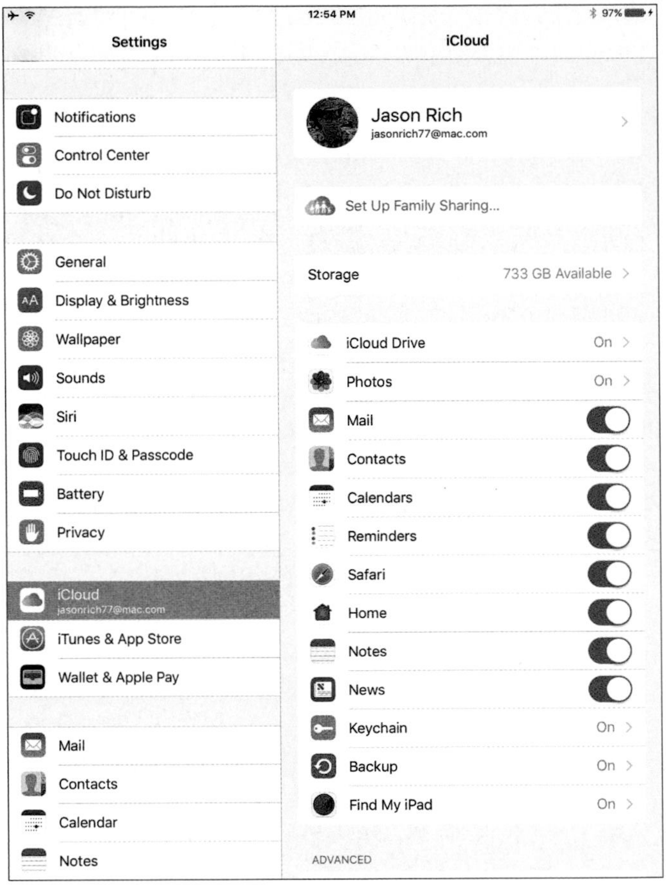

Figure 6.5

From your iPad, turn iCloud functionality on or off for specific preinstalled Apple apps from the iCloud menu in Settings.

4. Below the Account option is a list of all preinstalled iCloud-compatible apps on your iOS device. To the right of each listing is a virtual on/off switch. To turn on the iCloud functionality associated with a specific app, set its related virtual switch to the On position.

5. When you have turned on the iCloud functionality for all the apps that you want to synchronize via iCloud, press the Home button to exit Settings and save your changes.

6. Repeat this process on each of your iOS mobile devices. If you have an iPhone and an iPad, you must turn on the iCloud functionality for Contacts, for example, on both devices to keep Contacts data synchronized via iCloud on both devices.

> **NOTE** From the iCloud Drive Settings menu, there is a list of apps you have installed on your iPhone or iPad that enable you to store content, data, or files within iCloud Drive. Turn on or off the virtual switch for each app to activate this feature.
>
> To access the iCloud Drive menu, launch Settings, tap the iCloud option, and then tap the iCloud Drive option.

> **NOTE** After you've turned on the iCloud functionality for specific apps, to stay synchronized, each computer or device must have access to the Internet. For this use of iCloud on your iPhone or iPad, a cellular or a Wi-Fi Internet connection works fine. For certain other iCloud features, such as managing iCloud Photo Library functions or iCloud Backup, your iPhone or iPad requires a Wi-Fi Internet connection.

ACCESSING YOUR APP-SPECIFIC DATA ONLINE FROM iCLOUD.COM

Another benefit of using iCloud to sync your app-specific data is that using any computer or Internet-enabled device, you can visit www.iCloud.com to run online versions of iOS 10 preinstalled apps populated with all your app-specific data. To do this, log in to iCloud.com using your iCloud username and password (which is typically your Apple ID username and password). Online versions of the Mail, Contacts, Calendar, Photos, iCloud Drive, Notes, Reminders, Pages, Numbers, Keynote, News Publisher, Find Friends, Find My iPhone, and Settings apps are available. This is shown on a Mac using the Safari web browser in Figure 6.6.

Figure 6.6

Log in to www.iCloud.com to access your app-specific content using online versions of popular iPhone and iPad apps.

If you forget your iPhone at home, for example, you can still securely access your complete Contacts database, your schedule, your to-do lists, and your notes from any Internet-enabled computer, whether or not that computer is typically linked to your iCloud account.

After you log in to iCloud.com, click the onscreen app icon for the app you want to use. Then be sure to sign off from iCloud.com when you're finished. To do this, click your username in the top-right corner of the browser window, and then click the Sign Out option.

> **TIP**   From iCloud.com, it's possible to access and manage files you manually store in the iCloud Drive portion of your iCloud account. This includes non-app-specific files. To do this, log in to iCloud.com and click the iCloud Drive icon. You can then access or manage your files and folders from the iCloud Drive web browser window (shown in Figure 6.7).
>
> Near the top center of the iCloud Drive screen, from left to right, are command icons for creating a new file folder, as well as uploading, downloading, deleting, and/or sharing (via email) selected files.
>
> As discussed later in this chapter, the iCloud Drive app for the iPhone and iPad works almost exactly like this online iCloud Drive app, but from your mobile device.

Figure 6.7

From the iCloud Drive web browser window, accessible from iCloud.com, you can access and manage files and folders you've manually stored in this area of your iCloud account.

AUTOMATICALLY TRANSFERRING DOCUMENTS USING iCLOUD

In addition to the iCloud compatibility built in to many of the core (preinstalled) apps included with iOS 10, a growing number of other apps also offer iCloud compatibility and enable you to easily and automatically transfer or synchronize app-related documents and files.

If you turn on iCloud functionality in compatible third-party apps, when you create or revise a document or file, that revision is stored on your iOS device and on iCloud. It then syncs with that same app running on other iOS mobile devices, Macs, or PCs linked with your iCloud account.

Synchronization happens automatically and behind the scenes, assuming that your iOS devices and primary computer are connected to the Internet.

> **TIP** Many iCloud features are now accessible from Windows-based PCs; however, you must download and install the free iCloud for Windows software onto your PC, which is available from this page of Apple's website: www.apple.com/icloud/setup/pc.html.

As with all apps running on your iPhone or iPad, iCloud functionality must be turned on in compatible third-party apps. How to do this varies by app, but typically you do it from the app's Settings, Setup, or Preferences menu. You can also adjust this setting from the iCloud Drive submenu in Settings. To access it, launch Settings, tap the iCloud option, and then tap the iCloud Drive option.

CREATING A PHOTO LIBRARY USING iCLOUD

When it comes to photo sharing, backup, and syncing on an iPhone, iPad, or Mac, everything is now done through the iCloud Photo Library portion of your iCloud account. You can manage these tasks from the Photos app that comes bundled with iOS 10, as well as the macOS Sierra version of the operating system and Photos app for the Mac.

iCloud Photo Library automatically syncs your complete personal photo library with all the computers and mobile devices linked to the same iCloud account (including Windows PCs). Plus, it's possible to share specific albums (or a group of selected photos from within an album) with specific people, yet keep the rest of your photo library private.

To customize options related to iCloud Photo Library, launch Settings, tap the iCloud option, and then tap the Photos option. From the Photos submenu (shown in Figure 6.8 on an iPad), turn on the virtual switch associated with iCloud Photo Library, and if you want to be able to share certain albums with others, turn on the iCloud Photo Sharing option. You must do this on all your iOS mobile devices and from the iCloud Preference Pane on your Mac or Control Panel on PC computers.

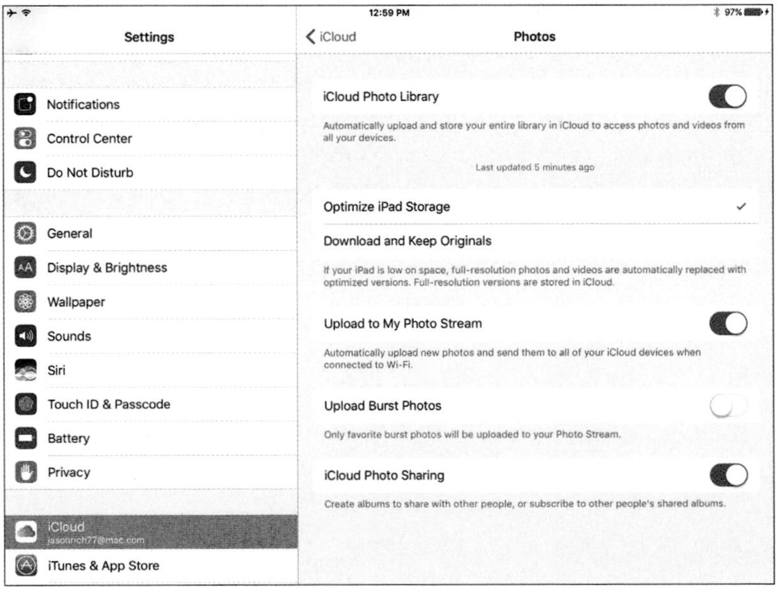

Figure 6.8

From the Photos menu in Settings on your iPhone or iPad (shown here), it's possible to customize the iCloud Photo Library feature.

NOTE   One goal of iCloud Photo Library is to give you full online access to your entire digital images library, anytime, from any of your computers or iOS mobile devices. As a result of this content being readily available via the Internet, the need to store digital images on your mobile device will be reduced, so you will ultimately be able to free up internal storage space on your iPhone or iPad.

Depending on the size of your entire digital photo library, it might become necessary, however, to purchase additional iCloud online storage space to store all of your digital images.

Meanwhile, if you have an older iPhone or iPad with limited internal storage space (such as 16GB), you might discover that your entire iCloud Photo Library doesn't fit on the device, especially if you have thousands of images.

If your iPhone or iPad's internal storage space is limited, access Settings, tap the iCloud option, tap the Photos option, and then select the Optimize iPhone Storage option (as opposed to the Download and Keep Originals option). Doing this enables you to work with lower-resolution versions of your images on your iPhone/iPad while keeping the full-resolution versions of those images in your iCloud account. Thus, your iCloud Photo Library (that gets stored in your iPhone or iPad) requires a lot less storage space.

USING A UNIQUE APPLE ID FOR iCLOUD

When you first create an iCloud account, you're encouraged to use your existing Apple ID and username. This is to entice Apple computer and mobile device users to use the same Apple ID to make all of their iTunes Store, App Store, and iBook Store purchases, plus use that same Apple ID to access Apple's online-based iMessage instant messaging service, use the FaceTime video-calling service, and use iCloud's other functionality.

To create and manage your Apple ID account(s), visit https://appleid.apple.com from any computer or Internet-enabled device. When you set up iCloud, try to use iMessage or FaceTime, or try to access the iTunes Store or iBook Store for the first time, you also have the option to create an Apple ID account.

TIP   From your iPhone or iPad, to view and manage your Apple ID account, launch Settings, tap the iTunes & App Store option, and then tap the Apple ID option. Tap the View Apple ID option to access and manage your account, or tap the iForgot option to recover a forgotten Apple ID username or password.

BACKING UP WITH iCLOUD

Another useful feature of iOS 10 is the capability to create a backup of your iOS device wirelessly and have the related backup files stored online ("in the cloud"). To use this iCloud Backup feature, your iOS mobile device must be connected to the Internet via Wi-Fi. Your primary computer is not needed, so the backup can be created from anywhere, and you can later restore your device from wherever a Wi-Fi Internet connection is present.

When activated, your iOS mobile device automatically creates a backup to iCloud once per day. For this to happen, your iPhone or iPad also must be connected to an external power source. However, at any time, you can manually create a backup of your device to iCloud from within Settings. This can be done when your device is running on battery.

Follow these steps to activate and use the iCloud Backup feature on an iPhone or iPad:

1. Connect your device to the Internet via a Wi-Fi connection.
2. From the Home screen, launch Settings.
3. Tap the iCloud option.
4. Scroll down and tap the Backup option.
5. Turn on the virtual switch that's associated with the iCloud Backup option.
6. Tap the Back Up Now option to manually begin creating a backup of your iOS mobile device at any time.

> **☑ TIP** The first time you use the iCloud Backup feature to create a wireless backup of your iOS device, the process could take up to an hour (or longer), depending on how much data you have stored on your device. After the process begins, a progress meter is displayed at the bottom of the Backup screen in Settings.
>
> In the future, the iCloud Backup process takes place once per day, automatically, when your iOS device is not otherwise in use. These backups save all newly created or revised files and data only, so subsequent iCloud Backup procedures are much quicker.
>
> At the bottom of the Backup screen within Settings, the time (and date, if it's not the current day) of the last backup is displayed.

The purpose of creating and maintaining a backup of your device is so that you have a copy of all your apps, data, files, content, and personalized settings stored if something goes wrong with your device. If and when you need to access the backup to restore your device using iCloud, when prompted, choose the Restore from iCloud option. Likewise, if your iPhone or iPad gets lost or stolen and you replace it, you can restore the content from your old device onto the new one.

> **☑ TIP** To be able to restore your iOS mobile device completely from an iCloud Backup, you also need to turn on and be syncing app-compatible apps. Turn on these app-specific features from the iCloud Control Panel screen, which is accessible by launching Settings and tapping the iCloud option.

SHARING PURCHASED CONTENT WITH FAMILY SHARING

Thanks to iCloud's Family Sharing feature, up to six people can share some or all of their content purchases, while each person retains his or her own private iCloud account. At the same time, a separate Family folder is set up in the Photos app that enables participating family members to share selected photos by placing them in this Family album. All the other photos, however, remain private.

> **✎ NOTE** When you set up Family Sharing, a separate Family calendar is automatically created in each participant's Calendar app. This calendar is shared with other family members, whereas all other Calendar-related data remains private.

To set up a Family Sharing account, one adult in the family needs to turn on this feature and then invite up to five other family members. Launch Settings, tap the iCloud option, and then tap the Set Up Family Sharing option (refer to Figure 6.4 or Figure 6.5).

One drawback to this feature is that the person setting up Family Sharing must choose one iCloud account associated with a credit card from which all purchases by all family members will be paid from this point forward. (This doesn't apply to gift cards, which are deducted from only the specific user's account.)

One useful feature of Family Sharing is the ability for family members to share their whereabouts with each other via the free Find My Friends app (which comes preinstalled with iOS 10). As you're setting up Family Sharing, you can activate this feature by tapping the Share Your Location option. Then, from the Family submenu screen, tap the Add Family Member option and enter the name or email address for each family member who will participate.

Remember, you need to select a single Shared Payment Method that can be used to purchase content via this account in the future. By using Family Sharing, parents can now preapprove their kids' spending for online content and in-app purchases, plus set spending limits.

As soon as this feature is set up and the family members respond to the email invitation to participate, each person's music, TV shows, movies, eBooks, and compatible apps become available to everyone else. However, it's possible for each family member to keep selected content purchases and/or photos private.

> 📝 **NOTE** It's a good idea for parents to set up the Family Sharing feature for their younger kids and create a separate Apple ID account for each child who the parent maintains control over. To do this, launch Settings, tap the iCloud option, tap the Family option, and then tap the Create an Apple ID for a Child option.

> ☑️ **TIP** Before a family member accepts a Family Sharing invitation, his iOS mobile device (or Mac) must already be signed in to his personal iCloud account.

When everyone is active with Family Sharing, to access each other's previously purchased content, launch the iTunes Store app, iBooks app (to access iBook Store), or the App Store app (to access apps), and tap the Purchased option. Select a family member from the displayed menu. The purchased content already acquired by that family member (using the person's own Apple ID account) is displayed and becomes downloadable by others. All new purchases are considered acquired by the primary account used to manage the Family Sharing option.

> ☑️ **TIP** If you're a parent, turn on the Ask to Buy option when setting up the Family Sharing feature. Then, anytime a child (under age 18) who is linked to the account wants to make a content purchase, the parent receives a text message asking them to approve the purchase. This approval is also required when a child wants to acquire free content.

In addition to the other Family Sharing features, events can be created and shared within an automatically created Family calendar using the Calendar app. Any participating family member can create an event with the Calendar app, like they normally would, and choose the Family calendar in the Calendar option in the New Event screen.

To view the Family calendar from the Calendar app, tap the Calendars option, and then tap the Family option to select the Family calendar for viewing.

Any participating member can add or delete events from the Family calendar; however, any other calendars being managed by each person's Calendar app remain separate and private.

> **NOTE** Just like the Family calendar accessible by all participating family members, a Family list is also created automatically in the Reminders app. This allows for centralized lists to be accessed and viewed by all participating family members. At the same time, by default, all other lists stored in each person's Reminders app are kept private (unless you opt to share your other lists as well).

> **NOTE** Using the Find My Friends app, it's possible to deactivate the Share My Location feature and block family members from viewing your current location. This cannot be done from a child's Apple ID/iCloud account if the account was set up as a Child Account.

Like all of iCloud's features and functions, what's possible with Family Sharing will evolve over time.

USING THE iCLOUD DRIVE APP

The iCloud Drive app enables you to access the individual folders that contain data, documents, files, photos, and other content that you manually stored online on your iCloud Drive.

> **NOTE** If iCloud Drive is not already installed on your iPhone or iPad, when you set up an iCloud account, you're prompted to install it onto your mobile device. However, you can also find the free iCloud Drive app in the App Store and install it anytime.

When you access a file, you can either preview it from within the iCloud Drive app or open and work with it using a compatible app. For example, if it's a Word document, you can open that document using the Word or Pages app. If it's a PDF file, you can open and view it using any PDF reader app.

iCloud Drive has its own app icon that appears on your device's Home screen. Tap the iCloud app icon to launch it. Your mobile device must have Internet access for this app to work.

If the app icon for iCloud Drive does not appear on your Home screen, launch Settings, tap the iCloud option, tap the iCloud Drive option, and then turn on the virtual switch associated with Show on Home Screen.

As soon as you launch the iCloud Drive app, default folders for specific apps are displayed, as are folders you created from your primary computer (shown in Figure 6.9).

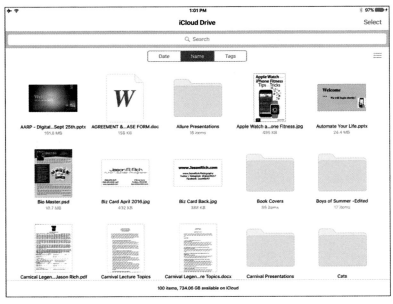

Figure 6.9
The main screen of the iCloud Drive app on an iPad when it's connected to the Internet.

Tap any folder to open it and view its contents, or tap any file icon or listing to preview it using the iCloud Drive app (in Figure 6.10, a Microsoft Word document has been selected).

When you're previewing content, tap the Share icon to access a menu that enables you to share that content via text message or email, or open that content in a specific (compatible) app already installed on your mobile device. In some cases, you will first need to tap the Download to View option that's displayed to view that content on your mobile device's screen.

To transfer the Microsoft Word file (previewed in Figure 6.10) that's stored on your iCloud Drive to the Microsoft Word app on the iPad being used, tap the Copy to Word icon displayed after tapping the Share icon (shown in Figure 6.11).

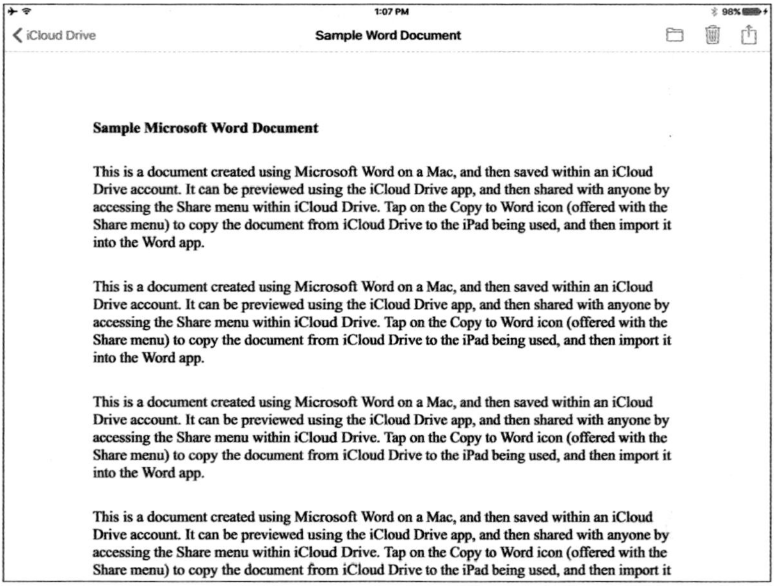

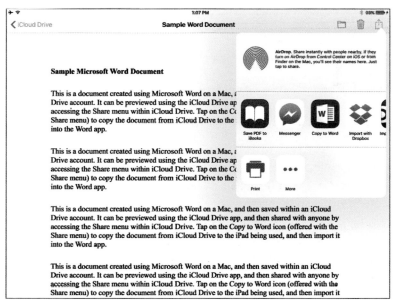

Figure 6.10

You can preview most types of files and content stored in iCloud Drive from directly within the iCloud Drive app by tapping its icon or listing. Shown here is a Microsoft Word document file.

Figure 6.11

When previewing a file, it's possible to open it in another compatible app (in this case Microsoft Word) and work with it, or share it via email with someone else.

As needed, the file or content is automatically downloaded from iCloud Drive, stored in your mobile device, and loaded into a compatible app.

> ☑ **TIP** As you're previewing content or files, tap the Trash icon to delete the file, or tap the Folder icon to move that file to a different folder within iCloud Drive. When you tap the Folder icon, a listing of folders in your iCloud Drive is displayed. Tap the listing for the folder where you want to move the file or content.

Located at the top of the screen when you launch the iCloud Drive app is a Search field. Type a keyword or search phrase to quickly find a file stored online in the iCloud Drive portion of your iCloud account.

To custom sort how the iCloud Drive folders and files are displayed on the screen, tap the Date, Name, or Tags tab displayed below the Search field. Tap the View icon, located to the right of these tabs, to switch between an icon view and a listing view of your stored folders and files. If you don't see these tabs, place your finger near the center of the screen and swipe downward, so you're looking at the very top of the screen (just below the Search field).

> ☑ **TIP** Tap the Select option in the top-right corner of the iCloud Drive app's screen to be able to select one or more files or folders by tapping them. As soon as you tap the Select option, the New Folder, Move, and Delete options are displayed at the bottom of the screen.
>
> After selecting one or more files, tap the New Folder, Move, or Delete option to handle that task. When you tap New Folder, you can create a new folder within your iCloud Drive account. Tap the Move option to move the selected file into a different folder. Tap the Delete option to delete the selected content.

When using the iCloud Drive app on an iPad, displayed at the bottom of the main screen is a summary of how many individual files are stored online, as well as how much of your allocated online storage space is still available.

Thanks to iCloud Drive, it's possible to store content online and not keep it stored on your mobile device (or computer). This frees up internal storage space. Yet, as long as your mobile device or computer has Internet access, the files stored in iCloud Drive are always accessible when they're needed.

You can access the same content that you can access from the iCloud Drive app on your mobile device from iCloud.com by clicking the iCloud Drive app icon when using the web browser of any Internet-connected computer.

When using a Mac, anytime you open a Finder window, there is an option for accessing your online-based iCloud Drive under the Favorites heading.

! CAUTION Anything you do in the iCloud Drive app in terms of creating new folders, moving files, or deleting content happens instantly. There is no "undo" option, and this affects what you can access via iCloud Drive from all your other computers and mobile devices linked to the same iCloud account.

MORE INFO Keep in mind that you are not required to use all of iCloud's various features. You can turn on only those features you believe are beneficial to you, based on how you typically use your iPhone and/or iPad and what content, data, and information you want to synchronize or back up to your iCloud account.

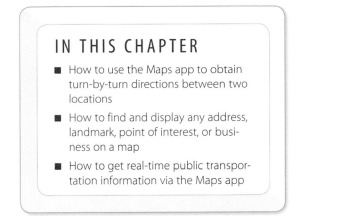

IN THIS CHAPTER

- How to use the Maps app to obtain turn-by-turn directions between two locations
- How to find and display any address, landmark, point of interest, or business on a map
- How to get real-time public transportation information via the Maps app

7

NAVIGATE AND INTERACT WITH YOUR WORLD USING THE REDESIGNED MAPS APP

One of the first things veteran iPhone and iPad users will discover when they launch the iOS 10 version of the Maps app is that it has been redesigned. It offers a more streamlined interface, but it also includes enhanced functionality and improved integration with Siri, Contacts, Calendar, and a handful of other apps, including Yelp!, Uber, Lyft, and OpenTable. In addition, the real-time mass transit information for buses, trains, subways, and ferries related to many major cities around the world has been expanded.

iOS 10 **WHAT'S NEW** When you're using the turn-by-turn, real-time navigation function of the Maps app and you need to find a nearby gas station, restaurant, or coffee shop, simply tap anywhere along the bottom of the screen (except for on the End button), and then tap the Gas Stations, Dinner, or Coffee icon.

If you tap the Gas Stations icon, for example, you see a listing of nearby gas stations. Tap the Go button that corresponds to the listing you'd like to choose. This also works with the Dinner and Coffee icons.

The Maps app automatically reroutes you to that gas station. After you've visited the gas station, Maps enables you to continue to your original destination without having to reenter any information into the app.

At the same time, your expected arrival time, the amount of time until you reach your final destination, and the current distance from your final destination will be updated to take into account the requested detour.

iOS 10 **WHAT'S NEW** To switch between using the iPhone's built-in speaker, a Bluetooth phone headset, or CarPlay (when applicable) while you're using the Maps app for real-time navigation, tap anywhere along the bottom of the screen (except for on the End button), and then tap the Audio icon.

From the Output heading on the Navigation Voice screen (shown in Figure 7.1), choose where you want the Maps app's audio to be played. Also from this screen, tap one of the volume options to change the volume of the voice prompts, and turn on the Pause Spoken Audio option if you want music, podcasts, or audiobooks, for example, to pause when the Maps app needs to speak.

As always, the Maps app requires continuous Internet access to function. Although the app works with a Wi-Fi connection, if you plan to use the app's turn-by-turn directions (Navigation) feature, you must use a cellular data connection (which uses up some of your monthly wireless data allocation with each use) because you'll be in motion and will quickly leave the wireless signal radius of any Wi-Fi hotspot.

That being said, you can use a Wi-Fi connection to preload driving or public transportation directions before your departure. If your route changes, however, your iOS mobile device isn't able to help if it can't connect to the Internet.

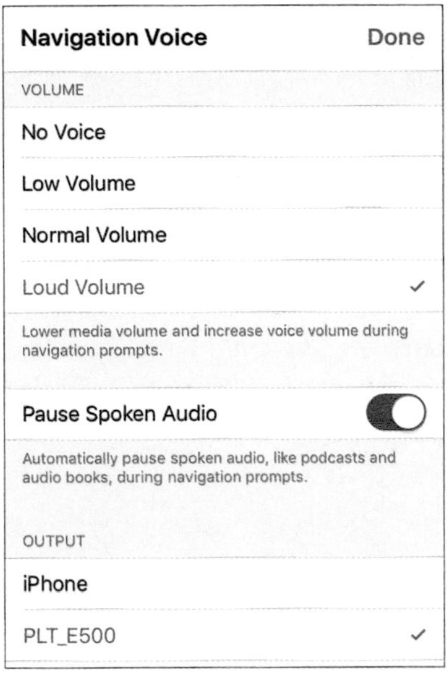

Navigation Voice	Done
VOLUME	
No Voice	
Low Volume	
Normal Volume	
Loud Volume	✓
Lower media volume and increase voice volume during navigation prompts.	
Pause Spoken Audio	⬤
Automatically pause spoken audio, like podcasts and audio books, during navigation prompts.	
OUTPUT	
iPhone	
PLT_E500	✓

Figure 7.1

The Navigation Voice menu (shown on an IPhone).

Using the Maps app with Siri (which is very convenient) requires even more cellular data usage.

> **NOTE** If you're wearing an Apple Watch that's paired with your iPhone, navigation information is automatically and simultaneously displayed on your watch.

> **TIP** To use the Maps app, the main Location Services feature in your iPhone or iPad (as well as Location Services for the Maps app) must be turned on. To do this, launch Settings, tap the Privacy option, and then tap Location Services. From the Location Services menu screen, turn on the virtual switch displayed near the top of the screen (associated with Location Services). Then, scroll down and tap the Maps option. Be sure that the While Using The App option is selected.

SETTING MAPS APP PREFERENCES FROM SETTINGS

Before the first time you use the iOS 10 edition of the Maps app (or anytime thereafter), launch Settings and then tap the Maps option to set or readjust app-specific options that allow you to customize your Maps experience.

From the Maps menu screen in Settings (shown in Figure 7.2), select the default Preferred Transportation Type for the way you'll most often be using the app. If you'll typically be in your car and want driving directions, choose Driving. If you'll most often be using the app while walking, choose the Walking option. If you rely mainly on public transportation to get around, select the Transit option. Of course, you can always override this default selection while actually using the Maps app.

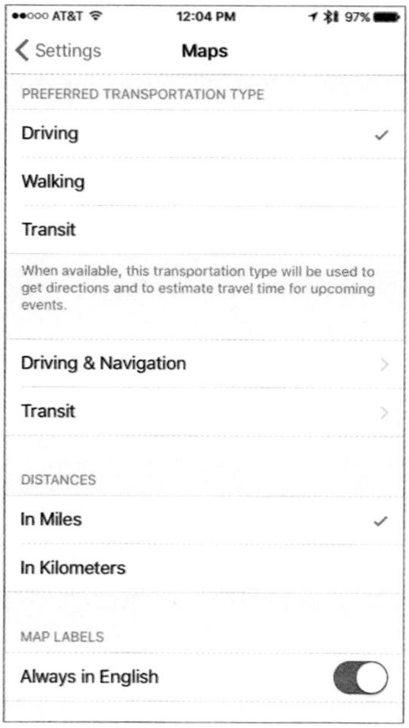

Figure 7.2

From the Maps menu screen within Settings, it's possible to customize the app.

Also from the Maps menu within Settings, tap the Driving & Navigation option to personalize preferences related to options used while navigating. For example, from under the Avoid heading, turn on the option related to Tolls or Highways if you want to avoid tolls or highways when the Maps app plans your routes.

From this submenu screen, it's also possible to turn on/off the onscreen compass display, plus set a default volume for the computerized voice that you hear when being provided with turn-by-turn navigation instructions.

iOS 10 WHAT'S NEW From the Maps menu within Settings (refer to Figure 7.2), it's possible to select whether the app should measure distances in miles or kilometers and whether all map labels should be translated into English. If your car is capable of communicating with your iPhone (via CarPlay or Bluetooth), use the Show Parked Location option so your parking location is recorded and temporarily marked in the app every time you park.

GETTING THE MOST FROM USING THE MAPS APP'S FEATURES

In addition to providing detailed maps, the Maps app is capable of displaying useful information within each map, including real-time, color-coded traffic conditions showing traffic jams, accidents, and construction, which can be graphically overlaid onto maps.

NOTE Mild traffic is showcased using orange, and heavy traffic is depicted in red. When construction is being done on a roadway, separate construction icons (in yellow or red) are displayed on the map.

Plus, when you look up a business, restaurant, point of interest, or landmark, the Maps app seamlessly integrates with Yelp! to display detailed information about specific locations.

The Yelp! information screens are interactive, so if you're using an iPhone and tap a phone number, you can initiate a call to that business or restaurant. Likewise, if you tap a website URL (on either an iPhone or iPad), Safari launches and the applicable website automatically loads and displays.

TIP To enhance the capabilities of the Yelp! integration, download and install the optional (and free) Yelp! app from the App Store. Without the Yelp! app, when appropriate, the Maps app transfers you to the Yelp! website. To be able to make restaurant reservations after using the Maps app to look up restaurants, also install the free OpenTable app onto your iPhone.

> **NOTE** Yelp! is a crowd-sourced online database. As of late 2016, it contained more than 102 million reviews related to businesses, stores, restaurants, hotels, tourist attractions, and points of interest throughout the world. Reviews are created by everyday people who share their experiences, thoughts, and photos. Beyond user-provided reviews, Yelp! offers details about many businesses and restaurants, often including hours of operation and menus.

> **NOTE** The OpenTable app is used to make reservations at more than 37,000 participating restaurants around the world. It also includes more than 750,000 detailed restaurant reviews written by app users. With the Open Table app installed on your iPhone, you can make reservations through the OpenTable app from within the Maps app or when using Siri. With a single onscreen tap, you can also call the desired restaurant. Using the Maps app, you can get navigation instructions to any selected restaurant.

Although Maps offers a lot of functionality packed into a standalone app, it's also designed to work with many other apps. For example, as you're viewing an entry in the Contacts app, when you tap an address, the Maps app launches and displays that address on a map. You can then quickly obtain detailed directions to that location from your current location, or from any address you select. This also works with any address displayed in almost any other app, such as Calendar, Mail, Messages, Notes, or Safari.

> **TIP** Any time you receive a text message or view a Calendar event that has an address included in it, iOS 10 automatically determines you're looking at an address and turns it into an active link. Tap this link to launch the Maps app and view the address or obtain directions to or from that address.

> **TIP** When creating or editing a Calendar event, by filling in the Add Location field, the iPhone or iPad is automatically able to calculate travel time from your current location to the destination and alert you about when it's time to leave, based on the anticipated travel time and current traffic conditions.

You can utilize many features built in to the Maps app using voice commands and requests, thanks to Siri. For example, regardless of what you're doing on the iPhone or iPad, it's possible to activate Siri and say, "How do I get home from here?," "Where is the closest Starbucks?," or "Where is the closest gas station?" and then have the Maps app provide you with the directions and map you need.

> ☑ **TIP** When you're viewing a map using the Maps app, tap the My Location icon (which looks like a northeast-pointing arrow) near the bottom-left corner of the screen to pinpoint and display your current location on the map. Your location is displayed on the map using a circular icon with an arrow inside (shown in Figure 7.3). In some cases, a pulsing blue dot is used to showcase your current location.

Current Location Icon

Figure 7.3

In Navigation mode, your current location is prominently displayed on the map. Tap the Location icon to display this information.

OVERVIEW OF THE MAPS APP'S SCREEN

The main screen of the iOS 10 edition of the Maps app sometimes displays a tiny compass in the upper-right corner of a map, as well as a map scale in the top-left corner of a map. The compass displays automatically when North isn't toward the top of the screen. The map scale appears if you're scrolling around a map using your finger or zooming in or out. From the Maps menu within Settings, it's also now possible to turn on the compass and have it continuously displayed whenever you're using the Maps app and viewing interactive maps.

When you launch the app, the top section of the iPhone's display showcases a map. Tap the Info (i) icon to change your map view. Options include Map, Transit, or Satellite. From the Maps Settings menu, turn on the virtual switch associated with Traffic to superimpose real-time traffic conditions on the maps you view (shown in Figure 7.4).

Figure 7.4

From the Maps Settings menu, choose your maps view (Map, Transit, or Satellite), plus turn on/off real-time traffic conditions.

Tap the My Location icon to pinpoint your current location on the map.

> **iOS 10 WHAT'S NEW** When looking at a map of your current location, the current temperature is displayed in the bottom-right corner of the map.

Just below the map is the Where Do You Want to Go? field. Tap this field and manually enter your desired destination. Keep in mind that as you enter content into this field, the Maps app can pull information from the Contacts app and other compatible apps, as well as from a vast database containing points of interest, businesses, and restaurants.

> ## ☑ TIP
>
> In the Where Do You Want to Go? field, instead of manually typing the address of your desired destination, you can type the name of a point of interest, airport, restaurant, service, or business. For example, if you type "Chinese restaurant" into this field, a listing of Chinese restaurants that are close to your current location will be displayed. However, if you want to find Chinese restaurants in another city and/or state, enter "Chinese Restaurants, White Plains, New York," for example.
>
> As you type in this field, the Maps app displays applicable search results. Tap a search result listing to select it.
>
> Alternatively, you can tap the empty Where Do You Want to Go? field, and then tap the Food, Drinks, Shopping, Travel, Services, Fun, Health, or Transport icon to seek out local businesses or services by category (shown in Figure 7.5). If necessary, tap a subcategory icon. Next, tap one of the search result listings that are of interest.
>
> When you tap a listing, information about it is displayed (shown in Figure 7.6). If it's a business or restaurant, for example, the business/restaurant name, phone number, address, website URL, and other details are displayed. Tap the Directions button to quickly obtain directions from your current location to the desired location.

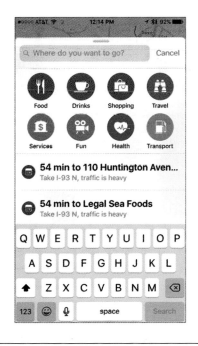

Figure 7.5

Instead of typing what you're looking for into the Where Do You Want to Go? field, tap one of the category icons, tap a subcategory icon (if applicable), and then tap a result listing.

Figure 7.6

When you look up a business, restaurant, service, or point of interest, details about it are displayed (based on content supplied by Yelp!). Tap the Directions button to obtain directions to that location.

Also displayed below the Where Do You Want to Go? field is a listing of past searches or destinations. Tap any of those listings to obtain directions to that listing's location.

> **TIP** While viewing any map, tap a listed point of interest or business that's displayed in the map to view details about it. The information window is fully interactive. For example, if you tap the phone number icon, a call to that business is initiated using the Phone app (on the iPhone).
>
> Tap the Directions button to obtain turn-by-turn directions from your current location to the selected destination.

Anytime you look up a listing in the Maps app, information appears in a window. Use your finger to drag this window up or down on the screen, allowing you to view more or less of its content (shown in Figure 7.7).

Drag this window up
or down by placing
your finger here.

Figure 7.7
*Anytime you look up information about a business, point of interest, restaurant, or service, details
about it are acquired from Yelp! and displayed in an adjustable-size window.*

> ☑ **TIP** In the Where Do You Want to Go? field, enter the name of any contact that has an entry stored in the Contacts app to find and display an address for that contact. Navigation details (directions) can be provided. The Maps app searches the contents of your iOS device (including the Contacts app), followed by a web-based search, if applicable.

VIEWING A MAP FROM MULTIPLE PERSPECTIVES

As you're viewing a map, place one finger on the screen and drag it around to
reposition the map. To rotate the map, place two fingers (slightly separated) on the
screen, and rotate your fingers clockwise or counterclockwise. To then return to
the north-up orientation, tap the compass icon.

Use a reverse-pinch finger gesture to zoom in or a pinch finger gesture to zoom
out. If you're using the Satellite or Flyover Tour view, it's possible to zoom in
very close, and then drag your finger around the map to take a bird's-eye tour of
the area.

> NOTE Flyover Tour is a newly enhanced Maps app feature that displays three-dimensional animations (from a virtual helicopter point of view) of a specific landmark or an entire supported city. When it's available, a Flyover Tour button is displayed.
>
> To see a demonstration of the Flyover Tour feature, in the Where Do You Want To Go? field, type "New York City," "San Francisco," "California," or "London, England," for example, and then tap the Search button.
>
> When the city map is displayed, below it you see a Flyover Tour button in addition to a Directions button. Tap the Flyover Tour button to view the visually stunning animated sequence.

USING THE MARK MY LOCATION OPTION

To mark your current location on the map, at any time, tap the Info icon to reveal the Maps Settings menu, and then tap the Mark My Location option. A virtual push-pin is added to the map. You can then tap the Edit Location button to fine-tune the stored address, or tap the Directions button to obtain directions to that location.

Tap the Share icon to share the marked location with other people via text message or email, for example. It's also possible to add the marked location to the Maps app's Favorites list, create a new Contacts entry using the address, or add the address to an existing Contacts entry by tapping one of the options displayed if you scroll down in the Marked Location window.

> TIP The Mark Location tool is ideal to help you remember where you parked your car. You must manually use this feature, unless your car is equipped with CarPlay or there's an established Bluetooth connection between your vehicle and your iPhone.

MANAGING YOUR FAVORITES LIST

The Maps app offers a Favorites list feature, which enables you to maintain a listing of places you commonly visit or want to be able to quickly refer to later. When looking at the information screen for any potential destination, scroll down and tap the Add to Favorites option to add that address to the Maps app's Favorites list.

To access your Favorites list, look below the Where Do You Want to Go? field, and scroll down to the bottom of the displayed search results. Tap the Favorites option. A listing of your Favorite locations is displayed. Tap any listing to obtain information or navigation directions.

Swipe from right to left across a Favorites listing to access a Remove and Share button. These enable you to manage your Favorites list.

SWITCHING THE MAP VIEW

Anytime you're viewing a map, you can switch between viewing perspectives. Options include

▪ **Maps**—This is the Maps app's standard view (shown in Figure 7.8). Roads and their names are displayed along with points of interest, businesses, and services (including gas stations, restaurants, and hospitals).

Figure 7.8

The standard Maps view of Manhattan's Times Square area is shown here on an iPhone.

▪ **Transit**—When applicable, this map view displays public transportation maps for trains, subways, buses, and/or ferries. This map view (shown in Figure 7.9) is particularly useful when you're relying on public transportation in a major city, like New York City or London.

▪ **Satellite**—Detailed satellite imagery is used to showcase maps (shown in Figure 7.10). When you choose this option, you can turn on/off virtual switches that allow traffic conditions and/or labels to be displayed, in addition to the multidimensional images.

Figure 7.9

Navigate your way around a city using a detailed public transit map. Shown here is the Times Square area of New York City on an iPhone.

Figure 7.10

The Satellite view utilizes detailed (multidimensional) satellite imagery to show a location on a map.

> ☑ **TIP** When you look up any business using the Maps app, if you then
> view the location of the business with the Satellite view, you can often determine
> the best place to park nearby. Consider dropping a pin on that location, and then
> using turn-by-turn directions to get you to that spot. There are also third-party
> apps, like Parker, that can help you find a parking spot or paid parking lot in a
> major city.

OBTAINING TURN-BY-TURN DIRECTIONS

To obtain navigation information to a particular destination, enter it into the Where
Would You Like To Go? field, or select it from a search result listing after you tap a
category, such as Food, Drinks, Shopping, Travel, Services, Fun, Health, or Transit.

Displayed immediately below a search result listing is a blue-and-white Directions
button. This button displays your current driving distance to that location. Tap
the Directions button to access the Maps app's navigation mode (shown in
Figure 7.11).

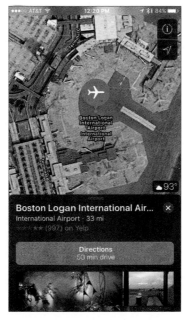

Figure 7.11
After you select a destination, tap the Directions button.

(iOS 10) WHAT'S NEW   By default, the iOS 10 version of the Maps app uses your current location as the default starting location. To change this and select any other starting location, after typing your desired destination into the Where Do You Want to Go? field and tapping the Directions button, tap the From My Location option that's displayed below the To information, and then manually enter your starting location.

For example, if you're currently in Boston, MA, but you want to see directions between New York's Time Square and New York's LaGuardia Airport, in the Where Do You Want to Go? field, type "LaGuardia Airport, New York." Tap the Directions button, and then tap the From My Location option. In the From field, type "Times Square, New York" (shown in Figure 7.12).

In the Start and End fields, you can enter a contact entry's name, a full address, a city and state, just a state, or just a country. You can use two-letter state abbreviations, and you don't have to worry about using upper- and lowercase letters. For example, you can type "New York, NY," "new york, ny," or "New York, New York," and get the same result. This goes for contacts or business names as well.

Next, tap the Route button. Choose your desired mode of transportation (Drive, Walk, Transit, or Ride), and then choose your selected route from up to three options. Tap the Go button to launch Navigation mode and begin receiving turn-by-turn directions.

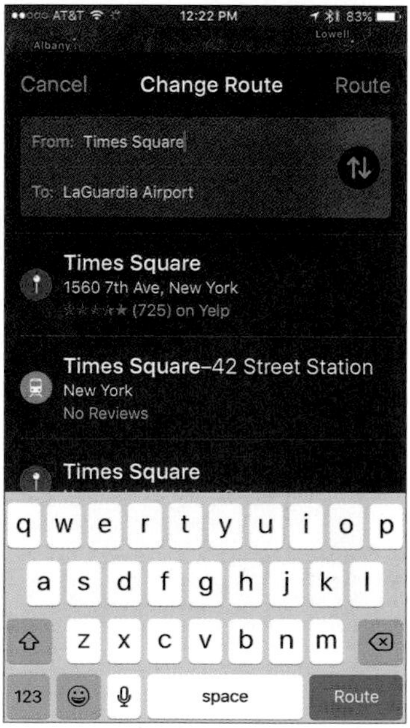

Figure 7.12

Fill in the From field to choose a starting location that is not your current location.

When you tap a destination option, the Maps app calculates your distance from it
and displays up to three separate routes on the map. The recommended route is
displayed with a dark blue line. Tap the route option you want to follow.

Below the map, tap the Go button to choose the selected route and driving directions. Alternatively, tap the Walk, Transit, or Ride icon to alter your mode of transportation (shown in Figure 7.13):

- **Drive**—Obtain real-time, turn-by-turn navigation directions for driving to
  your destination.

- **Walk**—Obtain real-time, turn-by-turn navigation directions for walking to
  your destination.

- **Transit**—Obtain real-time directions for using public transportation to reach
  your desired destination. This option is not yet available in all cities around
  the world. When it is available, the best option for using buses, trains, subways, and/or ferries are provided.

- **Ride**—Request a ride using Uber, Lyft, or another compatible taxi, limo, or
  ride-sharing service. Thus far, this feature is available only in certain major cities, and you must have the ride service's optional app (such as Uber or Lyft)
  installed on your mobile device.

Select a
Transportation
Option

Figure 7.13

*Choose a transportation option, and then receive real-time, turn-by-turn navigation information
to your destination.*

After you select the mode of transportation, tap the green-and-white Go button to begin receiving real-time, fully narrated, turn-by-turn directions to your destination.

Displayed in the main area of the screen is a detailed map that shows where you are and where you're headed. Along the top of the screen, information about the next turn or driving direction is listed. Along the bottom of the screen, your estimated time of arrival, the amount of time remaining in your trip, and the current distance between your current location and your desired destination is displayed (shown in Figure 7.14). This information continuously changes as you travel toward your destination and automatically updates based on your travel speed and traffic conditions.

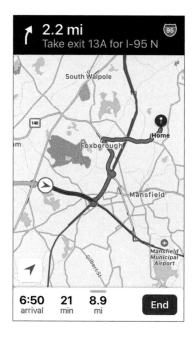

Figure 7.14

Navigation mode offers real-time, turn-by-turn directions, as well as detailed information about your current trip.

> **TIP**   Tap the End button to exit out of the navigation mode of the Maps
> app before reaching your destination.
>
> While you're using the navigation feature of the Maps app, you can utilize the App
> Switcher to switch between apps, and use the iPhone or iPad to run another app.
> The Maps app continues running in the background and alerts you of upcoming
> turns or directions.
>
> If you receive an incoming call on your iPhone, for example, the Phone app
> launches but the Maps app continues running in the background. When you
> switch to another app, with the navigation mode of the Maps app continuing
> to run, a blue bar pulses at the top of the screen that says Touch to Return to
> Navigation. Tap it to return to the Maps app (shown in Figure 7.15).

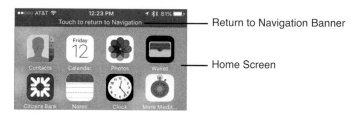

Return to Navigation Banner

Home Screen

Figure 7.15

*While you're using the Maps app for navigation, you can switch to another app but the Maps app
continues to run. Tap the Touch to Return to Navigation bar to return to the Maps app.*

Tap anywhere on the bottom Information bar (except on the End button) to reveal
an icon menu of additional options:

- **Gas Station, Dinner, or Coffee icon**—Take a detour and find the closest gas
  station, restaurant, or coffee shop, respectively.

- **Overview**—Switch to a different map view that showcases the entire route
  from your starting point to your selected destination. Tap the Resume icon to
  switch back to Navigation mode.

- **Details**—See a listing of all turns and directions you'll need to follow to reach
  your desired destination. Swipe down or up in this list (shown in Figure 7.16)
  to see upcoming directions. Tap Done to return to Navigation mode.

> **Note**   When using the Maps app's Navigation mode, you're warned
> about upcoming construction or traffic while you're driving. When applicable, the
> Maps app automatically recommends an alternative route, which you can accept
> or reject.

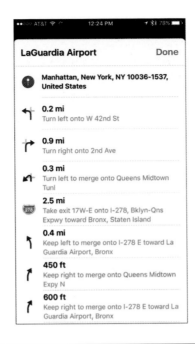

Figure 7.16

Tap the Details icon to view list of turns and directions you need to follow to reach your selected destination.

LOOKING UP CONTACT ENTRIES, BUSINESSES, RESTAURANTS, LANDMARKS, AND POINTS OF INTEREST

One of the other primary uses of the Maps app is to find and display addresses, contacts, businesses, points of interest, or landmarks on a map screen. To do this, launch the Maps app, and in the Where Do You Want to Go? field, enter what you're looking for.

The following are some things you can enter in this field:

■ A contact's name from your Contact's database. The Maps app looks up that contact's address that's stored in the Contacts app.

■ The specific name of any business or restaurant. (If it's not nearby, type the business or restaurant name, followed by a comma, and then the city, state, and/or country). The Maps app looks up the business or restaurant's address on the Internet, displays it, and gives you the option to receive directions to it.

- The type of business or restaurant you're looking for, such as Chinese Restaurant, Seafood Restaurant, Bank, Dry Cleaner, or Hospital. Enter just a business or restaurant type to find nearby listings, or include the city, state, and/or country to look up listings in other locations.

- The name of a point of interest or landmark. This can include the name of a major airport, or a landmark, such as the Statue of Liberty, Empire State Building, The White House, Disney World, The Golden Gate Bridge, London Eye, or Tower of London. You do not need to know the address for a point of interest. The Maps app maintains a vast database of them.

- Any full address that you manually enter (that is, street, city, state, country).

- The name of a city, state, or country.

> **☑ TIP** When looking up a famous landmark, you can often tap the Flyover Tour button (shown in Figure 7.17) to view a three-dimensional, animated, virtual tour of that landmark (from a visually impressive, helicopter-like viewing perspective).

Figure 7.17

See a Flyover Tour of a popular landmark (almost anywhere in the world) when you look it up using the Maps app.

> **☑ TIP** If you're looking for businesses or services in your immediate area, tap the My Location icon first, so the iPhone or iPad pinpoints your location, and then enter what you're searching for into the Where Do You Want to Go? field. No city or state needs to be entered.
>
> However, if you don't tap the My Location icon first, you must enter into the Where Do You Want to Go? field what you're looking for, followed by the city, a comma, and the state, to find local search results. Otherwise, the Maps app defaults to the last search location.

USING THE INTERACTIVE LOCATION SCREENS

Once search results are displayed, tap the desired result to view information pertaining to it that incorporates content from the Internet, Yelp!, and the Maps app. This information includes the phone number, address, website URL, hours of operation, and other information for that search result. The information displayed depends on whether it's a business, restaurant, point of interest, or tourist attraction. Photos (provided by other iPhone, iPad, and Yelp! users) are often displayed as well. When applicable, text-based reviews and star-based ratings from other iPhone, iPad, and/or Yelp! users are displayed for that business, point of interest, service, or restaurant.

Tap the More Info on Yelp! option to launch the Yelp! app or visit the Yelp! website to view more detailed information about that location.

Create New Contact, Add To Existing Contact, and Report a Problem options are also available.

> **☑ TIP** If you look up information about a restaurant, the information screen features Yelp!-related information, including the type of food served, the menu price range (using dollar signs), the hours of operation, and potentially a website link that enables you to view the restaurant's menu. You can also determine whether the restaurant delivers or accepts reservations.
>
> If reservations are accepted, use the optional OpenTable app to make reservations online. Activate Siri and say, "Make a reservation for [number of people] for [day and time]," or initiate a call from an iPhone to the restaurant by tapping the phone number field. When applicable, the Info or Yelp! screen for a business also tells you whether Apple Pay is accepted at that location.

USING THE MAPS APP'S FLYOVER VIEW

For a growing number of cities throughout the world, it's possible to take a virtual tour of the city using the Maps app's Flyover Tour mode. When this feature is available, type the city and state, or city, state, and country in to the Where Do You Want to Go? field.

For example, type "London, England" into the Where Do You Want to Go? field, and then tap the Search button. When the London map is displayed, tap the Flyover Tour button (shown in Figure 7.18).

Figure 7.18

Tap Flyover Tour to see a three-dimensional animated tour of the selected city.

An animated Fly Over tour, featuring popular landmarks and tourist attractions (including Buckminster Palace and the London Eye for the London tour) are displayed (shown in Figure 7.19). Simply watch the animated sequence on the screen.

A three-dimensional auto-scrolling map of the city is displayed, and you see an aerial virtual tour that showcases the city's most popular tourist locations and landmarks.

This feature isn't great for helping you navigate, but it is excellent for providing a quick overview of a city that you've never been to. Use this feature to help you get yourself acclimated, or to showcase the city's most famous landmarks that you might want to visit in person during your visit.

Figure 7.19
Take a three-dimensional virtual tour of almost any major city in the world.

> ☑ **TIP**   Use these quick tips for working with Maps:
>
> ☐ When using the Maps app, your iPhone or iPad accesses the Internet exten-
> sively. This drains the device's battery faster. If you often use this feature from
> your car, consider investing in a car charger that plugs into your car's 12-volt
> or USB jack. This way, your iPhone's/iPad's battery remains charged (and can
> recharge) while it's being used.
>
> ☐ Using the Maps app for Navigation via a cellular data Internet connection
> requires a significant amount of wireless data usage. Using this feature depletes
> your monthly cellular data allocation unless you're subscribed to an unlimited
> wireless service plan (or a plan with a generous amount of cellular data). Also,
> if you're using international roaming to access the Internet from abroad, using
> Maps with a cellular data connection can get very expensive.
>
> ☐ The Maps app works with iCloud and automatically syncs your Favorites list
> with all your other computers and mobile devices linked to the same iCloud
> account. You can also use the Handoff feature to switch from using your iPhone
> to your iPad or Mac (or vice versa) when using the Maps app, without having to
> reenter information.

> **WHAT'S NEW** Below the Where Do You Want To Go? field,
> when search results are displayed, the Maps app automatically displays locations
> listed in upcoming appointments in the Calendar app, as well as selected results
> from past searches (shown in Figure 7.20).

Info Icon

Current Location Icon

Addresses Related to
Upcoming Appointments
from the Calendar App

Figure 7.20

*Addresses associated with upcoming appointments from the Calendar app are displayed as
search results below the Where Do You Want to Go? field.*

SHOOT, EDIT, AND SHARE PHOTOS AND VIDEOS

Every day, more than 1.5 billion photos are taken on smartphones and tablets around the world. People love taking photos, and thanks to the two digital cameras built in to all the iPhone and iPad models released in the past few years, plus improvements made to the iOS 10 edition of the Camera and Photos apps, it has never been easler or more fun to shoot, edit, view, print, and share your digital images or video clips.

> **NOTE** In this chapter, the phrase, "newer iPhone and iPad models" refers to iPhone 6s, iPhone 6s Plus, or the iPhone 7 series, as well as many of the more recently released iPad Pro models.

> **NOTE** The Live Photo feature of the Camera app enables you to snap a photo but capture it as a two- to three-second mini-movie that can later be viewed as an animated image on any iPhone, iPad, iPod touch, Mac, Apple TV, or Apple Watch that's using the Photos app or is capable of displaying digital photos in other ways. For example, you can use a Live Photo as your custom watch face on the Apple Watch or as the Lock screen wallpaper on your iPhone or iPad.
>
> A Live Photo can still be treated as a regular digital image file. You can edit it, share it online, email it, or print it.

Whether you're using one of the latest iPhone models or an older iPhone (or any iPad model for that matter), it's possible to take crystal-clear photos and create large and vibrant full-color prints from your digital image files, or share those images using options offered by the Photos app's Share menu.

THE iPHONE 7 PLUS IS DIFFERENT FROM OTHER iPHONES WHEN IT COMES TO USING THE CAMERA APP

The iPhone 7 Plus is the first Apple mobile device to include a front-facing, 7MP FaceTime HD camera (which can be used to take photos, shoot video, or participate in video calls via FaceTime, Facebook Messenger, or Skype, for example). This smartphone model also includes two separate rear-facing cameras and a redesigned Quad-LED True Tone flash. As a result, when using the Camera app, the viewfinder screen looks somewhat different than earlier models.

> **NOTE** The older iPhone 6s, for example, offers a 5MP front-facing camera and just one rear-facing camera (that offers a 5x digital zoom feature), as opposed to 10x zoom capabilities offered by the iPhone 7 Plus.

When using any of the shooting modes, to switch between the rear-facing wide-angle and telephoto lenses, tap the circular 1x icon that appears near the bottom center of the viewfinder screen, just above the shooting mode menu (shown in Figure 8.1). Alternatively, place and hold your finger on the circular zoom intensify icon, and a redesigned zoom slider (shown in Figure 8.2) appears. Use this zoom slider, or a reverse-pinch/pinch finger gesture, to zoom in or out from the Camera app's viewfinder screen.

When you switch to the telephoto lens, 5x magnification will immediately be utilized. You can then increase the zoom intensity up to 10x. To switch back to the wide-angle lens, tap the circular 2x icon.

Figure 8.1

Tap the 1x circular icon to switch between the wide-angle and telephoto lenses of the iPhone 7 Plus.

When using the iPhone 7 Plus, you'll notice that, by default, the Camera app always initially utilizes the wide-angle lens with 1x (zero) zoom magnification. Using the reverse-pinch finger gesture or the zoom slider, you can adjust the zoom between 1x and 10x without manually switching between rear-facing cameras. The camera switch happens automatically when it's needed. The zoom slider's new look on an iPhone 7 Plus is shown in Figure 8.2.

! CAUTION When utilizing higher levels of the optical or digital zoom (higher than 5x, for example) with the iPhone 7 Plus, be sure to hold the smartphone very still when pressing the shutter button to snap a photo. Even the slightest movement can cause the image to appear blurry or pixelated, particularly in low-light situations (when not using the flash). The Camera app's built-in image stabilization will sometimes compensate for this (mainly in well-lit situations), but not always.

Figure 8.2
Press and hold your finger on the circular zoom intensity icon to make the redesigned zoom slider appear.

> **NOTE** The Camera Selection icon displayed in the bottom-right corner of the viewfinder screen is still used to switch between the front- and rear-facing cameras

The cameras built in to the iPhone 7 and iPhone 7 Plus now include what Apple refers to as Optical Image Stabilization, as well as improved body and face detection, among other features that work behind the scenes to help you automatically take clearer, more vibrant photos in a broader range of shooting situations.

If you opt to use the flash that's built in to the iPhone 7 or iPhone 7 Plus, instead of utilizing just two LEDs to create the True Tone flash, four auto-adjusting LEDs are now used. This enables the smartphone to better analyze the available light, and then utilize the flash to simulate but brighten the ambient light when taking a photo. This new Quad-LED True Tone flash should help reduce red-eye, overexposed subjects, and unwanted shadows that a typical camera flash often causes. Depending on the shooting situation, however, you'll often discover that you'll capture more authentic colors and lighting by turning on the HDR shooting mode instead of using the flash.

> **✓ TIP**   When using one of the latest iPhone models and viewing the Home screen, instead of launching the Camera app by tapping on its app icon, place and hold your finger gently on the app icon to reveal a Touch 3D menu that enables you to access the Selfie picture taking feature, record a video, record a slo-mo video, or take a regular photo by tapping one of the listed options (shown in Figure 8.3).

Figure 8.3

Quickly launch a specific feature of the Camera app directly from the Home screen by placing and holding your finger on the Camera app icon for about 2 seconds and using the iPhone's 3D Touch functionality.

GET ACQUAINTED WITH THE iOS 10 EDITION OF THE CAMERA APP

Regardless of which iPhone or iPad model you're using, you'll discover that some of the command icons displayed on the viewfinder screen when using the iOS 10 edition of the Camera app have been moved around, yet each performs the same function as it did before. Keep in mind that if you're using an older iPhone model (pre-iPhone 6s), not all of the features discussed in this chapter will be available to you.

! CAUTION The same iOS 10 version of the Camera app is installed on all iOS mobile devices. However, based on which iPhone or iPad model you're using, some of the features and functions of the Camera app might not be available to you.

Features such as the Selfie picture taking mode and the ability to shoot Live Photos, for example, work only with the latest iOS mobile devices that offer 3D Touch functionality built in to the device's touchscreen.

NOTE If you activate the iCloud Photo Library feature offered by the Photos app (which enables you to sync your digital images between all iOS mobile devices and computers linked to the same iCloud account), your main photo album where all your photos are stored, including all newly shot photos, is called All Photos. However, when iCloud Photo Library is turned off, the main album where you'll initially find all photos you take using your iPhone or iPad is called Camera Roll.

TAKING PHOTOS OR SHOOTING VIDEO

The Camera app is the primary app used to take photos or shoot HD video using the cameras that are built in to your iPhone or iPad.

LAUNCHING THE CAMERA APP

There are several easy ways to launch the Camera app:

- From the Home screen, tap the Camera app icon.
- From the main Lock screen, swipe from right to left.
- Tap the Camera app icon in the Control Center.
- On an iPhone with 3D Touch capabilities, press the Camera app icon displayed on the Home screen to reveal a pop-up menu for using specific Camera app features (refer to Figure 8.3).
- Activate Siri and say, "Launch the camera app." If you're using one of the newer iPhones or iPads, simply say, "Hey Siri, launch the Camera app," without having to press and hold down the Home button.
- If the Camera app is already running in the background, access the App Switcher and select the Camera app.

SHOOTING PHOTOS OR VIDEO

The iPhone and iPad each have two built-in cameras—one in the front and one on the back of the device. (As you now know, the iPhone 7 Plus has three built-in cameras.) The front-facing camera makes it easier to snap photos of yourself (that is, take a "selfie," or participate in video calls via FaceTime or Skype).

> **✓ TIP** When taking a selfie, consider using an optional selfie stick. These accessories cost between $15.00 and $30.00 and enable you to hold your iPhone farther away from your body as you're taking a picture of yourself, the people you're standing close to, and what's behind you—always using the front-facing camera. The selfie stick has a shutter button built in to its handle that enables you to control the iPhone's Camera app remotely.

The rear-facing camera (which enables you to take much higher-resolution photos or video) enables you to photograph or record whatever is in front of you. Tap the camera-shaped Camera Selection icon to switch between cameras.

The main camera viewfinder screen appears as soon as you launch the Camera app on an iPhone, iPod touch, or iPad. Figure 8.4 shows the main Camera app viewfinder screen on an older iPhone 5c, whereas Figure 8.5 shows the Camera app on the iPhone 6s (which offers the Live Photo feature). Figure 8.6 shows the Camera app's viewfinder screen on an iPad.

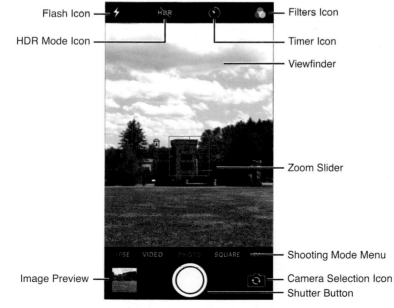

Flash Icon — Filters Icon
HDR Mode Icon — Timer Icon
Viewfinder
Zoom Slider
Shooting Mode Menu
Image Preview — Camera Selection Icon
Shutter Button

Figure 8.4

From the Camera app's main screen (shown here on the iPhone 5c), you can snap digital photos or shoot video.

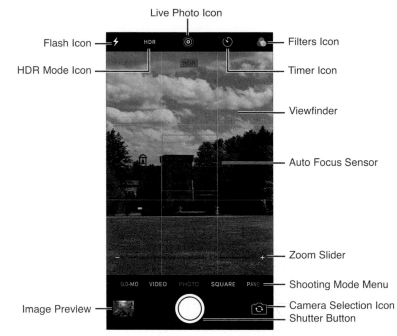

Live Photo Icon

Flash Icon

HDR Mode Icon

Filters Icon

Timer Icon

Viewfinder

Auto Focus Sensor

Zoom Slider

Shooting Mode Menu

Image Preview

Camera Selection Icon

Shutter Button

Figure 8.5
The Camera app on the iPhone 6s (or iPhone 6s Plus) or later has the Live Photo icon displayed at the top center of the screen.

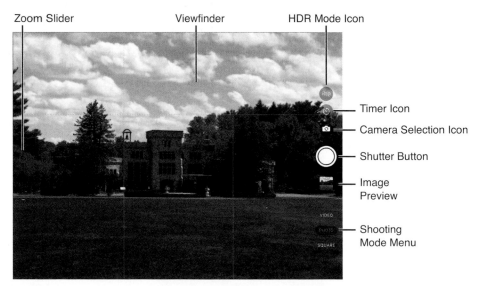

Zoom Slider

Viewfinder

HDR Mode Icon

Timer Icon

Camera Selection Icon

Shutter Button

Image Preview

Shooting Mode Menu

Figure 8.6
The Camera app looks slightly different on an iPad, but it offers much of the same functionality, depending on which iPad model you're using (shown here on an iPad mini 4).

WHAT'S NEW On an iPhone, the iOS 10 edition of the Camera app displays the Camera Selection icon in the bottom-right corner of the viewfinder screen. On an iPad, this icon is now located directly above the Shutter button.

TIP To snap a Live Photo, first tap the Live Photo icon at the top center of the viewfinder screen to turn on this feature. Then take a photo as you normally would by using any of the Camera app's other features and functions. The Live Photo feature works only when the Camera app is set to Photo mode (not Square, Time Lapse, or Pano mode, for example). It does still work, however, with the Timer feature turned on. Using the iOS 10 edition of the Photos app, it is now possible to edit Live Photos and keep their animation intact.

When using the Camera app on any iOS mobile device, the main area of the screen serves as your camera's viewfinder. What you see in this viewfinder is what will be captured in your digital photo.

On the iPhone, along the top and bottom of the screen are several command icons and options. When using the Camera app with an iPad, most command icons and options are displayed along the right margin of the screen.

NOTE If you're using an older iPhone or iPad model, some of the features and functions discussed in this chapter (such as HDR Auto mode, Live Photo, and Burst shooting mode) are not available to you.

To view the last photo you shot (or the last video clip recorded), tap the Image Preview thumbnail displayed in the bottom-left corner of the viewfinder screen (iPhone), or just below the Shutter button on an iPad. You can then use the Photo app's viewing and editing functions on that image or video clip.

At the bottom center of the screen on the iPhone is the camera's Shutter button. On the iPad, it's located in the right margin. Tap this to snap a photo or to start and stop the video recording process.

!CAUTION If you accidently press and hold the Shutter button for too long when trying to snap a single image, Burst shooting mode activates, and you'll wind up with several similar images taken in quick succession. To avoid this, be sure to quickly tap the Shutter button, not press and hold it down.

> **☑ TIP**   In Photo mode, if you press and hold the Shutter button, Burst shooting mode automatically activates on newer iPhone and iPad models. This feature enables you to shoot multiple photos in quick succession (several frames per second) without having to keep pressing the Shutter button.
>
> This feature is ideal for capturing a fast moving subject, for example, and enables you to capture an action or event that happens very quickly. You can always delete the unwanted (extra) photos after choosing your favorite image(s) from the sequence.
>
> Images shot using Burst shooting mode are placed in a separate album in the Photos app called Bursts.

UNDERSTANDING THE SHOOTING MODES

From the Shooting Mode menu offered on the latest iPhone models, your options include Time-Lapse, Slow-Mo, Video, Photo, Square, and Pano. Use your finger to manually scroll left or right to select your shooting mode. The active shooting mode is highlighted in yellow directly above the Shutter button.

On an iPad, the available shooting modes are displayed below the Shutter button in the right margin of the viewfinder screen. Scroll up/down to view and access them.

> **☑ NOTE**   If you're using one of the latest iPhones, the Selfie shooting mode enables you to snap a photo and use the smartphone's screen as your flash. You can access this feature from the Home screen using the Camera app's 3D Touch menu, or anytime you're using the front-facing camera (as long as the flash option is set to On or Auto).

Here's how you can use the six shooting modes:

■ **Time-Lapse**—Enables you to set up the Camera app to automatically keep snapping one photo at a time (the time interval is dynamically set by the iOS device) until you manually turn off this function. This feature works best if you mount the iOS mobile device on a tripod or use it with a stand. It's great for capturing changes that happen in a single scene over time, such as a sunrise or sunset. The content created when using the Time Lapse feature is stored in the Photos app as a video, not as a series of photos.

> **NOTE** When shooting with Time Lapse mode, the longer you leave the feature turned on (so the Camera app keeps taking photos automatically over an extended period of time), the longer the interval is between shots. Typically, if you leave this feature turned on long enough, the images are condensed into a 30- to 40-second mini-movie that shows the animated time-lapsed images.

- **Slo-Mo**—Enables you to shoot high-action video but play it back in slow motion. When using one of the latest iPhone models, it's possible to capture slow-motion video at up to 240 frames per second, as opposed to 120 frames per second using an older iPhone and some iPad models. This shooting mode is ideal if you're shooting a fast-moving subject or a high-action activity.

- **Video**—Enables you to shoot HD-quality video using your iPhone or iPad. Depending on which device you're using, it's possible to shoot at 30 or 60 frames per second. Keep in mind that your iPhone or iPad is ideal for shooting relatively short video clips. These HD video files take up a tremendous amount of storage space, so if you want to shoot long home videos, consider using a dedicated video camera.

> **NOTE** In Settings, you can select the video shooting resolution. The options vary based on the device you're using. If you're using an iPhone 6s, iPhone 6s Plus, iPhone 7, or iPhone 7 Plus, for example, you can shoot 4K resolution video at 30 frames per second (or you can choose a lower resolution, such as 720p or 1080p).
>
> To adjust the default video resolution on any iPhone or iPad, launch Settings, tap the Photos & Camera option, and then tap the Record Video option and/or Record Slo-Mo option.
>
> Keep in mind that the higher the resolution you select, the larger your video files will be. Larger files require more internal storage space in your mobile device.

- **Photo**—Used for taking most pictures. It allows you to snap regular, rectangular-shaped digital images at the highest resolution the front- or rear-facing camera that's built in to your iPhone or iPad is capable of.

> **TIP** The shooting resolution of the rear-facing camera can capture images and video at a much higher resolution than the front-facing camera. So, unless you're taking a selfie (a photo of yourself and whatever is behind you), you'll capture clearer, more vivid, and more detailed images and video using the rear-facing camera.

- **Square**—Automatically precrops images as you're shooting photos to be compatible with services such as Instagram. You wind up with square images.
- **Pano**—Launches the Camera app's panoramic mode, which is ideal for shooting vast landscapes, skylines, or large groups of people. You wind up with a long, rectangular image (shown in Figure 8.7).

Figure 8.7

The Pano (panoramic) shooting mode is ideal for shooting images of vast landscapes, large groups of people, or very wide areas.

> **TIP** In addition to the Time-Lapse option, the Camera app offers a Timer option. To turn on the timer, tap the Timer icon, and then set it for 3 or 10 seconds. Doing this determines how long the Camera app waits between the time you press the Shutter button and when an image is actually taken and saved. This feature is available on most iPhone and iPad models.

iPHONE 7 PLUS USERS: DISCOVER PORTRAIT MODE

Starting in late 2016, a free update to iOS 10, called iOS 10.1, was offered that introduced a new Portrait shooting mode to the Camera app. This new feature is available exclusively to the iPhone 7 Plus.

> **NOTE** To access the new Portrait mode built in to the Camera app, you must first upgrade your iPhone 7 Plus to iOS 10.1.

When taking pictures of people or objects, this new mode will help to ensure that your intended subject is in focus and displayed clearly but the background is slightly blurred. When you select Portrait mode, the rear-facing telephoto lens (5x zoom) of the iPhone 7 Plus is automatically selected, and a depth-of-field effect is utilized automatically.

Anytime you're using Portrait mode, be sure to tap the viewfinder screen directly over the intended subject to ensure that the Camera app's autofocus sensors focus in on your intended subject, as opposed to something else that appears in the foreground, background, or to either side of your subject.

> **NOTE** When using Portrait mode, your intended subject can be a person, pet, or any object that's clearly positioned in front of something else.

To use this new Portrait shoot mode, select it from the newly expanded shooting mode menu. (Again, this option appears only if you're using the iOS 10.1 version of the Camera app on an iPhone 7 Plus.) Portrait mode is listed between the Photo and Square shooting modes. After you select it, tap your intended subject. The autofocus sensor appears over your subject.

Using Photo mode, notice in Figure 8.8 that both the flower in the foreground and the historic Boston church in the background are in focus. When you switch to Portrait mode, however, and select the flower as your intended subject by tapping it (as shown in Figure 8.9), the flower stays in focus but the church in the background becomes slightly blurred. A Depth Effect message appears on the screen indicating that this feature is being utilized. This effect places more emphasis on your intended subject in the photo that's being taken.

Figure 8.8

Using Photo mode, your intended subject (in this case, a flower) and what's in the background (the historic church) appear in focus.

Figure 8.9

When selecting Portrait mode, the rear-facing telephoto lens of iPhone 7 Plus is used. Tap your intended subject, and the background automatically becomes blurred.

To recap, Figure 8.10 shows a photo taken using the Photo shooting mode, so both the flower and the church are in focus, while Figure 8.11 was taken using the new Portrait shooting mode.

Figure 8.10
This shot was taken using the Photo shoot-ing mode with the iOS 10.1 version of the Camera app on an iPhone 7 Plus.

Figure 8.11
This shot was taken using the new Portrait mode.

TIP Anytime your intended subject is located in front of something else, experiment using Portrait mode to tinker with the image's depth of field, and create visually interesting effects in your photos that draw more attention to your subject.

USING THE HDR SHOOTING FEATURE

The HDR feature offered by the Camera app stands for High Dynamic Range. You can use it only with the rear-facing camera. When turned on, this feature captures the available light differently, which can help you compensate for a photo that would otherwise be over- or underexposed. You can use this feature anytime, but it works extremely well in low-light situations.

When you take a photo using HDR mode, the iPhone or iPad actually captures several separate images simultaneously, and then automatically blends them into a single image in a fraction of a second. By doing this, it's possible to capture more depth and contrast, plus make better use of available lighting. The result is often a more detailed and vibrant photo.

You can decide whether the original photo and the HDR version of a photo are both saved in the All Photos/Camera Roll album, or if just the HDR version of the image should be saved. To make this adjustment, launch Settings, tap the Photos & Camera option, and then turn on or off the virtual switch associated with the Keep Normal Photo option.

Depending on which iPhone or iPad model you're using, you might have access to HDR Auto mode. This allows the Camera app to decide for you whether a photo benefits from this feature. Turning on HDR Auto mode takes some of the guess-work out of picture-taking, and often results in better-quality images.

The HDR button is displayed at the top of the Camera app's viewfinder screen on the iPhone, or above the Shutter button on the iPad. Tap it to toggle the HDR mode when taking photos.

On the latest iPhones and iPads there are three HDR-related options: On, Off, or Auto. (On older iPhone and most iPad models, only the On or Off options are avail-able.) If HDR Auto is available (shown in Figure 8.12), it enables you to consistently capture the most vibrant photos In a wide range of lighting situations.

Figure 8.12

On the latest iPhone and iPad models, set HDR mode to On, Off, or Auto mode by tapping the option at the top of the screen.

> **NOTE** When you turn on the HDR mode, this automatically turns off the flash that's built in to the iPhone (and some iPad Pro models).

USING THE BUILT-IN FLASH

On the iPhone (and some iPad Pro models), the flash icon enables you to control whether the built-in flash is used as you're shooting photos or video. Tap the Flash icon, and then tap the On, Off, or Auto option to toggle this feature.

The Auto option is offered only on the newer iPhone and iPad Pro models. The Auto option enables the smartphone to analyze the available light for you, and automatically determine whether the flash is needed.

> ✓ **TIP**   Keep in mind that even in low-light situations, you can often achieve better results if you shoot photos using the HDR shooting mode rather than using the flash.

> ✎ **NOTE**   Starting with the iPhone 5 series, the smartphone includes what Apple calls a True Tone flash. This is really two flashes that work together and emit light in different colors. As a result, the Camera app analyzes the available light in each shooting situation and enhances it, while monitoring the natural colors in a photo.
>
> The True Tone flash automatically reduces the red-eye effect when taking pictures of people, and can often reduce or eliminate unwanted shadows in photos. In the iPhone 7 and iPhone 7 Plus, the built-in flash utilizes four separate LEDs that work together, as opposed to just two.
>
> A True Tone Flash is also built in to the latest iPad Pro models.

> ✓ **TIP**   When using a newer iPhone model, if you activate the flash when using the front-facing camera, the screen of your iPhone automatically serves as a simulated flash to brighten up your face when the ambient light isn't adequate. Make sure the Camera app's flash option is turned on for this to work.

USING THE AUTOFOCUS AND EXPOSURE CONTROL OPTIONS

As you're looking at the Camera app's viewfinder and framing your shot, be sure to force the app to focus on your intended subject by tapping the screen directly over where your subject appears.

When you do this, the Autofocus Sensor box appears in the viewfinder, and the Camera app focuses on your intended subject (that is, what's in the box). What's behind, in front of, above, below, or to the sides of your subject may be slightly blurred.

If you're shooting people, however, the Camera app automatically identifies each person's face in a photo and focuses on those faces. An Autofocus Sensor box appears around each person's face.

> ☑ **TIP**   In addition to the Autofocus Sensor, depending on which iOS mobile device you're using, a manual Exposure Control slider might also be displayed. It looks like a sun-shaped icon that appears to the immediate right of the Autofocus Sensor.
>
> When this Exposure Control slider is displayed (see Figure 8.13), place your finger on the sun-shaped icon and slide it upward or downward to manually adjust the exposure before snapping the photo.

Autofocus Sensor

Figure 8.13

Whatever the autofocus center is centered on, such as someone's face, is what the Camera app will make sure is in focus as you take each photo.

SNAPPING A PHOTO

Snapping a single digital photo using the Camera app is simple. Follow these steps:

1. Launch the Camera app.
2. Make sure the shooting mode is set to Photo or Square.
3. Choose which of your device's two cameras you want to use by tapping the Camera Selection icon.
4. Compose your image by holding up your device and pointing it at your intended subject(s).

5. If desired, set the Timer feature.

6. To add a special effect to the image as you're shooting, tap the Filter icon, and then select one of the eight displayed filters by tapping its preview image (shown in Figure 8.14). The filter thumbnail serves as the shutter button for snapping a photo when you tap it. The Filters icon is now displayed in the top-right corner of the Camera app's viewfinder screen on the iPhone.

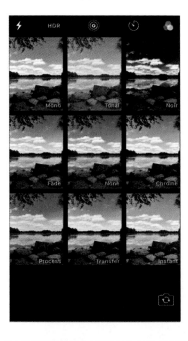

Figure 8.14

As you're shooting a photo, you can choose one of the eight image filters to add an effect. Choose None (in the center) to shoot without using a filter.

> **NOTE** You don't have to add a filter when you shoot the photo. You can always add a filter later when editing a photo using the Photos app.

7. Choose the intended subject of your photo, such as a person or an object. Tap your finger on the screen where your subject appears in the viewfinder. An Autofocus Sensor box appears on the screen at the location you tap (refer to Figure 8.13). Where this box is positioned is what the camera focuses on (as opposed to something in the foreground, background, or next to your intended subject).

8. If necessary, use the Exposure Control slider (the sun-shaped icon; refer to Figure 8.13) to manually adjust the exposure just before snapping a photo. You

can later adjust or correct a variety of problematic issues in a photo—including its exposure, contrast, saturation, color, and shadows—using the Photos app.

> **TIP** As you're holding your iPhone or iPad to snap a photo or shoot video, be sure your fingers don't accidentally block the camera lens. On the more recent iPhone and iPad Pro models, located near the rear-facing camera lens is a tiny True Tone flash. Keep your fingers clear of this, as well.

9. If you want to use the Camera app's zoom feature, use a pinch motion on the screen. A zoom slider (shown in Figure 8.15) appears directly above the Shooting Mode menu and the Shutter button. Use your finger to move the dot on the slider to the right to zoom in, or to the left to zoom out. Alternatively, use a pinch or reverse-pinch finger gesture to manage the zoom level while shooting. Remember, the iPhone 7 Plus displays the zoom intensity in a circular icon near the bottom center of the viewfinder screen. A zoom slider is not displayed. Use the reverse-pinch or pinch finger gesture to adjust the zoom intensity.

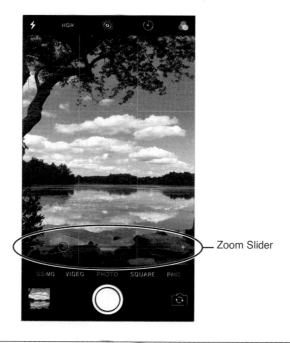

Zoom Slider

Figure 8.15

As you're framing your shot, zoom in (or out) on your subject using the onscreen zoom slider. Use a pinch finger gesture on the screen to make this slider appear, and then move it to the right or left to increase or decrease the zoom level.

10. Decide whether you want to use HDR mode or the built-in flash (iPhone or iPad Pro only) when taking the photo. (You can also choose neither of these options.)

11. When you have your image framed in the viewfinder, tap the Shutter button to snap the photo. Alternatively, press the Volume Up (+) or Volume Down (–) button on the side of your iPhone/iPad, which also serve as a Shutter button when using the Camera app.

12. The photo is saved in the All Photos/Camera Roll album of the Photos app. You can now shoot another photo or view the photo using the Photos app.

> **NOTE** All regular photos are automatically stored in the All Photos/ Camera Roll album as they're taken. The iOS 10 edition of the Photos app automatically also places selfies into a separate Selfies album and sorts your panoramic shots into a Panoramas album.
>
> Videos are placed in a separate Videos album, and slo-mo video clips are stored in an album called Slo-Mo.
>
> When you use the Burst shooting mode, these groups of images are clustered together and placed in the Bursts album.
>
> All these albums are automatically created for you. In the Photos app, you can move images into the Favorites album or any custom-named albums you create manually.

SHOOTING A PANORAMIC PHOTO

To take advantage of the panoramic shooting mode to snap a photo of a landscape, city skyline, or a large group of people, follow these steps:

1. Launch the Camera app.

2. Swipe the Shooting Modes menu, and select the Pano shooting mode.

3. Position your iPhone or iPad's viewfinder to the extreme left of your wide-angle shot. (When using the Pano shooting mode, hold the smartphone or tablet upright in portrait mode, unless you're shooting a very, very tall object).

> **TIP** If you tap the large arrow icon in the viewfinder, you can switch the panning direction from right to left, instead of left to right as you're capturing a panoramic shot.

4. Tap the Shutter button, and then slowly and steadily move (pan) your iPhone or iPad from left to right (shown in Figure 8.16).

Figure 8.16

When taking panoramic shots, the viewfinder screen looks very different on your iPhone or iPad.

5. The panorama slider moves from left to right as you capture your image. Tap the Shutter button again when you're finished, or continue moving the iOS device to the right until the entire length of the image has been captured.

> **TIP** If you pan the iPhone or iPad too fast or too slow while taking a panoramic shot, or if your hand isn't steady, you see a message that tells you what you're doing wrong. Although you can continue taking that shot, for the best results, tap the Shutter button to stop shooting, and then start again from step 1.

6. The panoramic photo is saved in the Panoramas album of the Photos app. You can then view, edit, or share it from within Photos. Like all images, it's also accessible from the All Photos/Camera Roll album.

> **TIP** When viewing a panoramic photo, hold your iPhone or iPad in landscape mode; however, when shooting a panoramic shot, hold it in portrait mode.

SHOOTING HD VIDEO

From the Camera app, you can easily shoot stunning HD video. Follow these basic steps for shooting video using your iPhone or iPad:

1. Launch the Camera app.

2. Select the Video shooting mode from the Shooting Mode menu. (If you want to shoot slow-motion video, select the Slo-Mo option, if it's offered by your iOS mobile device.)

> **NOTE** When you select the Video shooting mode, on the viewfinder screen the Flash icon, Timer, Shooting Mode Menu, Shutter button, and Camera Selection icon are all displayed. On the iPhone, the selected video resolution is displayed in the top-right corner of the screen.
>
> When you start actually filming video, some of these icons disappear, and on some iPhones and iPads, the Still Image Shutter button becomes accessible.

3. Tap the camera selection icon to choose which camera you want to use. You can switch between the front- and the rear-facing camera at any time.

> **NOTE** The newer iPhone models are capable of shooting 4K resolution video using the rear-facing camera.
>
> On any iPhone, set the video recording resolution by launching Settings, tapping the Photo and Camera option, and then tapping the Record Video and/or Record Slo-Mo options. The available options are listed on the Record Video submenu screen, as well the amount of internal storage space needed to record each minute of video.
>
> For example, when the iPhone 6s or iPhone 6s Plus records video in 4K resolution, this requires 375MB of internal storage space per minute of saved video content.

4. If applicable, tap the Flash icon (iPhone/iPad Pro) to turn on the flash and use it as a continuous light source while filming video.

5. Hold your iPhone or iPad up to the subject you want to capture on video. Set up your shot by looking at what's displayed in the viewfinder.

6. In the viewfinder, tap your intended subject to make the autofocus sensor appear. If necessary, and if your device supports this feature, you can also manually adjust the Exposure Control using the displayed slider.

7. When you're ready to start shooting video, tap the Shutter button. The red dot turns into a red square. This indicates you're now filming. Your iPhone or iPad captures whatever action you see on the screen, as well as any sound in the area.

8. As you're filming video, notice a timer displayed on the screen (shown in Figure 8.17). Your only limit to how much video you can shoot is based on the amount of available storage space in your iOS device, and how long the battery lasts. However, this app is designed more for shooting short video clips, not full-length home movies.

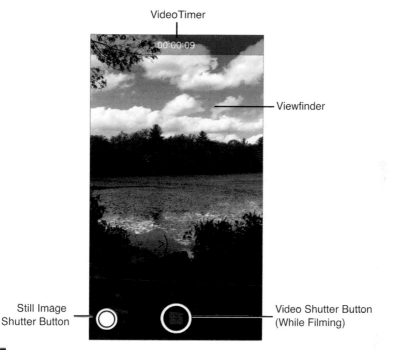

Video Timer

Viewfinder

Still Image Shutter Button

Video Shutter Button (While Filming)

Figure 8.17
When shooting video on your iPhone or iPad, make sure the timer is counting up. This indicates you're actually recording.

9. As you're filming, tap anywhere on the screen to focus on your subject using the app's built-in autofocus sensor.

10. To stop filming, tap the Shutter button again. Your video footage is saved. You can now view, edit, and share it from within the Photos app (or use an optional video editing app, such as iMovie).

> **TIP** Although the Photos app enables you to trim your video clips as well as view and share the videos, if you want to edit your videos, plus add titles and special effects, use Apple's feature-packed iMovie app, which is available from the App Store. For more information about iMovie, visit www.apple.com/apps/imovie.

> **✓ TIP**   Depending on which iPhone or iPad model you're using, at the same time you're shooting video, you might discover a second, circular (white) Shutter button displayed (refer to Figure 8.17). This second Shutter button is used to snap high-resolution digital images at the same time you're shooting HD video.

USING THE PHOTOS APP TO VIEW, EDIT, ENHANCE, PRINT, AND SHARE PHOTOS AND VIDEOS

Use the Photos app to view images stored on your iOS device or in your iCloud account. The iOS 10 version of the Photos app includes a robust selection of photo editing and image enhancement tools.

> **iOS 10 WHAT'S NEW**   The Photos app now has built-in face and object recognition and will automatically sort your images based on who or what appears in them.
>
> In addition, the Camera app uses the GPS (Location Services) capabilities of your mobile device to record the exact location where each photo is taken, and it also records the time and date. As a result, the Photos app's new Related feature is able to sort images based on location, who or what appears in your photos, and/or when they were taken and group those images together.
>
> When you tap the Albums icon in Photos, you'll discover that separate folders for People and Places have automatically been created. These folders are auto-populated with appropriate photos as you take them.

> **iOS 10 WHAT'S NEW**   Tap the Places option to view a world map that shows the places you've been where you've taken photos, as well as how many photos you took there (shown in Figure 8.18).
>
> Place your finger on this map and drag it around to reposition it. Use the reverse-pinch or pinch finger gestures to zoom in or out.
>
> Tap any location tag on the map to view the collection of photos taken there. For this feature to work, you must have the Location Services feature turned on for the Camera and Photos apps.

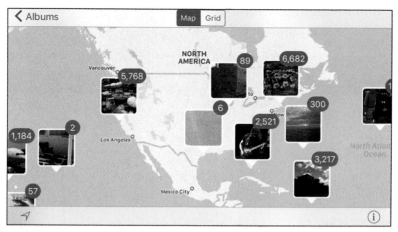

Figure 8.18

The new Places option in the Photos app enables you to see where in the world you've taken photos, and then quickly find and view those images.

> **NOTE** The All Photos/Camera Roll, Favorites, Videos, Selfies, Panoramas, Time-Lapse, Slo-Mo, Bursts, Screenshots, and Recently Deleted albums are also automatically created on your behalf in Photos. These albums are populated with appropriate photos and video clips as you take them or transfer them into your iPhone or iPad.
>
> If you opt to use third-party photography apps, additional albums may automatically be created to store images taken or edited using those apps.

EXPERIENCING PHOTOS AND VIDEOS WITH MEMORIES

The new Memories feature groups related images together automatically and can present them in an animated, movie-like format that can include a title, music, special effects, and cinematic transitions. To access this feature, tap the new Memories icon at the bottom of the Photos screen. The app uses your images and video clips to create a collection of animated presentations.

Thumbnails for the Memories that the Photos app has created are displayed (shown in Figure 8.19). Tap any Memory thumbnail to view, edit, and then share that Memory. From within the Photos app, you can share Memories just as you share a photo or video clip—on Facebook, for example.

When you tap one of the Memories thumbnails, the collection of images in it is displayed. Tap the Play icon to preview the Memory as is, or tap the Select option to choose specific images you want to delete from the Memory (shown in Figure 8.20).

Figure 8.19

The Photos app automatically creates Memories for you.

Figure 8.20

After selecting a Memory, you can view, edit, or share it from within the Photos app.

After tapping Select and choosing one or more images, tap the Share icon to share the selected images, or use the command icons displayed at the bottom of the Share menu to Copy, Hide, Print, or Duplicate these images.

As a Memory is playing, tap the screen to customize it. For example, choose a theme, like Happy, Uplifting, Epic, Dreamy, or Sentimental. Tap the Short or Medium option to determine the playback length of the Memory, or tap the Edit icon to fully customize the memory (shown in Figure 8.21).

From the Edit menu (shown in Figure 8.22), you can add a custom title to the Memory, select music to be played in the background, customize the duration of the animated presentation, and add/remove photos and video clips included in the Memory.

> **TIP** If you have video clips included in the memory, those need to be edited separately, as standalone videos (either using the Photos app or iMovie, for example). Those edited video clips can then be incorporated into an animated memory.

Figure 8.21

You can customize Memories that have been auto-created for you.

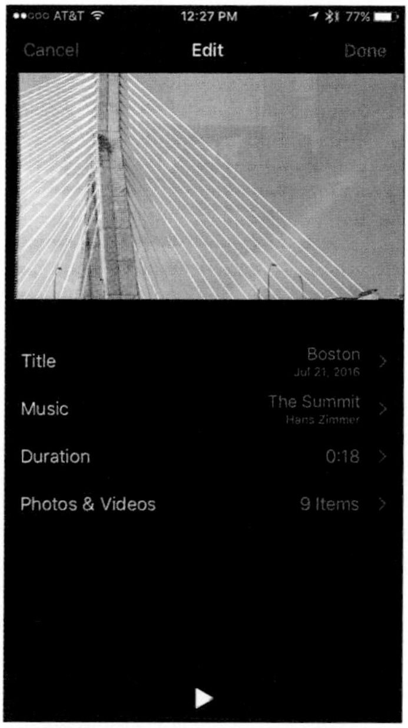

Figure 8.22

Create a title, and further customize a Memory from this Edit menu.

After making changes to the Edit menu, tap the Done option to save your changes to the Memory. Tap the Share icon to Share the Memory via email, text message, or by publishing it on Facebook or Twitter, for example.

> **TIP** In addition to the usual sharing options offered when you access the Share menu while working with Memories, if you have the YouTube app installed on your iPhone or iPad and have an active YouTube (Google) account, it's possible to upload your Memories directly to your YouTube channel from the Photos app.

> **TIP** When viewing a particular Memory, scroll down to the bottom of the thumbnail images that are included in that Memory. Here, you'll discover a Related heading, with additional Memories that are somehow related to the one you're viewing. There's also an Add to Favorite Memories option and a Delete Memory option.

NAVIGATING AROUND THE PHOTOS APP

Displayed at the bottom of the Photos app are a series of command icons. Use these to navigate your way around the app, find your images, and then use the tools offered by the app to manage your photo collection, edit your images, and ultimately share them.

You'll discover that the Photos app continues to be fully integrated with iCloud and allows you to create and manage your iCloud Photo Library, which is explained later in this chapter and in Chapter 6, "Use iCloud and the iCloud Drive App."

The main command icons in the Photo app include

■ **Photos**—Tap this option to sort and view all images stored in your iPhone/ iPad, based on the time and date, as well as the location where they were taken. Use your finger to scroll up or down this screen. To select and work with any of the images, tap the Select option, and then tap their image thumbnails. It's then possible to delete those images, share them (by tapping the Share icon), copy them into another folder (using the Add To option). Tap any single image to view it, and then use the Photos app's editing and management tools to work with that single image.

> ☑ **TIP** When you select the Photos option, images are sorted based on when or where they were shot. Years displays thumbnails of all images shot in a particular year and includes details about where those images were shot.
>
> Collections further breaks down a Years grouping to sort images based on when and where they were taken. Moments enables you to display thumbnails of images in a Collection that represent one location or date.
>
> As you're viewing thumbnails in the Moments view, tap one of them to view and work with a single image. Tap the < icon in the top-left corner of the screen to move backward between individual photos, Moments, Collections, and Years.

■ **Memories**—Access, view, edit, manage, and share Memories that are automatically created by the Photos app.

■ **Shared**—Access and manage images you've stored in custom folders, and/or that have been placed online using iCloud's Photo Sharing feature.

■ **Albums**—Access, view, and manage albums (folders), as well as individual images stored in each album. In addition to the albums that the Photos app has created and populated for you, it's possible to create and manage your own custom albums, and place groups of photos you select in them.

MOVING IMAGES BETWEEN ALBUMS

To copy selected images from one album to another as you're viewing thumbnails for images in a specific album, tap the Select option. Then, one at a time, tap the images you want to copy into another album. A check mark appears on each image thumbnail you select.

Tap the Add To option, and then tap which album from the displayed listing you want to move the selected images to. For example, you can choose the Family album if you have iCloud Family Sharing activated.

To create a new album from scratch, from the Add to Album screen, tap the New Album option. When prompted, type a title for the new album, and then tap the Save button.

Create as many separate albums as you need in the Photos app to properly group and organize your images. As you create a new album, it syncs with iCloud Photo Library if you have this feature turned on.

VIEWING AN IMAGE IN FULL-SCREEN MODE

When viewing thumbnails of your images, tap any single image thumbnail to view a larger version of it.

On the iPhone, the Share, Favorites, Edit, and Trash icons are displayed along the bottom of the screen, and the Details option is in the top-right corner of the screen. On the iPad (shown in Figure 8.23), these icons and options are grouped together near the top-right corner of the screen.

Along the bottom center of the screen are thumbnails for all the images stored in the Album you're currently accessing.

> **TIP** By tapping the Favorites (heart-shaped) icon associated with each image, you can place that image into a separate Favorites album, and then opt to view or share only those images.

As you're viewing a photo, tap it to hide or show the command icons and options available, which automatically appear and then disappear after a few seconds when you first open a photo.

Figure 8.23

When viewing a single image (shown here on an iPad), you can share it, add it to the Favorites folder, edit it, or delete it. Tap the Details option to view Related images.

To exit the single-image view and return to the multi-image thumbnail view, tap anywhere on the screen to make the command icons appear, then tap the left-pointing arrow icon in the upper-left corner of the screen.

Tap the Edit icon to reveal the Photo app's image editing options (shown in Figure 8.24).

iOS 10 WHAT'S NEW When you edit a photo containing people, the icon for the new Red Eye Fix tool is displayed. Tap it, and then follow the onscreen prompts to fix the ugly red-eye effect caused by the flash.

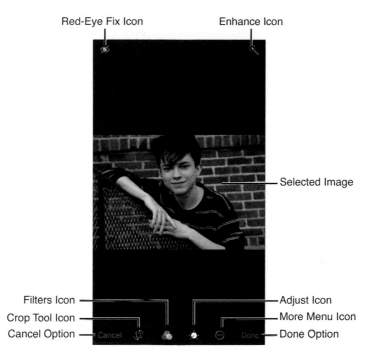

Red-Eye Fix Icon   Enhance Icon

Selected Image

Filters Icon
Crop Tool Icon
Cancel Option

Adjust Icon
More Menu Icon
Done Option

Figure 8.24
The Edit icons give you access to the Photo app's image editing tools.

TOOLS FOR EDITING PHOTOS

When you tap the Edit icon while viewing a single image, several command icons are displayed on the screen (refer to Figure 8.24). These icons provide the tools for quickly editing and enhancing your image. Your options are explained in the next sections.

> **NOTE** Animated photos taken using the Live shooting mode can now be edited using the tools built in to the iOS 10 edition of the Photos app. Editing these photos is done exactly the same way as editing a traditional (still) digital image.
>
> In the past, to edit a Live photo, the animated element needed to be removed. This is no longer the case. Edited Live photos can be viewed using the Photos app running on any iPhone, iPod touch, or iPad that's running iOS 10, the Apple Watch (running WatchOS 3), or any Mac that's running macOS Sierra.

WHAT'S NEW   The new Markup feature enables you to use your finger (or the Apple Pencil on compatible devices) to annotate or draw directly on an image (see Figure 8.25).

To access this feature, open and view a single photo, and then tap the Edit icon. From the Edit screen, tap the More (...) icon. Tap the Markup icon that's displayed as part of the More menu.

The new Markup screen is displayed (shown in Figure 8.26). From here, select your drawing or annotation tool and virtual ink color from the icons that are displayed at the bottom of the screen. It's also possible to select a thickness for the virtual drawing tool.

Once the annotation and drawing tool is selected, draw or write on the image itself. Tap the Text tool to add a text-based caption directly onto the image. Use the magnification tool to enlarge an area of the image. Tap the Done option to save your changes.

Whatever you draw or annotate in an image is saved and becomes part of that image. Thus, it's a good idea to create a duplicate image so you can keep the original and separately save the one you use the Markup features on.

Do this as you save the newly edited image the first time after using Markup. Alternatively, before using the Markup feature, open an image to view it, tap the Share icon, and then tap the Duplicate icon to create a copy.

Figure 8.25

Add text or draw on your photos using the new Markup feature.

Figure 8.26

The new Markup screen offers a collection of drawing and annotation tools, as well as virtual ink colors.

ENHANCE

The Enhance icon looks like a magic wand. When you tap it, you can use a one-touch editing tool that automatically adjusts multiple aspects of a photo at once, including its contrast, exposure, and color, to make the image look better and the colors appear more vibrant. You can turn this feature on or off, but it is not manually adjustable.

CROP

Use the Crop tool shown in Figure 8.27 to manually adjust the cropping of the image by dragging one of the corners of the white frame horizontally, vertically, or diagonally. The Crop tool also enables you to straighten a photo and readjust its angle by placing your finger on the straightening dial and moving it. Tap the Image Rotation icon to rotate the image 90 degrees.

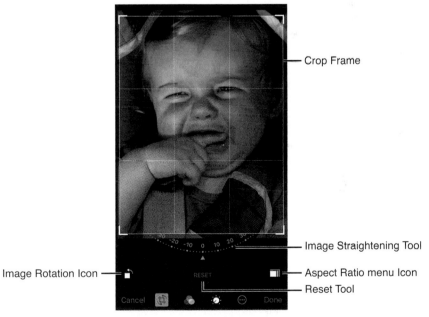

Crop Frame

Image Straightening Tool

Image Rotation Icon

Aspect Ratio menu Icon

Reset Tool

Figure 8.27

Tap the Crop icon to access tools for cropping, straightening, and/or rotating an image.

> ☑ **TIP**   After using any of the Crop-related tools, be sure to tap the Done option to save your changes. Alternatively, tap Cancel to exit out of this option without saving your changes.

> **✓ TIP** As you're cropping an image, tap the Aspect Ratio icon to select an aspect ratio, such as Original, Square, 3:2, 5:3, 4:3, 5:4, 7:5, or 16:9. Unless you need the image in a specific size, choose the Original option, and then use the Crop tool to adjust your image. Selecting an aspect ratio forces the basic dimensions to stay intact as you crop the image. This enables you to make accurately formatted prints later, without throwing off the image dimensions.

> **✓ TIP** Tap the Reset option to undo anything you've done using the Crop tool, Image Rotation tool, or Aspect Ratio tool.

FILTERS

The Photos app offers eight preinstalled special effect filters. After tapping the Filters icon, select the filter you want to apply to your image with a single onscreen tap. A preview of the altered image is displayed. To save the changes, tap Done. To discard the changes, tap Cancel, or tap another filter.

> **✏ NOTE** In addition to the filters that come preinstalled with the Photos app, third-party developers can now create optional filters you can use with the Photos app.

ADJUST

The Photos app enables you to edit or enhance many different aspects of a photo. Begin by tapping the Adjust icon. Then, from the Adjust submenu, tap the Light, Color, or B&W option. Each one of these options reveals a submenu that offers a variety of editing tools.

> **WHAT'S NEW** As you're using the various editing tools, press your finger gently on the image to toggle between viewing the original image and the edited version of the image you're working with. Doing this enables you to see the effect the editing tool is having on your image.

THE LIGHT TOOLS

When you tap the Light tool, a slider appears that enables you to manually increase or decrease the overall Light effect in the image being viewed (shown in Figure 8.28).

When you tap the Menu icon (after tapping the Light option), a submenu with options for Brilliance, Exposure, Highlights, Shadows, Brightness, Contract, and Black Point is displayed (shown in Figure 8.29).

Selected Image

Menu Icon

Light Slider

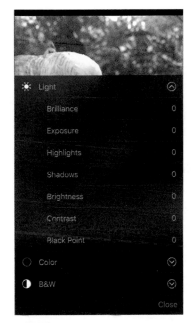

Figure 8.28

It's possible to use a slider to manually adjust the master Light tool.

Figure 8.29

The Light menu gives you access to seven additional tools you can use one at a time to edit your image.

Tap any of these options to reveal a separate slider you can use to manually adjust that option. Keep in mind that you can mix and match the use of these tools to create truly customized visual effects.

THE COLOR TOOLS

When you tap the Color icon, a master Color slider is displayed. Use your finger to manually adjust this feature. Tap the Menu icon to reveal additional color-related options, including Saturation, Contrast, and Cast.

Each of these tools (shown in Figure 8.30) has its own slider that you can manually adjust. Again, after making a change, be sure to tap Done to save your edits.

Alternatively, tap Cancel/Close to exit out of the selected editing tool without making any changes.

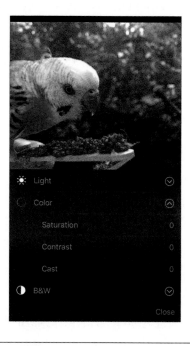

Figure 8.30

After tapping on the Color icon, tap the More menu icon to access tools for adjusting the Saturation, Contrast, and Cast in a photo.

THE B&W TOOLS

Tap the B&W icon to instantly convert a full-color image into black and white. It's then possible to manually adjust the black, white, and grayscale colors using the B&W slider.

By tapping the Menu icon after selecting the B&W editing tool, additional submenu options enable you to manually adjust the image's Intensity, Neutrals, Tone, and Grain, which all relate directly to the black-and-white effect. Upon tapping one of these options, a separate slider is offered, so you can adjust the intensity of the tool and the effect it has on your image.

After making a change, tap Done to save your edits or Cancel/Close to exit out of the selected editing tool without making any changes.

EDITING VIDEOS

When you tap the thumbnail for a video clip, you have the option of playing that clip from within the Photos app. The Share, Favorite, and Trash icons are displayed on the screen.

Tap the Edit icon to access the video trimming (editing) feature. To trim a video clip, look at the filmstrip display of the clip and move the left and/or right editing tabs accordingly to define the portion of the clip you want to edit and keep.

The box around the filmstrip display (representing the portion of the video you want to keep) turns yellow, and the Done option appears (see Figure 8.31). Before tapping Done, tap the Play icon to preview your newly edited (trimmed) video clip.

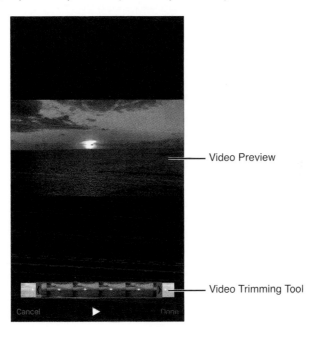

Video Preview

Video Trimming Tool

Figure 8.31

Use the Photos app to trim video clips, but use the optional iMovie app to fully edit videos.

After trimming the beginning and/or end of the video clip, tap Done to save your changes. The Save As New Clip option appears. Tap it. To gain access to a comprehensive and powerful set of video editing tools, download and install Apple's iMovie app onto your mobile device.

All videos you shoot and edit are stored automatically in the All Photos/Camera Roll album, as well as the separate Videos (or Slo-Mo album), which you can access by tapping the Albums icon at the bottom of the screen.

PRINTING PHOTOS

iOS 10 is fully compatible with Apple's AirPrint feature, so if you have a home photo printer set up to work wirelessly with your smartphone or tablet, it's possible to create prints from your digital images using the Print command in the Photos app. Follow these steps to print an image:

1. Launch the Photos app from the Home screen.

2. Tap any image thumbnail to view that image. You might need to open an album first by tapping the album's thumbnail if you have the Albums viewing option selected.

3. Tap the full-screen version of the image to make the various command icons appear.

4. Tap the Share icon.

5. Select the Print option.

6. When the Printer Options submenu appears, select your printer, determine how many copies of the print you'd like to create, choose the size of the desired print(s), and then tap the Print icon.

> **(iOS 10) WHAT'S NEW** The iPhone and iPad can also work with some Bluetooth compatible printers, such as the Polaroid Zip Mobile Photo Printer ($129.00, www.polaroid.com/zip-instant), which is shown in Figure 8.32.
>
> When using a printer that can communicate with your mobile device via Bluetooth (as opposed to AirPrint), a separate, proprietary app for that printer must be installed on your mobile device.
>
> In this case, images *cannot* be printed directly from the Photos app. Instead, when using the Polaroid Zip Mobile Photo Printer, for example, you'd need to import the desired images into the free Polaroid Zip app first.
>
> This import process takes just seconds. In the Polaroid Zip app, tap the Quick Print option, followed by the Gallery option. Then, select the desired image from the Photos app's albums that are displayed.
>
> The Polaroid Zip Mobile Printer is a tiny, battery-powered printer that works wirelessly with the iPhone or iPad. It allows you to create stunning 2" × 3" prints on premium ZINK photo paper in less than 20 seconds each.
>
> The ZINK photo paper offers a peel-off sticky backing, so the prints you make can become stickers.
>
> The Polaroid Zip Mobile Printer and separate packs of ZINK photo paper are available from Polaroid.com, Amazon.com, and many consumer electronics or photo specialty stores.

Figure 8.32

Create 2" × 3" prints from pictures you take on your iPhone or iPad almost anywhere (in less than 20 seconds) using the optional Polaroid Zip Mobile Printer.

> **MORE INFO** To print wirelessly from your iOS device using the AirPrint feature, you must have a compatible printer. To learn more about AirPrint, and to configure your printer for wireless printing from your iPhone or iPad, visit https://support.apple.com/en-us/HT201311.

THIRD-PARTY APPS FOR ORDERING PRINTS FROM YOUR IMAGES

If you want to order professional-quality prints directly from your iPhone or iPad, and have them shipped to your door in a few days, use one of several apps (such as FreePrints) available from the App Store.

The free KickSend app, for example, determines your current location, and tells you which one-hour photo labs are in close proximity. Upload your photos to the desired lab directly from your iPhone or iPad, and within 30 to 60 minutes, pick up your prints at the selected location. KickSend is easy to use, and works with partici-pating Walgreen's, CVS Pharmacy, Target, and Walmart locations.

The free Shutterfly app also enables you to order prints directly from your iOS mobile device, plus it gives you the option to create custom photo gifts, such as coffee mugs, mouse pads, iPhone cases, T-shirts, and other products that showcase your images. You can order enlargements, canvas prints, and other types of wall art that showcase your favorite photos.

SHARING PHOTOS AND VIDEOS

After you have selected one or more images, tap the Share icon to access the Share menu (shown in Figure 8.33).

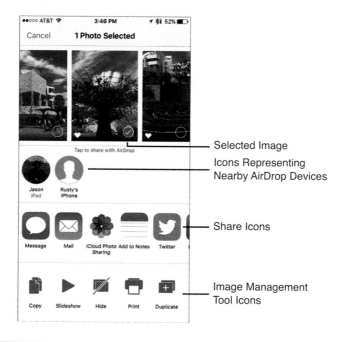

Figure 8.33

The Share menu offered by the iOS 10 edition of the Photos app offers some additional options, including a series of command icons that allow you to manage the selected image(s).

SENDING IMAGES WIRELESSLY VIA AIRDROP

If you're within close proximity to another Mac, iPhone, or iPad and the other computer or iOS mobile device also has the AirDrop feature turned on, you can wirelessly send images from within the Photos app using the AirDrop feature. This feature becomes active only when others nearby can receive an AirDrop transmission.

 **WHAT'S NEW**   Use the options available from the Share menu to share selected images via AirDrop, Text Message, Email, iCloud Photo Sharing, Twitter, Facebook, and Flickr.

App icons for third-party apps that are installed in your iPhone or iPad and that you can use for sharing images are also displayed here—for example, Instagram or Facebook Messenger.

From the Share menu, tap the Add to Notes icon to export a photo directly into a note in the Notes app, or tap the Save PDF to iBooks to export the image using the PDF file format so it can be viewed in iBooks.

Tap the More (...) icon to display a list of all apps installed on your iPhone or iPad that are compatible with the Photos app's Share menu. To make them appear in the Share menu, turn on the virtual switch associated with each app listing when viewing the Activities menu.

The bottom column of command icons displayed in the Share menu offer a selection of tools for managing the selected image(s). Here, you'll find the Copy, Slideshow, Hide, Print, Duplicate, AirPlay, Assign to Contact, Use As Wallpaper, Add to iCloud Drive, Save to Dropbox (if you have the Dropbox app installed and an active Dropbox account), and More (...) command icons.

☑ TIP   In the Share menu are options for iCloud Photo Sharing. To place photos online in a particular iCloud Photos album that you will ultimately want to share with other people, tap the iCloud Photo Sharing option, and then fill in the prompts offered in the iCloud window that appears.

To upload the selected images to iCloud Drive (which is different from iCloud Photo Library or iCloud Shared Albums), select the Add to iCloud Drive option. Refer to Chapter 6 for more information about iCloud Drive.

COPYING AN IMAGE TO ANOTHER APP

In the Photos app, it's possible to temporarily store a photo in your iOS device's virtual clipboard, and then paste that photo into another compatible app. To copy a photo into your device's virtual clipboard, follow these steps:

1. In the Photos app, select a single photo and view it in full-screen mode.

2. Tap the image to make the command icons appear.

3. Tap the Share icon.

4. Tap the Copy icon. The photo is now stored in the virtual clipboard.

5. Launch a compatible app and then hold your finger down on the screen to use the Paste option and paste your photo from the clipboard into the active app.

SHOWING IMAGES ON A TELEVISION VIA AIRPLAY

Instead of viewing an image in full-screen mode on your iPhone or iPad, tap the AirPlay icon and select Apple TV to wirelessly transmit the image to your HD television set. To use this feature with an HD TV, you need the optional Apple TV device. To use the feature with a Mac, be sure AirPlay on your Mac is turned on.

DELETING PHOTOS STORED ON YOUR iOS DEVICE

To delete one image at a time as you're viewing them in full-screen mode, simply tap the Trash icon.

To select and delete multiple images at once as you're looking at thumbnails, tap the Select button. Tap each thumbnail that represents an image you want to delete. A check mark icon appears in each image thumbnail to indicate that the image has been selected. Tap the Trash icon to delete the selected images.

> **!CAUTION** When you opt to delete a photo, it automatically gets deleted from the mobile device you're using, as well as from iCloud Photo Library and all computers and mobile devices that are linked to the same iCloud account.

TAKING ADVANTAGE OF iCLOUD PHOTO LIBRARY

Turn on the iCloud Photo Library feature from within Settings on all your iOS mobile devices, as well as from the iCloud Control Panel on your Mac and/or PC computers, and you'll be able to sync your entire digital photo library across all your computers and mobile devices, maintain an online backup of your images, and share groups of selected images (or entire albums) with other people.

To turn on iCloud Photo Library on each of your iOS mobile devices, launch Settings, tap the iCloud option, tap the Photos option, and then turn on the virtual switch associated with the iCloud Photo Library option. Use the other options in this submenu to customize the iCloud Photo Library feature on the device you're using.

Keep in mind that, based on how many digital photos are in your entire digital photo library, it might be necessary to upgrade your iCloud account and acquire additional online storage space (for a monthly fee). Refer to Chapter 6 for more information about using iCloud.

USING THE PHOTOS APP WITH iCLOUD'S FAMILY SHARING

One aspect of iCloud's Family Sharing feature is what Apple refers to as the Family Album. One single Family Album becomes accessible by up to six family members, who can then freely add, edit, delete, and share images stored in that Family Album. Everyone's other image albums remain private and separate from the Family Album.

When you turn on the Family Sharing feature in iCloud, the Family Album is automatically created. In the Photos app, you can move images from the All Photos album (or another album) into the Family Album, so they become viewable by participating family members.

GETTING ADDITIONAL PHOTOGRAPHY AND VIDEOGRAPHY FUNCTIONS

Instead of using the Camera app to take pictures, and the Photos app to edit, manage, print, and share your photos, you can browse through the hundreds of third-party photography- and videography-related apps available from the App Store that can be used with or instead of the Camera and Photos apps.

These optional apps can provide you with a much broader toolbox for taking and working with your digital images. To find these apps, visit the App Store and browse the Photo & Video category.

🔍 MORE INFO The following are ten of the more popular and powerful photo-editing apps available for the iPhone and iPad (in alphabetical order):

- Afterlight
- Enlight
- Facetune for iPad (iPad only)
- Photoshop Elements
- Photoshop Fix
- Photoshop Mix
- Pixelmator
- Pixomatic Photo Editor
- PortraitPro Tablet (iPad only)
- Snapseed

📝 TIP Many of these apps work nicely with the Apple Pencil (on compatible iPads) when it comes to detailed image editing.

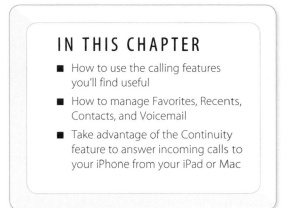

IN THIS CHAPTER

- How to use the calling features you'll find useful
- How to manage Favorites, Recents, Contacts, and Voicemail
- Take advantage of the Continuity feature to answer incoming calls to your iPhone from your iPad or Mac

9

MAKE AND RECEIVE CALLS WITH AN iPHONE

Although your iPhone is capable of handling a wide range of tasks, one of its core purposes is to serve as a feature-packed cell phone. Your iPhone makes and receives voice calls using a cellular network that's operated by the service provider you selected when the phone was activated. The Phone app that comes preinstalled on your iPhone offers a vast selection of calling features that make it easy to stay in touch with people.

WHAT'S NEW One of the new Phone app features offered by iOS 10 is automatic voicemail message transcription. When a caller leaves a voicemail message, the iPhone automatically transcribes that message (typically within a minute or two) and offers both text and audio versions of the message (shown in Figure 9.1).

To access this new feature, launch the Phone app and tap the Voicemail icon. Tap a listing for a new voicemail message. In addition to the familiar Play/Pause icon, as well as a slider for fast forwarding and rewinding through the audio message, a text-based version of the voicemail message is now displayed.

As you're viewing this text, tap the Share icon to forward the message to yourself or other people using any of the options offered by the Share menu, such as text message or email. It's also possible to export the text-based voicemail message transcription into a compatible app, such as Notes.

Keep in mind that, like the Dictation feature, the iPhone often has trouble accurately transcribing voice into text if the person speaking is in a noisy area or doesn't speak clearly. Consequently, this feature does not always provide 100-percent accurate voicemail transcriptions, especially for longer messages.

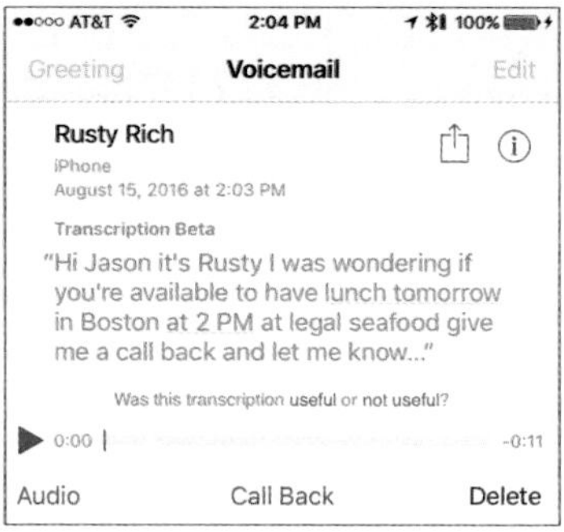

Figure 9.1

From the Voicemail screen in the Phone app, text-based transcriptions of incoming audio voicemail messages are now automatically created and displayed.

WHAT'S NEW When listening to incoming voicemail messages, if you want to edit the audio message, tap the Share icon associated with that message and then tap the Voice Memos option. Use the Voice Memos app that comes preinstalled with iOS 10 (or another compatible audio-editing app) to edit, archive, and/or share the edited audio file.

It's also now possible to export the audio and text-based transcription of a voicemail message to a cloud-based service, such as iCloud Drive or Dropbox, by tapping the Share icon associated with the message and then tapping the appropriate icon displayed within the Share menu.

After you set up and activate your new iPhone with a cellular service provider and choose a calling plan, the iPhone is capable of receiving incoming calls and enables you to make outgoing calls using the Phone app.

In the United States and throughout Europe, for example, a growing number of cellular service providers offer iPhone compatibility. Unless you acquire an "unlocked" version of the iPhone (which is not tied to any service provider), when you purchase the phone, you must decide which wireless service provider to sign up with. It's then often necessary to sign a service agreement, which can last up to two years.

If you purchase an "unlocked" iPhone with no service contract, it's possible to pay a month-to-month fee for pre-paid or pay-as-you-go cellular service. This requires you to pay the unsubsidized price for the iPhone itself, and then pay between $30 and $120 per month for voice, data, and text services.

> **NOTE** Many cellular service providers offer plans that enable you to pay for the iPhone over time and then upgrade to the newest model iPhone each year when it's released. For example, AT&T calls this the Next plan.
>
> Apple also offers the iPhone Upgrade Program, which is available from Apple Stores and Apple.com. It involves paying up to 24 monthly installments to purchase an unlocked iPhone outright or enables you to keep paying monthly installments but receive a brand-new iPhone (every 12 months) when a new model is released.
>
> When you receive a new phone, if it's before the 24 installments have been paid, the installment plan restarts, or you can pay off the balance for the phone you already have and keep it, but then begin paying installments on the newest iPhone model.
>
> The monthly installment varies, based on which model iPhone you acquire and how much internal storage space it contains. Keep in mind that the monthly installment you pay for the Apple Upgrade Program or AT&T Next, for example, does not include cellular service. The service is a separate fee, which is based on the plan you select from a compatible cellular service provider.
>
> One benefit to the Apple Upgrade Program is that AppleCare+ is included. To learn more about this program, visit www.apple.com/shop/iphone/iphone-upgrade-program.

Choose a wireless service provider that offers the best coverage in your area, the most competitively priced calling plan based on your needs, and the extra features you want or need. When looking at coverage area maps for various service providers, focus on 4G LTE coverage, as opposed to 3G or plain 4G service. Some wireless service providers, for example, offer better international roaming coverage than others, whereas some are more generous when it comes to monthly wireless data allocation.

Keep in mind that the iPhone hardware is slightly different based on which wireless service provider you choose, so you typically can't switch providers after you've acquired the iPhone (unless it's an unlocked iPhone).

TIP   For your iPhone to make or receive calls, it must be turned on and *not* in Airplane mode. Unless you're using the Call Over Wi-Fi function (which not all cellular service providers support), a decent cellular service signal, which is displayed in the upper-left corner of the screen in the form of dots, is also a necessity. The more dots you see (up to five), the stronger the cellular signal (which is based on your proximity to the closest cell towers).

WHAT'S NEW   From the Home screen of a compatible iPhone that offers 3D Touch capabilities, press and hold the Phone app icon to reveal a menu that gives you quick access to a handful of useful call-related features, including icons representing your most recently called contacts from the Phone app's Favorites list (shown in Figure 9.2).

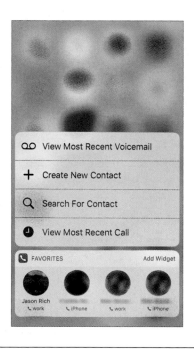

Figure 9.2

Use the iPhone's 3D Touch capabilities from the Home screen (on compatible iPhones) to gain quick access to useful call-related features.

ANSWERING AN INCOMING CALL

Regardless of what you're doing on your iPhone, when you receive an incoming call, everything else is put on hold and the Phone app launches automatically, unless the iPhone is turned off, in Airplane mode, or the Do Not Disturb feature is turned on, in which case incoming calls automatically go to voicemail.

To control the volume of the ringer, press the Volume Up or Volume Down buttons on the side of your iPhone; or to turn off the ringer (which causes the phone to vibrate when an incoming call is received), turn on the Mute button on the side of the iPhone.

> **TIP** While your iPhone is still ringing, you can silence the ringer and send the incoming call to voicemail after a 5- to 10-second delay by pressing the Power button or the Volume Up or Volume Down button one time. To send the incoming call immediately to voicemail, double press the Power button, or tap the Decline option displayed on the screen when the phone is not locked at the time the incoming call is received.
>
> You also can silence the iPhone's ringer by switching on the Mute button (located on the side of the iPhone). Your phone vibrates instead of ringing when an incoming call is received.
>
> To control the Vibrate feature, launch Settings, tap the Sounds option, turn on the virtual switch associated with Vibrate On Ring and/or Vibrate On Silent, and then tap the Ringtone option under the Sounds and Vibration Patterns heading to select a custom vibration pattern when incoming calls are received.
>
> Yet another way to be left alone is to put your phone in Do Not Disturb mode. This can be done automatically at certain predetermined times, or manually whenever you want to be left alone. To do this, access Control Center and tap the Do Not Disturb icon. Read more about the Do Not Disturb feature later in this chapter.

There are several ways to answer an incoming call. If you're doing something else on your iPhone and it starts to ring, the caller ID for the incoming caller appears, along with a green-and-white Accept button and a red-and-white Decline icon (as shown in Figure 9.3). Tap the Accept button to answer the call. If you tap Decline or wait too long to answer, the call automatically goes to voicemail.

If you're using your iPhone with EarPods, ear buds, or a headset with a built-in microphone, answer an incoming call by pressing the Accept button on the headset.

Figure 9.3

Your iPhone notifies you when an incoming call is received. You can then answer or decline the call. This screen appears as long as the phone is not locked when the incoming call is received.

☑️ TIP   When you receive an incoming call, displayed above the Decline and Accept buttons (or the Slide to Answer slider on the Lock screen) are two other options labeled Remind Me and Message (refer to Figure 9.3).

When you tap Message, a menu containing four prewritten text messages, along with a Custom button, is displayed. Tap one of the message buttons to send that message to the caller via text/instant message. Or tap the Custom button to type a custom message to send to that caller. The incoming call is automatically transferred to voicemail.

To customize the prewritten messages available from the Message option, launch Settings, tap the Phone option, and then tap the Respond with Text option. Displayed on the Respond with Text menu screen are three customizable fields under the heading "Respond With:" Tap one of these fields to replace one of the default messages with your own.

The other option for managing incoming calls is the Remind Me option. When you tap this button, the incoming call is sent to voicemail, but you can quickly set a reminder (and alarm) for yourself to call that person back in one hour, when you leave your current location, or when you get home. For these last two options to function, Locations Services related to the Phone app must be turned on from within Settings.

If the iPhone is in Sleep mode (or on the Lock screen and locked) when an incoming call is received, unlock the phone by swiping your finger from left to right on the Slide to Answer slider, which automatically takes the phone out of Sleep mode, unlocks it, and answers the incoming call (shown in Figure 9.4).

Figure 9.4

When an incoming call is received while the phone is in Sleep mode (locked), you need to unlock the phone to automatically answer it.

Of course, if your iPhone has a Touch ID sensor built in to the Home button, you're able to unlock the phone and answer a call simply by placing your finger on the Touch ID sensor.

Notice that the iPhone's Lock screen displays the Remind Me and Message icons but does not display an Accept or Decline button.

> **NOTE** Answering the phone using an optional Bluetooth headset automatically unlocks the phone if it's in Sleep mode.

> **☑ TIP** If you're too busy to answer an incoming call on your iPhone, you can let the call go to voicemail or set up call forwarding so that the incoming call is automatically rerouted to another phone number, such as your home or office number. To set up call forwarding and turn this function on or off, launch Settings and then tap the Phone option.
>
> From the Phone submenu in Settings, you can view your iPhone's phone number, set up and turn on call forwarding, turn on or off call waiting, and decide whether you want your iPhone's number to be displayed on someone's caller ID when you initiate a call.
>
> Also from Settings, you have the option of enabling the International Assist feature, which makes initiating international calls much less confusing.

After you answer an incoming call, you have a few additional options. You can hold the iPhone up to your ear and start talking or tap the Speaker icon to use your iPhone as a speakerphone. It's also possible to use the phone with a wired or Bluetooth (wireless) headset or CarPlay, which offers hands-free operation. The headset option is ideal when you're driving, plus it offers privacy (versus using the iPhone's speakerphone option).

> **! CAUTION** If you're driving, choose a headset that covers only one ear, use the Speaker option for hands-free operation, or use CarPlay. Refrain from holding the phone up to your ear or covering both ears with a headset. Make sure you're familiar with state and local laws in your area related to the use of cell phones while driving.

When using a Bluetooth headset, you don't need to hold the phone up to your ear to carry on a conversation. If you're using a headset, answer the call by pressing the headset's answer button when you receive an incoming call. There's no need to do anything on your iPhone.

When you're in a compatible car (or in a vehicle equipped with an iPhone Hands-Free Kit), take advantage of the vehicle's CarPlay or Hands-Free compatibility. This enables your phone to link to your vehicle and use the in-dash infotainment system, Siri, and/or the car's stereo system to make and receive calls, utilizing your vehicle's built-in microphone and stereo system speakers to interact with the other party. The call is still handled by your iPhone, but the iPhone is operated hands-free (and eyes-free).

USING THE HANDOFF FEATURE WITH CALLS

When Continuity/Handoff is activated, as long as your iPhone is within wireless proximity to your iPad or Mac (typically within 33 feet), it's possible to use your iPad (see Figure 9.5) or Mac to answer a call coming in to your iPhone.

Figure 9.5

When an iPhone and iPad are linked to the same iCloud account and have the Handoff option turned on, it's possible to answer an incoming call on the iPad (shown here).

> **NOTE** All Macs and iOS mobile devices that are set up to work with the Continuity/Handoff features must be linked to the same iCloud account and have Bluetooth and Wi-Fi turned on. Keep in mind that some older iPhones and iPads do not support these features. Likewise, only Macs purchased in 2012 or later (and running OS X Yosemite, El Capitan, or macOS Sierra) support this feature.

> **NOTE** When the Handoff feature is turned on and the iPhone is wirelessly linked with an iPad or Mac, you can initiate calls from that tablet or computer by tapping or clicking a displayed phone number that appears in the Contacts app, Safari, or another compatible app.

To set up this feature, start with your iPhone and launch Settings, tap the General option, and then tap the Handoff option. From the Handoff submenu, turn on the virtual switch that's associated with the Handoff option. Next, repeat this process on your iPad.

When the feature is turned on, your iPhone automatically maintains a wireless link to your iPad and/or Mac. When an incoming call is received, all connected devices ring, Caller ID information is displayed, and you can accept or decline the call from any connected device.

On the iPad or Mac, the tablet or computer acts like a speakerphone by taking advantage of the built-in microphone and speaker(s). You can also pair a Bluetooth wireless headset to your iPad and/or Mac, or you can connect a corded headset (with built-in microphone) to the tablet or Mac via the headphone jack.

MANAGING THE DO NOT DISTURB FEATURE

To activate and customize the Do Not Disturb feature, launch Settings and tap the Do Not Disturb option. To later enable or disable this feature, access the Control Center, and tap the crescent moon–shaped icon (shown in Figure 9.6).

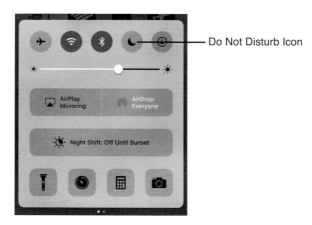

Do Not Disturb Icon

Figure 9.6

You can easily access the Do Not Disturb feature from Control Center.

When turned on, a moon icon is displayed on the iPhone's or iPad's status bar (at the very top of the screen), and all calls and alerts are silenced.

You can turn on or off this feature at any time, or you can schedule specific times you want Do Not Disturb to be automatically activated, such as between 11:00 p.m. and 7:00 a.m. on weekdays. From the Do Not Disturb menu in Settings, determine whether certain important callers are allowed to reach you even when the phone is in Do Not Disturb mode.

Keep in mind that when your iPhone is turned off, all incoming calls are forwarded directly to voicemail, and it is not possible to initiate an outgoing call. Likewise, incoming text messages, FaceTime calls, and other communications from the outside world are not accepted when an iPhone is turned off, in Do Not Disturb mode, or in Airplane mode. Instead, notifications for these missed messages are displayed in Notification Center (depending on how you set up Notification Center), in their respective apps, and potentially on the Lock screen when you turn on the device or turn off Airplane mode.

MANAGING CALLS IN PROGRESS

As soon as you answer an incoming call, the Phone app's display changes to the Call in Progress screen (shown in Figure 9.7). This screen contains several command icons, including Mute, Keypad, Speaker/Audio, Add Call, FaceTime, Contacts, and End. The caller's information and a call timer are displayed at the top of the screen.

Figure 9.7

Manage a call while you're engaged in it from this Call In Progress screen.

NOTE When you receive an incoming call, if the caller ID for that caller matches up with a contact entry stored in the Contacts app, that person's name, which number the call is from (Home, Work, Mobile, and so on), and the caller's photo (if you have a photo of that person linked to the contact) are displayed.

If there's no match in your Contacts database, the regular Caller ID data is displayed, which can include the person's name, phone number, and the city and state from which the call is originating. You might also receive calls labeled Private or Unknown.

TIP It's possible to block incoming calls from specific phone numbers. To block a caller, after receiving a call from the number you want to block, relaunch the Phone app (if necessary), tap the Recents option, find the listing for the incoming call, and then tap the Info icon associated with that listing. When the information screen for the caller is displayed, scroll down to the bottom of the screen and tap the Block This Caller option.

To add or remove phone numbers from your personal list of blocked phone numbers, launch Settings, tap the Phone option, and then tap the Call Blocking & Identification option.

The Call Blocking & Identification screen displays all phone numbers currently on your blocked list. To delete a number from this list (and accept calls from it again), swipe from right to left across the listing, and then tap the Unblock button.

Alternatively, tap the Edit option on the Call Blocking & Identification screen, and then tap the – icons associated with the listings you want to remove from the list. Tap the Done option to save your changes.

To add phone numbers to this list, you must first create a contact entry in the Contacts app that contains the phone number(s) you want to block. Then, from the Call Blocking & Identification screen, scroll down, and tap the Block Contact option. Select the contact entry you want to block, and that entry's phone number(s) is added to the block list.

Here's a summary of the command icons available to you from the Call in Progress screen during a phone conversation:

■ **Mute**—Tap this icon to turn off your iPhone's microphone. You can still hear what's being said to you, but the person you're speaking with cannot hear you. When you're ready to be heard again, turn off the Mute feature by tapping this icon again.

- **Keypad**—Replace the current Call in Progress screen with the numeric telephone keypad. This is necessary for navigating your way through voicemail trees (for example, when you're told to press 1 for English, press 2 to speak with an operator, press 3 to track an order, and so on).

- **Speaker (or Audio)**—Tap the Speaker icon to switch from Handset mode (in which you hold the iPhone up to your ear to have a phone conversation) to Speaker mode, which turns your iPhone into a speakerphone. If you're using your iPhone with an optional Bluetooth headset or CarPlay, a third Headset or CarPlay option (which may be listed as Headset, the name of your vehicle, or the name of your headset) is displayed, and this menu feature is labeled Audio as opposed to Speaker.

- **Add Call (+)**—During a conversation with someone, you can initiate a conference call and bring a third party into the conversation by tapping Add Call, as described later in this chapter.

- **FaceTime**—If the person to whom you're talking is also using an iPhone, iPad, or Mac, and both devices have access to a Wi-Fi Internet connection, tap the FaceTime icon to switch from a traditional voice call to a real-time video call using the FaceTime app. This is a free service.

> **✓ TIP** In addition to being able to launch FaceTime from the Phone app and switch from a normal call to a video call, you can use the separate FaceTime app to initiate a video or audio-only call from your iPhone that utilizes a Wi-Fi Internet connection, as opposed to a cellular network. (A few cellular service providers now allow FaceTime calls to be made using a 4G LTE connection, however.)

- **Contacts**—While you're conversing on the phone, you can access your Contacts database and look up someone's information by tapping this option.

- **End**—Tap the large red-and-white End button or press the end call button on your headset, if applicable, to terminate the call.

> **✓ TIP** Your phone conversation can continue while you're using other apps. To launch another app, press the Home button and tap the app icon from the Home screen. To access the app switcher, double press the Home button and then tap any app icon that appears.
>
> When you view the Home screen while still on the phone, a green-and-white banner shows, "Touch to return to call," along with a call timer. Tap this green bar to return to the Phone app.

RESPONDING TO A CALL WAITING SIGNAL WHILE ON THE PHONE

As you're chatting it up on the phone, if someone else tries to call you you hear a call waiting tone, and a related message appears on your iPhone's screen. You can control the Call Waiting feature from the Settings app.

When a second call comes in, the caller ID information of the new caller is displayed on the screen, along with several command icons and buttons (shown in Figure 9.8). These commands are End & Accept, Send to Voicemail, or Hold & Accept.

Figure 9.8

When you're on a call and you simultaneously receive another incoming call, in addition to hearing the call waiting signal, you're given several onscreen options.

If you place the first call on hold and answer the new incoming call (by tapping the Hold & Accept icon), you then have the opportunity to merge the two calls and create a conference call or switch between the two calls and speak with each person individually (while the other is on hold).

While engaged in a conference call on your iPhone, the names of the other parties on the call are displayed along the top of the screen, along with an Info icon. Tap the circular "i" icon to the right of this information to reveal a new screen that enables you to manage any of the parties involved with the conference call.

While you're engaged in a three-way call (with two other parties), you can tap the Add Call option again to add more parties to the conference call. How many parties you can add to a conference call is determined by your cellular service provider.

On the secondary Conference Call Info screen, associated with each name/Caller ID number is an End button and a Private button. Tap End to disconnect that party, or tap Private to speak with that party privately and place the other party (or parties) on hold. You can then reestablish the conference call by tapping the Back button to return to the previous Conference Call screen, and then tap the Merge Calls icon again.

MAKING CALLS FROM YOUR iPHONE

There are several ways to initiate a phone call from your iPhone; however, you typically must first launch the Phone app. Then, you can do the following:

- Dial a number manually using the keypad.
- Access a listing from your Contacts database (from within the Phone app), choose a number, and dial it.
- Use Siri (which is explained in Chapter 3, "Say It and Make It So Using Siri"). This can be done anytime, regardless of what app is running on your iPhone.

> **☑ TIP** If you're using one of the newer iPhone models and the "Hey Siri" feature is active, simply say "Hey Siri, call [name]" or "Hey Siri, call [name] at [location (such as home or work)]" to initiate a call.

- Redial a number from the Phone app's Recents call log.
- Select and dial a phone number from the Phone app's Favorites list.
- Dial a number displayed in another compatible app or iOS 10 feature, such as Maps, Messages, Mail, Safari, Contacts, or the Notification Center window. When you tap a displayed phone number, it dials that number and initiates a call using the Phone app.

MANUAL DIALING

To initiate a call by manually dialing a phone number, launch the Phone app and tap the Keypad option. Enter the desired phone number, one digit at a time, and press the green-and-white Call button to initiate the call.

> **✓ TIP** As you're manually entering a phone number, if you want to create a Contacts entry for it, tap the + icon in the top-left corner of the screen, and then tap the Create New Contact or Add to Existing Contact option.

> **✎ NOTE** You can also use the Cut, Copy, and Paste features of iOS 10 to copy a phone number displayed in another app, and then paste it into the phone number field on the Keypad screen. Or, if you tap a phone number displayed in the Contacts app, listed in an incoming email, or displayed in a web page while you're using Safari, for example, the Phone app automatically launches and a call to that number is initiated.

DIALING FROM A CONTACTS ENTRY

In the Phone app, you can look up any phone number stored in the Contacts app. Tap the Contacts icon at the bottom of the Phone app screen. When you tap a phone number in a Contacts entry, a call is initiated.

USING THE CALL OVER WI-FI CALLING FEATURE

Typically, when you initiate a call from your iPhone, it connects to the cellular network you've subscribed to, such as AT&T Wireless, Verizon Wireless, Sprint, or T-Mobile (if you're in the United States). Thanks to the Call Over Wi-Fi feature, if you're not in a good cellular network coverage area but your compatible iPhone is within range of a Wi-Fi hotspot, you can still make a call to any landline or other cellphone via the Internet.

Once you initiate a Wi-Fi call, if you leave the Wi-Fi hotspot, your call is automatically transferred to the cellular network's Voice Over LTE feature, if your cellular service supports this option. Likewise, if you're using the Voice Over LTE feature and a Wi-Fi signal becomes available, the call is seamlessly transferred to the Wi-Fi network.

If a Wi-Fi network is available, manually initiate calls using the Call Over Wi-Fi feature (rather than over a cellular network) by launching Settings, tapping the Phone option, and then turning the virtual switch associated with the Wi-Fi Calling option.

> **✓ TIP** If you're an iPad user, you can also make and receive Internet-based Voice-over-IP (VoIP) phone calls using Skype or a similar app. These calls can be made to or received from any landline or cell phone. You can participate in Skype-to-Skype calls for free. For other calls, Skype charges a very low per-minute rate (typically $0.02 or less per minute).
>
> In addition to VoIP calls, Skype can be used for free video calls with Mac, PC, iOS mobile device, Android mobile device, or Windows mobile device users. Using FaceTime for video or audio-only calls, however, works only with other Mac or iOS mobile device users.
>
> Skype is also ideal for saving money when you're making international calls from the United States, or to avoid hefty international roaming charges when you're calling home to the United States when traveling overseas.
>
> Yet another Internet calling option is to use the audio calling feature offered by Facebook Messenger to initiate calls with your Facebook friends.

MANAGING YOUR VOICEMAIL

Your unique iPhone phone number comes with voicemail, which enables people to leave you messages if you're not able to speak with them when they call. Just as with any voicemail service, you can record your outgoing message, play back missed messages from your iPhone, or call your iPhone's voicemail service and listen to your calls from another phone.

Using iOS 10's new Voicemail Transcription feature, you can read text-based versions of your incoming voicemail messages that your iPhone creates for you. As mentioned earlier in this chapter, this new feature works automatically.

RECORDING YOUR OUTGOING MESSAGE

To record your outgoing voicemail message, which is what people hear when they call your iPhone and you don't answer, follow these steps. Alternatively, you can have a computer-generated voice instruct callers to leave a message.

1. Launch the Phone app from the Home screen.
2. Tap the Voicemail icon, displayed in the lower-right corner of the screen.
3. In the upper-left corner of the Voicemail screen, tap the Greeting option.
4. From the Greeting screen, tap the Default option to skip recording a message and have a computer voice use a generic message. Alternatively, tap

the Custom option to record your own outgoing voicemail message and continue to step 5.

5. Tap the Record option that's also displayed on the Greeting screen. Hold the phone up to your mouth and begin recording your message.

6. When you're finished recording, tap the Stop option. You can play back your message by tapping the Play option, or tap the Save option to save your message and activate it.

PLAYING AND DELETING VOICEMAIL MESSAGES

It's possible to listen to audio voicemail messages either from your iPhone or by calling your iPhone's voicemail from another phone.

LISTENING TO VOICEMAIL FROM YOUR iPHONE

From your iPhone, follow these steps to listen to and then save or delete an incoming voicemail message:

1. Launch the Phone app from the Home screen, or by swiping a voicemail notification appearing on the Notification Center screen.

2. Tap the Voicemail icon displayed in the bottom-right corner of the screen.

3. Under the Voicemail heading at the top of the screen is a listing of missed voicemail messages. Tap a message to highlight it.

> **NOTE** When you see a blue dot to the left of a voicemail message listing, this indicates it's a new, unheard message. After you listen to the message, the blue dot disappears. When you tap the message to listen to it, the blue dot changes to a Pause/Play icon.

4. After a message is highlighted, tap the small Play/Pause icon (shown in Figure 9.9). The message begins playing. It might, however, take a few seconds for the message to load. Expect a brief pause before the message begins.

5. Displayed immediately below the message's Caller ID information is a transcription of the message. It appears a minute or two after the message is recorded by the caller.

Share Icon   Info Icon

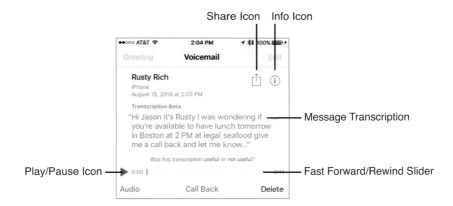

Message Transcription

Play/Pause Icon

Fast Forward/Rewind Slider

Figure 9.9

Listen to and manage incoming voicemails from the Phone app.

6. Near the bottom of the voicemail listing is a slider that depicts the length of the message, along with Speaker/Audio, Call Back, and Delete options. As your message plays, the timer slider moves to the right. You can listen to parts of the message again by moving this slider around with your finger.

> **TIP** Associated with each incoming voicemail message is a Share icon and an Info icon. Tap the Share icon to access a variety of options for sharing or exporting the voicemail message. Tap the Info icon to reveal information about the caller and, among other things, view options that enable you to call back that person or create a new contact for him/her in the Contacts app. It's also possible to keep the caller from reaching you in the future by tapping the Block This Caller option.

7. When you're finished listening to the message, either leave the listing alone (which keeps the message saved on your phone) or tap the Delete option to erase it. You also have the option of calling back the person who left the message by tapping the Call Back option.

8. To exit the voicemail options, tap any of the other command icons displayed at the bottom of the Phone app's screen, or press the Home button on your iPhone.

> **TIP** You might find it easier to listen to your voicemail messages via speaker phone, by first tapping the Speaker/Audio option that's displayed below the timer slider.

TIP If you accidentally delete an important voicemail, don't panic. From the voicemail screen, scroll to the very bottom of your voicemail message list and tap the Deleted Messages icon. Tap a message to highlight it, and then tap the Undelete icon.

CREATING AND USING A FAVORITES LIST

In the Phone app, you can create a Favorites list, which is a customized list of your most frequently dialed contacts. To access this list, launch the Phone app, and then tap the Favorites icon.

To add a contact to the Favorites list, tap the + icon in the upper-right corner of the screen. Select any listing from your Contacts database and tap it. When the complete listing for that entry appears, tap the specific phone number you want listed in your Favorites list. The newly created Favorites listing appears at the end of your Favorites list.

TIP Each Favorites entry can have one name and one phone number associated with it, so if a Contact entry has multiple phone numbers listed, choose one. If you want quick access to someone's home, work, and mobile numbers from your Favorites list, create three separate entries for that person.

When you create the entry in Favorites, the type of phone number (Home, Work, Mobile, iPhone, and so on) is displayed to the right of the person's name. A Favorites listing can also relate to someone's FaceTime identifier (their iPhone number, Apple ID, or the email address they used to set up their FaceTime account).

To edit the contacts already listed in your Favorites list, tap the Edit option in the upper-left corner of the screen.

TIP As you're viewing your Favorites list, tap the Info ("i") icon, shown to the right of each listing. This enables you to view that person's entire entry from within your Contacts database.

To dial a phone number listed in your Favorites list, simply tap its listing. The Phone app automatically dials the number and initiates a call.

ACCESSING YOUR RECENTS CALL LOG

The Phone app automatically keeps track of all incoming and outgoing calls. To access this detailed call log, launch the Phone app, and then tap the Recents icon at the bottom of the screen.

At the top of the Recents screen are two command tabs, labeled All and Missed, along with an Edit option. Tap the All tab to view a detailed listing of all incoming and outgoing calls, displayed in reverse-chronological order. Missed incoming calls are displayed in red. Tap the Missed tab to see a listing of calls you didn't answer. Tap the Edit option to delete specific calls from this listing, or tap the Info ("i") icon to view more details about that caller, including their recent call history with you.

> **✓ TIP** Missed calls are also displayed in the Notification Center window on your iPhone or as an icon badge or alert on your Home screen, depending on how you set up Notifications for the Phone app in the Settings app. To customize the Notifications options for the Phone app, launch Settings and tap the Notifications option. Then tap the Phone option. You can adjust how your iPhone alerts you to missed calls by personalizing the options on this Phone screen.

Each listing in the Recents call log displays the name of the person you spoke with (based on data from your Contacts database or the Caller ID feature) or their phone number. If it's someone from your Contacts database, information about which phone number (home, work, mobile, or such) the caller used appears below the name.

If the same person called you, or you called that person, multiple times in a row, a number in parentheses indicates how many calls were made to or from that person. This is displayed to the right of the name or phone number.

On the right side of the screen, with each Recents listing, is the time/date the call was made or received. To view the Contacts entry related to that person, tap the Info icon associated with the listing. At the top of a contact's entry screen are details about the call itself, including its time and date, whether it was an incoming or outgoing call, and its duration.

To call someone back who is listed in the Recents list, tap anywhere on that listing except for on the Info icon.

KEEPING TRACK OF USAGE

Some iPhone voice plans come with a predetermined number of talk minutes per month. Some plans offer unlimited night and weekend calling, but calls made or received during the day count against your monthly minute allocation.

If your plan does have a monthly allocation for talk minutes, if you go over your monthly minute allocation, you might be charged a hefty surcharge for each additional minute used.

> **✓ TIP** Each wireless service provider that supports the iPhone offers a free app for managing your wireless service account. It's available from the App Store. Use it to manage all aspects of your account, pay your monthly bill, and track your voice, data, and text-messaging use at any time. You can also set the alert option in the app to remind you each month when the bill is due for payment.

CUSTOMIZING RINGTONES

Thanks to the iTunes Store, you can purchase and download custom ringtones for your iPhone. You can use one ringtone as your generic ringtone for all incoming calls, or you can assign specific ringtones to individual people.

> **✓ TIP** iOS 10 comes with more than two dozen preinstalled ringtones. To shop for ringtones, launch Settings, select Sounds, and from the Sounds menu screen, tap the Ringtone option. Tap the Store option near the top-right corner of the Ringtone menu screen (within Settings).
>
> When you purchase and download a new ringtone, it becomes available on your iPhone's internal ringtones list. Most ringtones from the iTunes Store cost $1.29 each.
>
> Using a specialized app, such as Ringtone Designer, Ringtone Maker, or Ringtone Pro, it's also possible to create your own ringtones using music or audio from your iTunes library.

To choose a default ringtone for all your incoming calls, launch Settings and select the Sounds option. From the Sounds menu screen, scroll down to the Ringtone option and tap it. A complete listing of ringtones stored on your iPhone is displayed. Select the one you want to hear when you receive calls.

PICKING CUSTOM RINGTONES FOR SPECIFIC CONTACTS

To assign a custom ringtone to a specific contact so that you hear it when that person calls your iPhone, follow these steps:

1. Launch the Contacts app from the iPhone's Home screen.

2. From the All Contacts screen, find the specific contact with whom you want to link a custom ringtone. You can scroll through the listing or use the Search field to find a contact.

3. When the contact is selected and you're looking at that Contacts entry, tap the Edit option in the upper-right corner of the screen.

4. From the Info screen that displays that contact entry's data, scroll down to the Ringtone field and tap it (shown in Figure 9.10).

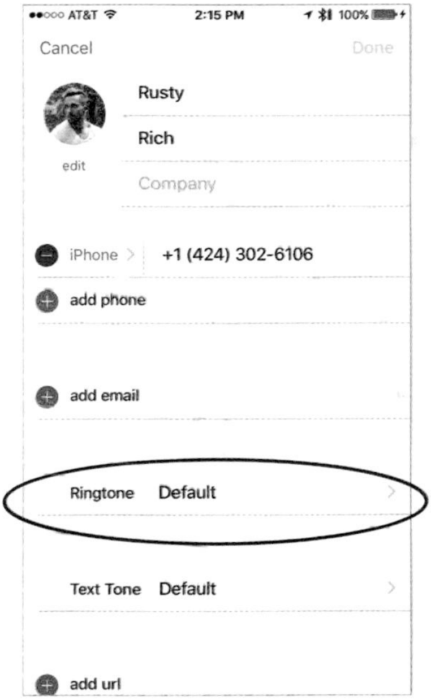

Figure 9.10

It's possible to choose a custom ringtone for each entry in the Contacts app.

5. When the Ringtone screen appears, select a specific ringtone from the list that you want to assign to the contact and tap it. You can choose a specific song (purchased from iTunes) or ringer sound that reminds you of that person (shown in Figure 9.11).

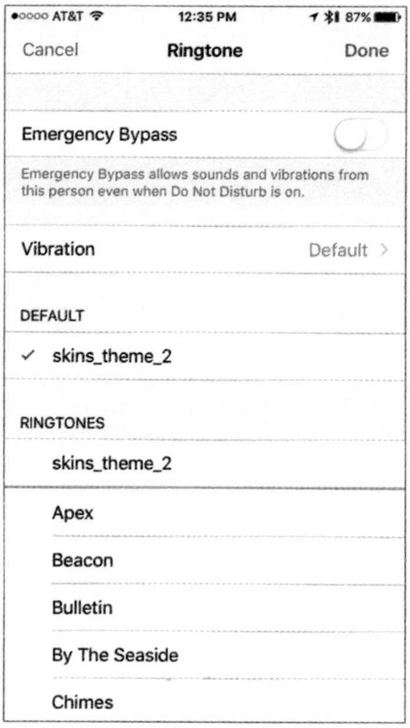

Figure 9.11

It's possible to select individual ringtones for each entry in your Contacts app database, or at least for the people you speak with the most.

6. Tap the Done icon to save your selection and return to the contact's Info screen.

7. When that contact calls you, you will hear the ringtone you just linked to that contact (as opposed to the default ringtone).

> **TIP** Also from a Contact's entry screen in the Contacts app, it's possible to choose a special vibration pattern for the phone when that person calls. To do this, tap the Vibration option and choose a vibration pattern from the Vibration menu, or scroll to the bottom of this screen and tap the Create New Vibration option to create a custom vibration pattern for that contact.

MORE INFO   Many states have outlawed using a cellphone while driving unless you have a wireless headset or hands-free (CarPlay) feature on your phone. Although the speakerphone feature of your iPhone counts as a hands-free feature, to ensure the best possible call quality while you're driving, invest in a wireless Bluetooth headset.

In addition to using a wireless Bluetooth headset while driving, you can keep it on your person throughout the day and use it whenever you make or receive calls using your iPhone.

Using a headset enables you to keep your hands free while you're talking so you can easily access other apps or iPhone features during a phone conversation.

Bluetooth wireless headsets are priced as low as $20 but can cost as much as $100. If you want to ensure the highest-quality phone conversations possible so that people can hear you and you can hear them even if there's background noise present, invest in a good-quality Bluetooth wireless headset that includes a noise-canceling microphone and a good-quality speaker. Plus, choose a headset that's comfortable to wear and that has a long battery life.

Apple's new, wireless AirPods work as stereo headphones when you place one AirPod in each ear. However, using just one AirPod (in one ear), it can be used as a wireless headset with the Phone app. To learn more about this optional $159.00 accessory, visit www.apple.com/airpods, or visit any Apple Store or authorized Apple dealer.

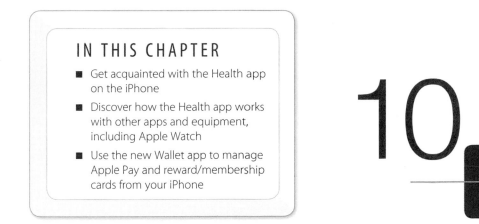

IN THIS CHAPTER

- Get acquainted with the Health app on the iPhone
- Discover how the Health app works with other apps and equipment, including Apple Watch
- Use the new Wallet app to manage Apple Pay and reward/membership cards from your iPhone

10

IMPROVE YOUR HEALTH AND MANAGE YOUR WEALTH USING YOUR iPHONE

Built in to iOS 10 are a vast assortment of tools available to app developers that make it possible to create cutting-edge apps related to health and fitness.

Because third-party app developers continue to utilize these tools, and fitness equipment and medical device manufacturers continue build iPhone compatibility and integration into their products, you can use your smartphone (and optional Apple Watch) to lead a healthier and more active lifestyle, eat a well-balanced diet, and get a good night's sleep.

NOTE Throughout this chapter, references to the Apple Watch refer to Apple Watch Series 1, Apple Watch Series 2, and the new Apple Watch Nike+ edition.

🔍 **MORE INFO**   If you're interested in learning much more about the health and fitness capabilities of your iPhone and the Apple Watch, pick up a copy of *Apple Watch and iPhone Fitness Tips and Tricks* (Que) by Jason R. Rich. This informative, full-color book is now available from wherever books are sold or from www.quepublishing.com. This book covers all aspects of improving and monitoring your fitness, activity, health, diet, sleep, and mental health using the iPhone and (optional) Apple Watch.

💬 **WHAT'S NEW**   The first time you launch the iOS 10 edition of the Health app, you have the opportunity to create or update your Medical ID profile in the app. To do this, tap the Update Medical ID button when prompted.

You also have the opportunity to sign up to be an organ donor through an organization called Donate Life. To do this, tap the Sign Up button (shown in Figure 10.1). If you're already a donor, tap I'm Already a Donor. To skip this option, tap Not Now.

You can become an organ donor at any time from within the app by tapping the Medical ID Icon at the bottom of the Health app's screen, scrolling to the bottom of the Medical ID screen, and then tapping Sign Up with Donate Life. Follow the onscreen prompts to complete the registration process.

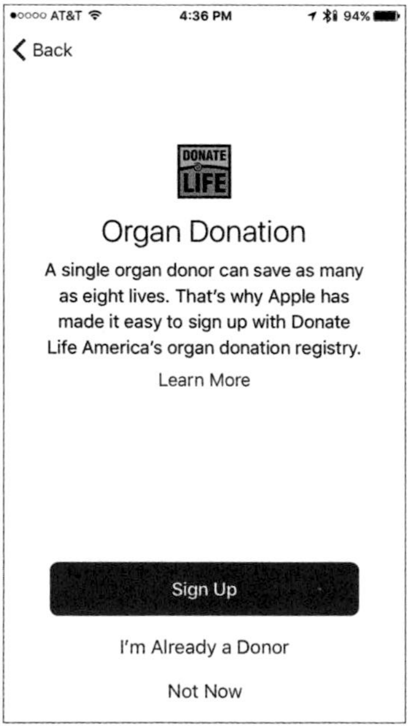

Figure 10.1

The iOS 10 edition of the Health app enables you to become an organ donor. Of course, this is totally optional.

DISCOVERING THE iPHONE-SPECIFIC HEALTH APP

Among all the other preinstalled app icons displayed on your iPhone's Home screen is an app called Health. On its own, the Health app can't do much. However, for people who are fitness, health, and/or nutrition conscious, the Health app works as a "dashboard" along with a growing number of other workout, fitness, diet, and lifestyle apps, and it can help you monitor and analyze your daily health, activity, food intake, and sleep patterns.

Beyond just working with other apps, the Health app is designed to integrate and communicate with optional equipment, including the Apple Watch, heart rate monitors, fitness/workout machines, digital weight scales, and various types of sleep and blood sugar monitors. The Health app is designed to gather information from these sources wirelessly and help you track your progress and/or share specific data with appropriate professionals, when applicable.

What's nice about the Health app is that it's fully customizable. You determine what data it collects automatically or what information you manually enter into it, and then you decide exactly how that data is used and whether it can be shared. If you ultimately choose to share certain information stored in the app—for example, sharing your fitness or workout progress with a personal trainer—you can still keep other medical data private.

(iOS 10) WHAT'S NEW When you tap the Health Data icon at the bottom of the Health app's screen, you see an updated and expanded menu of information the app can collect and manage.

Tap the Activity, Mindfulness, Nutrition, or Sleep buttons (shown in Figure 10.2) to manage information sorted into these categories.

Below these large buttons are options for collecting, analyzing, and storing data pertaining to Body Measurements (body fat percentage, body mass index, lean body mass); Health Records (Clinical Document Architecture [CDA]–formatted documents from your doctor or hospital that can be imported into the app); Reproductive Health (basal body temperature, cervical mucus quality, menstruation, ovulation test results, sexual activity, and spotting); Results (medical test results related to a dozen categories); and Vitals (updated vital sign information, including blood pressure, body temperature, and respiratory rate).

From the bottom of the Health Data screen, tap Watch the Overview Video to learn more about these features.

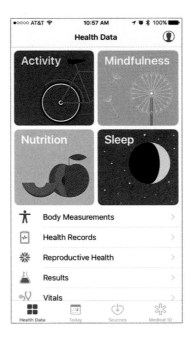

Figure 10.2

From the Health Data screen of the Health app you can track many different pieces of data.

> **✓ TIP** To discover what apps are designed to work with Health, visit the App Store, tap the Categories icon near the bottom of the screen, and then tap the Health & Fitness or Medical options.

GETTING STARTED WITH THE HEALTH APP

Without allowing your iPhone to communicate with the Apple Watch or other optional fitness or medical equipment, the Health app's capabilities are limited to being a secure personal database for medical, diet, sleep, and health-related information that you manually enter into the app or that you import from other apps installed on your iPhone.

To get started using the Health app, launch it from the Home screen. Displayed along the bottom of the screen are four command icons: Health Data, Today, Sources, and Medical ID. Tap the Health Data icon to access a menu of categories related to the types of data the Health app is capable of collecting, tracking, analyzing, and sharing.

> **☑ TIP** To create or edit your basic profile, tap the Health Data or Today icons and then tap the Me icon in the top-right corner of the screen.
>
> Tap the Edit option, and then fill in each of the fields related to your First Name, Last Name, Date of Birth, Sex, Blood Type, Fitzpatrick Skin Type, and Wheelchair. If you don't know how to fill in a particular field or don't have the necessary information, leave it blank. Tap the Done option to save your updated information.

You control which apps and optional equipment you want to use with the Health app by tapping the Sources icon. From here, you select which apps and equipment can transmit data to, or retrieve data from, the Health app. If no optional apps or equipment are being used, the word None is displayed under the Apps heading.

The Health app works best when used with the Apple Watch, a Bluetooth scale, a compatible fitness/activity tracker, and/or sleep monitoring device, for example.

> **✏ NOTE** When you pair your iPhone with the Apple Watch, the Activity app is automatically installed on your iPhone. This app collects your real-time activity data from the Apple Watch, and then formats and shares it with the Health app. It then displays your activity-related data in a variety of easy-to-understand and colorful formats.

Once you have an Apple Watch or another piece of compatible equipment linked with the iPhone, you're able to track your day-to-day activity using the Health app. To do this, tap the Today icon at the bottom of the screen.

At the top of the Today screen is a calendar view (shown in Figure 10.3). Use it to select the current day or a day from the past. Then below the Activity heading you see the information the Health app has collected, including Resting Energy, Activity Energy, Stand Hours, Exercise Minutes, Steps, Walking + Running Distance, Flights Climbed, and Heart Rate.

> **✏ NOTE** It's possible to customize what information is displayed on the Today screen. Tap any option listed to access customization options.

Figure 10.3
To view more information related to a specific category, such as Steps or Exercise Minutes, tap the banner related to that option.

USING THE MEDICAL ID FEATURE

Regardless of whether you use any additional apps or equipment with the Health app, consider using the Medical ID tool built in to the app. This is basically a digital summary of vital medical information that can be made available to doctors, paramedics, or medical personnel in case of an emergency.

To use the Medical ID component of the Health app, tap the Medical ID icon (in the lower-right corner of the screen). From the Medical ID welcome screen (shown in Figure 10.4), tap the Create Medical ID option, and then tap each field to manually enter medical information about yourself (shown in Figure 10.5).

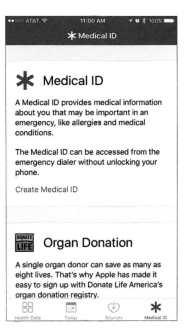

Figure 10.4
Tap the Create Medical ID option to enter your personal information.

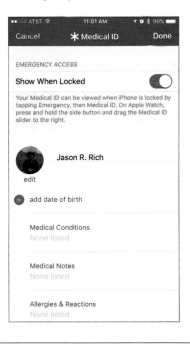

Figure 10.5
After you fill in the Medical ID component of the Health app with your personal data, medical professionals can access it in an emergency situation.

There are fields for your Name, Date of Birth, Medical Conditions, Medical Notes, Allergies & Reactions, Medications, Primary Care Doctor, Spouse, Emergency Contact, Blood Type, Organ Donor Information, Weight, and Height. Some of this information might already have been imported automatically from the Me section of the app or other health and fitness or medical apps you use. Fill in the additional fields with information that pertains to you.

For easy identification, include a photo of yourself in the app. Also, displayed at the top of this Medical ID Edit Screen is a virtual switch associated with the Show When Locked option. Turn on this option if you want a doctor or emergency medical professional to be able to access your Medical ID information from your locked iPhone, without knowing its passcode.

After you've added your personal information, tap Done to save it.

> ## ⌕ MORE INFO   In an emergency situation, to access the Medical ID
> information from a locked iPhone, press the Home button. The Enter Passcode screen is displayed.
>
> Located in the bottom-left corner of this screen is an option labeled Emergency. Tap this to access the emergency phone dialing screen. Next, tap the Medical ID option displayed in the lower-left corner to view the Medical ID information stored in the phone. Doing this does not grant someone full access to the phone.

MANAGING APPLE PAY AND MORE USING THE WALLET APP

Another app that comes preinstalled with iOS 10 (on the iPhone only) is called Wallet. It serves two main purposes—to securely store your debit card, major credit card, and store credit card information so you can use Apple Pay from your iPhone; and to store and help you manage various reward and membership cards from companies you do business with or organizations you belong to (such as AAA).

SETTING UP AND USING APPLE PAY FROM YOUR IPHONE

If you want to set up and begin using Apple Pay from your iPhone, you must be using an iPhone model that supports this feature and has a Touch ID sensor built in.

From the Wallet introductory screen, tap Add Credit or Debit Card, or tap the + icon to the right of the Apple Pay heading (see Figure 10.6). (Use the + to add cards after you have cards stored in the Wallet app.)

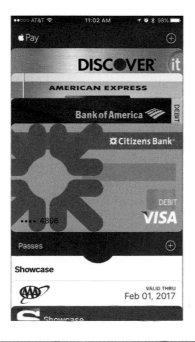

Figure 10.6

Use the Wallet App to create a virtual wallet that securely stores digital versions of your compatible credit and debit cards.

> **Note** Many of the more recently released iPad Pro and iPad mini models support Apple Pay, but only when you use it to make online purchases from supporting websites or when you're making in-app purchases. (You cannot currently make Apple Pay purchases at retail stores using any iPad.)

After you store information about at least one compatible credit or debit card in the Wallet app, use the app to make purchases/payments using Apple Pay at participating retail stores, when making in-app purchases (in compatible apps), or when making online purchases (from participating websites).

In a retail store, instead of handing a retail store's cashier your plastic debit or credit card, you simply need to hold your iPhone close to the cash register or credit card swiper, launch the Wallet app, select the debit or credit card you want to pay with (or use the app's default card that you preselect), and then place your finger on the iPhone's Touch ID sensor to authorize the purchase and make your payment.

MORE INFO Not all debit or credit card issuers (banks and financial institutions) currently support Apple Pay, although the list of supporting card issuers in the United States and Europe is growing rapidly. To determine whether your card issuer supports Apple Pay, enter your debit or credit card information into the Wallet app, or visit https://support.apple.com/en-us/HT204916.

To view an up-to-date list of retail stores, supermarkets, restaurant chains (and fast food establishments), pharmacies, and hotels, for example, that currently accept Apple Pay, visit www.apple.com/apple-pay/where-to-use-apple-pay. From this web page, scroll down to also view a list of third-party iPhone apps that accept Apple Pay.

There are several reasons why using Apple Pay is more secure than making a purchase using a traditional (plastic) debit or credit card. For example, the merchants do not see your name, nor do they receive your actual credit/debit card number, expiration date, security code, and/or card PIN.

The credit card issuer processes the payment using an encrypted code. Also, a purchase can be authorized only by you via Apple Pay using the Touch ID sensor to scan your fingerprint. So, even if someone steals your iPhone, they can't access your card details or use the card without your fingerprint scan.

NOTE If you're using Apple Pay to make a debit card purchase at a retail store, you might be required to enter the PIN associated with the card, a four-digit passcode you create when you first set up Apple Pay on your iPhone or provide a signature to complete a transaction. This varies and is determined by your financial institution, the retailer where you're making the purchase, and the amount of the purchase.

Meanwhile, if your traditional (plastic) credit or debit card gets stolen, the thief could use that card to make purchases until you call the card issuer and report the card lost or stolen. Unauthorized use of a credit/debit card by someone else, and potential identity theft, is no longer as much of a threat when using the Wallet app and Apple Pay.

ADDING CARD DETAILS TO THE WALLET APP

To add one or more credit or debit cards to the Wallet app, which is a process you need to do only once per card, tap the + icon to the right of the Apple Pay heading when you launch the Wallet app. (The phone must have Internet access to proceed.)

After viewing the Add Card Screen (shown in Figure 10.7), tap Next in the top-right corner.

Figure 10.7

Read this information screen about Apple Pay and the Wallet app; then tap Next.

The rear-facing camera of your iPhone becomes active. In a well-lit area, position your plastic credit or debit card within the onscreen frame, and your iPhone automatically scans the card and imports your name and card number into the Wallet app (shown in Figure 10.8). Confirm the displayed information, and tap Next.

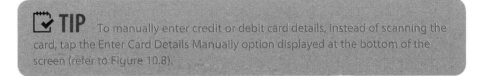

TIP To manually enter credit or debit card details, instead of scanning the card, tap the Enter Card Details Manually option displayed at the bottom of the screen (refer to Figure 10.8).

From the Card Details screen that appears next, enter the Expiration Date and Security Code from your card into the Wallet app (shown in Figure 10.9). At this point, the verification process varies based on the card issuer. Follow the onscreen prompts to complete the verification process, which typically takes 30 seconds or less.

Figure 10.8

Using the rear-facing camera built in to your iPhone, it's possible to scan each of your credit or debit cards into the Wallet app.

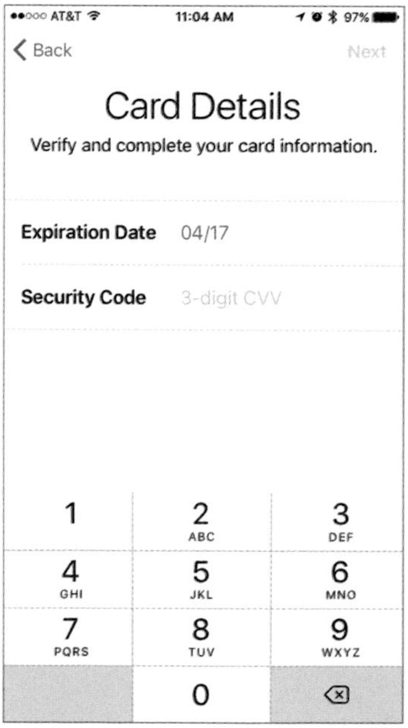

Figure 10.9

Enter the expiration date and security code when prompted for the debit or credit card you're storing in the Wallet app.

> **NOTE** Some card issuers require you to call the customer service number displayed on the card verification screen to activate your card in the Wallet app for use with Apple Pay.

After the credit or debit card has been verified and activated by your card issuer, a digital version of that card (that displays only the last four digits of the card number) is displayed in the Wallet app (refer to Figure 10.6). You're now ready to use that credit or debit card to make Apple Pay purchases. If you want to add additional cards to the Wallet app, repeat this process for each card.

> **NOTE** If you have an Apple Watch linked with your iPhone, after adding a new credit/debit card to the Wallet app, you're asked if you want the new card to be activated on the Wallet app in your smartwatch as well.

> **TIP** There are two ways to set the default card, which is the one preselected each time you launch the Wallet app.
>
> First, place your finger on one of the virtual cards displayed under the Apple Pay heading (refer to Figure 10.6), hold your finger down on the screen, and drag that card's graphic to the top of the pile. A message is displayed stating that the card you selected and placed at the top of the pile is now your default card.
>
> Alternatively, to select a default card, launch Settings, tap the Wallet & Apple Pay option, and then tap the Default Card option below the Transaction Defaults heading. Be sure to customize the Shipping Address, Email, and Phone Number fields as well.

Once you have one or more credit or debit cards stored in the Wallet app, when you're ready to make a payment at a retail location, launch the Wallet app and select the card you want to use by tapping the graphic for a card displayed below the Apple Pay heading.

When prompted by the cashier, hold the iPhone up to the cash register or credit card swiper, and then place your finger on the iPhone's Touch ID sensor for a few seconds to authorize the payment (shown in Figure 10.10).

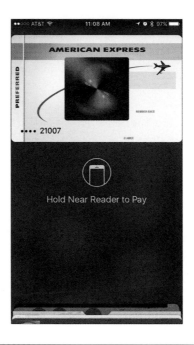

Figure 10.10
The only way to authorize Apple Pay to initiate a payment using the selected credit or debit card (or store credit card) is to use the Touch ID sensor to scan your fingerprint.

> **NOTE** When making an in-app or online purchase, you'll be prompted to confirm an Apple Pay payment by placing your finger on the phone's Touch ID sensor.

Once a purchase is finalized, a confirmation message is always displayed on your iPhone's screen.

> **TIP** There are two ways to launch the Wallet app. First, tap the Wallet app icon from the Home screen. Second, from the Lock screen, quickly double-press the Home button, without first having to unlock the phone and manually launch the Wallet app.
>
> To use this second option, be sure to turn on the virtual switch associated with the Double-Click Home Button option that can be found by launching Settings, and then selecting the Wallet & Apple Pay option.

To delete or edit a credit or debit card stored in the Wallet app, launch Settings, tap the Wallet & Apple Pay option, and then tap the listing for a card that appears below the Cards heading. Scroll to the bottom of the screen and tap Remove Card.

To change the Billing Address associated with the card, tap the Billing Address option.

USING THE WALLET APP TO MANAGE REWARD CARDS, MEMBERSHIP CARDS, AND MORE

A growing number of retail stores and organizations that have iPhone apps are beginning to support the Wallet app and allow users to manage their reward and/or membership cards from the Wallet app. For example, Dunkin' Donuts, Walgreen's, Panera, and AAA were among the first companies and organizations to support the Wallet app for this purpose. To use this functionality, it is often necessary to also install the app from that company.

In addition, most of the major airlines enable you to store Frequent Flier membership cards in the Wallet app and also manage digital versions of upcoming flight boarding passes.

Meanwhile, movie theaters and ticket services (like Ticketmaster and Live Nation) enable you to store digital tickets you purchase online in the Wallet app and present those tickets at the movie theater, event, or show.

Many movie theater chains that have reward programs also support the Wallet app to store membership card details, so you can view, manage, and redeem reward points earned from within the app.

> **☑ TIP**   To add membership or reward card details from participating companies and organizations into the Wallet app, launch the app and tap the + icon displayed next to the Passes heading. Next, scan the plastic card into the Wallet app by tapping the Scan Code to Add a Pass option.
>
> Alternatively, import the appropriate information directly from the store or organization's own iPhone app. Directions for how to do this are supplied in the compatible app.

After you set up Apple Pay to work with the Wallet app and begin storing compatible company/organization reward and membership cards in the app, you'll quickly discover that not only is Apple Pay more secure than making a purchase using a traditional, plastic credit/debit card but the checkout process is typically faster, plus you can dramatically slim down your actual wallet.

🔎 MORE INFO   To learn more about how Apple Pay and the Wallet app work, visit www.apple.com/apple-pay.

📝 TIP   To delete a card that's stored in the Wallet app, view that card with the app and then tap the Info (i) icon in the bottom-right corner of the screen. Tap the Delete option that appears there.

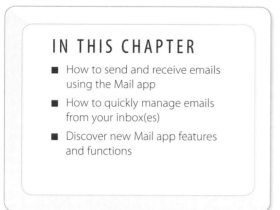

IN THIS CHAPTER

- How to send and receive emails using the Mail app
- How to quickly manage emails from your inbox(es)
- Discover new Mail app features and functions

11

SEND AND RECEIVE EMAILS WITH THE MAIL APP

If you're someone who's constantly on the go, being able to send and receive emails from virtually anywhere there's a cellular or Wi-Fi Internet connection enables you to stay in touch, stay informed, and be productive from wherever you happen to be.

The Mail app offers a comprehensive set of tools to help you compose, send, receive, and organize emails from one or more existing accounts. From your iPhone or iPad, it's possible to simultaneously manage your personal and work-related email accounts, as well as the free email account that's provided when you set up an iCloud account.

Before you can begin using the Mail app, it's necessary to set up your existing email accounts from within Settings.

> **NOTE** If you don't yet have an email account, there are several ways to get one. You can sign up for a free Apple iCloud account, which includes an email account. In addition, Google offers free Gmail accounts (http://mail.google.com), and Yahoo! offers free Yahoo! Mail accounts (http://features.mail.yahoo.com), both of which are fully compatible with your iOS device's Mail app.

ADDING EMAIL ACCOUNTS TO THE MAIL APP

Use the Add Account tool available in Settings to initially set up your iOS device to work with your existing email account(s). This process works with virtually all email accounts, including industry-standard POP3 and IMAP email services.

If you have an email account through your employer that doesn't initially work using the setup procedure outlined in this chapter, contact your company's IT department or Apple's technical support for assistance.

> **NOTE** The process for setting up an existing email account to use with your iPhone or iPad and the Mail app needs to be done only once per account.

Follow these steps to set up your iOS device to work with each of your existing email accounts:

1. From the Home screen, launch Settings.
2. Tap the Mail option.
3. Tap the Accounts option near the top of the Mail screen (in Settings).
4. Tap Add Account below the Accounts heading.
5. Select the type of email account you have. Your options include iCloud, Microsoft Exchange, Google Gmail, Yahoo! Mail, AOL Mail, Microsoft Outlook. com, and Other (shown in Figure 11.1). Tap the appropriate option. If you have a POP3 or IMAP email account that doesn't otherwise fall into one of the provided email types, tap the Other option and follow the onscreen prompts.

   If you have an existing Yahoo! email account, for example, tap the Yahoo! option. When the Yahoo! account setup screen appears (shown in Figure 11.2), enter your account name, email address, password, and a description for the account.

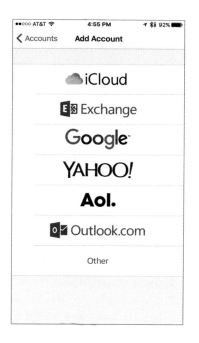

Figure 11.1

Choose the type of email account you'd like to add by tapping the appropriate option.

Figure 11.2

If you're setting up a Yahoo! Mail account, tap the Yahoo! option, and then fill in your existing account information.

> **☑ TIP**   As you're adding an email account from within Settings, the account name should be your full name (or whatever you want to appear in the From field of outgoing emails). You can opt to use just your first name, a family name (such as "The Anderson Family"), or a nickname, based on what you want to share with the recipients of your emails. The description can be anything that helps you personally differentiate that account from your other accounts, such as Home Email, Work Email, or Yahoo! Email. This is something that you see only on your device.

6. Tap Next. Your iOS device connects to the email account's server and confirms the account details you've entered. The word Verifying appears on the screen.

7. After the account has been verified, you see a new window with options. They're probably labeled Mail, Contacts, Calendars, Reminders, and Notes, although depending on the type of email account you're setting up, some of these options might not be available. They're used to determine what additional app-specific data can be linked with the Mail account, such as your Contacts database, the schedule from your Calendar app, your to-do list from the Reminders app, or your notes from the Notes app.

> **! CAUTION**   If you're already syncing app-specific data for Contacts, Calendar, Reminders, and/or Notes with iCloud, do not also sync them with Yahoo!, Google, or a Microsoft Exchange–compatible account, or you could wind up with duplicate records or entries in each app. Likewise, if you're already syncing your app-specific data with Google, don't also sync this information using iCloud.

8. Tap Save. An Adding Account message is briefly displayed, and details about the email account you just set up are added to your iOS device. The account is now ready to use via the Mail app.

9. If you have another existing email account to set up, from the Mail screen in the Settings app, tap the Add Account option again, and repeat the preceding procedure. Otherwise, exit the Settings app and launch the Mail app from the Home screen.

Depending on the type of email account you're setting up, the information for which you're prompted varies slightly.

> ✅ **TIP**   If you plan to set up a POP3 or IMAP email account, in addition to your existing email address and password, you might be prompted to enter your host name *[mail.example.com]* and outgoing mail server information *[smtp.example.com]*. Obtain this information from your email account provider, Internet service provider, or the IT department at your company before attempting to set up this type of account on your iPhone or iPad.

After the account is set up, it is listed in Settings under the Accounts heading when you tap the Mail option. From this same Mail screen, you can customize a handful of features pertaining to the Mail app and how it sorts, displays, and handles your messages.

> ✅ **TIP**   When you purchase a new iOS device, it comes with free technical support from AppleCare for 90 days. If you purchased AppleCare+ with your iOS device, you have access to free technical support from Apple for two years. This includes the ability to make an in-person appointment with an Apple Genius at any Apple Store and have someone set up your email accounts on your iPhone or iPad for you.
>
> To schedule a free appointment, visit www.apple.com/retail/geniusbar. Or call Apple's toll-free technical support phone number and have someone talk you through the email setup process. Call 800-APL-CARE (275-2273).

CUSTOMIZING MAIL OPTIONS FROM SETTINGS

To customize options available in the Mail app, launch Settings and select the Mail option. Displayed on the Mail submenu screen (shown in Figure 11.3 on an iPad) are a handful of customizable features for managing your email accounts.

> ✅ **TIP**   You should customize each email account separately. This includes how your iOS device displays new incoming email details in Notification Center, as well as how alerts or banners are utilized for each account. To set this up for each account, launch Settings, tap Notifications, select the Mail option, and then tap the listing for each of your email accounts. There's also a separate listing for VIP, which enables you to set separate alerts for important incoming emails from people included in the Mail app's VIP list that you create.

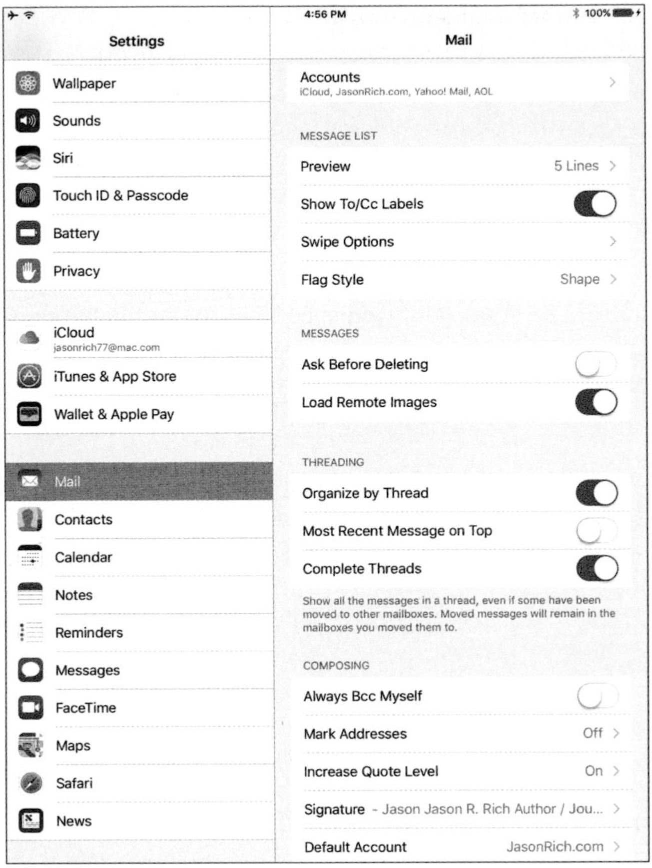

Figure 11.3

From Settings, you can customize a handful of settings relating to the Mail app.

---

iOS 10 WHAT'S NEW   As you're customizing Notifications related to the Mail app, in addition to having the ability to customize each of your email accounts separately, it's now possible to receive special Notifications related to email conversation threads. To do this, launch Settings, tap the Notifications option, tap the Mail option, and then tap the Thread Notifications option.

Thread Notifications refers to email correspondence with other people where there is back-and-forth dialogue through multiple but related email messages, where you and the person you're communicating with each tap the Reply option to respond to the previous message. The first time that Reply option is used, a new conversation thread is automatically created.

At the top of the Mail submenu screen within Settings, tap Accounts to view a listing of the individual email accounts you have already linked with the Mail app.

Below this account listing is the Fetch New Data option. Use this to determine how often your iOS device automatically accesses the Internet to check for and download new incoming email messages from each email account's server.

> ☑ **TIP**   From the Fetch New Data screen, either enable or disable the master Push feature. When turned on, your iPhone or iPad automatically accesses and displays new incoming emails as they arrive on your email account's server. When the Push feature is turned off, select how often you want to check for new emails. Your options include Every 15 Minutes, Every 30 Minutes, Hourly, or Manually. Customize this setting separately for each of your email accounts.
>
> The benefit of having the Fetch feature set to Manually is that you can greatly reduce your cellular data usage. This is important if you have a monthly data allocation through your cellular service provider. If you have an account that offers unlimited wireless data, or you utilize a Wi-Fi connection, this is not a concern. Using the Fetch feature can also help you extend your device's battery life.

> ✎ **NOTE**   Not all email accounts support the Push feature. The Fetch option might be selected for you, in which case, from the bottom of the Fetch New Data submenu screen in Settings, you'll need to select the Every 15 Minutes, Every 30 Minutes, Hourly, or Manually option for that account.

When you scroll down on the Mail submenu screen, you see the following customizable options relating to how the Mail app manages your email accounts and email messages:

■ **Preview**—As you look at your Inbox (or any mailbox) using the Mail app, determine how much of each email message's body text is visible from the mailbox summary screen, in addition to the From, Date/Time, and Subject. Choose None, or between one and five lines of the email message to preview.

> ☑ **TIP**   The Preview option also affects the email-related notifications that appear in the Notification Center if you assign it to continuously monitor the Mail app. You can adjust this in Settings by tapping the Notifications option in the main Settings menu.

- **Show To/Cc Label**—Decide whether to view the To and Cc fields when viewing the preview screen for emails.

- **Swipe Options**—This feature helps you manage the Inbox of your email accounts. As you're looking at the previews of each message in your Inbox, swipe across each message listing to access menu options. Configure which Mail-related command(s) become available to you by swiping across a message listing (shown in Figure 11.4).

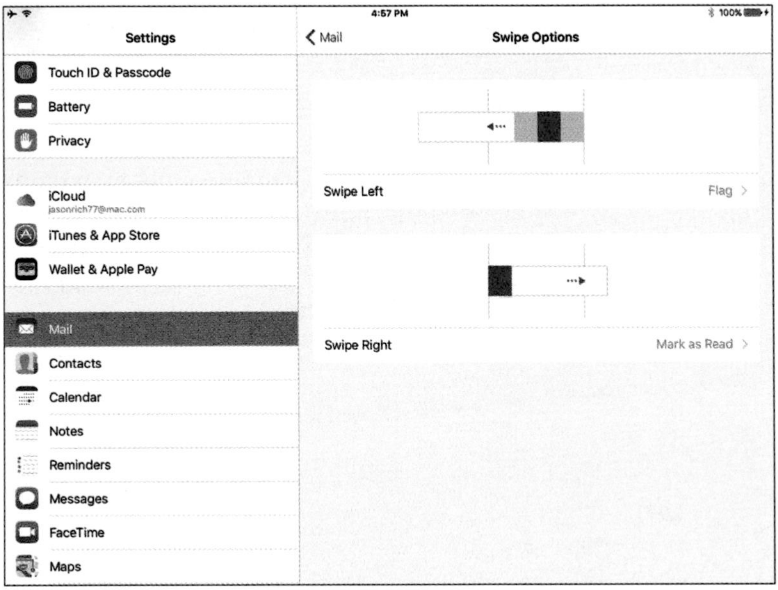

Figure 11.4
Access commonly used commands for managing incoming messages by swiping your finger across a message listing.

> **TIP**   Tap Swipe Options in the Mail submenu to determine which email management–related commands become available to you when you swipe across a message listing when viewing an Inbox.
>
> When you swipe from left to right, it's possible to choose whether the Mark As Read, Flag, Move Message, or Archive command is made available. If you select the None option, the left to right swipe feature is disabled.
>
> When you swipe right to left, choose whether the Mark As Read, Flag, or Move Message command becomes available, in addition to the Trash and More options (which are default options).
>
> Choose the email message commands you most often use to organize your incoming messages so you can access them faster (refer to Figure 11.4).

■ **Flag Style**—When you flag an email as important, the Flag style determines whether the Mail app displays a flag-shaped icon or a colored dot next to each flagged email message.

■ **Ask Before Deleting**—This option serves as a safety net to ensure that you don't accidentally delete an important email message from your iOS device. When this feature is turned on, you're asked to confirm your message deletion request before an email message is actually deleted. By default, with some email service providers, you cannot delete email messages stored on your email account's server. When you delete a message from the Mail app, it is deleted from your iPhone or iPad but is still accessible from other devices. Check with your mail service provider to see how this feature is set up and whether it is changeable.

■ **Load Remote Images**—When an email message has a photo or graphic embedded in it, this option determines whether the image is automatically downloaded and displayed with the email message. You can opt to refrain from automatically loading graphics with email messages to reduce the amount of data transferred to your iPhone or iPad (which is a consideration if you're connected to the Internet via a cellular data network). You still have the option to tap the placeholder icon in the email message to manually download the images in a specific message.

> **NOTE** In addition to reducing your cellular data usage, disabling the Load Remote Images option can help cut down on the amount of spam (unsolicited emails) you receive. Remote image loading can be tracked by the senders of spam and used to verify valid email addresses. When the senders are able to verify your address, they can send you more mail. If you don't load the image, your address is unverified to the sender.
>
> When turned off, displaying images embedded within an email requires an additional step on your part because you now must tap the image icon to load the image if you want to view it.

■ **Organize by Thread**—This feature enables you to review messages in reverse chronological order if a single message turns into a back-and-forth email conversation in which multiple parties keep hitting Reply to respond to messages with the same subject. When turned on, this makes keeping track of email conversations much easier, especially if you're managing several email accounts on your iPhone or iPad. If it's turned off, messages in your Inbox are displayed in reverse chronological order as they're received, not grouped by subject.

WHAT'S NEW Also available from the Mail submenu within Settings are the Most Recent Message on Top and Complete Threads option, which are displayed below the Threading heading. Turn on the Most Recent Messages on Top option to display the newest (most recent messages) first when viewing the conversation thread. Turn on the Complete Threads option if you want all messages within the thread to be displayed, even when some messages have been moved to other mailboxes.

When viewing an Inbox, tap the >> icon that's displayed to the right of the time/date a message was received to expand the thread and see listings for all messages within that thread, without first actually opening the latest message. To close the expanded thread in the inbox, tap the icon that contains two downward-pointing arrows.

- **Always Bcc Myself**—When this feature is turned on, a copy of every outgoing email is sent to your Inbox. Typically, all outgoing messages are automatically saved in a Sent folder related to that account. If your email account type does not enable you to access sent emails from another computer or device, using the Bcc Myself option compensates for this. When you send an email message from your iPhone/iPad, using this feature ensures that the message becomes accessible from your primary computer.

- **Mark Addresses**—With this option, you can enter a portion of an email address and then be alerted each time an email is received that meets that search criteria. For example, if you do business with many people who work at The Widget Company and their email addresses end with @Widget.com, anyone with an email address ending with @widget.com, such as johndoe@widget.com, sales@widget.com, or janedoe@widget.com, can be automatically flagged in your Inbox to get your attention. All you have to do is store "widget.com" in the Mark Address field. This feature is particularly useful if you work in a corporate environment.

- **Increase Quote Level**—When turned on, anytime you reply to a message or forward a message, the content of that original email appears indented, making it easier to differentiate between the message you add and the original message being replied to or forwarded. This option affects the message formatting, not the actual content.

- **Signature**—For every outgoing email that you compose, you can automatically add an email signature. The default signature is "Sent from my iPhone" or "Sent from my iPad." However, with this option you can create customized signatures for each email account. A signature might include your name, mailing address, email address, phone numbers, and so forth.

> **NOTE** From the Signature submenu screen within Settings, you can create a signature and use it with all email accounts by selecting the All Accounts option. However, you can assign different signatures to each of your accounts by selecting the Per Account option.

■ **Default Account**—If you're using the Mail app to manage multiple email accounts, when you reply to a message or forward a message, it is always sent from the email account to which the message was originally sent. However, if you tap the Compose New Email icon to create a new email from scratch, the email account from which the message is sent is whichever you have set up as the Mail app's default account. If you want to change this account for a specific email, simply tap the From field as you're composing a new email and select one of your other accounts.

VIEWING YOUR INCOMING MAIL

When you launch the Mail app, the Inbox for your various email accounts is displayed. You can opt to display incoming messages for a single email account or display the incoming messages from all of your email accounts by selecting the All Inboxes option.

Even though Mail enables you to simultaneously view incoming emails from multiple accounts within a single listing (on the same screen), behind the scenes, the app automatically keeps your incoming and outgoing emails and your various email accounts separate. So if you opt to read and respond to an email from your work-related Inbox, for example, that response is automatically sent out from your work-related email account and saved in the Sent folder for that account.

Viewing all the Inboxes for all of your accounts simultaneously makes it faster to review your incoming emails, without having to manually switch between email accounts.

If you have multiple email accounts being managed from your iOS device, to view all of your Inboxes simultaneously, or to switch between Inboxes, follow these steps:

1. Launch the Mail app.

2. The Inbox you last looked at is probably displayed. If only one email account is set up to work with your iPhone or iPad, the last email you viewed is displayed.

3. Tap the left-pointing, arrow-shaped Mailboxes option in the upper-left corner of the screen to select which Inbox you want to view. If you're looking at a particular account's Inbox, the arrow-shaped option is labeled with the name of the mailbox.

4. From the menu that appears, the first option displayed is All Inboxes. Tap it to view a single listing of all incoming emails, or tap any single email account that's listed on the Mailboxes screen.

> **(iOS 10) WHAT'S NEW**   If you receive an email from an automated email list that you're on, and the Mail app determines this, at the top of the message is a banner that states, "This message is from a mailing list." You're then given the option to unsubscribe to that list with a single tap of the screen. This feature, when used over time, can help you reduce the amount of spam or unwanted (and unsolicited) email you receive.

> **TIP**   Tap the VIP mailbox listing to view only emails from your various Inboxes that have been received from people you've added to your VIP list. When you tap the VIP option, these emails are displayed in a single list, although it is comprised of VIP messages from all the accounts you're managing on your iPhone or iPad.
>
> Below the VIP listing under the Inboxes heading is a Flagged listing. This enables you to view a separate mailbox comprised of only emails (and message threads) you've previously flagged as being important. Again, this is a comprehensive list from all the accounts you're managing on your iPhone or iPad. The Mail app keeps the messages sorted behind the scenes, based on which account each is associated with.

> **(iOS 10) WHAT'S NEW**   As you're viewing any Inbox (or All Inboxes) the new Filtered by Unread icon is in the bottom-left corner of the screen. Tap it to see only new, unread messages. Tap the icon again to turn off this feature and view all messages currently stored in the selected Inbox(es).

As you're viewing a listing of messages within All Inboxes, a specific inbox, or any mailbox, type a keyword, date, name, email address, or search phrase in the Search field to quickly find a particular message or message thread that contains the search word or phrase you entered.

iOS 10 **WHAT'S NEW** A >> icon displayed to the immediate right of the time/date an email message was received in your Inbox indicates that the message is part of an ongoing message thread. Tap the >> icon to display all messages in that thread within the Inbox. Tap the icon again to condense the message thread to a single message listing. Tap the message listing to open and view the entire message (as well as all previous messages in the thread).

COMPOSING AN EMAIL MESSAGE

From the Mail app, it's easy to compose an email from scratch and send it to one or more recipients. Just tap the Compose icon. On an iPhone, the Compose icon is in the lower-right corner of the screen in the Mail app. On an iPad, the Compose icon is in the top-right corner of the screen.

NOTE The Compose icon looks like a square with a pencil on it.

When you tap the Compose icon, a blank New Message email message template appears. Using the virtual keyboard, fill in the To, Cc, Bcc, and/or Subject fields (as shown in Figure 11.5). You must fill In the To field with a valid email address for at least one recipient. The other fields are optional.

Figure 11.5

Tap the Compose icon to create an email from scratch and send it from your iOS device.

It's possible to send the same email to multiple recipients by either adding multiple email addresses to the To field or adding additional email addresses to the Cc and/or Bcc fields.

The From field is automatically filled in with your email address. If you're managing multiple email addresses from the iPhone or iPad, the default address is used. If you want to change the address from which the email is being sent, tap the From field to select one of your other accounts. See the "Customizing Mail Options from Settings" section earlier in this chapter for information on changing the default account.

TIP As you fill in the To field when composing an email, the Mail app automatically accesses your Contacts database to match up entries. This feature can save you time, because you don't have to manually enter that entire email address. If you know that the person you're sending an email is already in your Contacts database, you can type that person's name in the To field.

The Mail app also remembers email addresses from people not in your Contacts database, but with whom you've corresponded in the past through email via the Mail app. Also, when you begin manually entering an email address, the Mail app offers suggestions. Either select a suggestion or continue typing.

Next, tap the Subject field and use the virtual keyboard to enter the subject for your message. As you do this, the subject appears at the very top center of the Compose window (replacing the New Message heading).

TIP When using almost any app with a Share menu, to compose and send an email that contains app-specific content without first launching the Mail app, tap the Share icon and select Mail from the Share menu.

A New Message screen appears with the related app-specific content already attached to that outgoing email message. Use the virtual keyboard to compose your email, and then tap the Send icon. The email message is sent and you are returned to the app you were using.

To begin creating the main body of the outgoing email message, tap in the main body area of the Compose Message screen, and begin using the virtual keyboard (or an optional external keyboard) to compose your message. You also have the option of tapping the Dictation key and then dictating your message using the Dictation feature.

! CAUTION If you have the Auto-Capitalization, Auto-Correction, or Check Spelling features turned on, as you type, the iPhone or iPad automatically corrects anything that it perceives as a typo or misspelled word. Be very careful when using these features because they are notorious for plugging in the wrong word into a sentence. Especially if you're creating important business documents and emails, make sure you carefully proofread whatever you type before sending it. Typically, these features are helpful, but they do have quirks that can lead to embarrassing and unprofessional mistakes.

To control the Auto-Capitalization, Auto-Correction, and Check Spelling features, launch Settings, tap the General option, select the Keyboard option, and then turn on or off the virtual switch associated for each option displayed in the Keyboard menu screen.

☑ TIP When turned on, the QuickType feature monitors what you're typing in real time and anticipates what you're about to type (based on the context of what you're typing). It then suggests appropriate words or phrases.

Use this feature to speed up and improve the accuracy of your typing. The QuickType suggestions are displayed as tabs just above the virtual keyboard (shown in Figure 11.6). Tap a suggestion tab to select that word and insert it into your message. Then continue typing.

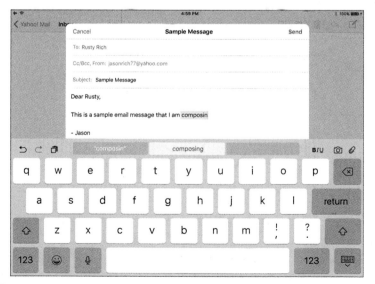

Figure 11.6

The QuickType feature works nicely when composing emails using the Mail app. Notice the suggested text displayed in tabs just above the virtual keyboard.

The signature you set up from within Settings for the selected From account is automatically displayed at the bottom of each newly composed message. You can return to Settings to turn off the Signature feature or change the signature that appears. A signature can also be edited or added manually, directly from the Compose screen, as you create or edit each message.

When your email is fully written and ready to be sent, tap the Send option. In a few seconds, the message is sent from your iOS device, assuming that it is connected to the Internet. A copy of the message appears in your Sent or Outbox folder. As a message is being sent, a "Sending" notification appears near the bottom of the Mail app's screen.

> **✓ TIP** The Mail app enables you to format your outgoing email messages and include **bold**, *italic*, and underlined text (as well as combinations, like ***bold-italic*** text).

On an iPhone (shown in Figure 11.7), you format text within an email message you're composing by typing the text as you normally would using the virtual keyboard. After the text appears in your email, hold your finger on a word to make the Select, Select All, Paste, Quote Level, Insert Photo or Video, and Add Attachment command tabs appear above that word.

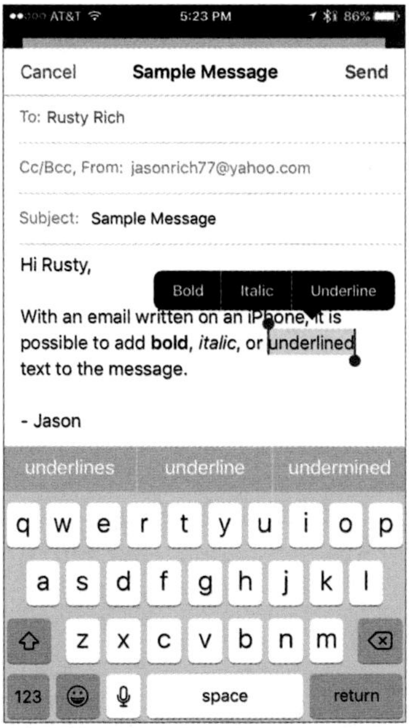

Figure 11.7

On an iPhone, you can format text after it's been typed in the Mail app. You can add bold, italic, and/or underlined text, for example.

Tap Select, and then use your finger to move the blue dots that appear to highlight the text you want to modify. When the appropriate text is highlighted in blue, tap the right-pointing arrow above the text (next to the Cut, Copy, and Paste commands), and then tap the **B**/U option. A new menu appears above the highlighted text with three options labeled Bold, Italic, and Underline. Tap one or more of these tabs to alter the highlighted text.

On an iPad, in the top-right corner of the virtual keyboard is a text formatting (**B**/U) icon, as well as an Attach Photo and a File Attachment icon (refer to Figure 11.6). By tapping this formatting icon and selecting a typestyle, you can format text in real time as you're typing. If you want to type using ***Bold/Italic*** text, for example, tap the B and I icons. Alternatively, you can use the Select command after text is typed, and adjust the typestyle using the directions outlined earlier for the iPhone.

Also on the iPad, tap the Attach Photo icon to select and import a photo (from the Photos app) into your email, or tap the File Attachment icon to attach a file, document, or photo that's stored in iCloud Drive to your outgoing email.

> **NOTE** On an iPhone, to insert a photo or file, place and hold your finger in the body of the email message where you want to insert the file. Tap the Insert Photo or Video option or the Add Attachment option to insert a photo or file, respectively.

> **TIP** When using any iPad model, to more accurately move the cursor around the screen (to select content to cut and paste, for example) place two fingers together on the screen (directly over the cursor), and then drag your fingers around on the screen. Also, if you're using an external keyboard with your iPad, press the Control, Command, or Options key to access available shortcuts (which are specific to the app you're currently using).

INSERTING A PHOTO OR VIDEO INTO OUTGOING MAIL

As you're composing an outgoing email, one way you can insert a photo or video clip that's stored in the Photos app into that email is to place and hold your finger anywhere in the body of the email where you want to embed the content.

> **NOTE** On the iPhone, tap the right-pointing arrow displayed to the right of the Select, Select All, and Paste commands to access the Insert Photo or Video option.

When the Insert Photo or Video tab is displayed, tap it. Select the photo you want to insert into the email by selecting an album and then tapping an image or video thumbnail. The photo/video you selected is previewed in the Choose Photo window. Tap the Use button to insert the photo or video into your email.

✓ TIP On the iPad, you also have the option to tap the camera icon that's above the virtual keyboard to insert a photo or video clip.

Repeat this process to include multiple images within an email, keeping in mind that the overall file size associated with the outgoing email is often limited by your email service.

✓ TIP When you insert a photo into an outgoing email you are prompted to choose the image size. Your options include Small, Medium, Large, and Actual Size. Each is accompanied by the file size of the image(s) you're sending. Tap one of these options when prompted.

On the iPad, tap the Images option to the right of the Cc/Bcc, From field, and then tap the Small, Medium, Large, or Actual Size tab on the newly displayed Image Size field to customize the image file size.

INSERTING AN EMAIL ATTACHMENT

To add a file attachment into an email you're composing, place and hold down your finger in the body of the email where you want to insert the file. From the menu that appears tap the Add Attachment option. Alternatively, if you're using an iPad, simply tap the File Attachment icon at the extreme right on the toolbar above the virtual keyboard.

Your iOS mobile device accesses your online-based iCloud Drive folders and enables you to select a file stored in your iCloud account (not in your iPhone or iPad).

✐ NOTE Refer to Chapter 6, "Use iCloud and the iCloud Drive App," for more information about managing files, data, photos, and documents using iCloud Drive.

Select the file you want to attach to the outgoing email by tapping its icon or listing, and then tap Done. The selected files are attached to the outgoing email message.

USING SELECT, SELECT ALL, CUT, COPY, AND PASTE

The iOS operating system offers Select, Select All, Cut, Copy, and Paste commands, which are accessible from many iPhone or iPad apps, including Mail. Using these commands, you can quickly copy and paste content from one portion of an app to another or from one app into another app, whether it's a paragraph of text, a phone number, or a photo.

> **☑ TIP** When using the iPad's Split Screen feature, you can display two apps at once on your tablet's screen and then easily select, copy, and paste content between the two apps.

To use these commands, use your finger to hold down on any word or graphic element on the screen for one or two seconds, until the Select and Select All tabs appear above that content. To select a single word or select the content you want to copy or cut, tap the Select tab. Alternatively, to select all the content on the screen, tap the Select All tab.

After text (or a graphic element, such as a photo) is selected, tap the Cut tab to delete the selected content from the screen (if this option is available in the app you're using), or tap the Copy tab to save the highlighted content in your iPhone or iPad's virtual clipboard.

Now, move to where you want to paste the saved content. This can be in the same email or document, for example, or in another app altogether. Choose the location on the screen where you want to paste the content, and hold your finger on that location for two or three seconds. When the Paste tab appears, tap it. The content you just copied to the virtual clipboard is pasted into that location.

> ☑ **TIP**   On the iPad, the Undo, Redo, and Clipboard icons are displayed above the virtual keyboard. Tap the Undo icon to go one step back and undo the last thing you did when composing the email. Tap the Redo icon to counteract what the Undo command just did.
>
> When you select content in an outgoing email, for example, the Cut, Copy, and Paste command icons are displayed on the top-left side of the virtual keyboard. Tap the scissor-shaped icon to use the Cut command. The icon that looks like two sheets of paper represents the Copy command, and the clipboard-shaped icon works as the Paste command.

> ☑ **TIP**   In the Mail app, as you use the Select, Select All, Cut, Copy, and Paste commands, notice a Quote Level option that appears on the menu above the highlighted text or content you select. Tap this to increase or decrease the indent of that content, which impacts how it's formatted on the screen.

SAVING AN UNSENT DRAFT OF AN EMAIL

To save a draft of an email without sending it, as you're composing the email message, tap the Cancel button that appears in the upper-left corner of the Compose message window. Two command buttons appear: Delete Draft and Save Draft. To save the unsent draft, tap Save Draft.

You can return to it later to modify and send it. To do this, from the main Inbox screen in Mail, tap the left-pointing Mailboxes icon that looks like an arrow displayed at the upper-left corner of the screen. From the Mailboxes screen, scroll down to the Accounts heading, and tap the listing for the email account from which the email draft was composed.

When you see a list of folders related to that email account, tap the Drafts folder. Tap the appropriate listing to open the email message. You can now edit the message or send it.

READING EMAIL

Just like the Inbox on your main computer's email software, the Inbox of the Mail app (shown in Figure 11.8 on an iPhone and Figure 11.9 on an iPad) displays your incoming emails.

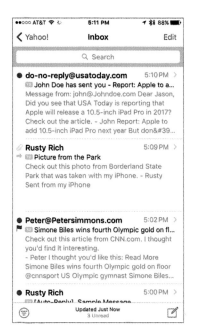

Figure 11.8

The Inbox screen of the Mail app displays a listing of your incoming emails on the iPhone.

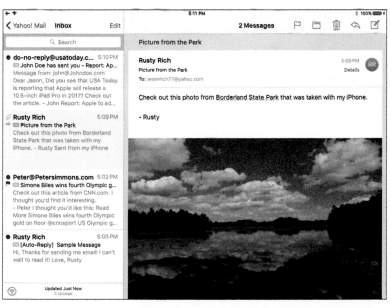

Figure 11.9

On the iPad, the Inbox provides a listing of your incoming emails on the left side of the screen (in the Inbox sidebar).

NOTE As you're looking at the Inbox for any of your email accounts (or the All Inboxes mailbox), to the left of each email message preview you might see a tiny graphic icon. A blue dot represents a new and unread email (or an email that has been marked as unread). A solid blue star represents a new and *unread* email from someone on your VIP list, and a gray star icon represents a *read* email from someone on your VIP list.

An orange flag-shaped icon to the left of an email preview means that you have manually flagged that message (or message thread) as urgent. Instead of a flag icon, a blue dot with an orange circle can be displayed indicating a message is urgent and unread. Just an orange dot will appear after it's read. You can choose between a flag or a dot icon from Settings.

A curved, left-pointing arrow icon means that you have read and replied to that message, whereas a right-pointing arrow icon means you've read and have forwarded that message to one or more people.

A bell icon means that the Notify Me option has been turned on in relation to that message.

If no tiny icon appears to the left of an email preview listing, the message has been read and is simply stored in that inbox (or mailbox).

When you're viewing your Inbox(es), a list of the individual emails is displayed. Based on the customizations you make from the Settings app that pertain to the Mail app, the Sender, Subject, Date/Time, and up to five lines of the message's body text can be displayed for each incoming message listing.

NOTE If you're using the Mail app on an iPad while holding the tablet in portrait mode, place your finger near the left side of the screen and swipe to the right to open the Inbox sidebar.

On the iPhone, when viewing your Inbox and the listing of incoming (new) email messages, tap any message listing to read that message in its entirety. When you do this, a new message screen appears. At the bottom of this screen is a series of command icons for managing that email.

WHAT'S NEW When you receive an email from someone whose contact information that's saved in your Contacts app has changed, you see a banner at the top of the message that states, "New Contact Info Found." Tap Add to automatically update that person's Contact entry with the new or updated information.

> **TIP** If you're using a newer iPhone model, take advantage of the 3D Touch features to quickly review emails. As you're looking at the Inbox listing, place and hold your finger gently on a specific email listing. A preview of that entire email message is displayed. If you want to open and read the message, press down on the screen a bit harder when the preview is visible.

On the iPad, the email message that's highlighted in gray on the left side of the screen is the one that's currently being displayed, in its entirety, on the right side of the screen. Tap any email listing on the left side of the screen to view the entire message on the right side of the screen. Use the icons at the top of the screen to manage that email.

At the top of the Inbox message listing are two command icons, labeled Mailboxes (or the name of the mailbox you're viewing) and Edit.

Located at the top of the Inbox message listing is a Search field. You might need to swipe your finger downward along the Inbox to reveal it. Tap the Search field to make the virtual keyboard appear so you can enter a search phrase and quickly find a particular email message. It's possible to search the content of the Mail app using any keyword, a sender's name, a date, or an email subject, for example. You can also use your device's Spotlight Search feature to quickly locate content within email messages.

> **(iOS 10) WHAT'S NEW** When using an iPad Pro with the 12.9-inch screen, the Mail app uses a three-pane view (as opposed to just two). On the extreme left is the Mailboxes pane. The middle pane is the selected Inbox message listing, and the right pane displays the selected message.

THE EDIT BUTTON

Located on top of a mailbox's message listing (to the right of its heading) is the Edit button. Tap this option to quickly select multiple messages from a mailbox, such as your Inbox, and delete or move the selected content to another mailbox (or folder), as shown in Figure 11.10.

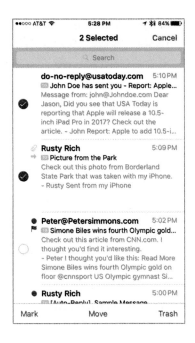

Figure 11.10

Tap the Edit button, and then manage your incoming messages, mark them, delete them in quantity, or move them to the Trash folder.

> **TIP** After tapping the Edit button, manually select one or more message listings to move or delete, or tap the Mark All option to select all the messages in that Inbox. You can use the Flag or Mark As Read/Unread options for all the selected messages.

> **TIP** If you tap the Mark button to the left of the Trash and Move buttons, you can then flag them or mark one or more emails as read or unread. You can also move selected messages to your Junk folder.

After you tap the Edit button, an empty circle icon appears to the left of each email message preview listing. To move or delete one or more messages from the current mailbox's listing (which could be your Inbox, VIP, Archive, or Junk mailbox), tap the empty circle icon for that message. A blue-and-white check mark fills the empty circle icon when you do this, and the Mark, Move, and Trash options are displayed at the bottom of the screen.

After you've selected one or more messages, tap the Trash button to quickly delete one or more messages simultaneously from the mailbox (which sends them to the Trash folder), or tap the Move button and then select to which folder you want to move those email messages. Tap the Mark option to Flag the message, mark it as unread, or move it to the Junk folder.

To exit this option without doing anything, tap the Cancel button displayed at the top of the Inbox listing, to the right of the Inbox heading.

DELETING INDIVIDUAL INCOMING MESSAGES

As you're looking at the listing of messages in your Inbox (or any mailbox), to delete individual messages, one at a time, swipe your finger from right to left over a message listing. Tap the red-and-white Trash option to delete the message.

Tap the More option to access a menu (shown in Figure 11.11) that offers the Reply, Reply All, Forward, Mark, Notify Me, and Move Message options. You can also tap the orange Flag option to flag or unflag that message.

Figure 11.11

After swiping from right to left across a message listing in your Inbox, tap More to reveal this menu.

TIP Another way to delete a message from your Inbox, or any mailbox, is to tap a message listing to view that message, and then tap the Trash icon.

VIEWING YOUR EMAILS

When a single email message is selected from the Inbox listing, that message is displayed in its entirety. At the top of the message, see the From, To, Cc/Bcc (if applicable), Subject, and the Date/Time it was sent.

In the upper-right corner of the email message is a blue Hide command. If you tap this, some of the message header information will no longer be displayed. To make this information reappear, tap the More option.

As you're reading an email, tap the flag icon to flag that message and mark it as urgent, or mark the email as unread. These options appear within a pop-up menu. When you flag a message, an orange flag (or an orange dot) becomes associated with that message, which is displayed in the message itself (to the right of the date and time) and in the Inbox (mailbox) in which the message is stored. Plus, from your Inboxes menu, if you tap the Flagged option, you can view a separate mailbox that contains only flagged (urgent) messages.

USING THE MAIL APP'S VIP LIST FEATURE

In addition to flagging individual messages as important, the Mail app can automatically highlight all emails sent from particular (important) senders, such as your boss, specific clients, close friends, or family members. Once you add a sender to your VIP List, all their incoming emails are marked with a star icon instead of a blue dot that represents a regular, new incoming email.

To add someone to your VIP list, as you're reading an email from that person, tap the From field (the name/email address). A Sender screen (iPhone) or window (iPad) appears. Tap the Add to VIP option. This adds and keeps that sender on your custom VIP list until you manually remove them. To later remove someone from your VIP list, read any of their email messages and tap the From field. When the Sender window appears, tap the Remove from VIP button (which has replaced the Add to VIP button).

> **TIP** From the Mailboxes menu, tap the VIP listing to view a special mailbox that displays only incoming emails from people on your VIP list. Using the VIP list feature helps you quickly differentiate important emails from spam and less important incoming emails that don't necessarily require your immediate attention.

DEALING WITH INCOMING ATTACHMENTS

The Mail app enables you to access certain types of attachment files that accompany an incoming email message. Dozens of file formats are compatible with the

Mail app. As you add third-party apps that support other file formats, they become recognized by the Mail app. This includes files related to text, photos, audio clips, video clips, PDFs, and eBooks, as well as iWork and Microsoft Office documents and files.

To open an attached file using another app, in the incoming email message, tap and hold down the attachment icon for one to three seconds. If the attachment is compatible with an app that's installed on your iPhone or iPad, you're given the option to transfer the file to that app or directly open or access the file using that app. If an incoming email message contains an attachment that is not compatible or accessible from your iOS device, you can't open or access it. In this case, you must access this content from your primary computer.

ORGANIZING EMAIL MESSAGES IN FOLDERS

You can easily move email messages into a folder, enabling you to better organize your emails. Here's how to do this:

1. From the Inbox listing, tap the Edit button located above the Inbox listing. Or, if you're viewing an email message, swipe your finger from right to left across the message listing.

2. Tap Move. A menu that offers various folders and options available for that email account is displayed.

3. Tap Move Message, and then tap the mailbox folder to which you want to move the message. The email message is moved to the folder you select.

> **NOTE** The Move option is also available by swiping from right to left across a message listing from your inbox and then tapping More.

> **TIP** As you're managing incoming and outgoing emails, the Mail app uses the default mailboxes that are already associated with that email account, such as Inbox, Drafts, Sent, Trash, and Junk. For some accounts, you are limited to only these default mailboxes. However, for many types of email accounts, you can create additional mailboxes and then move messages into those mailboxes to organize them.

FORWARDING, PRINTING, AND REPLYING TO MESSAGES

As you're reading incoming emails, it's possible to forward a message to someone else, reply to the message, or print the email by tapping the left-pointing, curved-arrow icon displayed when you're viewing an email. When you tap this icon, as you're reading any email message a menu offers the following options: Reply, Forward, Save Image, and Print. If the message you're viewing has more than one recipient, an additional option, Reply All, appears.

To reply to the message you're reading, tap the Reply (or Reply All) option. An email message template appears on the screen that already contains the content of the message you're replying to. Refer to the "Composing an Email Message" section for details on how to write and send an email message from the Mail app.

To forward the email you're reading to another recipient, tap the Forward icon. If an attachment is associated with the email, you're asked, "Include attachments from original email?" and offered two options: Include and Don't Include. Tap the appropriate response.

When you opt to forward an email, a new message template appears on the screen. However, the content of the message you're forwarding appears in the body of the email message. Start the message-forwarding process by filling in the To field. You can also modify the Subject field (or leave the message's original subject), and then add to the body of the email message with your own text. This text appears above the forwarded message's content.

> **TIP** To forward an email to multiple recipients, enter each person's email address in the To field of the outgoing message, separating each address with a comma (,), or tap the + to the right of the To field to add more recipients.

When you're ready to forward the message, tap Send, or tap Cancel to abort the message-forwarding process.

If you have an AirPrint-compatible printer set up to work with your iOS device, tap the Print option that appears when you tap the left-pointing curved-arrow icon as you're reading an email.

MORE INFO   Use these quick tips to manage your email:

- To refresh your Inbox, swipe your finger downward on the inbox screen (iPhone) or column (iPad).

- As you're reading email, if the text is difficult to see, you can automatically increase the size of all text displayed in the Mail, Contacts, Calendar, Messages, and Notes apps by adjusting the Accessibility option in Settings. To make this font size adjustment, launch Settings. Select the General option, and then tap the Accessibility option. From the Accessibility menu screen, tap the Larger Text option.

- While looking at the Home screen on a newer iPhone model, press and hold down on the Mail app icon to make the app's 3D Touch Pop menu appear. Four options appear, including All Inboxes (view the Inbox for all of your accounts on a single screen), VIP (view the VIP inbox), Search (enter a keyword or search phrase to find in any of your incoming or outgoing emails), and New Message (used to compose a new message from scratch).

- When using almost any app (Contacts, Calendar, Notes, Safari, Reminders, Messages, and so on), tap an email address in the app to compose and send an email to that person via the Mail app. The To field automatically includes the email address you tapped.

- When you see a new message notification displayed in the Notification Center screen, on an iPad, swipe across the listing from right to left, and then tap the View option to quickly open the Mail app and view that message. On an iPhone with Touch 3D, press and hold your finger on the message listing to see a preview of that message (along with a Trash and Mark As Read option). Tap the notification to launch the Mail app and read that message.

- When viewing your Inbox, to refresh it and load new messages that have been sent, swipe your finger downward in the Inbox. The message Updated Just Now displays at the bottom center of the Inbox screen or pane when your messages are up to date. Otherwise, the time and date that the Inbox was last updated is displayed. Your Inbox can refresh only when the iPhone or iPad has Internet access.

TIP   The Mail app also has a Notify Me feature. As you're reading an email, tap the flag icon and then select the Notify Me option to activate this feature for the message you're reading. Then, when you receive a response from anyone related to this email thread, you are automatically notified.

IN THIS CHAPTER

- Discover new ways to communicate using the Messages app
- How to send and receive text, audio, and video messages using your cellular service provider's text-messaging service
- How to take advantage of Apple's iMessage service to communicate with other iPhone, iPad, iPod touch, and Mac users

12

COMMUNICATE BETTER USING THE MESSAGES APP

According to Apple, Messages is the most frequently used app among iPhone and iPad users. As a result, out of all the apps that come preinstalled with iOS 10, the Message app has received the biggest overhaul. The changes made to the app aren't just cosmetic, however. The redesigned version of Messages includes a handful of new ways for users to communicate using words, audio, video clips, emojis, and animated graphics, particularly when the app is being used with Apple's iMessage service.

> **NOTE** iMessage is a free messaging service operated by Apple that utilizes the Internet. It enables iOS mobile device and Mac users to communicate with other iOS device and Mac users, as long as both users' devices have access to the Internet. This means you can send a message via iMessage if you are connected to the Internet via Wi-Fi or a cellular data network, unlike an SMS or MMS text message, which requires a cellular network connection.

WHAT'S NEW The iOS 10 edition of Messages now offers colorful animations, which allow users to emphasize a celebratory statement, for example, by displaying animated balloons, confetti, or fireworks on the entire screen as they send messages via iMessage.

Users can also create personalized handwritten notes, using their finger as a writing instrument on the screen (or the Apple Pencil with a compatible iPad Pro), and then send those notes as messages to other iMessage users.

Because people like to communicate using emojis, iOS 10 now includes a vast library of these whimsical, graphic characters, and makes it easier to insert them into outgoing text messages.

The Invisible Ink feature enables text messages to materialize on the recipient's screen when they swipe over them. Plus, when video clips, photos, and other animated graphics are included in a text message, that content can more easily be viewed from directly within the Messages app.

How to use these new features to communicate via the Messages app is discussed in this chapter.

NOTE When it comes to text messaging, all messages sent and received via a 3G/4G/LTE cellular network utilize the text messaging service offered by your cellular service provider. However, all messages sent and received when communicating with other Apple equipment users can be done through the free, Internet-based iMessage service.

Based on whom you're communicating with and whether a cellular or Wi-Fi Internet connection is available, the Messages app automatically determines whether cellular text messaging or iMessage should be used.

COMMUNICATING EFFECTIVELY WITH THE MESSAGES APP

Text messaging was designed to make communications between two or more people fast and easy. Today, "texting" has become a preferred and highly efficient form of communication.

In addition to sending and receiving text-based messages, the Messages app now supports the sending and receiving of photos, video messages, video clips, emojis, virtual handwritten messages, animated backgrounds, and audio messages.

> **NOTE** If the person you're communicating with via the Messages app has an entry in your Contacts app database, and that entry contains the person's photo, it is displayed in the Messages app; otherwise, the person's initials are displayed by default if the entry contains no photo. Or, if there's no Contacts entry at all for the person, a generic graphic might be used.

Most iPhone service plans have three components: voice, data, and text messaging. When you sign up with a wireless service, choose a paid text-messaging plan that allows for the sending or receiving of a predetermined number of text messages per month, or pay for an unlimited text messaging plan.

If your plan has no text messaging component, you are charged for every text message you send or receive. However, these days, most cellular service plans, especially family plans, come with unlimited text messaging.

There are different types of text messages. There are text-only messages (SMS, or Short Message Service), as well as text messages that can contain a photo or video clip (MMS, or Multimedia Messaging Service). These messages can be sent to the cell phones of one or more people simultaneously via the Messages app.

> **NOTE** The Messages app supports audio and video messages when used to communicate with other iMessage users. Instead of typing a message, use the app's audio recording interface to record a short audio message, and then send it to one or more recipients.
>
> Alternatively, it's possible to record and send a short video message (from within the Messages app) using one of the cameras that are built in to your iPhone or iPad. How to do this is explained shortly.

> **TIP** Thanks to the Handoff feature, if someone sends your iPhone a text message, the Messages app running on your iPhone can automatically forward the message to your iPad or Mac. Thus, you can send and receive messages via your iPhone's cellular network from any of your Macs or iOS mobile devices linked to the same iCloud account, as long as your iPhone is within about 33 feet of the iPad and/or Mac and Bluetooth is turned on.

> **☑️ TIP** From Settings, it's possible to set up the Messages app to store all of your text messages forever, or save internal storage space in your mobile device by adjusting the Keep Messages option to 30 Days or 1 Year. To do this, launch Settings, tap the Messages option, and then tap the Keep Message option.

> **✏️ NOTE** Be sure to use options available within Settings to customize the functionality of the Messages app. To do this, launch Settings, tap the Messages option, and then customize one setting at a time in this submenu (shown in Figure 12.1 on an iPad). Start by turning on the virtual switch that's associated with the iMessage service, so you can use the app's new features and functions when communicating with other Apple iPhone, iPad, or Mac users.

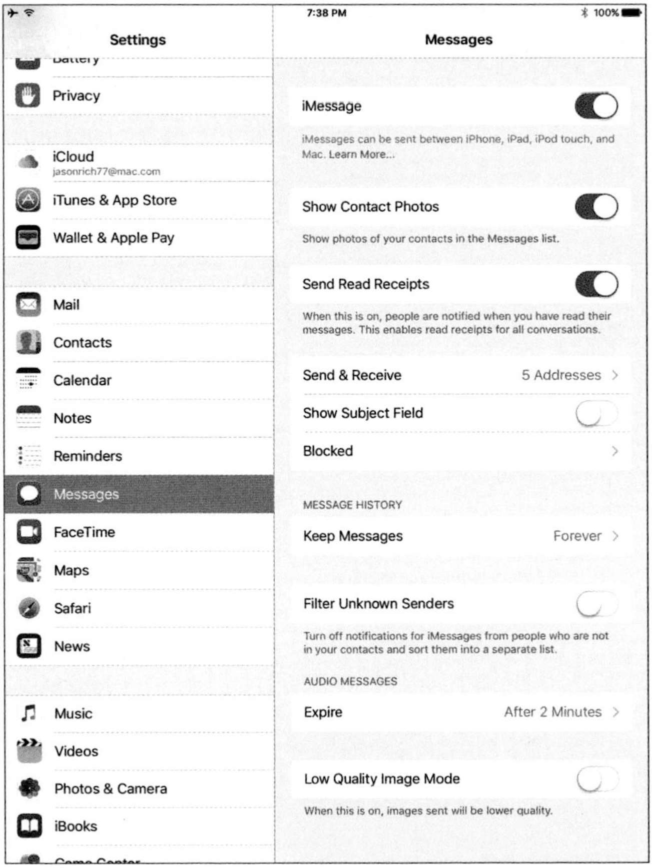

Figure 12.1

Customize a handful of Messages-related functions from this newly expanded menu in Settings.

USING THE MESSAGES APP WITH APPLE'S iMESSAGE SERVICE

Unlike the text-messaging services available through cellular service providers, Apple's iMessage service is free of charge, and it allows for an unlimited number of messages to be sent and received. The service also taps into your iPhone's or iPad's other functions and allows for the easy sharing of photos, videos, locations, and contacts; plus, it works seamlessly with Notification Center and Siri.

iMessage enables you to participate in text-based, real-time conversations. When someone is actively typing a message to you during a conversation on iMessage, a bubble with three periods in it appears to indicate that the other person is typing.

When you use cellular-based text messaging via the Messages app, it is possible to send messages to, or receive messages from, any other cell phone (located anywhere in the world), regardless of a user's wireless service provider.

> **! CAUTION** When communicating with people via cellular-based text messaging who are outside your home country, international texting rates apply. Likewise, international texting rates apply if you're traveling overseas and send text messages via a cellular network to recipients in your home country or abroad.
>
> Receiving (but not responding to) text messages while abroad is typically free, but check with your cellular service provider before you leave home. Again, using iMessage to send/receive messages is always free.

> **NOTE** In addition to using iMessage, some people who are active on Facebook use Facebook Messenger as a way to communicate in real time using text-based instant messages (which can also include photos, video clips, emojis, and other content).
>
> Internet-based audio calling and video calling via the free Facebook Messenger app are also possible. Facebook Messenger enables you to communicate with other Facebook Messenger users for free. The optional app is available from the App Store and is separate from the official Facebook app, which is used to access the Facebook social media service.

SETTING UP A FREE iMESSAGE ACCOUNT

Because traditional text messaging is tied to a cell phone, which has a unique phone number, there is no need to have a separate username or account name when using the text-messaging feature through your cellular service provider.

If you know someone's cell phone number, you can send a text message to that person from your cell phone (and vice versa). However, because iMessage is web based, before using this service, you must set up a free iMessage account.

The first time you launch the Messages app to use it with the iMessage service, you're instructed to set up a free account using your existing Apple ID. Or, instead of using your Apple ID, tap the Create New Account option to create an account that's linked to another existing email address.

> **NOTE** iPhone users can associate their cell phone number with their iMessage account to send and receive text messages using this service. However, you can use an Apple ID and/or an existing email address as well. To make it easier to communicate via iMessage, it's now possible to associate your cellular phone number, Apple ID, and/or other email addresses to the same iMessage account.

To do this, you must complete the information requested from the New Account screen. When the requested New Account information is entered, tap Done. When you simply enter your existing Apple ID/iCloud account information to set up your iMessage account, and then tap Sign In, the initial process for establishing an iMessage account is quick.

> **TIP** Just as when you're using FaceTime, the unique Apple ID, email address, and/or iPhone phone number you use to set up your iMessage account is how people find you and are able to communicate with you. So if you want someone to be able to send you messages via iMessage, that person must know the iPhone phone number, Apple ID, or email address you have set up to work with the iMessage service.
>
> Likewise, to send someone a message via iMessage, you must know the iPhone phone number, Apple ID, or email address the recipient used to set up his or her iMessage account. Again, because it's now possible to link an iPhone phone number, Apple ID, and email addresses to the same account, this makes it easier for people to find you or for you to find other people to establish a conversation via iMessage.

> **NOTE** When you send a text message, it is displayed in a blue text bubble if you're using the iMessage service. However, if you're using your cellular service provider's texting service, your text bubbles are displayed in green. Depending on your cellular service plan, charges may apply.

BENEFITS TO USING iMESSAGE

The biggest benefits to using iMessage over other text-messaging services are that it's free and you can send/receive an unlimited number of messages. The Messages app itself also nicely integrates with other features, functions, and apps on your iPhone or iPad.

Thanks to iOS 10, you can also utilize more than just generic text within your messages, as you'll discover shortly.

Another convenient feature of iMessage is that you can begin a text message–based conversation using your iPhone, for example, and switch to using your iPad or Mac to continue that conversation. This, however, is also possible with all types of text messaging via the Messages app if you turn on the Handoff feature.

WORKING WITH THE MESSAGES APP

The Messages app on the iPhone has two main screens: a summary of conversations labeled Messages, and an actual conversation screen labeled at the top of the screen using the name of the person(s) with whom you're conversing. The conversation screen has handful of icon-based commands that give you access to the app's features and functions.

On the iPad, the Messages screen is divided into two main sections (or panes). On the left is a listing of your previous conversations. When Messages is running, the right side of the iPad screen is the active conversation window. From here, you can initiate a new conversation or respond to incoming messages, one at a time.

Whether you're using an iPhone or an iPad, switching between conversations requires just one or two onscreen taps. Plus, thanks to group messaging, it's possible to communicate with two or more people at the same time and have everyone in the group be able to read and respond to all messages sent by all group members.

CREATING AND SENDING A TEXT MESSAGE

The first time you launch Messages, the New Message screen is visible, the cursor flashes on the To field, and the virtual keyboard is displayed. If you have contact information stored in the Contacts app, as soon as you start typing in the To field, Messages attempts to match existing contacts with the name, cell phone number, or email address you're currently typing. When the intended recipient's name appears, tap it.

> **TIP** To initiate a conversation with someone else, tap the New Message icon that appears in the upper-right corner of the Messages screen on the iPhone or next to the Messages heading on the upper-left side of the iPad's screen.

To quickly search your Contacts database to find one or more recipients for your text messages, tap the blue-and-white plus icon in the To field as you're composing a new message. A scrollable list of all contacts stored in Contacts displays, along with a Search field you can use to search your contacts database from within the Messages app.

> **TIP** If you're using an iPhone, to use your cellular service provider's SMS text-messaging service to send a message to another cell phone user, enter the recipient's cell phone number in the To field of a new message. This applies if the person doesn't have an entry in your Contacts database.
>
> If you're using an iPhone or an iPad to send a message to another iOS mobile device or Mac user via iMessage, in the To field, enter the recipient's Apple ID, cell phone number, or the email address that user has linked with their iMessage account.
>
> In your Contacts database, you can create a separate field for someone's iMessage username, or when viewing the person's Contacts listing, simply tap the appropriate contact information based on how you want to send the text message.

After filling in the To field with one or more recipients, if you have the Subject feature turned on (from within Settings), tap the optional Subject field to create a subject for your text message, and then tap the blank message field to begin typing your text message. If you're sending only text in your message, however, just enter the text, and then tap the Send icon.

WHAT'S NEW As soon as you type something into the message field, the Send icon is displayed. This icon looks like an upward-pointing arrow in a circle. Simply tap this icon to send the message. However, to access some of the new features built in to the Messages app, press and hold down this icon to access the Send with Effect options.

The Send with Effects menu has two tabs at the top: Bubble and Screen. Tap the Bubble option to reveal the Slam, Loud, Gentle, and Invisible Ink features. Any of these options add an attention-getting animation to the text bubble when you're using iMessage to communicate.

If you choose Invisible Ink, the message is sent using invisible virtual ink (shown in Figure 12.2). The recipient must swipe their finger over the incoming message to make the message readable on their screen.

After choosing one of these options, tap the Send icon.

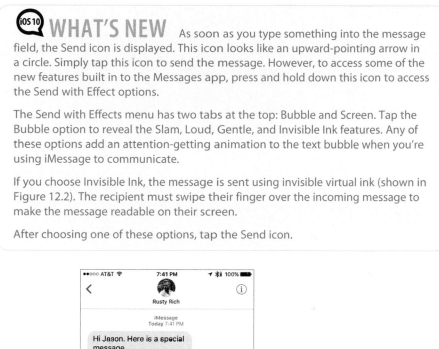

Invisible Ink
(Swipe to Reveal Text)

Figure 12.2

Here, a message is received using the Invisible feature. Swipe across this message to display the text in a readable format.

Before you start typing a message in the Messages app, while the message field is still blank, to the right of the message field is a microphone icon (rather than a Send icon). Press and hold down this icon to record a short audio message that will be sent as an audio file to the intended recipient.

WHAT'S NEW To send an animated background with a message, first fill in the message field with text, or use another iMessage feature to create or collect content to send. Then, instead of pressing the Send icon, press and hold the Send icon to reveal the Bubble and Screen tabs.

Tap the Screen tab, and then scroll right to left to toggle between the animated balloons, confetti (shown in Figure 12.3), laser, fireworks, or shooting star animated sequence, which will be displayed across the entire background of the message area in the Messages app.

After you select a screen animation, tap the Send icon. The recipient will receive your message and the full-screen animation you selected.

Figure 12.3
Send an attention-getting, full-screen animation with your message.

> **NOTE** Sending an audio file by tapping the microphone icon to the right of the message field is different from using iOS 10's Dictation feature, which enables you to speak into your iPhone or iPad and have the device transcribe what you say into text. To use the Dictation feature in Messages, tap the microphone key at the bottom of the virtual keyboard (to the immediate left of the space bar).

Instead of sending basic text to the intended recipient or recording an audio message, when using Messages to communicate via the iMessage service, tap the Menu (>) icon to the left of the message field (see Figure 12.4) to reveal three additional icons, each of which gives you access to new features.

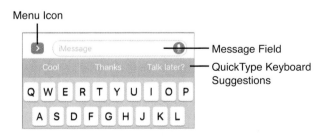

Figure 12.4
Tap on the > icon to access three additional command icons, which provide new ways to communicate via the iMessage service.

iOS 10 WHAT'S NEW After tapping the Menu (>) icon to the left of the message field, you see three new icons (shown in Figure 12.5). Tap the camera icon to snap a photo (using one of the iPhone or iPad's built-cameras) so that you can send that photo to the intended recipient in a message via iMessage. Alternatively, you can swipe from left to right and then select a pre-shot photo or video clip that's currently stored in the Photos app. (Tap the Photo Library button to do this.) After you select one or more photos, each gets embedded into the outgoing message, and thumbnails for them appear in the Message field. Tap the Send icon to send the photos or pre-shot video clips to the recipient(s).

When you tap the camera icon, a mini version of the Camera app's viewfinder screen is displayed. Use the camera selection icon to switch between the front- and rear-facing cameras, and then snap a photo by tapping the Shutter button (shown in Figure 12.6). That photo is then added to the message field, and it will be sent when you tap the Send icon.

Alternatively, after tapping the camera icon, swipe from right to left and then choose a recently shot photo stored in the Photos app. Another option is to swipe from left to right and then tap the Photo Library button to choose any photo(s) or video clip(s) stored in the Photos app.

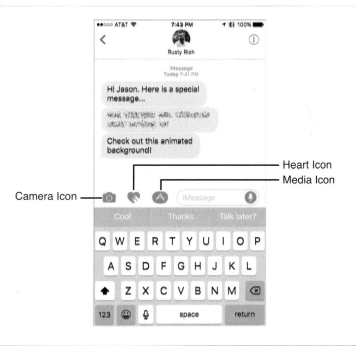

Figure 12.5

After tapping on the Menu (>) icon, three icons for accessing new tools in the Message app are displayed.

Figure 12.6

In Messages, you can use the Camera app to snap a photo and quickly embed it in an outgoing message, without separately (and manually) launching the Camera app.

iOS 10 WHAT'S NEW After tapping on the Menu (>) icon, tap the heart icon to record a video clip or still photo, and at the same time, annotate over the video/photo using virtual ink. You use your finger (or the Apple Pencil on a compatible iPad) as your drawing/annotating tool.

The annotation and drawing screen shows a handful of new finger gestures that you can use to overlay an animated tap, fireball, kiss, heartbeat, or heartbreak graphic. Figure 12.7 shows the menu of finger tap commands available, and Figure 12.8 shows what the recipient sees when an animated Kiss is received. As soon as you create one of these Digital Touch animations, it is automatically sent to the recipient, without you having to tap the Send icon.

Tap the Video icon to capture a short video sequence or still image and then annotate or draw on it. This can be done in real time or after shooting. After finishing your annotations/drawing (shown in Figure 12.9), tap the Send icon to send your photo or video clip.

Figure 12.7

Use one of these Digital Touch finger gestures, or annotate a photo or video in real time.

Figure 12.8

This is what a received animated Kiss looks like when it's sent via iMessage.

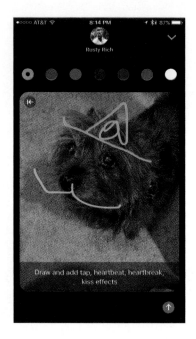

Figure 12.9
Shoot a short video clip (or a still image) and then annotate it with virtual ink before sending it via iMessage.

iOS 10 **WHAT'S NEW** After tapping the Menu (>) icon, tap the Media icon to embed what looks like a handwritten message, a song that's stored in your iPhone or iPad, or an animated GIF. Scroll right to left to switch between media cards, and select what you want to send.

For example, from the selection of simulated handwritten messages, choose between a Hello, Thank You, Happy Birthday, Congratulations, Thinking of You, I'm Sorry, or Awesome message by tapping its thumbnail (see Figure 12.10). You can also compose a handwritten message, which is discussed in the next section.

When viewing the music menu, tap a thumbnail that represents a recently played song from the Music app (shown in Figure 12.11) to share it.

From the animated GIFs menu (which pulls content from the Internet), select an animated graphic that helps to convey a message you want to send. Keep scrolling down to view a vast selection of GIFs (see Figure 12.12). Tap the thumbnail for the one you want to send.

In the Find Images and Videos search field that's displayed just above the GIF thumbnails, type a keyword or search phrase to help you quickly find an appropriate GIF to send.

After tapping the Media icon, tap the Menu icon (four ovals) in the lower-left corner of the screen. This gives you access to four command icons. Tap the Store icon to visit the App Store and search through third-party apps designed to integrate with the Messages app. For example, you can find free and paid apps that allow you to add animated stickers to your messages.

Tap Recents to see what graphic features you've used recently in your messages and quickly access them again. Tap the Music icon to search through music available in the Music app, or tap Images to search your mobile device and the Internet for images and animated GIFs you can send via the Messages app.

Figure 12.10

Select a simulated handwritten message to send via iMessage to the desired recipient. After you select a message, you can add a text-based comment in the message field, or simply tap the Send button.

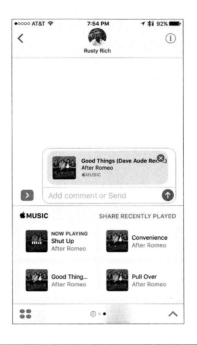

Figure 12.11
Select a recently played song from the Music app to share with someone via iMessage.

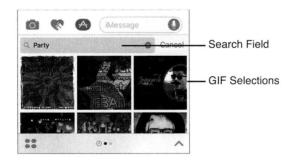

Figure 12.12
Choose an animated GIF to help you convey a message using graphics.

SENDING YOUR OWN HANDWRITTEN MESSAGE

In addition to the pre-created, simulated handwritten messages you can choose
in the Messages app (when communicating via iMessage), you can also handwrite
on the iPhone or iPad's screen to compose your own handwritten messages, which
you can send to others as a graphic.

On the iPhone, to compose a handwritten message, tap the empty message field and then rotate the iPhone to landscape mode. A large white text box appears. Use your finger to draw or write using your finger, and then tap the Done option to transfer your handwritten note to the message field. Alternatively, select a prewritten note from the thumbnails displayed along the bottom of the screen, or tap the keyboard icon to return to the traditional keyboard without composing a handwritten note.

On the iPad, tap the message field to make the iPad's virtual keyboard appear. Instead of typing a message, however, tap the Draw key, which is displayed between the 123 and Hide Keyboard key on the virtual keyboard.

In the white box that appears (shown in Figure 12.13), use your finger or the Apple Pencil (on compatible iPad Pro models) to handwrite or draw your message using virtual ink. Tap Done to continue.

Figure 12.13

Write or draw something using your finger or the Apple Pencil.

What you wrote is transferred to the message field. You can now tap the Send button or add a text-based message using the virtual keyboard (to accompany the handwritten graphic message), and then tap the Send icon (shown in Figure 12.14).

Figure 12.14
Preview your message, and then send it after it's transferred to the message field.

> **NOTE** After your handwritten/drawn message is transferred to the message field, if you choose to cancel (not send it), tap the X icon in the top-right corner of the graphic.

> **TIP** The majority of the animated graphic options available to you in the Messages app work only with iMessage. When sending a traditional text message via a cellular text-messaging service, you can, however, attach a photo or video clip by tapping the Menu (>) icon and then tapping the camera-shaped icon.

RECORDING AND SENDING AN AUDIO MESSAGE

When using iMessage, it's possible to record and send short audio messages via the Messages app. To do this, launch Messages, select the person you want to send the message to, and then press and hold your finger on the microphone icon to the right of the message field. This begins the recording process. Simply start speaking into your iPhone or iPad.

When you're finished recording, lift your finger from the microphone icon. You can delete the audio message by tapping the X icon. Tap the Play icon to preview your audio message before sending it. You send your audio message to the intended recipient by tapping the Send icon or by swiping your finger upward.

Using the Messages app, it's also possible to receive an incoming audio message. Instead of text being displayed, an audio message icon is displayed (see Figure 12.15). Tap it to play the message.

Play Icon

Received Audio Message

Figure 12.15

This is what it looks like when an audio message is received via the Message app. Tap the Play icon to listen to the message.

> ✅ **TIP** In Settings, set up the Messages app to automatically delete audio messages or animated graphic messages after a predetermined amount of time, or keep them forever (or until you manually delete them). Storing audio messages or animated graphics requires additional internal storage space in your iPhone or iPad. To adjust this setting, launch Settings, tap the Messages option, and then tap the Expire option under the Audio Messages heading.
>
> It's also possible to set up the Messages app with the Raise to Listen feature. When this feature is turned on, if you receive an incoming audio message, it automatically plays when you pick up the iPhone and hold it up to your ear.

> ✅ **TIP** Using the iPad's Split Screen feature, you can keep the Messages app running on one side of the screen (and engage in one or more conversations) while at the same time you continue working with another app altogether.

PARTICIPATING IN A TEXT-MESSAGE CONVERSATION

As soon as you tap Send to initiate a new message conversation and send an initial text, audio, photo, animated graphic, or video message, the New Message window transforms into a conversation window, with the recipient's name displayed at the top center. Displayed on the right side of the conversation window are the messages you've sent. The responses from the person you're conversing with are left-justified and displayed In a different color on the screen with text bubbles (shown in Figure 12.16).

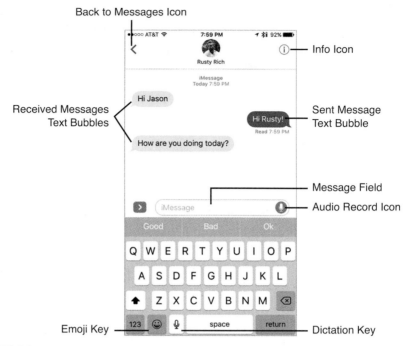

Figure 12.16
A sample text message conversation via the Messages app on an iPhone.

As the text-message–based conversation continues and eventually scrolls off the screen, use your finger to swipe upward or downward to view what's already been said.

> **TIP** Whenever there's a pause between the sending of a message and the receipt of a response, the Messages app automatically inserts the date and time in the center of the screen so that you can later easily track the time period during which each conversation took place. This is particularly helpful if there are long gaps and the conversation takes place over time.

COMMUNICATING WITH EMOJIS

Anytime you're engaged in a conversation using the Messages app, in addition to using the virtual keyboard to type text messages, you can tap the Emoji key (between the 123 and Dictation keys on the virtual keyboard) to access hundreds of graphic emojis.

In addition to many different face emojis, which you can use to graphically depict emotions, iOS 10 now offers hundreds of different themed emojis sorted into nine categories. After tapping the Emoji key on the keyboard, tap any emoji category icon at the bottom of the screen, or scroll from right to left (or left to right) between the emoji screens (shown in Figure 12.17).

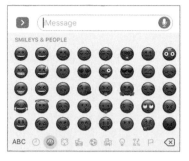

Figure 12.17

Choose from hundreds of nonanimated emojis to insert into a message.

To add an emoji to your text message, simply tap the emoji you want, and it will appear In the message field. Tap the ABC option (in the lower-left corner of the screen) to return to the regular virtual keyboard.

> **iOS 10 WHAT'S NEW** As you're typing a message using text in the Messages app, a new feature automatically enables you to swap specific words with those emojis related to those words, without you having to search for the emojis. While you're typing, if you use a word like "happy" or "sad" that has a related emoji, that emoji is displayed in a tab as part of the QuickType keyboard, above the regular virtual keyboard keys.
>
> To turn on this feature, press and hold down the Emoji key on the keyboard and turn on the virtual switches associated with Shortcuts and Predictive.
>
> When you're finished typing a text-based message, tap once on the Emoji key. Words in your messages that correspond to emojis are highlighted in orange. Tap any of those words to see a list of emojis that relate. Tap an option to replace the word in your message with the selected emoji (shown in Figure 12.18).

Figure 12.18

The Messages app scans your outgoing text messages and suggests applicable emojis to insert.

GENERATING A QUICK RESPONSE TO A MESSAGE AND ADDING EMPHASIS

Anytime you receive a message via the iMessage service, if you want to quickly send an emphasized graphic response, simply press and hold your finger on the text bubble you want to respond to. Within a second or two, a menu bubble appears that contains six "emphasized" responses, which are large graphic icons. Your options include a heart, thumbs up (shown in Figure 2.19), thumbs down, the message "Ha Ha," exclamation points, or a question mark.

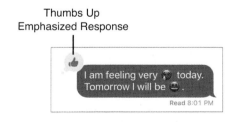

Figure 12.19

Send an emphasized response to any text message in the form of a graphic icon that gets attached to the text bubble you're responding to.

Tap your desired response, and it is automatically sent (and attached to the text bubble you responded to). There is no need to tap the Send icon.

RESPONDING TO AN INCOMING MESSAGE

Depending on how you set up the Messages app in Settings, you can be notified of an incoming message in a number of ways. Notification of a new message can be set to appear in Notification Center. Or, if the Messages app is already running, a new message alert is heard and a new message listing appears on the Messages screen (iPhone) or under the Messages heading on the left side of the iPad screen.

If you already have the conversation screen open and a new message from the person you're conversing with is received, that message appears on the conversation screen. Meanwhile, if you're an Apple Watch user, the messages you receive are automatically displayed on your watch's screen as well. This includes all new graphic-oriented message features available through iMessage.

> ☑ **TIP**   When a new message arrives, a blue dot appears to the left of the new message's listing (under the Messages heading on the iPad or on the Messages screen on the iPhone). The blue dot indicates it's a new, unread message.

To read the incoming message and enter into the conversation window and respond, tap the incoming message listing. If you're looking at the listing in Notification Center, for example, and you tap it, the Messages app launches and the appropriate conversation window automatically opens.

After reading the incoming text message, use the virtual keyboard to type your response in the blank message field, and then tap the Send icon to send the response message. You can also use one of the Messages app's other new features for composing a graphic, audio, photo, or video message.

RELAUNCHING OR REVIEWING PAST CONVERSATIONS

From the Messages screen on the iPhone, or from the left side of the screen on the iPad, when the Messages app is running, it's possible to view a listing of all saved conversations. Each listing displays the person's name, the date and time of the last message sent or received, and a summary of the last message sent or received. Tap any of the listings to relaunch that conversation in the Conversation window. You can either reread the entire conversation or continue the conversation by sending a message to that person.

> ### ☑ TIP
> By tapping one listing at a time, you can participate in multiple conversations at once.
>
> On the iPhone, to exit the conversation screen you're currently viewing, tap the left-pointing arrow icon in the upper-left corner of the screen (labeled Messages). On the iPad, tap one of the other listings under the Messages heading on the left side of the screen.

From the Messages screen on the iPhone (or the Messages listing on the iPad on the left side of the screen), tap the Edit icon, and then tap the red-and-white icon next to a conversation to quickly delete the entire conversation.

> ### ⓘⓞⓢ10 WHAT'S NEW
> While engaged in a conversation via the Message app, tap the Info icon displayed at the top-right corner of the conversation screen. The Details screen appears (see Figure 12.20). From the Details screen, it's possible to quickly initiate a FaceTime, voice, or text message conversation with that person. You can also use your iPhone or iPad's GPS capabilities to send your exact location to that person.
>
> The recipient receives a map that displays your exact location. They can then tap this Maps icon, and then tap the Directions to Here option to obtain turn-by-turn navigation directions from their current location to yours.
>
> To temporarily refrain from receiving messages from the person, from the Details screen, turn on the virtual switch associated with the Do Not Disturb feature to block them. Turn off this feature to once again receive their messages.
>
> If you want the recipient to know when you have read their messages after they've been received by you, turn on the virtual switch associated with the Send Read Receipts option. This option is set separately for each person you communicate with via Messages.
>
> Scroll down in the Details screen to see a collection of all images or attachments that have been shared during the entire conversation with that person (that's taken place using Messages).
>
> Tap the Images tab to view the images/photos, or tap the Attachments tab to view other content that's been shared.

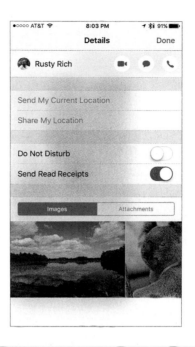

Figure 12.20

The Details screen in Messages enables you to access information about specific people you're communicating with and manage that conversation.

PARTICIPATING IN A GROUP CONVERSATION

If you participate in a group messaging conversation and it becomes too active and annoying, it's possible to opt out of the discussion. To do this, from the conversation screen, tap the Details option, and then turn on the Do Not Disturb feature. Turn off this virtual switch if you want to rejoin the conversation later.

To exit out of the conversation altogether, tap the Details option and select the Leave This Conversation option.

Also from the Details screen, it's possible to add new people to the group conversation by tapping the Add Contact option.

> **TIP**   It's possible to use Siri to dictate and send text messages using your voice. To do this, activate Siri and say something like, "Send text message to Rusty Rich." When Siri says, "What would you like it to say?" speak your message, and then confirm it. When prompted, tell Siri to send the text message you dictated. Siri can also be used to read your newly received text messages, so that you don't have to look at or touch the iOS device's screen.

TIP   To start a group message, launch the Messages app, tap the Compose icon from the Messages screen (or pane), and enter the cell phone number (or iMessage contact info) for one person at a time in the To field. Separate each recipient with a comma, or tap the + icon to the right of the To field. All the recipients you add to the To field will become part of the group message.

When engaged in a group message conversation, the name and profile image (if available) of each participant is displayed at the very top of the conversation screen. Tap the Info (i) icon to add or delete people from the group and manage the group conversation.

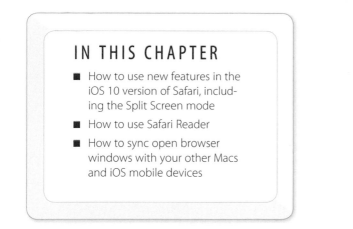

IN THIS CHAPTER

- How to use new features in the iOS 10 version of Safari, including the Split Screen mode
- How to use Safari Reader
- How to sync open browser windows with your other Macs and iOS mobile devices

13

SURF THE WEB MORE EFFICIENTLY USING SAFARI

Chances are, if you know how to use a Mac or PC, you already know how to surf the Web using a browser such as Safari, Microsoft Edge, Firefox, or Google Chrome on your computer.

The Safari web browser on your iPhone (shown in Figure 13.1) or iPad (shown in Figure 13.2) offers the same basic functionality as the web browser for your desktop or laptop computer, but it's designed to maximize the iPhone or iPad's touchscreen and screen size.

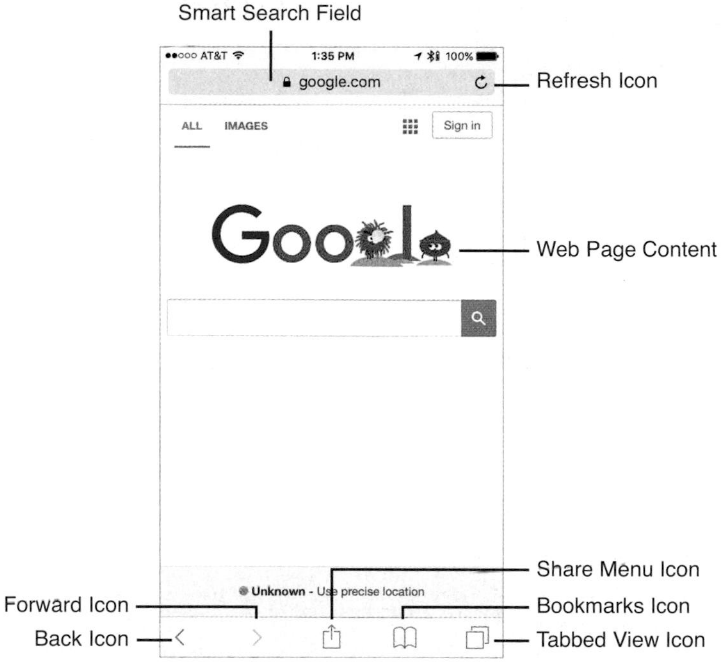

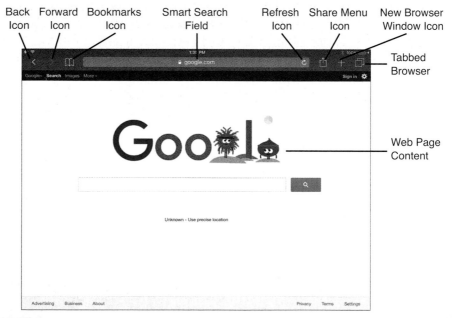

Figure 13.1

The main screen of the Safari web browser on the iPhone.

Figure 13.2

The main screen of the Safari web browser on the iPad.

 **WHAT'S NEW** Perhaps the most anticipated feature offered by the iOS 10 version of Safari is the capability to use Split Screen mode and have two independent web browser windows open at the same time on the iPad.

To use this new feature, launch Safari, and in the Smart Search field, type the first website address (URL) you want to visit.

Next, tap the + icon to open a second browser window, and enter the website address (URL) for the second website you want to visit. Two browser tabs are now displayed below the Smart Search field (see Figure 13.3).

Place your finger on either browser tab and drag it down and to the left or right side of the screen. Release your finger, and Split Screen mode launches. At this point, the two browser windows are running independently of each other (as shown in Figure 13.4).

To close one of the browser windows, tap the X icon near the top-left corner of the window you want to close.

Browser Window Tabs

Figure 13.3

When two browser tabs are open, drag one down and to the edge of the screen.

Figure 13.4

Two web browser windows can now be viewed side-by-side.

> **☑ TIP**   Using the Handoff function, you can begin surfing the Web using
> Safari on one of your supported Macs or iOS mobile devices and then pick up
> exactly where you left off on another, as long as all the equipment is linked to the
> same iCloud account. (Only iOS devices with the Lightning connector and 2012
> Macs and newer support this feature.)
>
> To turn on the Handoff feature, launch Settings, tap the General option, and then
> tap the Handoff option. From the Handoff submenu, turn on the virtual switch
> associated with the Handoff feature. This must be done on each device. Also turn
> on your device's Bluetooth feature.

CUSTOMIZING YOUR WEB SURFING EXPERIENCE

As you'd expect from your iPhone or iPad, surfing the Web is a highly customizable
experience. For example, you can hold your device in portrait or landscape mode
and, on most websites, you can also zoom in on or zoom out of speciflc areas or
content. To do this, use the reverse-pinch finger gesture (to zoom in) or the pinch
gesture (to zoom out), or double-tap a specific area of the screen to zoom in or
out. Keep in mind that zooming does not work when you're viewing a mobile-
optimized website.

To further customize your web surfing experience, launch Settings and tap the
Safari option. The Safari submenu (shown in Figure 13.5) offers a handful of customizable options. Here's a summary of what each is used for:

■ **Search Engine**—The Smart Search field is used to enter specific website
   addresses (*URLs*) and to find what you're looking for on the Web via a search
   engine, such as Google, Yahoo!, Bing, or DuckDuckGo. This option enables
   you to select your default (favorite) Internet search engine.

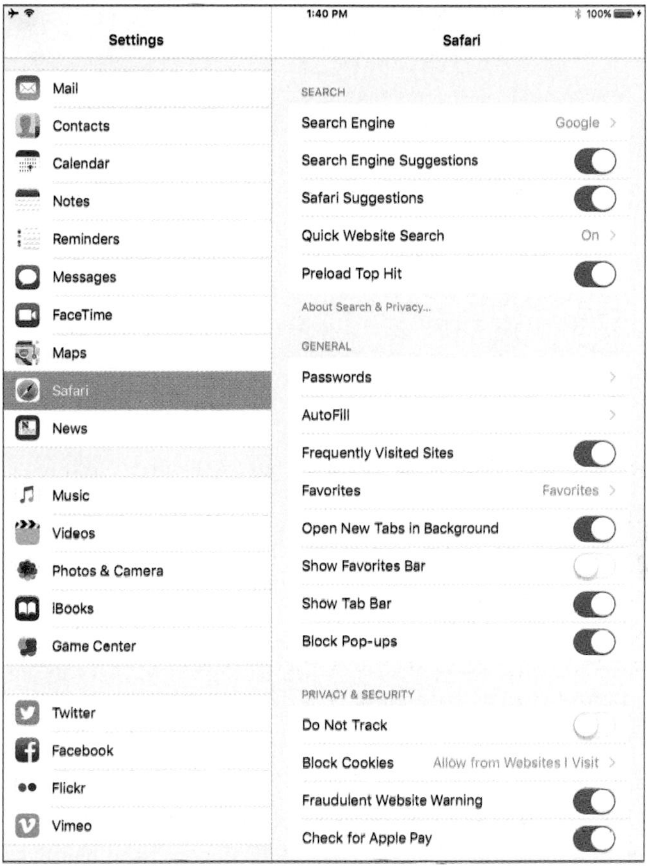

Figure 13.5

Customize your web surfing experience when using Safari from within Settings on your iOS device.

> **NOTE** DuckDuckGo.com is a search engine that does not track your web surfing behaviors or activities, so it offers a more private experience. However, you can use Safari's enhanced Privacy features to prevent your web surfing activities from being tracked, regardless of which search engine you're using.
>
> From the Safari menu in Settings, turn on the virtual switch associated with the Do Not Track option (refer to Figure 13.5).
>
> It's also possible to open a private browsing session by tapping the browser window icon and then tapping the Private option.

TIP The Safari-related Settings options, labeled Search Engine Suggestions, Safari Suggestions, Quick Website Search, and Preload Top Hit can be turned on or off from within Settings.

Search Engine Suggestions, for example, automatically offers additional (related) search term suggestions when you enter a website address or search term in Safari's Search field. Spotlight Suggestions shows related websites when you perform a search using the Search feature in the iOS 10 version of Safari.

Quick Website Search can be used to search a specific website for a specific term. For example, enter "Wiki New York" into the Search field to access the Wikipedia website and display information related to New York.

Turn on the Preload Top Hit option if you want your favorite and most frequented websites to be displayed first when performing a relevant search.

These options determine when website suggestions are offered when using Safari's Search field, Spotlight Search, or other search-related functions.

- **Passwords**—Safari can automatically store the passwords you create and use to access various websites. By accessing this feature, you can view the stored database of website-related passwords collected by Safari and edit this database by tapping the Edit option.

- **Autofill**—When turned on, this feature helps you fill in online-based forms by remembering your responses and automatically inserting your information into the appropriate fields. It also pulls information from your own Contacts app entry. Autofill is particularly useful when shopping online.

  To customize this option and link your personal contact entry to Safari, tap the AutoFill option, turn on the Use Contact Info option, and then tap My Info to select your own Contacts entry.

  You can also set whether Safari remembers names and passwords for specific websites you visit, as well as credit card information that you use to make online purchases. Tap the Saved Credit Cards option to add or edit credit card information you have securely stored in Safari for use when making online purchases. This functionality is part of what Apple calls iCloud Keychain.

- **Frequently Visited Websites**—Turn on this feature to display websites you frequent the most often when performing a search, as well as before you enter information into Safari's Search field or into Spotlight Search.

- **Favorites**—This feature serves as a shortcut for accessing websites you frequently visit or that you have favorited. As you begin typing a website address or website name into the Search field, Safari accesses your Favorites list and auto-inserts the appropriate website URL. When you tap the Search field, a screen with icons representing sites in your Favorites list is displayed. Your Favorites list of websites automatically syncs between your Macs, PCs, and iOS mobile devices that are linked to the same iCloud account. This option now enables you to choose a specific folder where your favorite bookmarks are stored in the device you're using.

> **TIP** If you've created custom Bookmark folders when using Safari on your Mac, you can access and manage them from your iOS mobile device. Plus from the Favorite option within Settings, it's possible to make one of these custom folders your default.

- **Open Links (iPhone only)**—Any time a new web page opens as a result of you tapping a link, this feature determines whether the new browser window is opened as the new active browser window or opened in the background as a tabbed browser window.

- **Open New Tabs in Background (iPad only)**—Any time a new web page opens as a result of you tapping a link, this feature determines whether the new browser window is opened as the new active browser window or opened in the background as a tabbed browser window. How this option works depends on options you have selected on the Safari submenu of Settings.

- **Show Favorites Bar (iPad)**—When you turn on the virtual switch associated with this feature, your Favorites Bar displays across the top of the Safari screen, just below the row of command icons and the Search field. The default setting for this feature is off because it utilizes some of your onscreen real estate.

- **Show Tab Bar (iPad)**—When turned on, if multiple browser windows are open in Safari, tabs for each window are displayed along the top of the screen, just below the row of command icons and the Search field. The default setting for this feature is on. This makes it faster and easier to quickly switch between open browser windows.

- **Block Pop-Ups**—When turned on, this feature prevents a website you're visiting from creating and displaying extra windows or opening a bunch of unwanted browser tabs. The default for this option is turned on because this makes for a more enjoyable web-surfing experience.

- **Do Not Track**—By default, when you surf the Web using Safari, the web browser remembers all the websites you visit and creates a detailed History list that you can access to quickly revisit websites. By turning on the Do Not Track feature, Safari does not store details about the websites you visit.

- **Block Cookies**—Many websites use cookies to remember you and your personalized preferences when you're visiting that site. Cookies contain data that gets saved in your iPhone or iPad and is accessible by the websites you revisit. When this option is turned on, Safari does not accept cookies from websites you visit. Thus, you must reenter site-specific preferences and information each time you visit that site. The Block Cookies submenu offers four options: Always Block (meaning all cookies are blocked), Allow from Current Websites Only, Allow from Websites I Visit, and Always Allow (meaning no cookies are blocked).

- **Fraudulent Website Warning**—Turn on this feature to help prevent you from visiting impostor websites designed to look like real ones, which have been created for the purpose of committing fraud or identity theft. It's not foolproof, but this feature gives you an added level of protection, especially if you use your iOS device for online banking, shopping, and other financial transactions.

- **Check for Apple Pay**—When turned on, this features checks to see whether Apple Pay is set up and will work to make purchases on the website you're visiting.

- **Clear History and Website Data**—Use this feature to delete the contents of Safari's History folder in which details about all the websites you have visited are stored. At the same time, cookies (data pertaining to specific websites you've visited) are also deleted.

- **Use Cellular Data**—This option enables your iPhone or iPad to use the cellular data service (as opposed to a Wi-Fi Internet connection) to download Reading List information to your device from your iCloud account so that it can be read offline. The option is available on all iPhones, as well as iPads with Cellular + Wi-Fi capabilities.

- **Advanced**—View details about website-specific data that Safari has collected. You can manually delete this information. You also can enable or disable the JavaScript feature.

USING TABBED BROWSING WITH SAFARI

Safari's main screen contains the various command icons used to navigate the Web. On the iPhone, these icons are displayed along the bottom of the Safari screen, while the smart Search field is displayed along the top of the screen.

If you're using Safari on an iPad, the Title bar displays all of Safari's command icons along the top of the screen, unless you're using Split Screen mode, in which case the icons are displayed along the bottom of the screen.

Immediately below the Title bar, if you have the option turned on, your personalized Favorites Bar is displayed. Below the Favorites Bar, the Tabs bar becomes visible if you have more than one web page loaded in Safari at any given time (and you have this featured turned on).

SWITCHING BETWEEN WEB PAGES ON AN iPHONE

The iPhone version of tabbed browsing involves Safari opening separate browser windows for each active web page. Tap the Tabbed View icon located in the bottom-right corner of the Safari screen to quickly switch between open browser windows (shown in Figure 13.6), because only one at a time can be viewed.

Figure 13.6

Safari's Tab view is shown here on the iPhone. To open a new page, tap the + at the bottom center of the screen, or tap a web page preview thumbnail to open it.

> **✓ TIP** If you press on the + option for a second or two, a Recently Closed Tabs menu screen appears. You can easily reopen a previously visited but closed browser window by tapping an item listed (which is based on your personal web surfing history).

When you're viewing the Tab View screen, tap the New Browser Window (+) icon to create a new (empty) browser window, and then manually surf to a new website by typing a URL or search term into the Smart Search field, selecting a favorite icon, or selecting a bookmark.

> **✓ TIP** When viewing the Tab View screen in Safari, tap the Private option to turn on the Private web surfing mode only for the newly open browser windows. This prevents Safari from storing details about the websites you visit and syncing this information with your iCloud account. When you're using this privacy feature, the background color of Safari's toolbar changes to dark gray.

To switch between active (viewable) browser windows that are open, simply tap one of the web page thumbnails displayed. Swipe up and down to scroll through the browser window thumbnails. To close a window (tab), tap its X icon.

> **✓ TIP** To access browser windows open on your other computers or iOS mobile devices, scroll down to the bottom of the Tab View screen (on the iPhone) to see listings for open browser windows on your Mac(s) and/or other iOS mobile devices linked to the same iCloud account. Tap any of these listings to pick up exactly where you left off on that other device.

Tap Done to exit the Tab View screen and return to the main Safari web browser screen. Alternatively, tap any web page thumbnail displayed in the Tab View screen to open that browser window and continue your web surfing experience at the selected web page.

USING TABBED BROWSING ON THE iPAD

When you tap a link in a web page that causes a new web page to automatically open, a new tab in Safari is created and displayed. Tabs are shown in Figure 13.7, and each represents a separate open browser window.

Figure 13.7
On the iPad, open browser window tabs are displayed along the top of the screen. Tap a tab to quickly switch between open browser windows.

> **NOTE** Keep in mind that on the iPad, tabs are not displayed if the Show Tab Bar option is turned off from the Safari submenu of Settings. Turning off Show Tab Bar and Show Settings Bar enables you to save onscreen real estate that can then be used to display more of the web pages you're visiting. Having these features turned on, however, makes switching between browser windows and reloading frequently visited websites faster and more convenient.

As you're viewing a web page, to simultaneously open another web page, tap the New Browser Window (+) icon near the top-right corner of the Safari screen (between the Share and Tab View icons). When you do this, a new tab is created for an empty browser window. This enables you to visit a different web page without closing the web page(s) you're currently viewing.

The Tab bar can display multiple tabs at once. To instantly switch between web pages, tap the desired tab. The website name (or web page title) is displayed in the tab for easy reference.

To close a tab, tap the small x that appears on the left side of that tab (refer to Figure 13.7).

> **☑ TIP** As you're surfing the Web using your iPad, tap the Tab View icon in the top-right corner of the screen to display all the open browser windows on each of your other Macs and/or iOS mobile devices linked to the same iCloud account. Tap any of these preview windows or listings to open that browser window on your iPad and pick up exactly where you left off when using the other computer or device.

CLEANING UP SCREEN CLUTTER WITH SAFARI'S READER OPTION

Safari Reader enables you to select a compatible website page; strip out graphic icons, ads, and other unwanted elements that cause onscreen clutter; and then read just the text (and view related photos) from that web page.

The Safari Reader works only with compatible websites. If the feature is available while you're viewing a web page, the Reader icon (as shown in Figures 13.8 and 13.9) is displayed before that web page's URL on the extreme left side of the Smart Search field.

Reader Icon

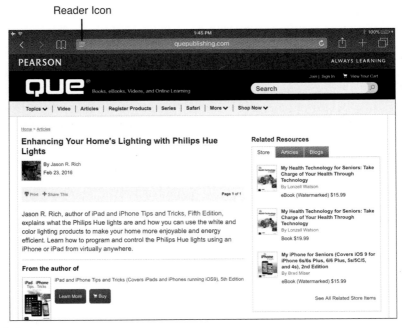

Figure 13.8

An article from QuePublishing.com, without the Reader feature active (shown on an iPad in landscape mode).

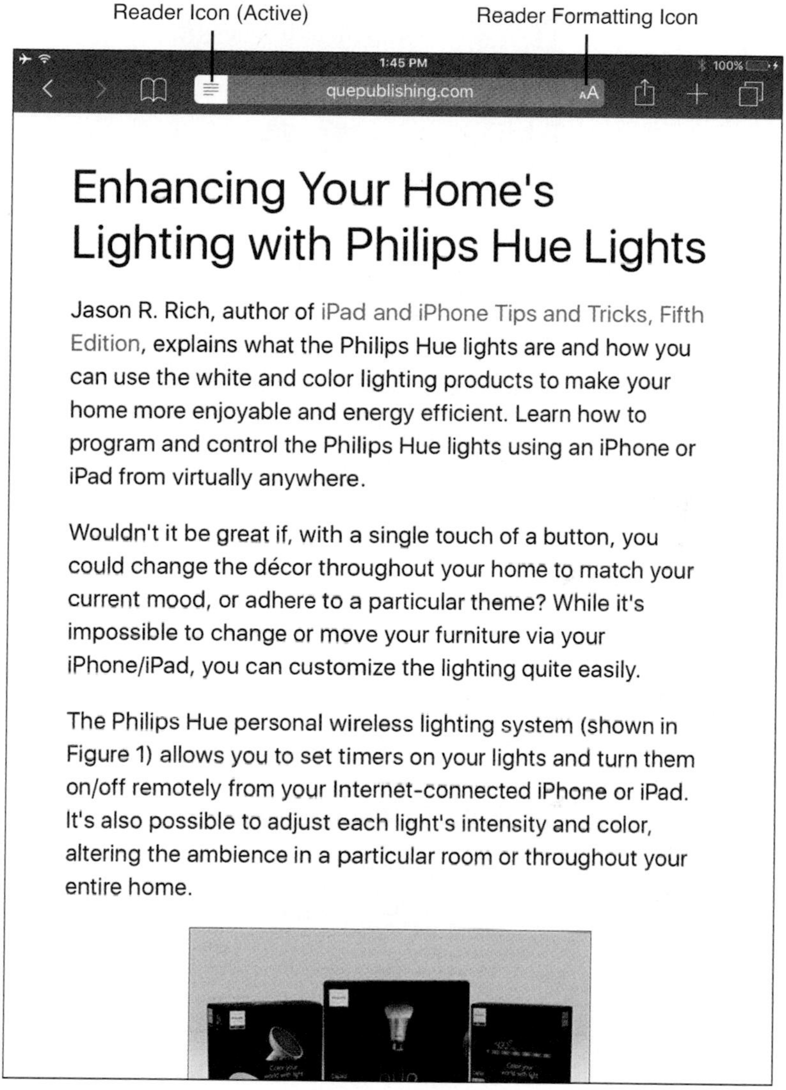

Reader Icon (Active) Reader Formatting Icon

Enhancing Your Home's Lighting with Philips Hue Lights

Jason R. Rich, author of iPad and iPhone Tips and Tricks, Fifth Edition, explains what the Philips Hue lights are and how you can use the white and color lighting products to make your home more enjoyable and energy efficient. Learn how to program and control the Philips Hue lights using an iPhone or iPad from virtually anywhere.

Wouldn't it be great if, with a single touch of a button, you could change the décor throughout your home to match your current mood, or adhere to a particular theme? While it's impossible to change or move your furniture via your iPhone/iPad, you can customize the lighting quite easily.

The Philips Hue personal wireless lighting system (shown in Figure 1) allows you to set timers on your lights and turn them on/off remotely from your Internet-connected iPhone or iPad. It's also possible to adjust each light's intensity and color, altering the ambience in a particular room or throughout your entire home.

Figure 13.9

The same article from QuePublishing.com but with the Reader feature active (shown on an iPad in portrait mode for easier viewing).

☑ **TIP**   When using the Reader feature, tap the AA icon on the right side of the Smart Search field in Safari to access a menu that enables you to change the font used to display the text, as well as decrease or increase the size of the text (shown in Figure 13.10).

Figure 13.10
Use this menu to adjust the font and font size used to display the text when using Safari's Reader feature.

Tap the Reader icon a second time to return the web page to its normal appearance.

CREATING AND MANAGING READING LISTS

As you're surfing the Web, you might come across specific web pages, articles, or other information that you want to refer to later. In Safari, it's possible to create a bookmark for that website URL and have it displayed as part of your Bookmarks list or as part of your Favorites Bar. Another option, however, is to add a web page to your Safari Reading List. In addition to just storing the web page's URL, Reading List stores the actual content of that page for later viewing (including offline viewing).

> **NOTE** The Reading List feature downloads entire web pages for offline viewing, as opposed to simply storing website addresses that you can refer to later. Although this feature downloads text and photos associated with a web page, it does not download animated graphics, video, or audio content associated with that page.

To add a website or web-based article to your personalized Reading List for later review, tap the Share icon, and then tap the Add to Reading List icon in Safari's Share menu.

To later access your Reading List to view any of the stored web pages or articles, tap the Bookmarks icon, and then tap the Reading List tab. Figure 13.11 shows an example of a Reading List. The Reading List tab looks like eyeglasses.

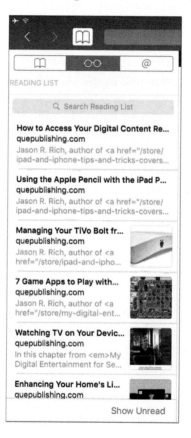

Figure 13.11

Creating a Reading List is another way to store links related to specific content on the Web that you want to easily be able to find again and access later.

TIP Like your Bookmarks list and Favorites Bar, the items stored in your Reading List automatically sync with your iCloud account and are almost instantly made available on any other computer or iOS device linked to your iCloud account.

WORKING WITH BOOKMARKS

When you tap the Bookmarks icon on an iPad, the Bookmarks menu appears along the left side of the screen. It remains visible until you tap the Bookmarks icon again. On the iPhone, when you tap the Bookmarks icon, the Bookmarks menu is displayed on a new screen in the Safari app.

At the top of the Bookmarks menu are three tabs. The leftmost tab (shaped like a book) is the Bookmarks tab. When you tap it, your saved list of website bookmarks is displayed. The center tab is the Reading List tab. Tap it to reveal your reading list (refer to Figure 13.11).

The Shared Links tab (represented by the @ symbol) enables you to see a list of website links shared with you by your Contacts, as well as subscriptions to RSS feeds or social media accounts (including Twitter). Set this up by tapping the Subscriptions option in the lower-right corner of this menu.

After you tap the Subscriptions option, add compatible social media accounts (such as Twitter), or if you're visiting a website or blog that has an RSS feed associated with it, visit that site and tap the Add Current Site option to make it a subscribed feed. From the Subscriptions panel, you can then delete a subscribed feed by tapping its corresponding – icon.

SHARING WEB CONTENT IN SAFARI

The iOS 10 version of Safari makes sharing web links and managing web page content extremely easy, thanks to a handful of available options offered by the expanded Share menu. The Share menu (shown in Figure 13.12), which you access by tapping the Share icon, offers a variety of features for sharing, printing, and managing web page content.

> **NOTE** The options available to you from the Share menu vary depending on several factors, including the content you're viewing as well as whether you have Facebook, Twitter, and other third-party apps set up to work with iOS 10.

> **TIP** If you have the AirDrop feature turned on, when you access the Share menu, the AirDrop option is available. This enables you to wirelessly share content with nearby (compatible) Mac, iPhone, iPad, or iPod touch users. Some older Mac and iOS mobile device models don't support AirDrop.

Figure 13.12

Safari's expanded Share menu offers a handful of ways to store, manage, print, and share web page content.

The following options are often available from the Share menu but vary based on the content you're viewing and how you have integration with some Sharing-related options set up:

- **Message**—Send details about the web page you're currently viewing to one or more other people via text message using the Messages app (without having to leave Safari).

- **Mail**—To share a website URL with others via email, select the Mail option. In Safari, an outgoing email window appears.

    Fill in the To field with the recipient's email address and tap the Send icon. The website URL automatically is embedded in the body of the email, with the website's heading used as the email's subject. Before you send the email, you can add text to the body of the email message and/or change the subject.

- **Reminders**—Create a new item in one of your lists in the Reminders app that contains the web page URL and content that you're currently viewing. Tap Options to choose which Reminders list the web page content should be added to, add a date/time and/or location-based alert, set a Priority, and add optional text-based notes with the new reminder.

- **Notes**—Use this feature to gather the content from the web page you're viewing and quickly export it to a note in the Notes app. After tapping the Notes app icon on the Share menu, tap the Choose Note option to select an existing note in the Notes app to add the web page content to, or select the

New Note option to create a new note from scratch. You can also add text-based notes to the web page content by tapping the Add Text to Your Note option.

- **Twitter**—Tap this option to create an outgoing tweet that automatically has the selected website URL attached. When the Twitter window appears, enter your tweet message (up to 140 characters). Tap the Send icon when the message is composed and ready to share with your Twitter followers.

> **TIP** If you're managing multiple Twitter accounts from your iOS mobile device, in the outgoing tweet window, tap the From field, and then select from which of your Twitter accounts you want to send the tweet you're composing.

- **Facebook**—Thanks to Facebook integration within iOS 10, it's possible to update your Facebook status and include details about the web page you're currently viewing.

- **Other Compatible Third-Party Apps**—A growing number of third-party apps enable you to export content from Safari to be imported into another app. When you have one or more of these compatible apps installed on your iPhone or iPad, app icons for them are displayed in the Share menu.

- **More (Top)**—Located to the extreme right of the app icons related to Safari's Share feature is a More (…) icon. Tap it to customize which app icons appear in Safari's Share menu. You can reorder these app icons by placing your finger on an app icon's Move icon and dragging it up or down in the Activities list. Tap Done to save your changes.

- **Add To Favorites**—Add a listing for the website you're currently viewing to your Safari Favorites list. This list syncs with iCloud and will be updated on all the Macs, PCs, and iOS mobile devices that you have linked to the same iCloud account.

- **Add Bookmark**—Tap this option to add a bookmark to your personal Bookmarks list. When you opt to save a bookmark, an Add Bookmark window appears. Here, you can enter a title for the bookmark and decide whether you want to save it as part of your Bookmarks menu or in your Favorites Bar. It's also possible to create separate subfolders in your Bookmarks menu to organize your saved bookmarks.

> **NOTE** When using Safari on the iPhone, you can maintain a Favorites list; however, to conserve onscreen space, a Favorites Bar is not displayed across the top of the Safari screen like it is on an iPad. Instead, on an iPhone, the Favorites list is displayed as an additional Bookmark folder when you tap the Bookmarks icon.
>
> When using an iPad, if you turn off the Show Favorites Bar option (found on the Safari submenu within Settings), this is also the case.

- **Add to Reading List**—Instead of adding a web page URL to your Bookmarks list or Favorites Bar, you can save it in your Reading List for later reference.

- **Add to Home Screen**—Save a website URL in the form of a Home screen shortcut icon.

- **Open in News**—Transfer the web content you're viewing in Safari to the News app, where it will be formatted and become viewable like any news article that's accessible from the For You screen.

- **Copy**—Use this command to copy the URL for the web page you're looking at to the virtual clipboard that's built in to iOS 10. You can then paste that information into another app.

- **Print**—Wirelessly print a website's contents to any AirPrint-compatible printer that's set up to work with your iOS mobile device. To print a web page, tap the Print command. From the Printer Options screen, select the printer you want to use, and then choose the number of copies you want printed. Tap the Print icon at the bottom of the Print Options window to send the web page document to your printer.

- **Find On Page**—Quickly search the open web page for a keyword or search phrase. When you tap this icon, the iPhone's or iPad's virtual keyboard appears, along with a new Search field. Type what you're looking for, and the matching text is highlighted in yellow in the web page you're viewing. Use the up and down arrow icons to scroll through the various search results one at a time. Tap Done to exit this feature.

- **Request Desktop Site**—Anytime you visit a website using the iOS 10 edition of Safari, if a mobile version of the website is offered, that's the version that automatically loads. A mobile website has been custom formatted to accommodate the smaller iPhone or iPad screen size (compared to a full-sized computer monitor). However, if you'd prefer to switch to viewing the Desktop version of the website, tap the Request Desktop Site icon, and if available, this version of the website loads. You can then use the zoom in and zoom out finger gestures, as well as swipe finger gestures to navigate around the web page.

■ **More (Bottom)**—This More (…) icon is located to the extreme right of the second row of command icons displayed in the Share menu. From the Activities menu, adjust the order in which the command icons are displayed in the Share menu, plus customize some options that relate to third-party apps and your ability to share Safari content with those apps.

CREATING, MANAGING, AND SYNCING SAFARI BOOKMARKS

Your iOS device automatically syncs your Bookmarks and related Safari data with your other iOS mobile devices, as well as the compatible web browsers on your primary computer(s).

To activate iCloud sync functionality as it relates to Safari, launch Settings and then tap the iCloud option. When the iCloud Control Panel appears, make sure your iCloud account is listed at the top of the screen, and then turn on the virtual switch associated with the Safari option. This must be done on each of your iOS mobile devices just once.

Once this feature is turned on, your Bookmarks list, Favorites Bar, open browser windows (tabs), Safari Reading List, and Keychain data are automatically and continuously synced with your iCloud account. Thus, when you add a new bookmark while surfing the Web on your iPad, for example, within seconds that same bookmark appears in your Bookmarks list on your iPhone and on Safari that's running on your Mac.

> ☑ **TIP** For Windows PC users, if you download the optional iCloud for Windows software (www.apple.com/icloud/setup/pc.html), your Bookmarks and related web browser data on your PC sync with your iOS mobile device(s) and Mac(s), and vice versa. Simply add a check mark to the Bookmarks option displayed in the iCloud Control Panel.
>
> This feature is compatible with the Microsoft Edge, Firefox, and Chrome web browsers. When prompted, simply select which web browser you want to sync your Safari bookmarks and data with.

SYNCING USERNAMES AND PASSWORDS USING iCLOUD

When the iCloud Keychain feature is turned on (on each of your iOS mobile devices and Macs), any time you enter a username and password for a website you visit, Safari stores that information and syncs it in your personal iCloud account. Then, any time you revisit that website on any of your Macs or iOS mobile devices that are linked to the same iCloud account, your username and password for that website are remembered and you're automatically logged in.

NOTE iCloud Keychain also remembers credit card information you use when making online purchases from a website. All usernames, passwords, and credit card details are stored using 256-bit AES encryption to maintain security.

WHAT'S NEW Safari now supports Apple Pay and enables you to make online purchases when you visit participating websites. Instead of manually entering your credit card details when making an online purchase, select the Apple Pay option, and then place your finger on the Touch ID sensor to confirm the purchase.

To set up this feature, launch Settings, tap the Wallet & Apple Pay option, and then tap the Add Credit or Debit Card option to link one or more of your credit or debit cards to your Apple Pay account.

Be sure to select your default shipping address, email address, and phone number to make the checkout process faster when shopping online.

To turn on and begin using iCloud Keychain, launch Settings and tap the iCloud option. Then, from the iCloud Control Panel, turn on the virtual switch associated with the Keychain option. Follow the onscreen prompts that walk you through the feature's built-in security precautions.

Next, return to the main Settings menu and tap the Safari option. Tap the AutoFill option, and turn on the virtual switches associated with Use Contact Info, Names and Password, and/or Credit Cards. Also, tap the My Info option and select your own entry from your Contacts app database.

NOTE For your security, online banking, credit card, and financial websites do not support iCloud Keychain. When you visit these websites, Safari might remember your username but you must manually enter your password each time.

When using this feature, it's a good strategy to also activate the Passcode Lock feature of your iOS mobile device to prevent unauthorized people from accessing personal information when using your iPhone or iPad to surf the Web.

> **TIP** If you also want iCloud Keychain to store your credit card details for when you shop online, turn on the virtual switch associated with the Credit Cards option. Then, tap the Saved Credit cards option and enter your credit card details. You need to do this only once.

Using iCloud Keychain, you no longer need to remember the unique usernames and passwords that you associate with each of the websites you frequently visit. Plus, to make your web surfing experience even more secure, you can use the built-in Password Generator feature to create highly secure passwords for you (which the web browser then remembers).

LAUNCHING YOUR FAVORITE WEBSITES VIA HOME SCREEN ICONS

A time-saving alternative to creating bookmarks for your most frequented websites is to create a Home screen shortcut icon for each of these websites. When you do this, an icon for that website is displayed on your device's Home screen. When you tap it, Safari launches and the selected website automatically loads.

To create a Home screen icon, surf to one of your favorite websites. After it loads, tap the Share icon, and then tap the Add to Home Screen button.

The Add to Home window appears. It displays a thumbnail image of the website you're visiting and enables you to enter the title for the website (which is displayed below the icon on your device's Home screen). Next, tap the Add option in the upper-right corner of the window.

After you create a Home screen icon for a web page, it can be treated like any other app icon. You can move it around on the Home screen, add the icon to a folder, or delete the icon from the Home screen.

> **TIP** Without manually launching Safari, it's possible to look up and access web content using the Spotlight Search feature built in to iOS 10. Plus, Siri is also fully compatible with Safari. Activate Siri and use verbal commands like, "Launch Safari," "Search the web for *[topic]*," or "Google *[topic]*." It's also possible to ask a question and have Siri search the Web for the answer.

WHAT'S NEW If you're using an iPhone with 3D Touch capabilities, press and hold down the Safari app icon on the Home screen to reveal a pop-up menu that offers some commonly used web surfing functions (shown in Figure 13.13).

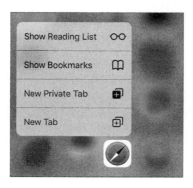

Figure 13.13

This 3D Touch menu is displayed when you press and hold down the Safari app icon on a compatible iPhone's Home screen.

IN THIS CHAPTER

- Get acquainted with the Calendar, Contacts, and Reminders apps
- How to create and collaborate with others using the Notes app
- How to stay organized, on time, and productive with your iOS mobile device
- How to sync your app data across all your devices and iCloud

14

USE CALENDAR, CONTACTS, REMINDERS, AND NOTES

Veteran iPhone or iPad users will quickly discover that the Contacts, Calendar, Reminders, and Notes apps that come bundled with iOS 10 have the same core functionality as before, but each has been given a few minor tweaks to enhance their functionality.

These four apps continue to be fully compatible with iCloud, which makes synchronizing your app-related data straightforward. Plus, from any computer or mobile device that's connected to the Internet, it's possible to access the online versions of these apps, which are automatically populated with all of your most current app-specific data. (To do this, visit www.iCloud.com and sign in using your Apple ID/iCloud account information.)

Plus, in Notification Center, the Calendar and Reminders apps can easily be set up so alerts, alarms, and notifications related to your schedule and lists are consistently displayed as part of the Today or Recent screen. (To have the information appear

on the Today screen in Notification Center, set up and use the app-specific widget. App-specific alerts, alarms, and notifications are otherwise displayed in Notification Center's Recent screen.)

> **NOTE** The features and functions offered by the Calendar, Contacts, Reminders, and Notes apps are virtually identical on all iOS mobile devices, as well as on the Mac. However, due to varying screen sizes, the location of specific command icons, options, and menus often varies. After you get to know how each app works in general, you can easily switch between the iPhone, iPad, Mac, and/or the iCloud.com online-based versions of these apps without confusion.

CUSTOMIZING EACH APP IN iOS 10

With iOS 10, more options are offered within Settings for customizing your experience using the Contacts, Calendar, Reminders, and Notes apps. Launch Settings, and tap the app name to view that app's submenu. Then, adjust each option to customize your experience using that app.

Elsewhere in Settings, additional app-specific options related to Contacts, Calendar, Reminders, and Notes can also be adjusted. For example

- To adjust iCloud-specific settings related to these apps, launch Settings and tap the iCloud option. Then turn on or off the virtual switch associated with each app.

- To adjust Notification-related options pertaining to these apps, launch Settings and tap the Notifications option. Then tap the app name.

- To adjust Location Services options pertaining to these apps, launch Settings, and then tap the Privacy option. Turn on the master Location Services option, and then from the Location Services submenu, tap the app name.

- To adjust which third-party apps have access to information stored in your Contacts database or in Calendar, Reminders, or Notes, tap Settings, select the Privacy option, and then tap the app name.

- To adjust sounds related to each of these apps, launch Settings, tap the Sound option, and then tap the submenu option related to an app-specific setting. For example, tap Calendar Alerts or Reminder Alerts to select the sound you'll hear each time the Calendar or Reminders apps generates an alert or alarm.

SYNCING APP-SPECIFIC DATA WITH ONLINE-BASED APPS

To sync your Calendar, Contacts, Reminders, and/or Notes data with iCloud, Yahoo!, Google, or Microsoft Exchange–compatible software, you need to make a one-time change in Settings. Launch Settings, and tap the option for an app you want to sync (Calendar, Contacts, Reminders, or Notes). From the submenu screen for that app, tap the Accounts option.

Tap the Add Account option and choose iCloud, Microsoft Exchange, Google, Yahoo!, Outlook.com, or Other. (Tap the Other option if you use a scheduling, contact management, list management, or note-taking software that's not otherwise listed.)

When prompted, enter your name, email address, password, and an account description (as well as any other requested information). After your account is verified, a menu screen in Settings related to that account lists app-specific options, such as Mail, Contacts, Calendars, Reminders, and/or Notes.

Turn on the virtual switch associated with any or all of these options. Your iPhone or iPad can automatically and continuously sync your app-specific data on your iOS device with your online-based account. So, if you turn on the virtual switch associated with Calendars, for example, your schedule data is continuously synchronized.

If you turn on the virtual switches for multiple options, Settings sets up each app appropriately to sync with the chosen account. In Figure 14.1, for example, a Yahoo! account is being set up to sync with an iPhone's Mail, Contacts, Calendar, Reminders, and Notes app.

Figure 14.1

From Settings you can sync existing online or PC/Mac software–based contact management, scheduling, list management, and/or note taking applications with the Contacts, Calendar, Reminders, and/or Notes apps running on your iPhone or iPad.

To sync scheduling and/or contact-related data with Facebook, launch Settings and tap the Facebook option. When prompted, enter your Facebook username and password. Then, near the bottom of the Facebook menu screen in Settings, turn on the virtual switch that's associated with Calendars and/or Contacts.

Periodically tap the Update All Contacts option as you add new online Facebook friends. Calendar and/or Contacts data is imported from Facebook and incorporated into your Calendar and/or Contacts apps. This includes profile pictures and birthday information for your online friends who also have an entry in your Contacts database.

SYNCING APP-SPECIFIC DATA WITH iCLOUD

The Calendar, Contacts, Reminders, and Notes apps work seamlessly when syncing data between your iOS mobile devices, Mac(s), and PC(s) that are linked to the same iCloud account. To set up this feature, launch Settings, tap the iCloud option, and then turn on the virtual switches associated with Contacts, Calendars, Reminders, and/or Notes. This needs to be done only once, but It must be done separately on each device or computer that's linked to the same iCloud account.

> **NOTE** By setting up app-specific data syncing for Contacts, Calendar, Notes, and Reminders via iCloud, your data automatically gets imported into the online version of these apps that are available via iCloud.com (www.iCloud.com). So, when you sign in to iCloud.com using your Apple ID and password, and then launch the online version of Contacts, Calendar, Notes, or Reminders, all of your current app-specific data is available to you. This can be done from any computer or mobile device that's connected to the Internet, even if that computer or device is not normally linked to your iCloud account.

GETTING ACQUAINTED WITH THE CALENDAR APP

With its multiple viewing options for keeping track of the scheduling information stored in it, the Calendar app is a highly customizable scheduling tool. In the Calendar app, any appointment, meeting, activity, or entry that you create and store within the app is referred to as an *event*.

Because the Calendar app can manage and display multiple color-coded calendars at once, when you create a new event, be sure to choose which calendar it gets stored in. For example, you can maintain separate calendars for Work, Personal, Family, and/or Travel.

In Calendar, you can also share some or all of your schedule information with colleagues and maintain several separate, color-coded calendars to keep personal and work-related responsibilities, as well as individual projects, listed separately, while still being able to view them on the same screen.

> **TIP** When you turn on iCloud's Family Sharing feature, a separate color-coded calendar labeled Family is created in the Calendar app. This calendar can be accessed by up to five other family members. Thus, your teens can add details about their after-school activities, sports practices, or drama rehearsals, and weekend family events can be posted for all to see. Plus, everyone can keep tabs on upcoming vacation dates.
>
> Although the Family calendar data is viewable by anyone with Family Sharing access, events stored in other calendars remain private, or viewable only by people you invite to see the information.

CONTROLLING THE CALENDAR VIEW

Launch Calendar from your iOS device's Home screen, and then choose which viewing perspective you'd like to use for your schedule data. Regardless of which view you're using, tap the Today option to immediately jump to the current date on the calendar. The current date is always highlighted with a red dot.

> **TIP** From the Home screen of an iPhone that has 3D Touch capabilities, press and hold your finger on the Calendar app icon to show your next upcoming appointment (event), plus access a shortcut for creating a new event. Tap + Add Event to quickly launch the Calendar app and access the New Event screen.

> **TIP** If event-related information is displayed in an incoming email, such as an upcoming airline flight reservation or restaurant reservation, the Mail app displays an Add Event banner near the top of the email. Tap this banner (which includes a tiny Calendar app icon) to import the event details from the body of the incoming email directly into the Calendar app as a new event.

On the iPad, switching between Calendar views is as easy as tapping the Day, Week, Month, or Year tab displayed at the top center of the Calendar app screen.

On the iPhone and iPad, the Calendar app opens on the last view option that you were using previously. However, on the iPhone, you also have access to a detailed Day, Week, Month, or Year view, as well as a Listing view, which works with the Month or Day view.

> ### ☑ TIP
>
> When the Month calendar view is selected on an iPhone, tap the Listing icon (near the top-right corner of the screen) to display a list of events for the current day (or the day you select). This information is displayed below the month view of the calendar (shown in Figure 14.2).
>
> When you select the Day view in the Calendar app, the Listing icon shows you all your appointments, hour-by-hour, in a scrollable format that enables you to quickly see your schedule for the previous or upcoming days in addition to the currently selected day.

Figure 14.2

The Listing icon in the Calendar app provides an additional way to format and view your schedule on the iPhone's screen.

The Year view shows mini calendars for the entire year (see Figure 14.3). To switch from the Year view to the Month view, tap any month in the Year view.

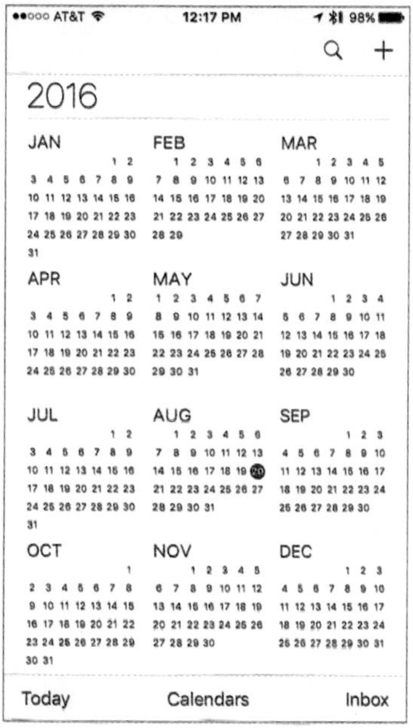

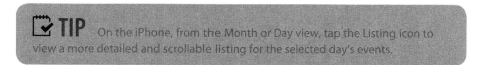

Figure 14.3

Shown here is the Calendar app's Year view on the iPhone.

From the Month view, switch to the Week view by rotating your iPhone from portrait to landscape mode. In other words, hold your smartphone sideways. Also from the Month view, to switch to the Day view, tap a day displayed in the calendar. From the Month view, any day that displays a gray dot in it has event details associated with it.

> **TIP** On the iPhone, from the Month or Day view, tap the Listing icon to view a more detailed and scrollable listing for the selected day's events.

The Year, Month, Week, and Day views in the iPhone version of the Calendar app can be switched in a hierarchical order. If you're in the Day view, for example, you can switch back to the Month view by tapping the Back icon (a left-pointing arrow), which is in the top-left corner of the screen.

Whether you're using the Calendar app on an iPhone or iPad, your Calendar view options include the views described in the following sections.

DAY VIEW

This view displays your events individually, based on the time each event is sched-uled. When using the iPad version of the app, this information is displayed on a split screen. On the left is an hour-by-hour summary of your day, and on the right is a synopsis of the events for that day.

> 📝 **NOTE**   On the iPhone, the Day view (shown in Figure 14.4) displays a week's worth of calendar dates near the top of the screen. Below that, the selected date is displayed, followed by an hour-by-hour rundown of your events.
>
> On the iPad, the Day display is split into two sections. The selected date, along with a week's worth of calendar dates, is displayed at the top of the screen, fol-lowed by a summary listing of appointments and/or events displayed on the left side of the screen. Details about one selected appointment or event are displayed on the right side of the screen by tapping it.

Use the Day view of the Calendar app to see a detailed outline of scheduled events for a single day. Swipe your finger to scroll up or down to see an hour-by-hour summary of that day's schedule.

Figure 14.4

The Day view of the Calendar app lets you see your schedule broken down one day at a time in one-hour increments.

Swipe right or left along the week's worth of calendar days to see upcoming or past dates and to view another day's schedule. Tap a specific day to switch to that date's Day view.

> **☑ TIP** To quickly find an event, tap the Search icon, and then enter any relevant text to help you find the item you're looking for that's stored in the Calendar app. You can also do this with Spotlight Search, or you can make a verbal request using Siri. In the Search field, enter a date, time, name, business, meeting location, or other pertinent information. Tap a search result to view that event listing in detail in the Calendar app.

> **☑ TIP** Displayed in the bottom-right corner of the Calendar screen is the Inbox option. If there's a number within parentheses next to the word Inbox, one or more potential event listings have been sent to you from other people. Tap the Inbox option to view a list of events found in other apps, as well as event invitations from others. Tap Add to Calendar or Ignore for each one.

WEEK VIEW

The Week view uses a grid format to display the days of the week along the top of the screen and time intervals along the left side of the screen (shown in Figure 14.5 on an iPhone). With it, you're given an overview of all events scheduled during a particular week (Sunday through Saturday).

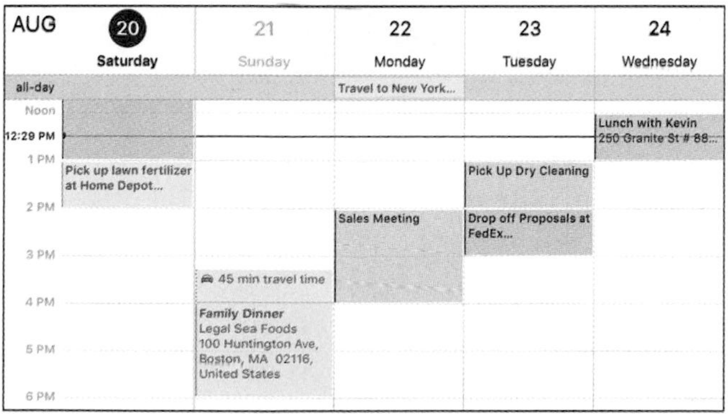

AUG	**20**	21	22	23	24
	Saturday	Sunday	Monday	Tuesday	Wednesday
all-day			Travel to New York...		
Noon					
12:29 PM					Lunch with Kevin 250 Granite St # 88...
1 PM	Pick up lawn fertilizer at Home Depot...			Pick Up Dry Cleaning	
2 PM			Sales Meeting	Drop off Proposals at FedEx...	
3 PM					
4 PM		🚗 45 min travel time			
5 PM		Family Dinner Legal Sea Foods 100 Huntington Ave, Boston, MA 02116, United States			
6 PM					

Figure 14.5

The Calendar app's Week view shown on an iPhone. The horizontal red line indicates the current time.

Scroll along the dates displayed near the top of the screen to quickly view your schedule for past or future weeks.

> ☑ **TIP** To fine-tune this or any other Calendar app view, tap the Calendars option near the bottom center of the screen. A listing of the separate color-coded calendars that the Calendar app is managing is displayed. Tap a listing to add or remove it from the Calendar view you're looking at.
>
> When you remove a calendar from the calendar view, this does not delete any data; it simply hides the events that are stored in that particular calendar from the display.

MONTH VIEW

This view enables you to see a month's worth of events at a time. On the iPhone, tap any single day to immediately switch to the Day view and review a detailed summary of events slated for that day. From the Month view, use your finger to scroll up or down to look at past or future months. On the iPad, use the Day, Week, Month, or Year tabs, located at the top of the screen, to switch Calendar views.

YEAR VIEW

The Year view enables you to look at 12 mini calendars, with minimal detail displayed (refer to Figure 14.3).

ENTERING A NEW EVENT

Regardless of which calendar view you're using, follow these steps to enter a new event:

1. Tap the New Event (+) icon displayed in the upper-right corner of the screen. This causes a New Event window to be displayed (shown in Figure 14.6).

2. The first field in the New Event window is labeled Title. Using the virtual keyboard, enter a title for the event.

3. If a location is associated with the event, tap the Location field located below the Title field and enter an address or location. Entering information into the Location field is optional. You can be as detailed as you want when entering information into this field.

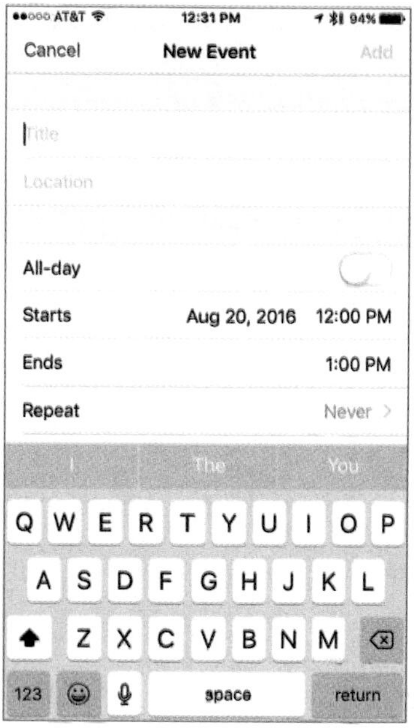

Figure 14.6
Add a new event to the Calendar app from the New Event screen.

📝 **TIP**   Many apps integrate and share scheduling information with the Calendar app. By entering a location, your iOS mobile device can calculate travel time to the event from your current location and give you ample warning related to when you need to leave. The Maps app can also use the location information to provide directions to that event. The more precise Location information you include in this field, the more helpful your iPhone or iPad's various other apps will be.

If you ask Siri a question related to an event's location, such as "Where is my next meeting?" or "How do I get to my next appointment?," the event's location information is used.

📝 **NOTE**   Many of the fields in the New Event screen are optional; in other words, only fill in the fields that are relevant to the new event you're creating. However, the more information you include, the more useful Maps, Siri, and Spotlight Search will be later when you want to refer to event information.

4. If the event lasts for the entire day, turn on the All-Day virtual switch; otherwise, to set the time and date the event begins, tap the Starts field. Use the scrolling Date, Hour, Minute, and AM/PM dials to select the start time for your event.

5. After entering the start time, scroll down and tap the Ends option, and again use the scrolling Date, Hour, Minute, and AM/PM dials to select the end time for your event.

> 🗒 **NOTE**   If the new event you're creating repeats every day, every week, every two weeks, every month, or every year, tap the Repeat option, and choose the appropriate time interval. The default for this option is Never, meaning that it is a nonrepeating, one-time-only event.

6. Turn on the virtual switch associated with the Travel Time option to add between 5 minutes and 2 hours of travel time to that event by tapping one of the listed options. So, if this event turns out to be 1 hour away from your previous event scheduled on the same day, 1 hour's worth of travel time can be added to your schedule. However, if you have a specific location entered in the Location field, your iPhone or iPad can calculate the travel time from wherever you happen to be prior to that event.

> 🔘 **WHAT'S NEW**   Because the Maps app now tracks real-time traffic conditions and integrates with the Calendar app, you will be notified when you need to leave for your next appointment based on the calculated travel time that takes into account current traffic. For this to work, a detailed address for the event must be included in the Location field. You also need to provide a starting location and the mode of transportation you'll be using—driving, walking (when applicable), or public transportation. The Travel Time feature for the event must be turned on (shown in Figure 14.7).

7. If you're managing several calendars in the Calendar app, tap the Calendar option to select in which calendar the new event will be placed. The default calendar is called Home, but you can change this in Settings.

8. To invite other people to the event, tap the Invitees option and, when prompted, fill in the To field with the invitees' names or email addresses. Use their name if they already have a contact entry in the Contacts app; otherwise, enter an email address for each person separated by a comma. The people you add as invitees are sent an email allowing them to respond to the invite. The Calendar app keeps track of RSVPs from event attendees and displays this information in the app.

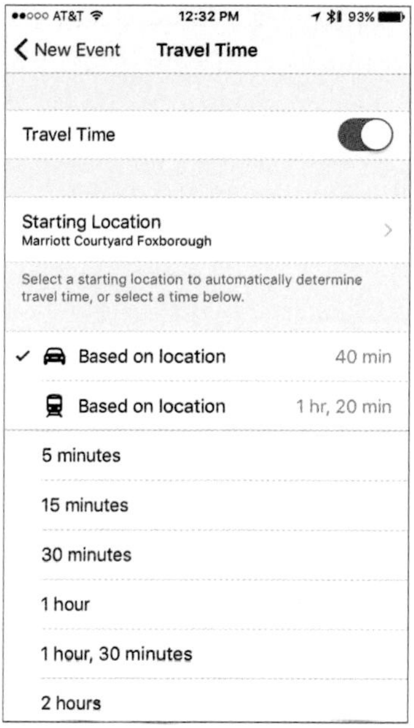

Figure 14.7

Based on traffic conditions, the Calendar app can tell you when to leave for your upcoming appointment.

9. To set an audible alarm for the event, tap the Alert option. The Event Alert window temporarily replaces the Add Event screen. In the Event Alert window, tap the option for how much advance notice you want before the scheduled event. Your options include None, At Time of Event, 5 minutes, 15 minutes, 30 minutes, 1 hour, 2 hours, 1 day, 2 days, or 1 week before the event. Once you tap a selection, you are returned to the Add Event screen.

> **TIP** A Second Alert option is also available from the Add Event screen. If you want to add a secondary alarm to this event, tap the Second Alert option and then set it.

10. Tap the Show As option to classify how you want an event to appear in your calendar. The default option is Busy. This is information others can see if you opt to share specific calendars with other people.

11. Tap the URL field to add a website address associated with the event.

12. Tap the Notes field to add text-based notes you want to associate with the new event. It's also possible to paste content from other apps into the Notes field.

13. Tap the Add option to save the event. Tap the Cancel icon to exit without saving any new information.

> **📝 NOTE** As soon as you create a new event, that information syncs with your iCloud account and all other computers and/or mobile devices that you have linked to that account. If you have the Calendar app set up to sync with another scheduling app or online service, your new data syncs with that app.
>
> This near-instant data synchronization also applies if you delete an event.

USING SIRI TO ENTER NEW EVENTS

Instead of manually entering event information into your iPhone or iPad using the virtual keyboard, or importing/syncing scheduling data from another computer or device, you always have the option to use Siri. Refer to Chapter 3, "Say It and Make It So Using Siri," for more information.

> **✅ TIP** Using Siri, say something like, "When is my next appointment with [name]?" You can also say, "Show me my schedule for Wednesday," or ask, "What's on my calendar for July 7?" to quickly find an event. If you enter information into the Location field as you're creating events, you can later ask Siri, "Where is my next meeting?"

VIEWING INDIVIDUAL APPOINTMENT DETAILS

From any view in the Calendar app, tap an individual event to display the details related to it. When you tap a single event listing, a new Event Details screen opens (shown in Figure 14.8). Tap the Edit option to modify any aspect of the event listing, such as its title, location, start/end time, alert, invitees, or notes.

At the bottom of an event listing (scroll down), a map showing the event's location is provided if the Location field has been filled in.

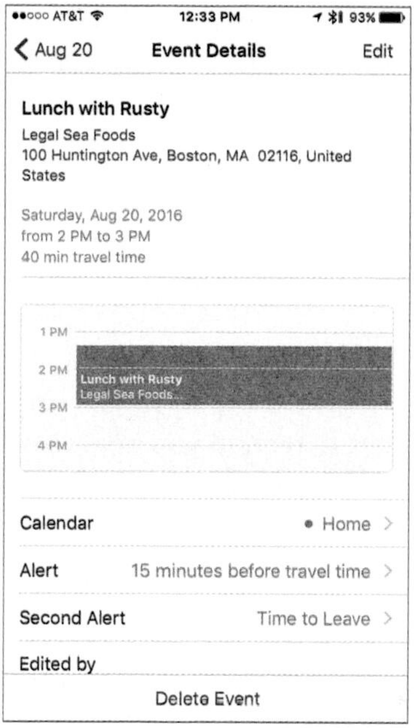

Figure 14.8

Detailed information about each event stored in the Calendar app can easily be viewed.

To delete an event entry entirely, tap the red-and-white Delete Event option at the bottom of the Edit window.

> **TIP** The Calendar app works with several other apps, including Contacts and Notification Center. For example, in Contacts, you can enter someone's birthday into an entry, and that information can automatically be displayed in the Calendar app in a separate Birthdays calendar.
>
> To display birthday listings in Calendar, tap the Calendars button displayed near the bottom center of the screen in the Calendar app, and then tap the Birthdays option to add a check mark to that selection. All recurring birthdays stored in Contacts appear in Calendar.
>
> There are also two options related to the Facebook app that enable you to display all the birthdays for your online Facebook friends, and/or all Facebook Events related to your account in the Calendar app. You can find it under the Facebook heading of the Show Calendars screen/window.

> ✓ **TIP**   In addition to viewing the various calendar views offered in the Calendar app, use the in-app Search or Spotlight Search options to find individual events.

CUSTOMIZING THE CALENDAR APP

There are many ways to customize the Calendar app beyond choosing between the various calendar views. For example, you can set audible alerts and/or use onscreen alerts and banners to remind you of events. You can also display Calendar-related information in the Notification Center and/or on the Lock screen.

> ✓ **TIP**   To customize the audio alert generated by the Calendar app, launch Settings and then select the Sounds option. Tap the Calendar Alerts option and choose a sound from the menu. Choose the None option from the Calendar Alerts menu to set up Calendar so it never plays audible alerts or alarms.

From the Calendar submenu within Settings, determine how far back in your schedule you want to sync appointment data between your primary computer and your iOS device(s) by tapping the Sync option. Your choices include Events 2 Weeks Back, Events 1 Month Back, Events 3 Months Back, Events 6 Months Back, and All Events. All Events is the default option.

Tap the Time Zone Override option, and then turn on the virtual switch associated with this feature if you want the Calendar app to always show event dates and times in your home time zone, regardless of which other time zone you've traveled to. After you turn on the virtual switch associated with this feature, tap the Time Zone option to select a home time zone.

> ❗ **CAUTION**   If you're traveling in another time zone but enter a new event that will take place in the future when you return to your home time zone, when entering the Start time for the new event, be sure to tap the Time Zone option and select your home time zone. Otherwise, the time you enter for the new event will remain in the time zone you're in and will not automatically adjust when you return home.

USING THE CONTACTS APP TO KEEP TRACK OF PEOPLE

The Contacts app stores information pertaining to the people in your life, as well as companies you do business with.

> **NOTE** Contacts is a powerful and customizable contact management database that works with many other apps that also came preinstalled on your iPhone or iPad, including Mail, Calendar, Safari, FaceTime, and Maps, as well as optional apps, like the official Facebook and Twitter apps. It's also fully compatible with Siri and Spotlight Search, along with a growing selection of optional third-party apps.

Your personal contacts database might include people you work with, customers, clients, family members, people from your community with whom you interact (doctors, hairstylist, barber, dry cleaners, and so on), your real-world friends, and your online friends from Facebook, for example.

> **TIP** When you're using an iPhone with Touch 3D capabilities, from the Home screen, press and hold your finger on the Contacts app icon to view a menu that enables you to see the most recent contacts you've been in communication with, as well as quickly create a new contact entry or view your own entry in the Contacts database (which is referred to as My Info).
>
> Be sure to create an entry for yourself in your Contacts database and populate it with as much information as possible, because many other apps will access this information in the future for a variety of reasons.

> **NOTE** As you receive incoming emails, if the sender includes their details in their email and this information is not stored in your Contacts app already, you have the ability to add it. This is also true if the sender updates their contact information and it doesn't match what's stored in the Contacts app. In the Mail app, as you're reading the email, you're given the opportunity to create a new contact or update the existing contact's entry in the Contacts app.
>
> For this feature to work, launch Settings, tap the Contacts option, and then turn on the virtual switch associated with the Contacts Found in Apps option.

DETERMINING WHAT INFORMATION TO STORE IN CONTACTS

Chances are, the same contacts database that you rely on at your office or on your personal computer at home can be synced with your iPhone or iPad and made available to you using the Contacts app. Of course, Contacts can also be used as a standalone app, enabling you to enter new contact entries as you meet people and need to keep track of details about them using your iOS mobile device(s).

The information you maintain in your Contacts database is highly customizable, which means you can keep track of only the information you want or need. For example, in each contact entry, it's possible to store a vast amount of information about a person or company, including multiple phone numbers, addresses, and email addresses. Each field is labeled for easy reference. A Contact entry can include someone's home, work, and cell phone numbers.

> **NOTE** To include some fields that aren't provided by default, tap the Add Field option and select a field type from the submenu.

It's also possible to customize your contacts database to include additional information, such as each contact's photo, as well as detailed and freeform notes related to a contact.

When you're using the Contacts app, your entire contacts database is instantly searchable using data from any field in the database, so even if you have a database containing thousands of entries, you can always find the person or company you're looking for in a matter of seconds, using a wide range of search criteria. This can be done using the Search field in the Contacts app, using the Spotlight Search feature, or with Siri.

INTEGRATING THE CONTACTS APP WITH OTHER APPS

After your contacts database has been populated with entries, Contacts works with many other apps on your iPhone and/or iPad. Here are just a few popular examples:

- When you compose a new email message in Mail, begin typing someone's full name or email address in the To field. If that person's contact information is already stored in Contacts, the relevant email address automatically displays in the email's To field.

- If you're planning a trip to visit a contact, pull up someone's address from your Contacts database, and then quickly obtain driving directions to the person's home or work location from the Maps app. To do this, simply tap their displayed address.

■ Activate Siri and request directions to any person or company with an entry stored in your Contacts database. For example, activate Siri and say, "How do I get to John Doe's house from here?"

■ If you include each person's birthday in your Contacts database, that information can automatically be displayed in the Calendar app and be set up to remind you (in advance) to send a card or gift.

■ As you're creating each Contacts entry, include a photo of that person—by activating the Camera app from the Contacts app to snap a photo, by using a photo stored in the Photos app that you link to the entry, or by acquiring profile photos from social media accounts. For example, to automatically insert profile photos of Facebook friends into the Contacts app, see the section "Add a Photo to a Contacts Entry" later in this chapter.

■ When using FaceTime, create a Favorites list of people you often engage in video calls with, compiled from entries in your Contacts database.

■ From the Messages app, access your Contacts database when filling in the To field as you compose new text messages to be sent via iMessage, text message, or instant message. This means that you can simply type the person's name in the To field, as opposed to their cell phone number or iMessage username.

■ If you're active on Facebook or Twitter, you have the option of adding each contact's Facebook and/or Twitter username to their Contacts entry. When you turn on the Facebook feature, the Contacts app automatically downloads each entry's Facebook profile picture and inserts it into your Contacts database.

When you first launch the Contacts app, its related database is empty; however, you can create and build your database in two ways:

■ Sync the Contacts app with your primary contact management application on your computer, network, or online (cloud)-based service, such as iCloud or Microsoft Outlook.

■ Manually enter contact information directly into the Contacts app.

> **📝 NOTE** The Contacts app that comes preinstalled with iOS 10 is 100 percent compatible with and extremely similar to the Contacts app that comes bundled with OS X Yosemite, OS X El Capitan, or macOS Sierra on the Mac. Thus, be sure to set up each version of the app to sync with each other via iCloud, so you always have access to your entire Contacts database.

As you begin using this app and come to rely on it, it's possible to enter new contact information or edit entries either on your iOS mobile device or using your primary contact management application and keep all the information synchronized, regardless of where the entry was created or modified. Remember, it's also possible to access and work with your Contacts database from iCloud.com using any computer.

VIEWING YOUR CONTACTS

On the iPhone, the All Contacts screen displays an alphabetical listing of all entries in your Contacts database. Along the right side of the screen are alphabetic tabs, and a Search field is located near the top of the screen.

> **NOTE** If you've used the Contacts app previously and it has been running in the background, the last contact entry you viewed will be displayed when you relaunch the app.

On the iPad, near the middle of the screen are alphabetic tabs. A listing of all contacts is displayed along the right side of the screen. Displayed in the top-left corner is a Search field. Use it to find any content stored in the Contacts app. Alternatively, use the Spotlight Search feature or Siri to quickly locate information stored in this app.

> **TIP** Tap the Search field to quickly find a particular entry by entering any keyword associated with an entry, such as a first or last name, city, state, job title, or company name. Any content in your Contacts database is searchable from this Search field.
>
> You can also tap a letter tab on the screen to see all entries "filed" under that letter by a contact's last name, first name, or company name, depending on how you set up the Contacts app using the Mail, Contacts, Calendars option in Settings.

To see the complete listing for a particular entry, tap its listing from the Contacts screen (iPhone) or Contacts listing (iPad). On the iPhone, a new screen shows the specific contact's information (shown in Figure 14.9). On the iPad, the selected contact listing is displayed on the right side of the screen.

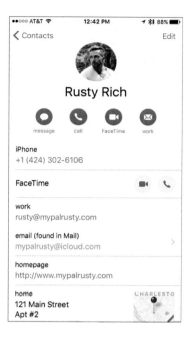

Figure 14.9

A sample contact entry from the Contacts app displayed on an iPhone.

WHAT'S NEW   Based on the information stored in the Contacts database about a particular person, when you view their listing, displayed just below their name and photo (if applicable) are up to four active icons: Message, Call, FaceTime (VIdeo), and Mail. Tap any of these icons to quickly initiate contact with that person using the method that corresponds to the icon (refer to Figure 14.9).

If an entry does not contain information related to a phone number, iMessage username (or cell phone number), FaceTime (Video) username, or email address, these icons aren't active for that entry.

If the person is a friend on Facebook and you have Facebook set up to sync information with Contacts, a tiny Facebook logo is in the upper-left corner of the contact's profile photo.

CREATING A NEW CONTACTS ENTRY

To create a new Contacts entry, tap the New Contact icon (which looks like a plus sign). The New Contact screen opens.

> ✎ **NOTE**   As you're creating each Contacts entry, fill in whichever fields you want. You can always edit a contact entry later to include additional information. The more information you enter, however, the more data the Contacts app will be able to share with Siri and other apps running on your mobile device.

The New Contact screen displays several empty fields related to the entry, starting with the First Name field (shown in Figure 14.10).

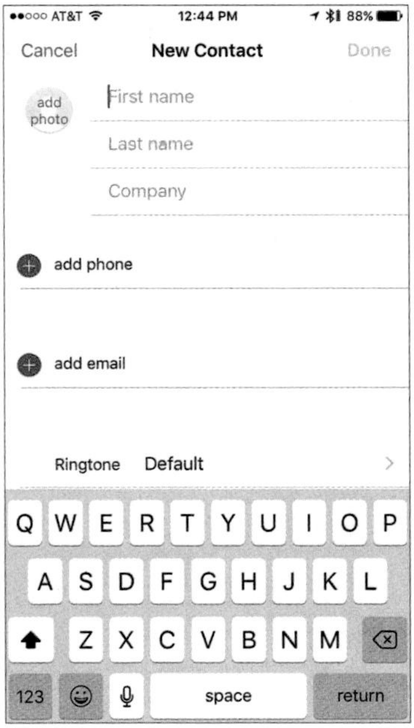

Figure 14.10

From this New Contact screen, create a new contact and include as much information pertaining to that person or company as you want.

Some fields, including Phone, Email, and Mailing Address, enable you to input multiple listings, one at a time. So you can include someone's home phone, work phone, and mobile phone (iPhone) numbers in the entry, for example. Likewise, you can include multiple email addresses, and/or a home address and work address for an individual.

> **☑ TIP** One of the available fields when creating a new Contact entry is labeled Add Related Name. Use this field to add the names of your contact's mother, father, parent, brother, sister, child, friend, spouse, partner, assistant, manager, or other. You can also add your own titles for the Related People field.

> **☑ TIP** It's possible to change the label associated with certain fields (which are displayed in blue) by tapping the field label itself. This reveals a Label menu that offers selectable options for that field. For example, the Label options for the Add Phone field include Home, Work, iPhone, Mobile, Main, Home Fax, Work Fax, Pager, and Other. At the bottom of this Label window, tap the Add Custom Label option to create your own label if none of the listed options applies.
>
> Tap the label title of your choice. A check mark appears next to it, and you are returned to the New Contact screen.

At the bottom of the New Contact screen is the Add Field option. Tap it to reveal a menu containing a handful of additional fields you can add to individual Contacts entries as applicable.

> **☑ NOTE** If there's a field displayed that you don't want to use or display, simply leave it blank as you're creating or editing a Contacts entry.

Each time you add a new mailing address to a contact's entry from within the New Contact screen, the Address field expands to include a Street, City, State, ZIP, and Country field.

After you have filled in all the fields for a particular entry, tap Done. Your new entry is saved and added to your contacts database. It is then synced with your other computers and/or mobile devices.

ADDING A PHOTO TO A CONTACTS ENTRY

To the immediate left of the First Name field is a circle that says Add Photo. When you tap this field, a submenu with two options—Take Photo and Choose Photo—is displayed. If the entry already has a photo associated with it, the Edit Photo and Delete Photo options are also displayed. (You're able to do this only when editing a Contact entry.)

Tap Take Photo to launch the Camera app from within the Contacts app and snap a photo to be linked to the Contacts entry you're creating. Alternatively, tap the Choose Photo option. In this case, the Photos app launches so that you can choose any digital image that's currently stored on your iOS mobile device. When you tap the photo of your choice, a Choose a Photo window displays on the Contacts screen, enabling you to move and scale the image.

> **TIP** As you're previewing the image, use a pinch or reverse-pinch finger motion to zoom in or out, and then hold your finger down on the image and reposition it within the frame.

After cropping or adjusting the selected photo, tap the Use icon in the upper-right corner of the Choose Photo window to link the photo with that contact's entry. The photo you link with an entry is displayed by other apps, like Mail, Messages, and FaceTime, that use the Contacts app data.

> **TIP** If you use an iPhone, or FaceTime on your iPhone or iPad, from the Ringtone option in the New Contact screen, select the specific ringtone you will hear each time that particular contact calls you. Your iPhone or iPad has many preinstalled ringtones. From the iTunes Store, you can purchase and download thousands of additional ringtones, many of which are clips from popular songs, movies, or TV shows.
>
> To purchase a new ringtone, as you're creating or editing a contact entry, tap the Ringtone option, and then tap Buy More Tones. (Your iPhone or iPad must have Internet access.) You'll be connected to the iTunes Store and will be able to purchase additional ringtones at a cost of $1.29 each.

> **WHAT'S NEW** As you're creating or editing an entry, if the person is important to you and you want them to be able to reach you even if the iPhone or iPad's Do Not Disturb feature is turned on, tap the Ringtone option, and then turn on the virtual switch associated with Emergency Bypass.

EDITING OR DELETING A CONTACT

To edit a contact, tap its listing from the All Contacts screen to display the contact details, and then tap the Edit option displayed in the upper-right corner of the screen. Tap any field to modify it. Delete a field by tapping the red-and-white – icon associated with it, and then tap the Delete button that appears to the right of the entry.

You can also add new fields in an entry by tapping any of the green-and-white + icons and then choosing the type of field you want to add.

When you're finished editing a Contacts entry, tap Done.

> **☑ TIP** To delete an entire entry from your Contacts database, as you're editing a contact entry and looking at the Contact screen for that entry, scroll down to the bottom of it, and tap the Delete Contact option that's displayed in red.
>
> Keep in mind that if you have your Contacts database syncing with iCloud or another contacts database, the contact you delete is removed from all your computers and devices that are connected to the Internet within seconds. There is no "undo" option.

SHARING CONTACT ENTRIES

From the main Contacts screen that displays your list of contact entries, tap the contact listing you want to share. When the contact's entry is displayed, scroll toward the bottom of the entry until you see the Share Contact option. Tap it. Then choose to share the contact's details with someone else via AirDrop, text/instant message (via the Message app), or email (via the Mail app).

The entire Contacts entry you selected (stored in .vcf format) will already be embedded in the outgoing email or text/instant message. When you've filled in all the necessary fields, tap the blue-and-white Send icon. Upon doing this, you are returned to the Contacts app.

When the recipient receives your email or message and clicks the attachment (the contact entry you sent), it automatically is imported into their contact management application as a new entry, such as in the Contacts app running on a Mac, iPhone, or iPad.

> **ⁱᐤˢ¹⁰ WHAT'S NEW** One way to share your current location with a contact is to view that contact's entry and tap the Share My Location option. You can then choose to share your location for one hour, until the end of the current day, or indefinitely.

🔎 **MORE INFO** Here are some additional quick tips for using Contacts:

■ If someone shares a Contacts entry with you via email, when you're viewing the incoming email on your iPhone or iPad, tap the email's attachment. The Contacts entry that was emailed is displayed in a window. At the bottom of this window, as the recipient of the contact's information, tap the Create New Contact or Add to Existing Contact option to incorporate this information into your Contacts database.

■ As you're creating or editing a contact entry, in the Notes field, enter as much information pertaining to that contact as you want using freeform text. It's also possible to paste content from another app into this field using the iOS's Select, Copy, and Paste commands, and using the app switcher to quickly switch between apps.

■ When creating or editing contacts, it's important to associate the correct labels with phone numbers, email addresses, and address data. For each phone number you add to a contact's entry, for example, it can include a Home, Work, Mobile, iPhone, or Other label (among others). For many iOS 10 functions that use data from your Contacts database to work correctly (including Siri), it's important that you properly label content you add to each Contacts entry.

■ Every field in a contact entry is interactive when you view it. If you tap a phone number, for example, you initiate a call to that person using the Phone app (iPhone). When you tap an address, you can obtain directions to that location via the Maps app or simply see the address displayed on a map. Tap an email address to compose and send an email to that person (via the Mail app). If multiple options are available, such as to call, FaceTime, or message someone from a phone number, a phone, FaceTime, and/or message icon is displayed.

CREATING AND MANAGING LISTS WITH THE REMINDERS APP

Use the Reminders app to easily manage multiple lists simultaneously, and if necessary, add alarms and deadlines to individual list items. Plus, it's possible to be reminded of responsibilities, tasks, or objectives exactly when you need this information, based on your geographic location or a predetermined time and date.

The Reminders app works nicely with Siri, Notification Center, and iCloud, which makes synchronizing your app-related data a straightforward process.

> ☑ **TIP** When using an iPhone with 3D Touch capabilities, press and hold your finger on the app icon for the Reminders app when viewing the Home screen. This reveals a pop-up menu that enables you to quickly add items to specific lists you've already created in the app, plus you can view upcoming reminders associated with a list or list items.

Using Reminders, create as many separate lists as you need to properly manage your personal and professional life, or various projects for which you're responsible.

> ☑ **TIP** Reminders enables you to color-code lists. Tap the Edit button to the right of a list's title, and then tap the Color option. Seven different colors are displayed. Tap your selection. The list title is displayed in the selected color.

> (iOS 10) **WHAT'S NEW** Just like the iOS 10 edition of the Notes app, Reminders now has a Sharing/Collaboration feature. To use it, tap the Edit option for a list you've created, and then tap the Sharing option. From the Share With screen, tap the Add Person option. In the To field, fill in the name or email address of one or more people, and then tap the Add option.
>
> The person or people you opt to share a list with will receive a notification, which they need to accept in their version of Reminders.
>
> At that point, any of the collaborators can view and/or modify the list. The list owner (that is, the person who created and first shared the list) can later revoke access to the list by people who were previously invited.

Because your iPhone or iPad has Location Services (GPS) capabilities, it always knows exactly where it is. Thus, it's possible to create items in your to-do lists and associate one or more of them with an alarm that alerts you when you arrive at or depart from a particular geographic location, such as your home, office, or a particular store.

In addition, you can have a reminder alarm set to warn you of an upcoming deadline. This can be displayed on your device's screen in Notification Center, or as separate alerts or banners, depending on how you have the Reminders app set up to work with the notifications options offered by your iPhone or iPad (which is adjustable from within Settings).

As you're setting up an alarm, if you want it to repeat every day, every week, every two weeks, every month, or every year, tap the Repeat option and make your selection. By default, the Never option is selected, meaning the alarm does not repeat.

> **☑ TIP**   Just as you do for other apps, to set up Reminders to work with Notification Center and/or display onscreen alerts or banners, launch Settings, tap the Notifications option, and then tap the listing for the Reminders app. You can then customize the settings in the Reminders submenu screen.

STAYING UP TO DATE WITH REMINDERS

When you launch Reminders for the first time on the iPad, the control center for this app appears on the left side of the screen. On the right side of the screen is a simulated sheet of lined paper.

Tap the Add List option in the bottom-left corner of the screen to create a new list from scratch. However, if you've already been using the Reminders app on another iOS mobile device or Mac that's linked to the same iCloud account, all your lists synchronize with the iPhone or iPad you're currently using.

When you create a new list from scratch, it is displayed on the right side of the screen using the temporary heading New List. Enter a title for the new list and then associate a color with it. Tap Done when you're ready to begin populating the list with items (as shown in Figure 14.11 on an iPad).

On the iPhone, to create a new list from scratch as you're looking at a list, place your finger near the center of the screen and swipe down. Next, tap the + icon to the right of the Search field. From the Create New screen, tap the Reminder or List option (shown in Figure 14.12).

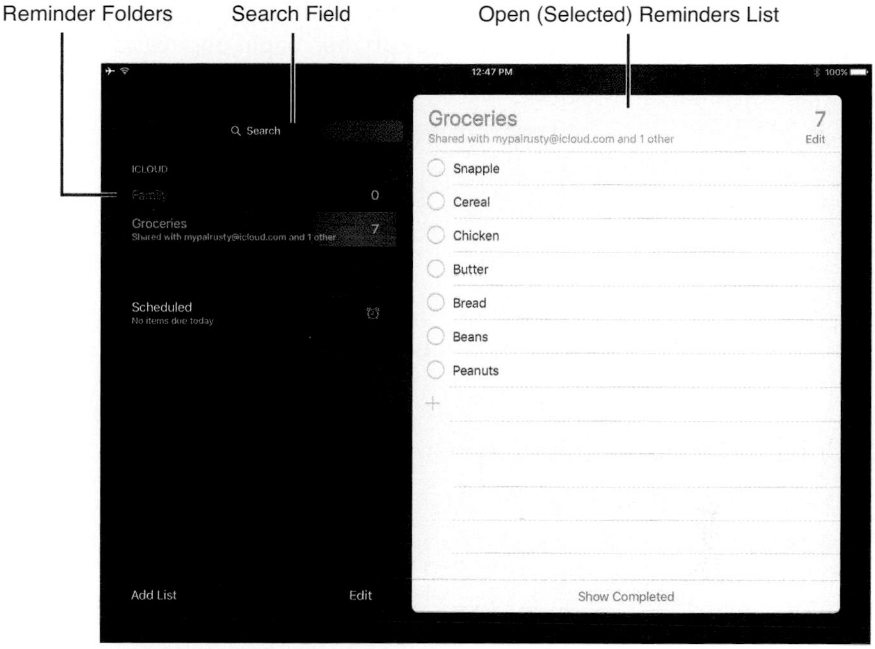

Reminder Folders   Search Field   Open (Selected) Reminders List

Figure 14.11

Using Reminders, it's possible to create and manage one or more lists. Each list can have as many separate items as you want.

Figure 14.12

Once you create a new list, give it a name, assign a color to it, and add collaborators, if you desire. Then populate the list with items, one at a time.

Select the List option, and then type the name of the list and associate a color with it (shown in Figure 14.13). Tap Done. You can then begin populating the list with items or repeat this process to create another list.

Figure 14.13

When you create a new list, give it a title and assign a color to it.

When viewing a list, tap an empty line of the simulated sheet of paper to add an item or tap the + icon at the bottom of the list. The virtual keyboard appears. Enter the item to be added to your to-do list. Next, tap the Return key on the keyboard to enter another item, or tap the Info icon (the blue *i* with a circle around it) to the right of the newly added item to associate an alarm, priority, and/or notes with it (see Figure 14.14). When you're finished adding new list items, tap Done.

To set a date-specific alarm, turn on the virtual switch associated with Remind Me on a Day option, and then tap the Alarm option to set the date and time.

To set a location-based alarm for that item, enter the Details screen by tapping the Info icon, and then turn on the virtual switch associated with the Remind Me at a Location option. Select a location, or enter an address, and then decide whether you want to be alerted when you arrive or when you leave that destination by tapping the When I Arrive or When I Leave tab.

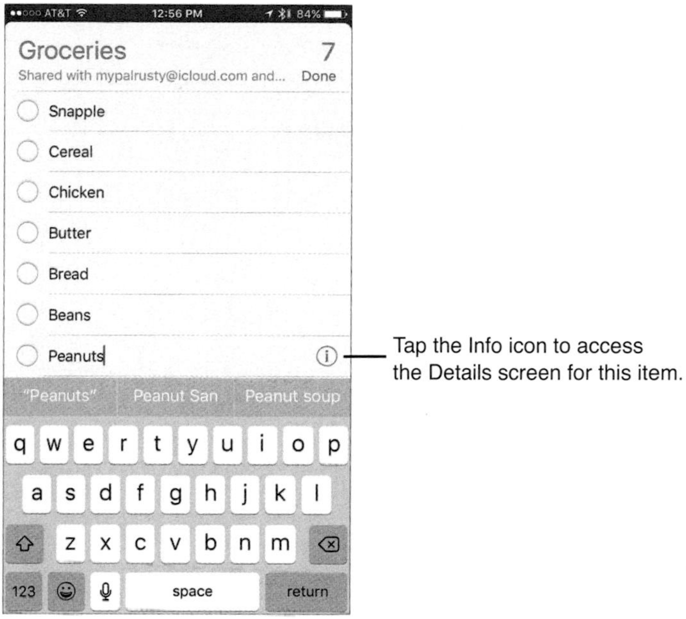

Tap the Info icon to access the Details screen for this item.

Figure 14.14

After creating a list item, tap its Info icon to add an alarm, priority, and/or freeform notes to it.

✓ TIP   You have the option to set a priority with each list item. Your priority options include None, Low (!), Medium (!!), and High (!!!). Although setting a priority for a list item displays that item with one, two, or three exclamation points to signify its importance, adjusting an item's priority does not automatically change its position in the list. You must manually rearrange the order of items on a list.

To do this, while looking at a list, tap the Edit button. Then place your finger on the Move icon (three horizontal lines) associated with the list item you want to move, and drag it up or down to the desired location in the list. Tap the Done button to save your changes.

✎ NOTE   After tapping the Info icon associated with an item, tap the Notes option to add freeform, text-based notes to it (see Figure 14.15). Use the virtual keyboard to type notes or the Dictation feature to dictate notes. You can also copy and paste content from other apps into this field.

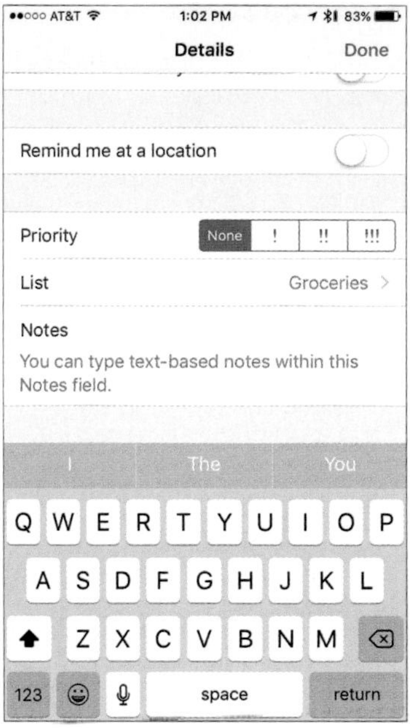

Figure 14.15
Every list item can have freeform notes associated with it. You can add as much note content as you want in this field.

Different alarms can be associated with each item in each of your lists. You also have the option to create a list item but not associate any type of alert or alarm with it. When an alarm is generated for a list item, a notification can automatically appear in Notification Center, assuming that you have this feature turned on.

> **TIP** One additional feature of the Reminders app is that you can display a separate list associated with each day on the calendar. When you use the Remind Me on a Day option, a date becomes associated with that item. Then, to review upcoming items related to a particular day tap the Scheduled option.

> **TIP** At the bottom of every to-do list on the iPad is a new Show Completed option. Tap this to display all items originally added to the list you're viewing that have since been moved to the Completed list.

To delete an item from a to-do list, swipe your finger from right to left across the item. A More button and a Delete button are displayed. Tap Delete to confirm your selection, or tap the More button to reveal the Info menu options related to that item. Remember, as soon as you make changes to a list item, if you have iCloud functionality turned on for the Reminders app and have access to the Internet, your additions, edits, or deletions automatically sync with iCloud.

DELETING AN ENTIRE TO-DO LIST

If you want to delete an entire list, enter the list and tap the Edit button, and then tap the Delete List option displayed at the bottom of the screen. A warning pops up asking you to confirm the deletion.

On the iPad, you can also locate the list you want to delete from the column on the left, and swipe your finger from right to left across it. When the Delete button appears, tap it. You also have the option of tapping the Edit button, and then tapping the — icon associated with the list you want to erase. In Edit mode, it's possible to change the order of your lists by placing your finger on the Move icon (three horizontal lines) that's associated with a list and dragging it up or down.

To exit Edit mode, tap Done.

TAKING NOTES OR GATHERING INFORMATION USING THE NOTES APP

In addition to typed notes, the Notes app enables you to create, gather, and manage information, including photos, drawings, and handwritten content.

> **iOS 10 WHAT'S NEW** After receiving a major revamp in iOS 9, the biggest update to the iOS 10 edition of the Notes app is the capability to collaborate with other people. Read more about it in the "Using the New Collaboration Feature" section.

Use the Notes app to keep track of memos, brainstorm ideas, take notes in meetings or classes, gather content from other apps that you want to store in one place, or for anything else that you'd use a traditional notebook and writing instrument to document.

iOS 10 **WHAT'S NEW**   Added to the iOS 10 edition of Notes is the capability to password-protect individual notes. To do this, open a note and tap the Share icon associated with it. From the Share menu, tap the Lock Note icon. When prompted, create a password for the note, verify it by typing it again, and in the Hint field enter something that will help you remember the password (see Figure 14.16).

Turn on the virtual switch associated with the Use Touch ID option so you'll be able to unlock notes by scanning your fingerprint using the Touch ID sensor that's built in to the Home button.

Keep in mind that if you forget the password you assign to a note, there is no way to recover or unlock it unless you're using a newer iPhone/iPad with a Touch ID sensor, and you previously turned on the Use Touch ID option.

Also, notes that utilize the Collaboration feature can't be locked with a password.

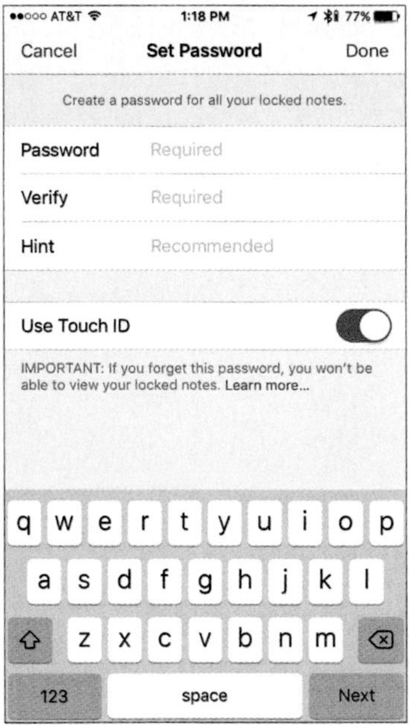

Figure 14.16

Protect a note from being accessed by unauthorized people by adding a password lock to it.

> **✓ TIP** When using an iPhone with 3D Touch capabilities, from the Home screen, place and hold your finger on the app icon for Notes to open a pop-up window that enables you to view your most recently created or edited note, create a new note, create a new checklist, take a photo and store it in a note, or create a sketch to be added to a note.

When using the Notes app, displayed directly above the virtual keyboard (used for typing note content) are several command icons (shown in Figure 14.17 on the iPhone).

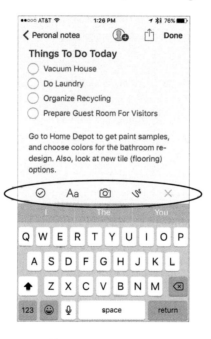

Figure 14.17

The Notes app displays special command icons directly above the virtual keyboard.

On the iPad only, in the top-left corner of the keyboard tap the Undo/Redo icon to reveal additional command icons that enable you to use the Undo, Redo, or Copy/Paste commands.

On either the iPhone or iPad, tap the check mark icon to begin creating and formatting an interactive checklist in your note.

Tap the Formatting option to quickly format text that you're typing into the Notes app.

In the top-right corner of the virtual keyboard are the Camera and Sketch command icons. Tap the Camera icon to import an image stored on your mobile device (from the Photo Library), or tap the Take Photo or Video option to use the device's built-in camera to snap a photo or shoot a video to be imported into the note you're working with.

Tap the Sketch icon to access the Notes app's drawing tools, which can also be used for handwriting on your phone's or tablet's screen using your finger or the Apple Pencil (on an iPad Pro).

USING THE NEW COLLABORATION FEATURE

After someone creates a note in the Notes app, that person has the ability to invite other people to view and modify that note and collaborate in real time. While composing or viewing a note, tap the new Collaboration icon (shown in Figure 14.18) and then add people who you want to collaborate with.

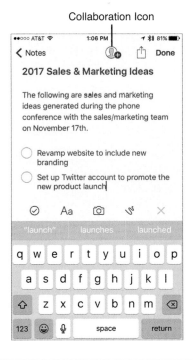

Figure 14.18

To launch the Notes app's new Collaboration feature, as you're working with a note, tap the Collaboration icon.

It's possible to invite collaborators via Message, Mail, Twitter, Facebook, or other compatible third-party apps. After choosing how you want to invite the one or more collaborators (shown in Figure 14.19), fill in the To field, when applicable, with the name, email address, or iPhone phone number. Figure 14.20 shows a collaboration invitation being sent via email. The Note is already embedded in the message. If you want, type an additional message, and then tap Send.

Figure 14.19

Choose how want to invite collaborators by tapping the appropriate icon for Message, Mail, and so on.

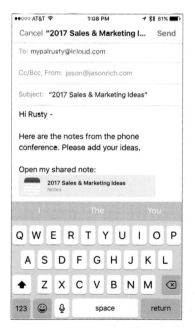

Figure 14.20

Decide how you want to invite collaborators (via email or text message, for example), and then fill in the To field with their name, email address, or phone number, based on the option you selected.

The recipient will receive your message and can click the provided Notes link. The note opens in their iOS 10 (or macOS Sierra) version of the Notes app (running on their iPhone or iPad). Any time a collaborator makes a change to the shared note, the updated version is immediately shared with the other collaborators, assuming each person's iPhone, iPad, or Mac has Internet access. Changes are highlighted in yellow for a few moments (see Figure 14.21), and then they automatically blend with the rest of the note. The collaborators will see, almost instantly, any changes you make to the note.

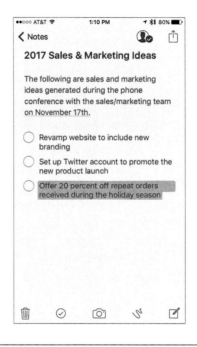

Figure 14.21

Changes made by others to a note are initially highlighted in yellow to get your attention. The yellow highlight fades after a few seconds.

Notes that are shared using the new Collaboration feature are stored in the original composer's online-based iCloud account. The collaborators have access to only the shared note, not all of the composer's notes that are stored in the Notes app.

After the collaboration tool becomes active a Collaboration icon appears to the left of the note's title (see Figure 14.22).

The person who set up the collaboration feature for a note can also revoke anyone's collaboration privileges. To do this, tap the Add Collaborator icon, and from under the People heading, tap the person you want to remove from list of people with collaboration privileges. Next, tap the Remove Access option related to that person.

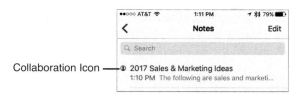

Collaboration Icon

Figure 14.22

Notes that have the Collaboration feature active display a Collaboration icon to the left of their title.

To quickly remove everyone's access to the Note and turn off the collaboration feature for just that note, tap the Stop Sharing option below the People heading.

CREATING AND MANAGING NOTES APP FOLDERS

Think of the Notes app as a digital notebook. Each note stored in the app is a separate page that can have its own title and content. Individual notes are stored in folders, which are basically virtual notebooks. Each folder can also be custom named.

Begin by creating one or more virtual notebooks (folders) in the Notes app. You do this from the Folders screen (shown in Figure 14.23) by tapping the New Folder option, choosing where the content should be stored (in iCloud or only on your mobile device), and then typing a title for that folder.

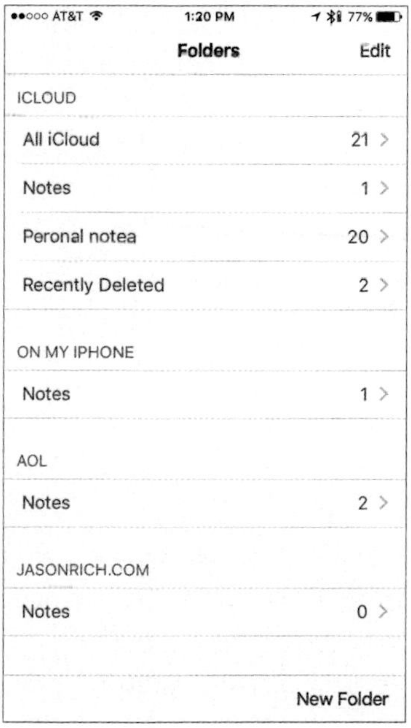

Figure 14.23

From the Folders screen, create one or more folders (virtual notebooks) within which you store your individual note pages.

To edit folders already created in the Notes app, access the Folders screen and then tap the Edit option. You can then select and delete entire folders created using the Notes app.

> ✏ **NOTE** Notes created using other apps that were synced with or imported into the Notes app can't be deleted or managed from the Folders screen.

CREATING INDIVIDUAL NOTES

From the Folders screen in the Notes app, tap the folder (notebook) within which you want to create a new note. When the screen for that folder opens, a listing of individual notes stored in it is displayed. If the folder is empty, only command icons are displayed on the screen.

To open and view, edit, or work with an existing note in a folder, access the Folder screen and tap that note's title/listing.

To create a new note from scratch, tap the Compose icon. On the iPhone, this icon is located in the bottom-right corner of the screen. On the iPad, it's located in the top-right corner of the screen.

The first line of text in a note becomes its title. Each time a new note is created, the time and date are automatically recorded and displayed. After typing the title for the note, tap the Return key and start typing your note's content. You can type as much content as you want in each virtual note page (refer to Figure 14.17). The note page extends infinitely downward.

As you're typing content, use the command icons at the top of the virtual keyboard to help you format the text or add checklists, for example. Tap the Emoji key on the virtual keyboard to add Emoji characters, or tap the Dictation key to use iOS 10's Dictation feature to speak into the app and have what you say translated into text and then imported into the note.

> **(iOS 10) WHAT'S NEW** To determine whether photo and video content you capture in the Notes app also gets stored in the Photos app, launch Settings, tap the Notes option, and then turn on the virtual switch associated with the Save Media to Photos option.
>
> Because the Notes app is designed to work with iCloud, if you want to be able to store notes in your iPhone or iPad (not just in the cloud), from the Notes submenu in Settings, turn on the virtual switch associated with the On My iPad Account or On My iPhone Account.

> **☑ TIP**   To delete the note you're currently working with, tap the Trash icon. The note will be deleted from the iPhone or iPad you're using, as well as from your iCloud account.
>
> To retrieve an accidentally deleted note, visit the Folders menu screen and tap the Recently Deleted option. From there you can select one or more accidentally deleted notes and move them into a different folder using the Move command. Tap the Move or Move All option, and then choose which folder the notes should be transferred to.

Keep in mind that using iOS 10's Select, Copy, and Paste commands, you can select content from other apps, copy it into the iPhone or iPad's virtual clipboard, and then paste that content into a note in the Notes app. This is easier if you're using an iPad and take advantage of the Split View feature to operate two apps at once on the tablet's screen.

Some apps (such as Safari) offer integration with the Notes app and include an Add to Notes option in the Share menu. Access this feature from a compatible app to export content from the app directly into a note within the Notes app.

MOVING NOTES BETWEEN FOLDERS

After notes are created and stored in particular folders, you can manually move them between folders. To do this, access the Folders screen and tap the folder that contains the notes you want to move. Next, tap the Edit option. Tap the listing for each note you want to move to select it.

Once one or more note listings have been selected, tap the Move To option and select which folder you want to move the notes to. At this point, the notes are removed from their current folder and moved into the newly selected folder. Instead of tapping the Move To option, delete the selected notes by tapping the Delete option.

CREATING INTERACTIVE CHECKLISTS IN NOTES

Using the checklist tool built in to the Notes app, it's easy to add and format interactive checklists into a note. To do this, place the cursor where you want to insert the list and tap the Checklist icon. The first empty circle is displayed. To the right of this icon, type your first list item, and then tap the Return key. Now, add second, third, and fourth items, and keep going until your list is complete (refer to Figure 14.17).

Later, when you tap one of the circles, a check mark is added to it, indicating that the item has been completed. In a note, add as many separate checklists as you

want, and each list can have any number of items. The various lists can be sur-
rounded by other types of content.

Remember, with the new Collaboration feature, multiple people can contribute to
a list, so those other people can add or delete items from a checklist or mark items
as completed.

USING THE DRAWING TOOLS IN THE NOTES APP

Using the Sketch tools built in to Notes, it's possible to draw or handwrite content
using your finger or the Apple Pencil (when using an iPad Pro). To do this, tap the
Sketch icon. The Sketch screen is displayed. At the bottom of this screen are three
virtual writing/drawing tools, including a pen, highlighter, and pencil (shown in
Figure 14.24 on an iPad).

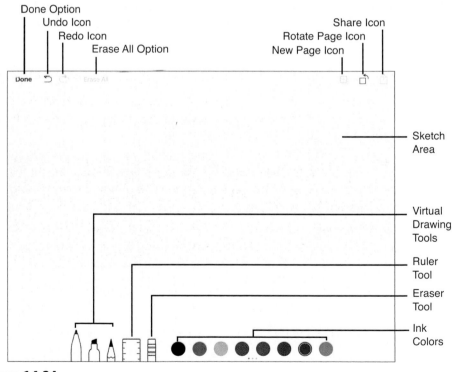

Figure 14.24

The Sketch tools include several virtual writing instruments and a selection of virtual ink colors.
(Only active icons and options are displayed in bright yellow.)

> **NOTE** On the iPhone, to view all of the Sketch tools and the virtual ink icons, rotate the phone to Landscape mode.

Tap the Ruler icon to make a virtual ruler appear on the screen, which you can then drag around, reposition, or rotate.

> **TIP** To drag the ruler, place and hold one finger on the ruler and move it around on the screen. To rotate the ruler, place two fingers (separated) on the ruler and rotate your fingers clockwise or counterclockwise.

To erase content that you've drawn on the screen, tap the Eraser tool, and then move your finger on the screen over the areas you want to erase. If you want to delete everything on the screen, however, tap the Erase All option.

After choosing a virtual writing instrument, tap an ink color. Swipe your finger across the ink colors to view all the available colors, and then tap the desired color.

When you're ready, use your finger, an optional stylus, or an Apple Pencil (when working with an iPad Pro) to draw or handwrite on the screen. You can switch ink colors or writing instruments as often as you choose.

> **TIP** To undo your last action, tap the Undo icon, or to redo that option you just undid, tap the Redo icon.
>
> If you want to rotate the entire virtual page you're drawing on, tap the Rotation icon. To share just the drawn content, not the entire note, tap the Share icon.

To save your work, tap Done. The content you've drawn is incorporated onto the note page you were previously working on, which can also include typed text and/or photos, for example.

> **NOTE** A single note can contain multiple sketches that were created separately.

SHARING NOTES

As you're viewing a note, tap the Share icon to access the Share menu. From here, you can share the contents of the note via AirDrop, text message, email, Facebook, or Facebook Messenger, for example, or use any listed third-party app that's compatible with the Notes app.

> **NOTE** The Share option is different from the new Collaboration option that allows multiple people to compose, edit, and view the same note, in almost real time. The Share option simply gives the person you share the note with a copy of the note in its current form. They will not see any future edits you make, and you will not see any changes they make unless the note is shared again.
>
> The Collaboration tool differs in that it enables all collaborators to always be working with the most up-to-date version of the note, as anyone makes any changes to it.

From the Share menu, it's also possible to copy content from a note to the device's virtual clipboard and then paste it into another app. Tap the Print icon to print the contents of the note using an AirPrint-compatible printer that's wirelessly connected to your iPhone or iPad.

> **MORE INFO** While the Notes app has become more powerful and versatile, a handful of other note-taking and virtual notepad apps for the iPhone and iPad offer a broader selection of tools or take a vastly different approach to composing, collecting, and organizing information.
>
> For example, there's Evernote (www.evernote.com) or Microsoft OneNote (www.onenote.com), which work across all computer and mobile device platforms and allow notes to be synced and shared easily.
>
> Meanwhile, iPhone/iPad-specific apps, like NotePad+, InkPad, SmartNote, Notability, Penultimate, and dozens of others, are available from the App Store. When using an iPad Pro, many of these third-party note-taking apps work with Apple Pencil and enable you to handwrite or draw on the tablet's screen to create note content.
>
> Choose a note-taking app that best suits your current work habits and needs.

15

GET ACQUAINTED WITH THE MUSIC, VIDEOS, AND iTUNES STORE APPS

What do eight-track tapes, vinyl records, cassettes, and CDs have in common? These are all outdated methods for storing music that have been replaced by digital music players. The music in your personal library can now be kept in a purely digital format, transferred via the Internet, shared with family members, and listened to on a digital music player, such as your iPhone or iPad.

With iOS 10, Apple has once again redesigned the Music app, giving it a more streamlined interface, along with more powerful features for experiencing digital music.

GETTING TO KNOW THE ALL-NEW MUSIC APP

The Music app serves as a full-featured digital music player, enabling you to play music. However, before playing your music, you first must load digital music files into your iOS mobile device or choose to stream music from the Internet. There are several ways to do this, including the following:

■ Purchase digital music directly from the iTunes Store (using the iTunes Store app) on your iPhone or iPad. An Internet connection is required.

> **◻ NOTE** When you activate the iCloud Family Sharing feature, you can share some or all of your iTunes Store digital content purchases with up to five other family members. You decide what content gets shared and have the option of keeping some of your content private, so it's only available through your iCloud account on all of your own iOS mobile devices and Macs. Family Sharing needs to be set up only once. See Chapter 6, "Use iCloud and the iCloud Drive App."

■ Purchase music using the iTunes software on your primary computer (used to connect to the iTunes Store) and then transfer content purchases and downloads to your iPhone or iPad using the iTunes Sync process or through iCloud.

■ "Rip" music from traditional CDs, convert it into a digital format using your primary computer, and then transfer the digital music files to your iOS device. For this, the free iTunes software on your computer or other third-party software is required.

■ Upgrade your iCloud account by adding the optional iTunes Match service, which costs $24.99 per year, so you can access your entire digital music library via iCloud, whether that music was purchased from the iTunes Store, ripped from your own CDs, or purchased/downloaded from other sources. To learn more about iTunes Match, visit www.apple.com/itunes/itunes-match.

■ Shop for and download music from another source besides the iTunes Store, load that music into your primary computer, convert it to the proper format, and then transfer it to your iPhone or iPad using the iTunes Sync process, or use a specialized app to experience that content.

> **NOTE** The Apple iTunes Store offers the world's largest collection of digital music that's available for purchase and download. This includes more than 40 million songs and albums, such as the latest hits, new music from the biggest bands and recording artists, as well as music from up-and-coming and unsigned artists/bands. You can also find classic songs and oldies from all music genres.
>
> Apple Music subscribers (who pay $9.99 per month) can stream most of the iTunes Store's music collection and listen to it on an unlimited, on-demand basis.

The Music app is used to play and manage digital music. If you want to watch videos, TV show episodes, or movies that you've purchased and/or downloaded from the iTunes Store, use the Videos app.

> **TIP** Instead of storing music on your iOS mobile device, you also have the option to stream music via the Internet. One way to do this is via the Music app and the Apple Music service.

To experience the free podcasts available from the iTunes Store, use Apple's Podcasts app. To access a vast collection of educational and personal enrichment content available from the Apple Store, also for free, take advantage of the iTunes U service. To do this, use the free iTunes U app.

Meanwhile, if you want to stream and watch videos from YouTube, use the official (free) YouTube app available from the App Store. There are also free apps available for all the popular streaming video services, like Netflix, Hulu, and Amazon Prime Video, as well as the streaming music services that compete with Apple Music, such as Spotify, iHeartRadio, and Pandora.

Remember, streaming content requires no internal storage space in your iPhone or iPad, but you do have to have a continuous Internet connection. Although the apps offered by the various streaming video and music services are free, a monthly subscription fee is charged by most of these services. This fee, which is typically less than $10.00 per month, enables you to stream as much content as you want, on an unlimited basis, during each month you're a paid subscriber.

> **NOTE** When you *stream* content from the Internet, it gets transferred from the Internet directly to your iOS device. However, your iPhone or iPad does not save streamed content. Streaming content from the Internet requires using a specialized app, which is provided by the source of the content.

GETTING STARTED WITH THE MUSIC APP

The all-new iOS 10 edition of the Music app continues to serve multiple purposes when it comes to experiencing music content. For example, it enables you to play songs or albums that are stored in your iPhone or iPad and that you own. You can also use the app to create, manage, and play back custom song playlists that you create or acquire. Plus, when your iPhone or iPad has a continuous Internet connection, it's possible to experience the Apple Music service or use the Music app's Radio feature to stream music programming from the Internet, including Apple's Beats 1 global radio station.

DISCOVERING THE APPLE MUSIC SERVICE

You can use a free three-month trial subscription to the Apple Music service, but you'll ultimately need to pay $9.99 per month for an ongoing individual subscription. Apple Music is accessible from the Music app. A $14.99 Family Membership plan (giving up to six people access to the service) is also offered.

Apple Music enables users to stream (and in some cases temporarily download) almost any music available from the iTunes Store, on an unlimited, on-demand basis. In addition, exclusive music from independent bands, artists, and musicians is offered, and you're allowed to access precreated playlists that have been compiled by other users.

> **NOTE** Music content you experience via Apple Music is streamed from the Internet, not purchased. One benefit to this on-demand aspect of the listening experience is that songs from Apple Music can be incorporated into your personalized playlists and temporarily stored on your mobile device even if you don't own them.

Another useful feature of Apple Music is that you can quickly select one or more artists, songs, albums, or music genres that you love, and the service recommends similar music based on your personal tastes. This is a great tool for discovering new, up-and-coming artists and bands or for previewing new music from some of your favorite artists or bands.

> **MORE INFO** You can learn more about Apple Music by visiting www.apple.com/music.

iOS 10 WHAT'S NEW   When you tap the For You icon displayed at the bottom of the Music app's screen, one newly added feature is called My New Music Mix. Based on your music preferences and listening history, the Music app recommends a selection of new music compiled just for you. This happens automatically every week.

Tap the My New Music Mix banner (shown in Figure 15.1) to access this playlist containing 25 songs from new, up-and-coming, and well-established artists.

When viewing the playlist (shown in Figure 15.2), tap the iCloud option to download all the songs (if you're an Apple Music subscriber), or scroll down to pick and choose which songs you want to download (and purchase, if applicable). Tap the More icon (…) to manage the new playlist, just as you would any other playlist..

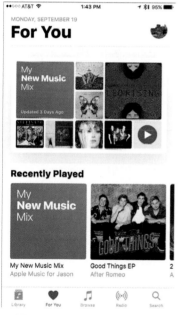

Figure 15.1

Automatically discover new music every week using Apple's My New Music Mix feature, which is part of the Music app.

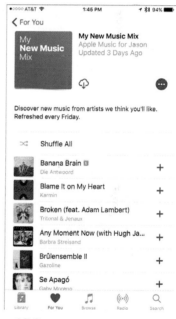

Figure 15.2

Treat the weekly My New Music Mix selection of recommended music as a new playlist each week. You can manage the contents of this playlist, just like you would for any other.

USING THE MUSIC APP: A QUICK TUTORIAL

The Music app is designed to give you total control over your music-listening experience. When you launch the iOS 10 edition of the Music app from the Home screen on your iPhone or iPad, along the bottom of the screen you see a handful of new command icons. These include Library, For You, Browse, Radio, and Search (see Figure 15.3). Tap any of these icons to manage and experience music via the Music app or Apple Music.

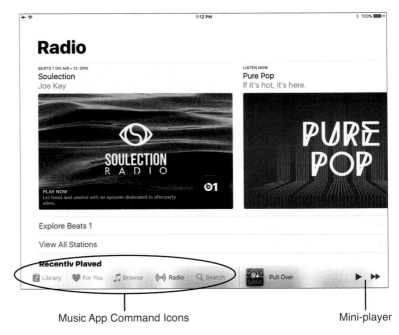

Figure 15.3

The Music app offers a new selection of icons displayed at the bottom of the screen. The Radio icon is selected here on an iPad.

You can also access the Music app's Radio feature, which is used to stream free music programming to the iPhone or iPad you're using.

Here's a quick summary of what each command icon is used for:

- **Library**—Access any music that you own and that's stored in your mobile device or your iCloud account. On the iPhone, after you tap the Library option, you can sort your music collection by Playlists, Artists, Albums, Songs, or Downloaded Music (just tap the appropriate option; see Figure 15.4). Scroll down to see the selection of newly acquired music under the Recently Added heading.

  On the iPad, tap the Library command icon at the bottom of the screen, and then tap the Library option in the top-left corner of the screen to re-sort the music. As you can see in Figure 15.5, options include Recently Added, Playlists, Artists, Albums, Songs, and Downloaded Music.

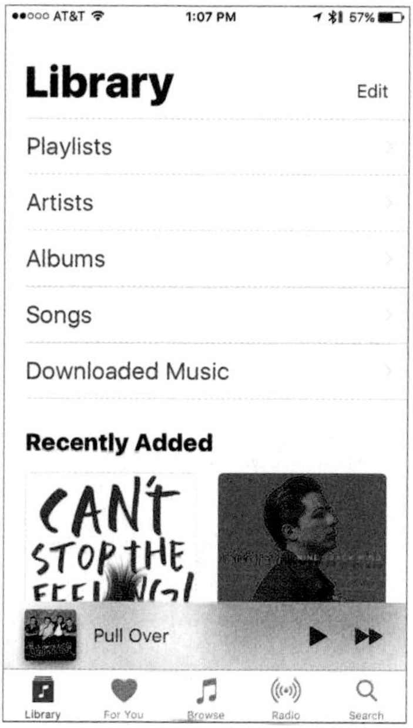

Figure 15.4

View and sort the music that you own (or have downloaded) onto your iPhone by tapping the Library command icon.

Library Pull-down Menu Option

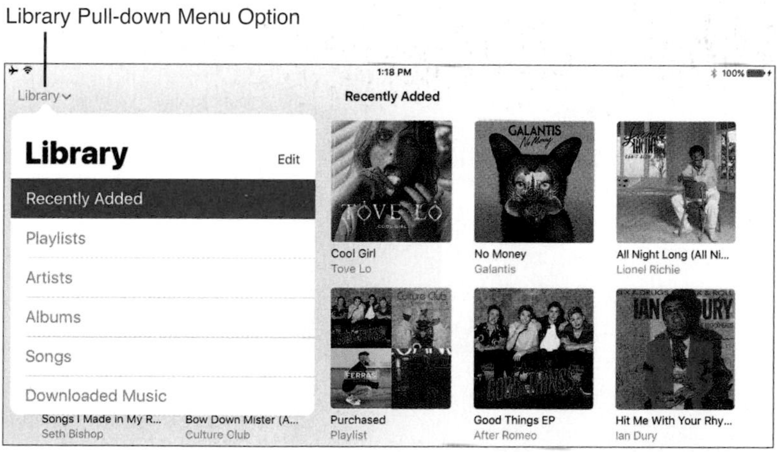

Figure 15.5

View and sort the music that you own (or have downloaded) onto your iPad by tapping the Library command icon and then choosing a sort option from the Library menu.

WHAT'S NEW   When you select the Downloaded music option, only music that is currently stored in your iPhone or iPad is displayed as being available to listen to.

NOTE   Regardless of which option you choose to sort and display your available music within Library, when you tap a listing, that music's Information screen is displayed. From here, you can select and play that music, access the More (…) menu, quickly find more music from that artist/band, or obtain suggestions for similar music that you might like.

When music is stored in your iPhone or iPad, you see the word Downloaded. You can then play that music by tapping its listing, whether or not your mobile device has Internet access.

If you see an iCloud icon associated with the music (shown in Figure 15.6), the music is available to you but isn't stored in your mobile device. Thus, you'll need an Internet connection to stream the music from the Internet (by tapping the music title) or to download the music to your mobile device (by tapping the iCloud icon associated with the song or album.)

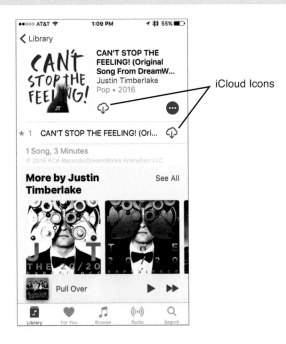

Figure 15.6

If you see the word Downloaded, the selected music is already stored in your mobile device. But if you see an iCloud icon associated with a music listing, you can stream or download that music via the Internet.

> **TIP**   When viewing the Library menu on an iPhone or iPad, tap the
> Edit option to add and display more sorting options, including Video, Genres,
> Compilations, and Composers. Use the Move icon associated with each listing to
> reorganize the menu order, and then tap Done to save your changes.

■ **For You**—Based on past music purchases, your music listening habits
using the Music app, and information about your musical tastes that you
provide to the app (by tapping the Love or Dislike icons as you listen to
music, for example), the Music app recommends music you might be interested in and provides collections of curated playlists. An Internet connection is required.

> **iOS 10 WHAT'S NEW**   The first time you use the For You feature of the
> Music app, provide the app with information about your personal music tastes by
> tapping the Profile icon in the top-right corner of the screen. Next, tap the Choose
> Artists For You option.
>
> You will be presented with a series of quick activities that will help the app get to
> know you better. For example, when you see the Tell Us What You're Into screen
> (see Figure 15.7), tap the music genres you enjoy listening to, such as Pop, Dance,
> Classical, or Hits. Tap Next to continue.
>
> From the Choose Your Favorites screen, tap some of your all-time favorite record-
> ing artists or bands. Tap More Artists to see a larger selection or, after choosing
> your favorites, tap Done.
>
> Tap the Profile icon again, and this time, from the Account menu screen, tap
> the Find More Artists and Curators. From this screen (shown on an iPhone in
> Figure 15.8), you have the option to choose curated playlists created by some of
> your favorite artists/bands, plus find more playlists from other artists/bands the
> Music app thinks you will enjoy (based on your music preferences).
>
> For each artist playlist you want to follow and enjoy using the Connect feature
> (which is discussed shortly), tap the @ symbol, and make sure a small + icon
> appears to the left of it.

Figure 15.7

Help the Music app get to know your personal music taste by selecting the music genres you enjoy.

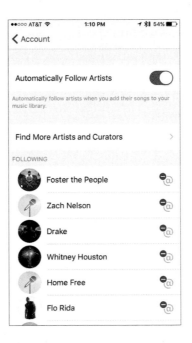

Figure 15.8

Access curated playlists and music hand-selected by some of your favorite bands and artists.

WHAT'S NEW To customize your public profile, which is accessible to people you share your music and/or playlists with, tap the For You command icon, and then tap the Profile icon. Tap your name at the top center of the Account window and edit how you want your full name to appear. In the @nickname field, it's possible to create a public nickname for yourself using alphanumeric characters and the underscore (_).

Tap the profile photo icon to add a profile photo of yourself. Tap Done to save your changes.

TIP When viewing the For You section of the Music app, tap any music selection, curated playlist, or music listing to begin streaming that music (if you subscribe to Apple Music); otherwise, only music you own will be accessible.

As you're viewing the For You music selection screen, tap a song title to jump to and play that song. Tap the Add (+) icon to add that track to your Library and download it to your mobile device so you can play it offline (for as long as you subscribe to Apple Music).

Tap the song's More (…) icon to access a menu (shown in Figure 15.9) that enables you to add/remove the selected (and playing) song to your Library, create a custom Radio station based on the song, or add it to a Playlist. You can also select the Play Next, Play Later, or Share Playlist option.

Figure 15.9
Tap the More (…) icon to view this menu. These options help you manage the music available to you, plus share your thoughts about the music you're hearing.

> **(iOS 10) WHAT'S NEW** When listening to music via the Music app, tap the Love (heart-shaped) icon to indicate you really like the music you're listing to (refer to Figure 15.9), or tap the Dislike icon to indicate you don't like the song. Doing this regularly helps the Music app and Apple Music service get to know your music preferences, so it can more accurately recommend music you'll like in the future.

■ **Browse**—This tool (shown in Figure 15.10 on an iPad) enables you to seek out new music, new playlists, music videos, and new albums, again based on your music preferences. After tapping the Browse command icon, choose from options including New Music, Curated Playlists, Top Charts, or Genres. Tap any of the album thumbnails or music listings to play the music that's being promoted. You'll discover the selection of music and curated playlists changes regularly.

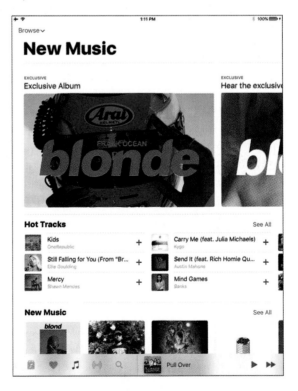

Figure 15.10
Use the Music app's Browse tool to discover music that will appeal to you, based on your personal preferences and past listening habits.

■ **Radio**—Previously called iTunes Radio, this steaming music service enables you to listen to (stream) customized, online radio stations that feature music based on your preferences and listening habits. Choose a recommended station (shown in Figure 15.11 on an iPhone), or tap the View All Stations option to explore the programming that's offered. Tap the Beats 1 option to tune in to this 24/7 live global broadcast produced by Apple. To utilize this free feature, a continuous Internet connection is required.

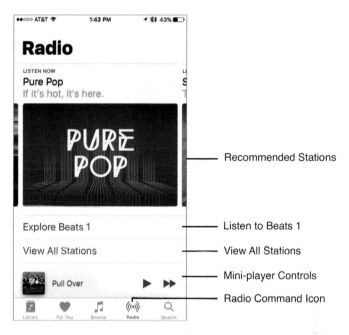

Figure 15.11

Choose from hundreds of streaming radio stations, based on the type of music you want to hear at any given moment.

> 📝 **NOTE** Using the Radio option, it's possible to choose a station to listen to based on an artist, album, or music genre you enjoy; however, you can't select the actual music selections that are played or choose the song order. However, from the Now Playing screen or mini-player, it's possible to skip a song (press the Fast Forward button) or tap the More (…) icon to access a menu (shown In Figure 15.12) that allows you to further manage the currently playing song.

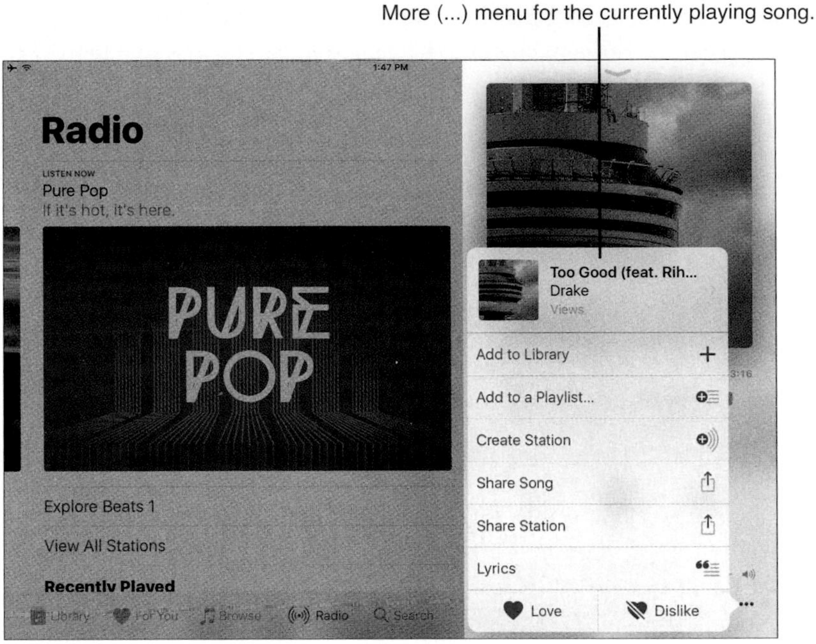

More (...) menu for the currently playing song.

Figure 15.12
While listing to a streaming radio station, access the Now Playing screen, and then tap the More (...) icon to view this menu.

(iOS 10) WHAT'S NEW   Listening to a streaming radio station via the Music app can be an interactive experience. From the Now Playing screen, tap the More (...) icon to create a new station based on the currently playing song selection, share the song with someone else, see the lyrics from the song that's playing (which is available for a growing selection of songs), and/or tap the Love or Dislike icon. From the main Now Playing screen, you always have the option to tap the Fast Forward option to skip to the next song, which is listed under the Up Next heading.

Tap any displayed album title or band/artist's name to view more information, see additional music from that band/artist, or learn about similar bands/artists.

■ **Search**—Apple's music collection is continuously expanding. Whether you're looking for a particular song, album, artist, band, or composer, tap the Search icon, and then type any search word or phrase into the Search field (shown in Figure 15.13) to find what you're looking for. This can also include a song lyric. A continuously updated Trending Searches list is displayed, so you can see what other people are searching for.

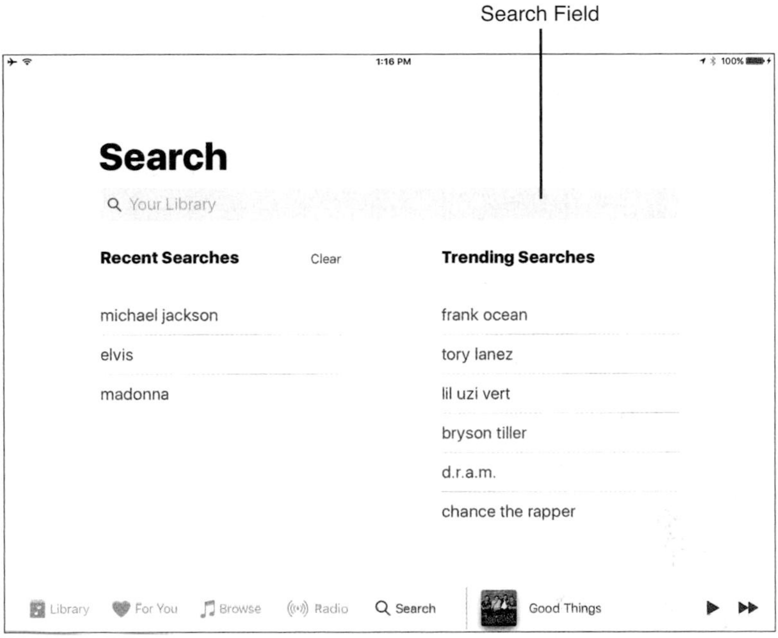

Search Field

Figure 15.13

Search Apple's vast and ever-expanding digital music collection to find what you're looking for within seconds.

TIP Apple Music and the Music app work seamlessly with Siri. So, if there's a song you want to hear, simply activate Siri and say, "Play *[song title]*" or "Play music from *[a band or artist's name]*" or "Play *[album title]*." Assuming the requested music is part of Apple's extensive and ever-growing digital music library, the song or album will begin streaming to your iPhone or iPad and play within seconds, assuming an Internet connection is available.

WHAT'S NEW Anytime music is selected or playing via the Music app, near the bottom of the screen a newly redesigned mini-player is displayed (see Figure 15.14). It enables you play/pause the music or quickly access the app's Now Playing screen, so you have lots of options when it comes to controlling the music that's playing on your iPhone or iPad.

Figure 15.14

Use the mini-player to control the selected music in the music app or quickly access the Now Playing screen.

TAKING ADVANTAGE OF THE NOW PLAYING SCREEN

Any time music is selected or playing in the music app, you'll see the mini-player controls displayed near the bottom of the screen, just above the app's command icons on an iPhone (refer to Figure 15.14) or in the lower-right corner of the screen on an iPad (refer to Figure 15.10).

Play/Pause and Fast Forward icons are displayed, and depending on the source of the music there might also be a Rewind icon (if you're streaming music, rewind isn't an option). The song title and album artwork is also displayed. To switch to the Now Playing screen (iPhone) or pane (shown in Figure 15.15 on an iPad), tap the mini-player with your finger.

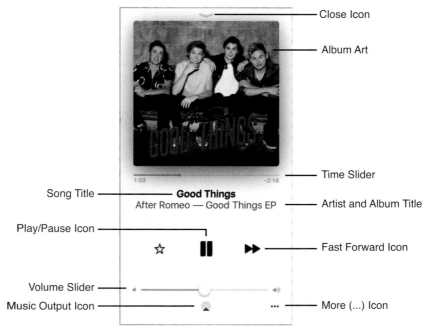

Figure 15.15

The Now Playing pane in the Music app (iPad) for a song being heard via a streaming Radio station.

The Now Playing screen/pane displays album artwork, the title of the song being played, the title of the album the song is from, the artist/band, a time slider, a volume control slider, and command icons.

In Figure 15.16, the Music Output icon is below the volume slider. Tap it to switch between the iPhone's internal speaker(s), Apple TV, or Bluetooth/AirPlay speakers or headphones that are wirelessly linked to your smartphone. Tap the More (…) icon to access a music management menu (shown in Figure 15.17).

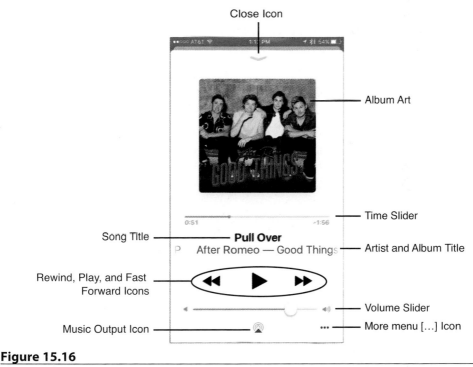

Figure 15.16

The Now Playing screen on an iPhone.

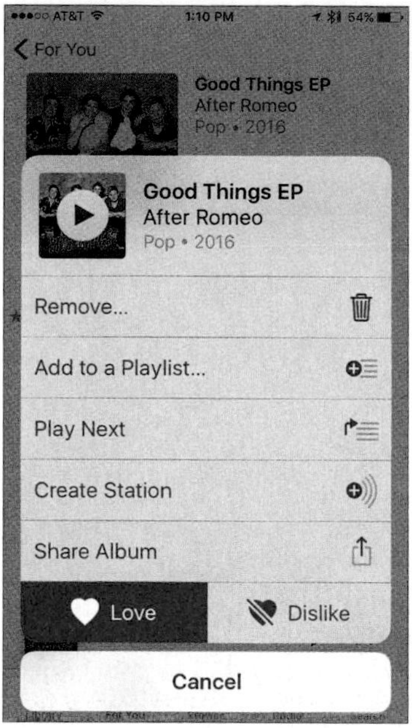

Figure 15.17
This menu offers a handful of options for managing the currently playing song/album.

> **TIP** Scroll down the Now Playing screen (iPhone) to access the Up Next heading, along with the Repeat and Shuffle icons. Tap the Repeat icon to continue repeating the same song. Tap the Shuffle icon to play music from the selected album or playlist in a random order.

On an iPad (refer to Figure 15.15), the Now Playing options are displayed in a pane along the right side of the screen. At the very bottom is the Add icon (which is used to add the song to your Library), the Music Output icon, and the More (…) icon.

> **TIP** To close the Now Playing screen/pane and return to the mini-player view, tap the downward-pointing Close icon at the top center of the screen (iPhone) or the top center of the Now Playing window (iPad).

USING CONTROL CENTER'S MUSIC CONTROLS

Once music is playing (or streaming) on your iPhone or iPad, there's no need to keep the Music app open. Press the Home button to return to the Home screen, and then begin working with another app, or access the app switcher (by pressing the Home button twice) to reopen an app that's already running in the background. The music that's playing (or streaming) continues to play, even after you exit the Music app. At this point, you can reopen the Music app at any time or take advantage of the new Music Controls that are accessible from Control Center.

Regardless of what you're doing on the iPhone or iPad, place your finger near the bottom of the screen and swipe upward to access the Control Center. Then swipe your finger horizontally, from right to left, to access the new Music Controls (see Figure 15.18).

Figure 15.18

Take charge of music that's playing on your iPhone or iPad using these Music Controls accessible from Control Center.

Music Controls displays information about music that's currently playing, plus offers an interactive time slider; Play/Pause, Rewind, and Fast Forward icons; a Volume slider; and a Music Output menu. (The Rewind icon isn't displayed when you're streaming music.) When video is playing, you can also access the Music Controls window.

CREATING CUSTOM PLAYLISTS USING THE MUSIC APP

Playlists are used to create a custom selection of songs. If you're an Apple Music sub-scriber, you can create a playlist from any music that's part of Apple's vast and ever-growing music collection. You can also share playlists with other people and acquire curated playlists from Apple's music experts and/or your favorite artists/bands.

However, if you're not an Apple Music subscriber, the music that can be added to playlists is limited to music stored on the mobile device you're using (or those in your iCloud account that you own).

> **NOTE** Think of a playlist as being like a custom mix tape. You decide what songs are included, how many songs are included, and the order in which those songs will be played (or they can be played in a random order using the Shuffle option).
>
> Using the Music app, it's possible to create or access an unlimited number of playl-ists, so you can have separate playlists for different types of activities or moods, for example.

Thanks to iCloud, when you create a playlist, it almost instantly syncs between your iPhone, iPad, and all other computers linked to your iCloud account. Thus, all your playlists are always accessible when and where you want to experience them.

> **TIP** When playing a playlist comprised of music stored on your iPhone or iPad, no Internet connection is required. However, if the music is being streamed from your iCloud account or via the Apple Music service, a continuous Internet con-nection is required (unless you first download each song selection in the playlist).

CREATING A PLAYLIST ON AN iPHONE

Follow these steps to create and save a custom playlist using the Music app on your iPhone:

1. Launch the Music app on your iPhone.
2. Tap the Library command icon in the bottom-left corner of the screen.
3. From under the Library heading, tap the Playlists option (see Figure 15.19).
4. From the Playlists screen, tap New Playlist.
5. Enter a custom title for the playlist in the Playlist Name field (shown in Figure 15.20).

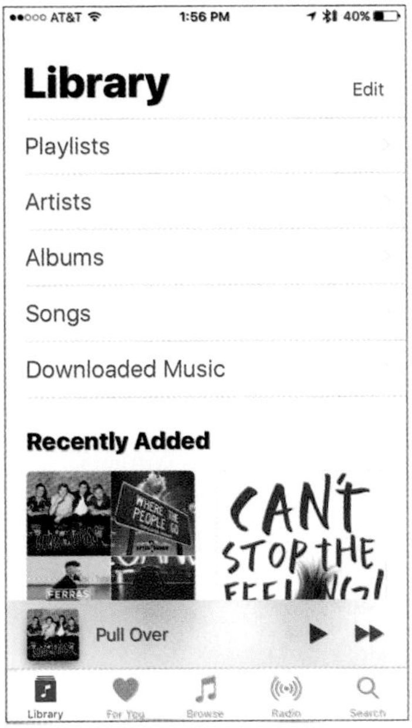

Figure 15.19

Tap the Playlists option to create, manage, or play a playlist stored in the Music app.

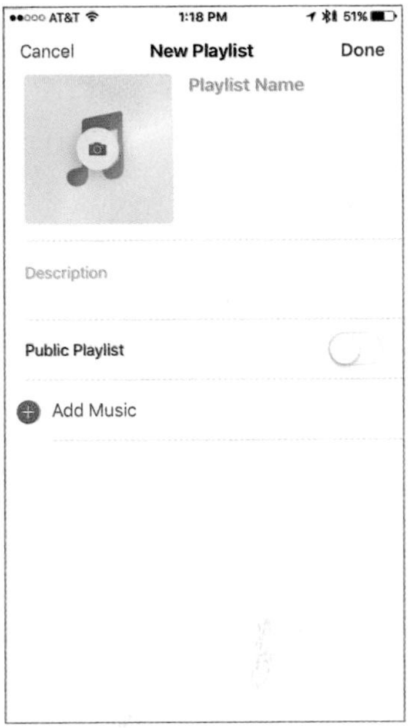

Figure 15.20

Fill in the Playlist Name and Description fields, and select an optional photo/graphic for your playlist.

6. In the Description field, type a short description of the playlist. For example, type "Favorite Song Compilation."

7. Tap the Artwork icon to import any image that you want to associate with that playlist. You can either take a photo using the iPhone's or iPad's camera or select a photo already stored on the device. (If you don't add your own artwork, artwork is created for you using album art from music featured in your playlist.)

8. Turn on the virtual switch associated with the Public Playlist option if you want to share this playlist with others.

9. Tap Add Music.

10. From the Library screen, locate the music you want to add. Select the Artists, Albums, Songs, Videos, Genres, Compilations, Composers, or Downloaded Music option to determine how your available music options will be sorted (see Figure 15.21).

11. If you select Songs, for example, all the songs currently stored on your iPhone or accessible via your iCloud account are displayed in alphabetical order by artist (as shown in Figure 15.22). Each song has an Add (+) icon to the right of its listing. Tap this icon to add the song to your playlist.

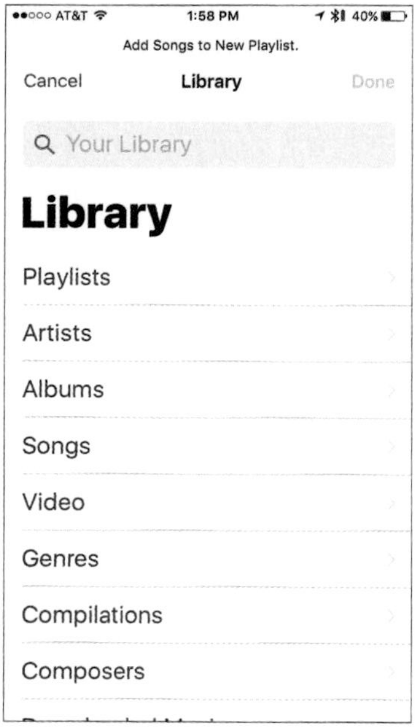

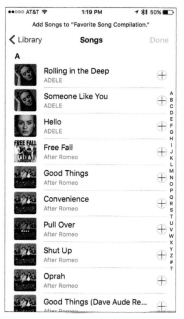

Figure 15.21

Select how you want the music stored on your iPhone to be displayed.

Figure 15.22

Tap the + icon associated with each song you want to add to your playlist.

NOTE If you selected Artists or Albums, for example, after tapping the Add Music option, a list of artists whose music you have stored on your iPhone or iPad, or a list of albums (or partial albums) you have stored on your iOS device, is displayed. Tap a listing to view individual song titles, and then tap the Add icon associated with each song you want to add. If you select Artists, initially a list of that artist's albums is displayed. Tap an album to reveal individual songs.

12. One at a time, add as many separate songs, from as many different artists or albums as you desire, to the playlist you're creating. Tap Done when you've finished compiling the list of songs to be added to your playlist.

13. A summary screen for your playlist is displayed (shown in Figure 15.23). To the right of each song listing is a Move icon. Place your finger on any of these icons and drag it up or down to rearrange the order of the songs.

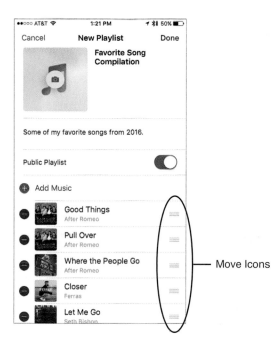

Move Icons

Figure 15.23
Tap a Move icon and drag to rearrange the order of songs.

14. Tap Done to save your newly created playlist.

15. Along with the playlists that are precreated for you, such as My Top Rated, Recently Added, Recently Played, and Top 25 Most Played, for example, your new playlist (see Figure 15.24) is displayed when you tap the Library command icon, and then tap the Playlists option. You will likely need to scroll down to view it.

16. Tap the playlist listing to access that playlist.

17. Tap any song listing within the playlist to begin playing it.

> 📝 **TIP** To edit the contents of a playlist, from the playlist screen while a playlist is being played, tap the Edit option. Alternatively, while a song from a playlist is playing, access the Now Playing screen, and then tap the More (…) icon to remove the currently playing song from the currently selected playlist.
>
> To delete a playlist, tap the Library icon followed by the Playlists option, and then tap the More icon associated with the playlist title. From the More menu, tap the Delete from Library option, and, when prompted, confirm your decision by tapping the Delete Playlist option.

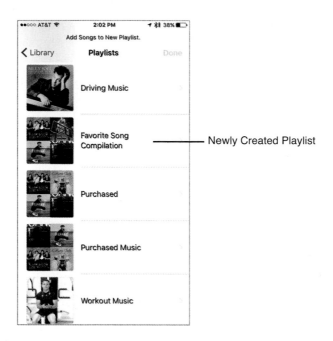

Newly Created Playlist

Figure 15.24
Access or manage a playlist by tapping its listing displayed below the All Playlists heading.

> **TIP** Regardless of what you're doing on your iPhone, it's also possible to begin playing a playlist, or any song, by activating Siri and issuing a command like, "Play *[playlist title]* playlist." You can also ask Siri to play a particular song, or music from a specific artist, for example.

CREATING A PLAYLIST ON AN iPAD

To create a Playlist using the iPad, begin by launching the Music app on your tablet, and then tap the Library option. Next, tap the Library pull-down menu in the top-left corner of the screen (shown in Figure 15.25 with the Albums option active); to create or manage a playlist, tap the Playlists option.

Continue by tapping the New option near the top-right corner of the screen (see Figure 15.26). Starting at step 5, follow the steps outlined in the previous section.

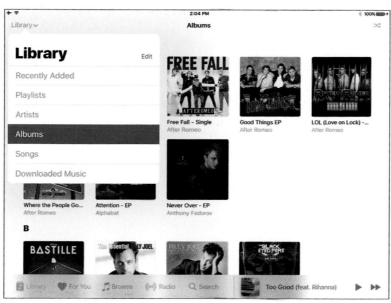

Figure 15.25
Create a new playlist on your iPad, or manage existing playlists, by tapping the Playlist menu option.

Figure 15.26
Create a new playlist from scratch, starting from this New Playlist screen.

CUSTOMIZING THE iTUNES STORE AND MUSIC APPS

To customize some of the features associated with the iTunes Store and Music apps, launch Settings and tap the iTunes & App Store and then the Music option, one at a time.

After tapping the iTunes & App Store option, for example, from under the Automatic Downloads option, turn on the virtual switch associated with Music if you want songs you purchase on other computers or mobile devices that are linked to the same iCloud account to automatically be downloaded to the iPhone or iPad you're currently using. If this feature is turned off, you always have the option of manually downloading that music.

> **✓ TIP** If you have a preset cellular data monthly usage allocation, turn off the virtual switch associated with Use Cellular Data. This prevents you from auto-matically downloading content from the iTunes Store using a cellular (3G/4G/ LTE) connection, which would otherwise quickly use up your monthly data allocation.

After tapping the Music option within Settings (see Figure 15.27), one at a time, turn on/off the virtual switches associated with each customizable option, or when applicable, tap an option to customize features from a submenu.

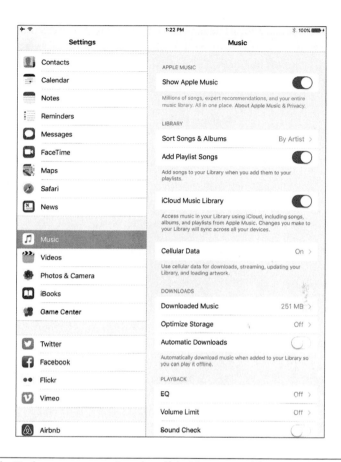

Figure 15.27
Shown here on the iPad, you can customize a handful of features and functions that are associated with the Music app from within Settings.

CONNECTING WITH YOUR FAVORITE BANDS AND ARTISTS

One feature of the Music app that was introduced with iOS 9 and has been reworked in the iOS 10 is called Connect. With it, you can select your favorite artists and bands and then view public posts from them. These posts might include text-based messages, candid photos, a sampling of new music, or video clips, for example. Not all artists and bands support this feature, but those that do use Connect as one way to stay in contact with their fans (in much the same way they'd also use Facebook, Twitter, Instagram, or Snapchat, for example).

To access the Connect feature and potentially see posts from your favorite bands and artists, tap the For You command icon, and then scroll down to the Connect Posts heading (shown in Figure 15.28).

Figure 15.28
Read posts from your favorite bands and recording artists.

To customize the list of bands and artists you follow via the Connect feature in the Music app, tap the Following option to the right of the Connect Posts heading. Alternatively, tap the profile icon (in the top-right corner of the screen), and then tap the Find More Artists and Curators option.

Next, automatically follow artists/bands you enjoy listing to music from by tapping the virtual switch associated with the Automatically Follow Artists option. Otherwise, from the Following screen (shown in Figure 15.29), tap the Find More Artists and Curators option to view a list of participating artists and bands, based on your music preferences and listening habits.

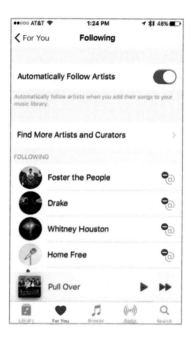

Figure 15.29

You choose which recording artists and bands you follow using the Connect feature in the Music app.

Underneath the Following heading (on the Following screen) is a listing of artists and bands you already follow. To remove an artist or band from this list, tap the @ symbol associated with their lIsting.

iOS 10 WHAT'S NEW Any time you tap a recording artist or band's name, an information screen for that artist/band is displayed on the screen (see Figure 15.30). This information screen displays biographical information about the artist/band, as well as details about their latest music releases, top songs, albums, videos, and (when applicable) content they've published using the Connect feature.

Tap the More (…) icon, and then tap the Follow on Connect option to begin following that artists or band through the Music app's Connect feature.

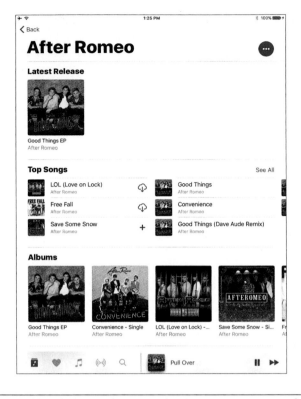

Figure 15.30
Tap any recording artist's or band's name when using the Music app to view an information screen for that band/artist.

STREAMING MUSIC VIA THE INTERNET

The Music app's Radio feature offers a free music streaming service operated by Apple. This service does not enable you to create custom playlists or choose the songs you hear, but it does enable you to create customized radio stations that play music that the service predicts you'll enjoy. However, if you subscribe to the Apple Music service, you can create and stream any music you want—either individual songs, entire albums, or custom playlists—pulling from Apple's vast and ever-expanding digital music collection.

There are also many other free and subscription-based streaming music services that you can enjoy from your iPhone or iPad. To use one of these services, such as Pandora, iHeartRadio, Amazon Cloud Player, or Spotify, for example, you need to download and install the app for that service, set up an account, and, if applicable, pay for a subscription.

In addition, virtually every radio network and local radio station in the world, as well as SiriusXM Satellite Radio, has proprietary apps that allow you to stream live programing from the Internet directly to your iOS device. An AM, FM, or satellite radio receiver is not required, but you do need a continuous Internet connection.

USING THE VIDEOS APP TO WATCH TV SHOWS, MOVIES, AND MORE

After you purchase and download TV show episodes or movies from the iTunes Store, you can enjoy that video content by using the Videos app. You can also view it on your primary computer using the iTunes software and share it between devices via iCloud. If you have Apple TV, it's possible to stream videos from your iOS device to your home theater system.

iOS 10 WHAT'S NEW When using iOS 10 on your iPhone or iPad, music videos can still be acquired and downloaded from the iTunes Store, but you can now watch them using the Music app instead of the Videos app.

To access acquired music videos from within the Music app, tap the Library option and then tap the Video option. A listing of music videos you have stored in your mobile device (or that are available to you via iCloud) are displayed.

A vast selection of music videos can be streamed for free, however, using the optional YouTube or VEVO apps.

NOTE The first time you launch the Videos app, if no video content is stored in your mobile device, the app automatically redirects you to the iTunes Store app, so you can acquire compatible video content to watch.

On the iPad, select the Purchased option to access TV shows and movies you've previously purchased or acquired from the iTunes Store, and download them to the device you're using for no additional charge. On the iPhone, do this by tapping on the More icon, and then tapping the Purchase option. That content will have an iCloud icon associated with it, as opposed to a Free or Price icon.

Tap the iCloud icon to download the content. It will then be displayed under the appropriate category (such as TV Shows) in the Videos app.

Read more about using the iTunes Store app to acquire and purchase content later in this chapter.

After you download or transfer iTunes Store video content to your iPhone or iPad, it is accessible from the Videos app. When you launch the Videos app, you see multiple content-type options displayed on the screen, based on the types of video content stored on your device. Figure 15.31 shows the TV show episodes that have been downloaded and are ready to view. (Notice that the TV Shows option at the top center of the screen has been selected.)

Figure 15.31

Use the Videos app content tabs to view the video content that you have stored on your iPhone or iPad that's downloaded and ready to watch.

> ☑ **TIP**   In Settings, tap the Videos option, and then turn on the virtual switch for the Show iTunes Purchases option to view all compatible content you've purchased or acquired from the iTunes Store, including content stored in your iCloud account but that has not been downloaded to the iOS device you're using (see Figure 15.32).
>
> After turning on Show iTunes Purchases, when using the Videos app to view content, thumbnails that display an iCloud icon represent content stored in iCloud but not on the device you're using.

These content types are labeled TV Shows, Rentals, and Movies. On the iPhone, they're displayed near the bottom of the screen; on the iPad, they're displayed near the top center.

> ☑ **NOTE**   If you have rented movies from the iTunes Store (as opposed to purchasing them), a Rentals option is displayed in addition to or instead of a Movies tab. Movie rentals can be viewed only on the device on which they were rented, and they cannot be transferred from one iOS mobile device to another. It is possible, however, to use AirPlay to play rented movies from your iPhone or iPad on an HD TV equipped with Apple TV.

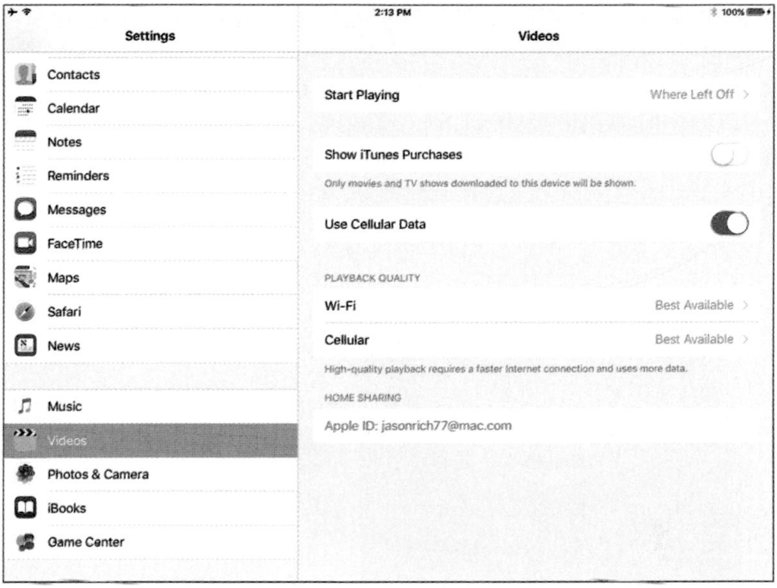

Figure 15.32

After turning on the Show iTunes Purchases option from within Settings, you see all content you've previously acquired from the iTunes Store, based on which content option you choose.

When you tap the TV Shows, Movies, or Rentals option, a thumbnail graphic representing each piece of viewable content is displayed. To begin playing a video, tap its thumbnail graphic.

> **TIP** When looking at the graphic thumbnails for TV shows you own, the number displayed in a blue circle near the top-right corner indicates how many episodes of that particular TV series you own. Tap the thumbnail to see a listing of specific episodes and then view them.

To delete video content from your iPhone, access the listing for that particular TV show episode or movie, and then swipe your finger from right to left across the listing. Tap the Delete button to confirm your decision.

On the iPad, to delete video content, tap the Edit button near the top-right corner of the screen, and then tap the X icon that appears on the movie thumbnail listing(s) you want to delete. After you delete iTunes Store–purchased content from your iPhone or iPad, it's always possible to redownload it from your iCloud account for free.

To shop for additional video content from the iTunes Store while using the Videos app, tap the Store option.

To play a video, tap a thumbnail representing the video that you want to watch. If you've downloaded a TV show, for example, a new screen appears listing all episodes from that TV series currently stored on your iOS device (as shown in Figure 15.33). These episodes are sorted by season, if applicable. Tap the episode of your choice to begin playing it, or tap the Play icon.

Figure 15.33
Multiple episodes of the same TV series are grouped together for easy access and viewing.

For movies, a similar information screen pertaining to that content is displayed. Tap the Play icon to begin watching that video content.

> **TIP** When playing video content, hold your iPhone or iPad in either portrait or landscape mode. However, the video window is significantly larger if you position your iOS mobile device sideways and use landscape mode.
>
> If applicable, based on the video content you're watching, you can instantly switch between full-screen mode and letterbox mode as your onscreen viewing option by tapping the icon displayed in the upper-right corner of the screen.

> **TIP** If you're using one of the newer iPad models to watch a video using the Videos app, you have the option to use the Picture in Picture feature. After you start playing a TV show or movie, for example, tap the Picture in Picture icon. The video window shrinks and displays Enlarge, Play/Pause, and Close icons in it. Tap the Play icon to continue playing your video in the smaller screen, or the Pause icon to pause it.
>
> As the video is playing, place and hold your finger on the video window to move it around in the iPad's screen. It's then possible to launch another app and use that app as the video continues playing in its smaller window.
>
> To adjust the size of the Picture in Picture window, place two fingers in the window and perform a reverse-pinch finger gesture.
>
> Other popular apps used for streaming video content, like YouTube, HBOGo, Netflix, Amazon Video, and Hulu, also support the Picture in Picture feature, but the appearance and location of the Picture in Picture icon, or the method for activating this feature, varies. For example, when the Netflix app is playing a video, press the Home button to activate the Picture in Picture feature, and also access the Home screen so you can launch another app.

Typically, while video content is playing, it displays in full-screen mode or letterbox mode. Tap anywhere on the screen to reveal the onscreen command icons used for controlling the video as you're watching it. When a video is playing, these controls disappear automatically after a few seconds. Tap anywhere on the screen to make them reappear.

> **NOTE** If you're watching a purchased movie acquired from the iTunes Store, below the Play, Rewind, and Fast Forward controls you might discover additional tabs that enable you to access movie-related "extras" that would otherwise be made available as part of the DVD or Blu-ray version of the movie. Tap any of these tabs to access the bonus content, which is movie-specific.

Along the top center of the screen is a time slider. On either end of this slider are timers. To the left is a timer that displays how much of the video you've already watched. On the right of the slider is a timer that displays how much time in the video remains. Tap the Done button in the upper-left corner of the screen to exit the video you're watching.

> ✅ **TIP** To manually fast forward or rewind while watching a video, place your finger on the dot icon that appears on the time slider and drag it left or right.

Near the bottom center of the screen as you're watching video content are the Rewind and Fast Forward icons. Tap the Rewind icon to move back by scene or chapter, or tap the Fast Forward icon to advance to the next scene or chapter in the video (just as you would while watching a DVD). Press and hold the Rewind or Fast Forward icon to rewind or fast forward while viewing the onscreen content. You can rewind or advance by a few seconds at a time.

Tap the Play icon to play the video. When the video is playing, the Play icon transforms into a Pause icon, used to pause the video.

> ✏️ **NOTE** If you pause a video and then exit the Videos app, you pick up exactly where you left off watching the video when you relaunch the Videos app. This information is automatically saved.

Use the volume control slider to manually adjust the volume of the audio. This can also be done using the volume control buttons on the side of your device or the volume buttons on your corded headphones (if applicable).

Located near the lower-right corner of the screen while a video is playing (when the controls are visible) are the Captions and AirPlay icons. (On newer iPad models, the Picture in Picture icon is also displayed in the lower-right corner of the screen.) Tap the Captions icon to adjust captions and/or switch between audio languages, if the video content you're watching supports these features. If not available, the text-bubble icon is not visible.

Tap the AirPlay option to stream the video from your mobile device to your television set or home theater system via an Apple TV. If you have Bluetooth- or AirPlay-compatible speakers, it's possible to stream just the audio from a TV show or movie, for example, to external speakers or wireless headphones.

> **NOTE** You must use Wi-Fi to stream video from your iOS mobile device to your HD television via Apple TV. Both the iOS mobile device and Apple TV must be linked to the same wireless network.

> **TIP** From the iTunes Store, you can purchase TV show episodes (or entire seasons from your favorite series), as well as full-length movies. In addition, you can rent certain movies.
>
> When you rent a movie from the iTunes Store, it remains on your device for 30 days before it automatically deletes itself, whether or not the content has been viewed. However, after you press Play in the Videos app and begin watching rented content, you have access to that video for only 24 hours before it deletes itself. During that 24-hour period, you can watch and rewatch the movie as often as you'd like.
>
> The first time you tap Play to watch a rented movie, you're prompted to confirm your choice. This starts the 24-hour clock and allows the rented movie to begin playing.
>
> Unlike movies you purchase from the iTunes Store (that you can load into all of your computers and/or iOS mobile devices that are linked to the same iCloud account), rented movies can be stored on only one computer, Apple TV, or iOS mobile device.

USING THE iTUNES STORE APP TO MAKE PURCHASES

The iTunes Store app comes preinstalled with iOS 10 and you use it to acquire music, movies, TV shows, and ringtones. To utilize this app (shown in Figure 15.34 on an iPad), your iOS mobile device requires Internet access. For smaller-sized files, such as songs, albums, or ringtones, a cellular data connection works. However, for larger-sized files, such as TV show episodes and movies, you must use a Wi-Fi Internet connection to download the content.

Figure 15.34
Use the iTunes Store app to purchase music, TV shows, and movie content and acquire free music and video-based content.

> **NOTE**   Like the App Store, from the iTunes Store you can view detailed descriptions and reviews of content before purchasing (or renting) it. It's also possible to preview the content or watch a movie's trailer(s). Tap the Details tab to read a description and access previews (shown in Figure 15.35), or tap the Reviews tab to see star-based ratings and read reviews.
>
> The process for purchasing content from the iTunes Store is virtually identical to using the App Store, so refer to Chapter 4, "Find, Buy, and Use Third-Party Apps," for more information.

On the iPhone, displayed along the bottom of the iTunes Store screen are five command icons: Music, Movies, TV Shows, Search, and More (...). Tap the More (...) icon to access the Tones (Ringtones), Genius, Purchased, and Downloads options.

On the iPad, seven command icons are displayed along the bottom of the screen, which from left to right are Music, Movies, TV Shows, Top Charts, Genius, Purchased, and Downloads. The Search field is displayed in the top-right corner of the screen.

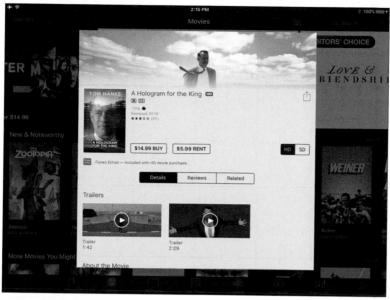

Figure 15.35

Tap any content's listing to view a detailed Description screen. From here, you can watch a preview/trailer(s), scroll down to read a description, and access star-based ratings and reviews (by tapping the Reviews tab).

To shop for music (or acquire free music), tap the Music icon. To purchase or rent movies, tap the Movies icon. For TV shows (either individual episodes or entire seasons of a series), tap the TV Shows icon. Use the Search feature to quickly find available audio or video content using keywords.

> **TIP** After you tap the More (...) icon on the iPhone, tap Purchased to view all past purchases from the iTunes Store. As content is downloading, you can view the progress of that download by tapping the Purchased icon.

Just like when using the App Store to acquire new apps for your mobile device, when you make a purchase from the iTunes Store, all charges are automatically billed to the credit or debit card you have linked with your Apple ID or offset against any credit your account might have from redeemed gift cards.

> **☑ TIP** It's possible to redeem an iTunes gift card and add the credit to the Apple ID account used for making online purchases from the iTunes Store, App Store, or iBook Store. When you select the Redeem option, you can scan a physical gift card using the camera built in to your iOS mobile device, so you don't have to manually type the long redemption code.

When you make a purchase from your iPhone or iPad, it immediately gets downloaded to that device and, at the same time, gets stored in your iCloud account. The online storage space required for purchased iTunes Store content is provided free of charge, and does not count against the 5GB of free online storage space your iCloud account comes with. The same content can then be downloaded and experienced on your other Macs and iOS mobile devices that are linked to the same iCloud account.

> **☑ TIP** The iTunes Store offers a Complete My Season feature for TV show seasons. If you purchase one or more single episodes of a TV series (from a specific season), you can later return to the iTunes Store and purchase the rest of the episodes from that season at a reduced, prorated price (based on how many episodes from that season you already own). This feature works just like the Complete My Album feature for your music but relates to TV shows.

FINDING TV EPISODES YOU WANT TO PURCHASE

When shopping for TV show episodes to purchase and watch using the iTunes Store app, tap the TV shows command icon. Shows are displayed by series name. The search results display the TV show by season number and by available episodes.

> **✐ NOTE** Purchasing most single TV episodes from the iTunes Store costs $1.99 (standard definition) or $2.99 (high definition). A discount for acquiring a complete season of a TV series is offered.
>
> The price to purchase movies varies, but the rental price is typically $3.99 (standard definition) or $4.99 (high definition).
>
> Most individual songs available from the iTunes Store cost between $0.69 and $1.29, and album prices vary.

In addition to purchasing one TV show episode at a time, the iTunes Store gives you the option of purchasing the entire season all at once, at a discounted rate, plus you can choose between high definition (HD) or standard definition (SD) video quality. The HD versions of TV shows have much larger file sizes and take up much more internal storage space in your device, but they look much better when you watch them.

To save money, purchase an entire season of your favorite show's current season. This is called a Season Pass. Then, when a new episode airs each week and becomes available from the iTunes Store (about 24 hours later), it can be downloaded to your iOS device and made available to you via iCloud using a Wi-Fi Internet connection. You'll also receive a weekly email, plus Notification Center alerts from Apple telling you when each new episode in your Season Pass is available.

When you shop for TV episodes from the iTunes Store (via the iTunes app), they're commercial free and available to watch whenever you want. They're also permanently accessible via your iCloud account to be downloaded to any computer, iOS device, or Apple TV device that's linked to the same iCloud account. Once an episode is downloaded to your iPhone or iPad, you no longer need an Internet connection to watch it.

> **☑ TIP**   Each week, the iTunes Store offers free episodes of featured TV shows. To discover which episodes are being offered, launch the iTunes Store app, tap the TV Shows icon, scroll to the bottom of the screen, and under the TV Shows Quick Links heading, tap Free TV Episodes. Then, from the Free TV Episodes screen, look under the Free Full-Length Episodes heading to see what's currently available.

STREAMING VIDEO CONTENT

To stream video content from the Internet, you must use a specialized app, based on where the content originates from on the Internet.

Whenever you're streaming video content, you can pause the video at any time. Depending on the app, you also can exit the app partway through a video and resume watching it from where you left off when you relaunch the app later.

Streamed TV programming and movies may or may not include commercials, based on the service you use to access it. For example, if you use the app from your cable TV service provider or from specific TV networks to stream on-demand programming using your iPhone or iPad, TV commercials are included if the original broadcast programming included commercials.

If you subscribe to a fee-based video streaming service, like Netflix, Amazon Prime Video, or Hulu, streamed content is offered commercial-free.

> [📝] **NOTE**   A Hulu Limited Commercials subscription ($7.99/month) includes commercials, whereas a Hulu No Commercials subscription ($11.99/month) offers the same programming selection but with no commercials.

> (iOS 10) **WHAT'S NEW**   One benefit to subscribing to a streaming video service, like Netflix, Hulu, Amazon Prime Video, or CBS All-Access, is the ability to watch award-winning programming produced exclusively for that service. For example, CBS All-Access offers a new and original *Star Trek* television series, called *Star Trek: Discovery* (premiering in 2017) that could only be watched via this service.
>
> Meanwhile, Netflix offers a growing selection of original series and movies, such as *Orange is the New Black*, *House of Cards*, *Stranger Things*, and *Grace and Frankie*. Amazon Prime Video's original series include *The Man in the High Castle* and *Mozart in the Jungle*, and original series from Hulu include *The Path*, *12.22.63*, and *Chance*.

> **!CAUTION**   When traveling on airplanes with Wi-Fi service, keep in mind that streaming video services are typically blocked and do not work. So, to watch video content, you need to acquire it first, and then download it to your mobile device before the flight.

The capability to stream content from the Internet gives you on-demand access to a wide range of programming; however, streaming audio or video content requires a tremendous amount of data to be transferred to your iOS device. Therefore, if you use a cellular data connection, your monthly wireless data allocation will quickly get used up. When you're streaming Internet content, it's best to use a Wi-Fi connection, unless you have an unlimited cellular data plan.

Not only does a Wi-Fi connection often allow video data to be transferred at faster speeds and at a higher resolution, there's also no limit to how much data you can send or receive.

Keep in mind that many cable television service providers (such as Xfinity/Comcast and Time Warner), as well as satellite TV service providers, individual television and cable TV networks (ABC, NBC, CBS, FOX, USA Network, Lifetime, SyFy, and so on), and even specific TV shows, often have their own proprietary apps available for streaming content from the Internet directly to your mobile device.

When you stream TV episodes from the Internet using a specialized app, this programming does not get stored on your iOS device, and is available only when your iPhone or iPad has a constant connection to the Internet while you're watching that content. In many cases, a Wi-Fi connection is required.

NOTE In addition to streaming TV and movie programming using the apps offered by cable TV and satellite providers, some of these apps now allow certain programming to be downloaded and watched offline. A growing number of these apps also now offer the ability to stream live programming.

For example, if you have a TiVo Bolt or TiVo Bolt+ digital video recorder (www.TiVo.com) connected to your television set for recording your favorite shows, most of that programming can be downloaded to your mobile device and later watched offline, or streamed from your TiVo to your mobile device when an Internet connection is available.

The ability to download and store some TV show and movie content is also offered by the Amazon Prime Video streaming service, and Netflix is expected to introduce this feature in 2017.

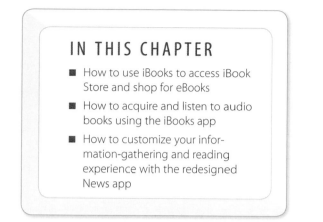

IN THIS CHAPTER

- How to use iBooks to access iBook Store and shop for eBooks
- How to acquire and listen to audio books using the iBooks app
- How to customize your information-gathering and reading experience with the redesigned News app

16

CUSTOMIZE YOUR READING EXPERIENCE WITH iBOOKS AND THE REDESIGNED NEWS APP

Thanks to Apple's iBooks app, you can easily acquire and read eBooks on any iOS mobile device (or Mac).

If you have a Mac, iPhone, or an iPad, you can use iCloud to sync your eBook library and related bookmarks between computers and iOS mobile devices (that are linked to the same iCloud account). As a result, all your books, even if you've acquired hundreds of them, are available to you regardless of which Mac or iOS device you're using.

Anything having to do with shopping for, downloading, installing, and then reading or listening to eBooks or audiobooks (that have been acquired from the Apple's iBook Store) is handled with the iBooks app.

The iBooks app has three main purposes. First, it's used to access Apple's online-based iBook Store. From iBook Store, you can browse an ever-growing collection of eBook titles

(including traditional book titles from bestselling authors and major publishers that have been adapted into eBook form). Although some eBooks are free, most must be paid for.

> **TIP** As with purchases from the iTunes Store or App Store, eBook and audiobook purchases made from iBook Store are charged to the credit or debit card associated with your Apple ID. You can also pay for iBook Store purchases using prepaid iTunes gift cards.

Second, the iBooks app is used to transform your smartphone or tablet into an eBook reader, which accurately reproduces the appearance of each page of a printed book on your device's screen, regardless of the device's screen size.

iBooks offers many features that make reading eBooks on your iOS device a pleasure. For example, when you stop reading and exit the iBooks app (by pressing the Home button), the app automatically saves the page you're on using a virtual bookmark, and then later reopens to that page when the iBooks app is restarted.

> **NOTE** You are allowed to install copies of your eBooks on all computers and devices that are linked to the same iCloud account, so you do not have to purchase the same eBook multiple times.

Third, the iBooks app is also used to acquire and listen to audiobooks. To find and purchase audiobooks, access iBook Store, tap the Featured or Top Charts icon, and then tap the Audiobooks tab to see a listing of available audiobooks. Tap the Categories option and then choose an audiobook category to narrow your search, or use the Search field to find the title you're looking for.

CUSTOMIZING iBOOKS SETTINGS

To customize settings related to iBooks, launch Settings and tap the iBooks option (shown in Figure 16.1 on an iPad). There are a variety of options you can adjust by turning on or off the virtual switches associated with each feature.

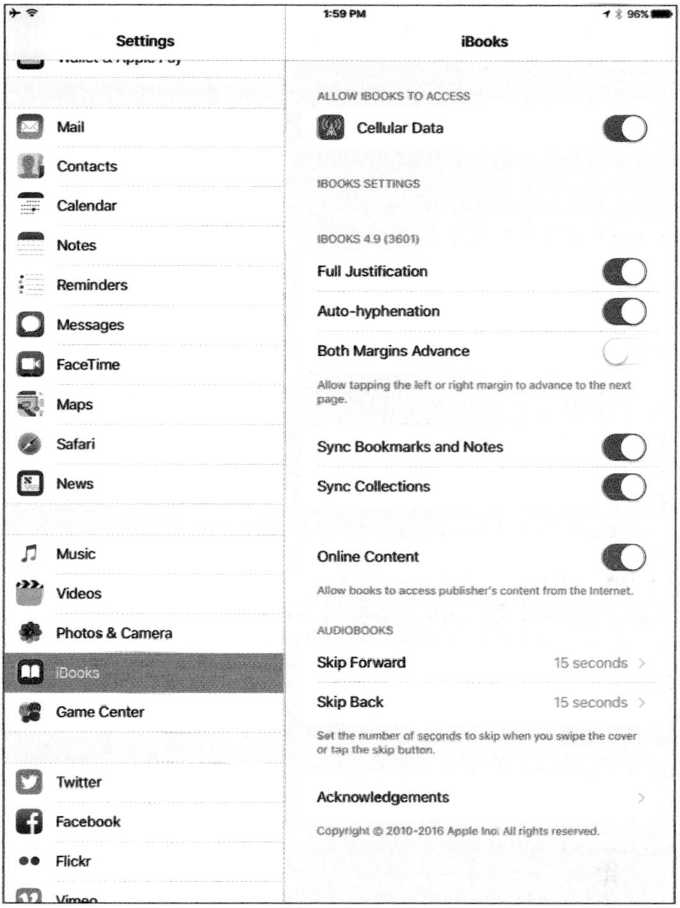

Figure 16.1
From within Settings, it's possible to customize a handful of options related to the iBooks app.

TIP At any time, an eBook's content can be updated by the book's author or publisher. By turning on the Online Content option that's part of the iBooks menu in Settings, your iPhone or iPad can update eBooks you've already acquired when and if new content related to a previously purchased book becomes available. To do this, from the iBooks app, tap the Purchased icon, and then tap the Updates option. Tap the Update button associated with each book that's listed to download that free update.

iBooks enables you to store and manage a vast library of eBooks on your iOS device, the size of which is limited only by the storage capacity of the device itself. Plus, all your iBook Store purchases automatically are saved to your iCloud account. Thus, from your iCloud account, you can easily redownload eBook titles you've previously purchased when you want to access a particular eBook that is not currently stored on your device.

ORGANIZING YOUR PERSONAL eBOOK LIBRARY

When you launch iBooks, the main My Books Library screen is displayed (shown in Figure 16.2 on an iPad). If it's not displayed, tap the My Books command icon at the bottom of the screen. Thumbnails of the book covers in your digital eBook library are displayed. Tap the menu near the top center of the screen to determine which eBook titles are displayed. The current option is the label for the pull-down menu, so it might say All Books or Books, for example.

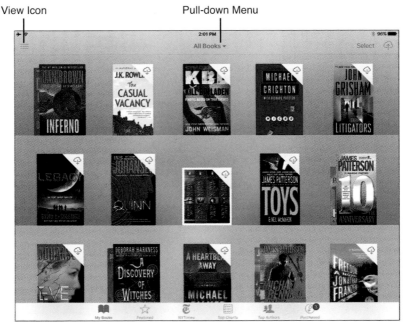

Figure 16.2

Tap the My Books command icon at the bottom of the iBooks screen to see your virtual bookshelf, which displays your eBook titles.

> ☐📝 **NOTE** When you have not yet opened a newly acquired eBook in iBooks,
> a blue-and-white New banner appears on its cover thumbnail on the Library
> screen. If you've only downloaded the free sample for a book, a red-and-white
> Sample banner is displayed as part of the eBook's cover thumbnail.

Select the All Books option to display all eBooks you've acquired, including titles
stored in your iCloud account but not currently stored on your actual iPhone or
iPad. These titles display an iCloud icon in the top-right corner of their thumbnail
(refer to Figure 16.2).

Audiobooks stored in your iPhone or iPad are displayed on the virtual bookshelf
with a headphone icon near the bottom-left corner of the audiobook's thumbnail
image.

To hide the eBooks stored in your iCloud account and display only eBooks currently stored on your iPhone or iPad, turn on the Hide iCloud Books virtual switch
near the bottom of the Collections window, which appears when you tap the All
Books option (see Figure 16.3).

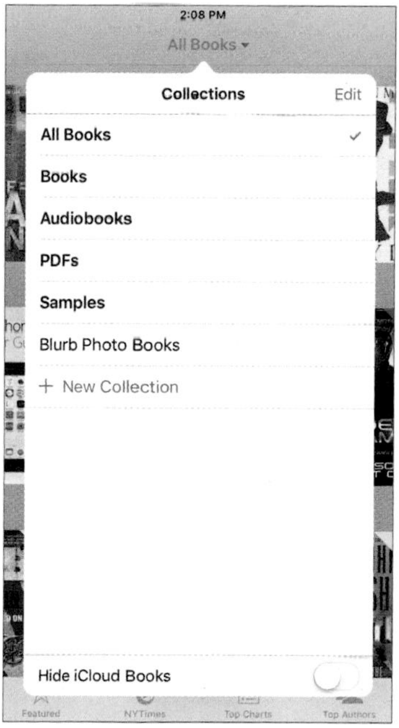

Figure 16.3
*From the Collections menu, create new Collection folders, each of which can have a custom title,
like Summer Reading or Blurb Photos Books.*

> **✓ TIP** To change how the eBooks and audiobooks are displayed on the screen, tap the View icon (located in the top-left corner of the screen). This allows you to toggle between the virtual bookshelf view and a listing view. The listing view displays each book's title and author, along with a tiny thumbnail of the cover artwork. When viewing the list view, tap the Most Recent, Titles, Authors, or Categories tab at the top of the screen to quickly re-sort your titles.

From the Collections menu, you can manually sort your eBook library into separate Collections, each of which can have a custom name. To do this, tap the Edit option to the right of the Collections heading, or tap the + New Collection option that's listed as part of the Collections menu (see Figure 15.3).

After you've created additional Collections, you can easily move eBooks into a specific Collection to organize them. To do this, return to the main Library screen and tap the Select option. Next, tap one or more eBook thumbnails that you want to transfer from the default All Books Collection into a specific Collection. As each eBook title is selected, a blue-and-white check mark icon appears in the lower-right corner of its thumbnail.

Tap the Move icon, and when the Collections menu appears, tap the name of the Collection you want to move the selected eBooks into.

> **✓ TIP** In addition to eBooks that have been formatted to be read using the iBooks app, this same app can also be used to view PDF files. When PDF files are transferred into the iBooks app, they automatically are placed in a separate Collection, called PDFs.

To delete eBooks stored on your iPhone or iPad (but keep them in your iCloud account), from the Library screen, tap the Select option, tap the eBook(s) you want to delete, and then tap the Delete option near the top-left corner of the Library screen.

> **✓ TIP** A cellular or Wi-Fi Internet connection is needed to load eBooks into the iBooks app from iBook Store. However, after an eBook is loaded into the app, you no longer need an Internet connection.

NAVIGATING THE iBOOKS APP

Displayed along the bottom of the Library screen in the iBooks app running on an iPhone are five command icons (shown in Figure 16.4). Here's how to use several of these options to find the eBook(s) you're looking for from Apple's online iBook Store:

- **My Books**—Tap this icon to access the Library screen and view your personal eBook collection. Place your finger near the center of the screen and swipe down to make a Search field appear at the top of the screen. Use this tool to find any eBook or audiobook by typing a keyword, title, search phrase, or author's name.

- **Featured**—Access iBook Store and browse through books that Apple considers to be "featured" titles (refer to Figure 16.4). An Internet connection is required.

Figure 16.4

These five command icons are displayed at the bottom of the screen when using an iPhone.

> **☑ TIP** After tapping the Featured button, scroll to the bottom of the screen to access the Apple ID *[your username]* button, the Redeem button, and the Send Gift button. Tap the Apple ID button to manage your Apple ID account. Tap the Redeem button to redeem iTunes gift cards and add credit to your Apple ID account. Tap Send Gift to send someone you know an eBook as a gift. You must know the recipient's email address to do this.

- **Top Charts**—Tap this option to display the charts listing the bestselling eBooks in iBook Store (and also seek out audiobooks). Near the top of the screen, Books, Audiobooks, and Top Authors tabs are displayed. Tap the Books tab to discover multiple charts, including a chart for Paid eBooks and Free eBooks. Tap the Audiobooks tab to search for audiobooks. Tap the Top Authors tab to view an alphabetical listing of popular authors who have books available from iBook Store.

- **Search**—Tap the Search option to reveal a Search field, within which you can type any book title, author name, keyword, or search phrase that helps you locate a specific book. Tap any listing to view the description for that book.

- **Purchased**—Tap this option to quickly find and reload any eBook or audio-books you've previously purchased.

> ☑️ **TIP** When viewing the Purchased screen, tap the Updates, Books, or Audiobooks option to locate purchased books by type. Tap Updates to see if any of your books have free updates available. When applicable, tap the Update but-ton for a book to download the new edition.
>
> After tapping the Books or Audiobooks option, tap the All or Not on This iPhone/ iPad tab to determine what content is displayed. The All option displays all books (or audiobooks) whether each title is stored in your mobile device or in your iCloud account. The Not on This iPhone/iPad option displays only titles stored in your iCloud account, that are not currently stored in your mobile device.

When using the iBooks app on an iPad, displayed along the bottom of the screen are six command icons (shown in Figure 16.5). The NYTimes icon enables you to browse the bestseller list from *The New York Times*. When you tap the Top Authors icon, you can search for eBooks and audiobooks from specific authors.

This same content is available on the iPhone. To access NYTimes charts, tap the Top Charts option, and then scroll down to the *New York Times* headings. Then tap the See All option to view the entire *New York Times Bestsellers List* for a specific cat-egory, such as Fiction or Non-Fiction.

To find a book based on its author, while using an iPhone, tap the Search option, and in the Search field, enter the author's name.

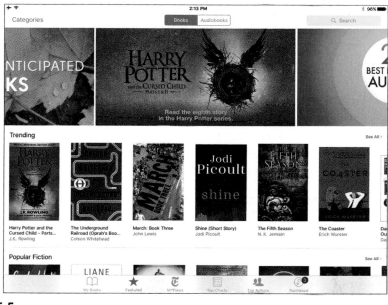

Figure 16.5

*As you'd expect, the Featured screen when viewed on the iPad reveals a lot more information
than what you see when viewing the same screen on an iPhone.*

> ☑ **TIP** When accessing the Featured, Top Charts, or Top Authors section
> of the iBook Store on an iPad, the Search field is in the top-right corner. On the
> iPhone, tap the Search command icon at the bottom of the screen to access the
> Search field.
>
> Use Search any time you know the title of a specific book you're looking for. In this
> field, you can also search for eBooks based on an author's name, keyword, genre,
> or any search phrase. Tap any listing to display that book's description. If you
> already know what you're looking for, using the Search field is typically the fastest
> way to find it.

The My Books, Features, Top Charts, Top Authors, and Purchased command icons
at the bottom of the iPad screen serve the same purpose as they do when you're
using the iPhone version of iBooks.

> ☑ **TIP** The Top Charts list can be customized to show titles from a spe-
> cific category or genre. To choose a specialized Top Chart listing, first tap the
> Categories option and select a specific category.

> **NOTE** It is possible to download and read eBooks acquired from sources other than iBook Store using iBooks; however, the eBooks must be a compatible file format. The iBooks app works with PDF files (or eBooks in PDF format), as well as eBooks created in the industry-standard ePub format.

LEARNING MORE ABOUT SPECIFIC eBOOKS WHILE VISITING iBOOK STORE

As you add books to your eBook library, the cover art for each title is displayed on the Library screen. Tap the My Books icon near the bottom of this screen to view the Library screen.

To see an alternative listing view of the Library screen, tap the Listing icon. Figure 16.6 shows this Listing view. To return to the default Thumbnail view, tap the icon showing six squares that's in the top-left corner of the screen.

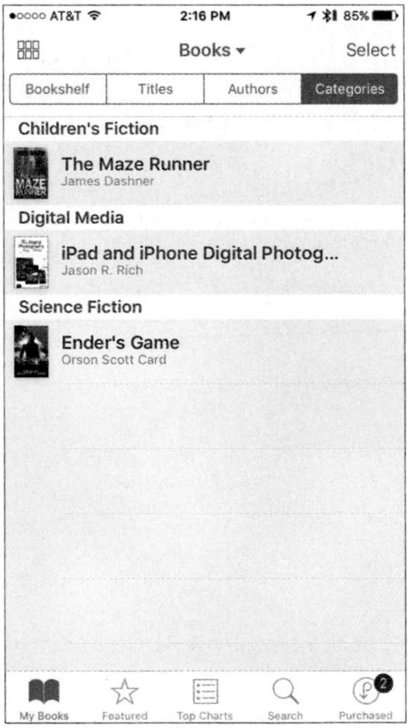

Figure 16.6
The Listing view is shown here.

FINDING A SPECIFIC eBOOK—FAST

Use the Search field to enter the eBook title, author's name, subject, or keyword that's associated with what you're looking for. Entering a specific book title reveals very specific search results. However, entering a keyword relating to a topic or subject matter reveals a selection of eBook suggestions that somehow relate to that keyword.

Tap any listing to reveal a more detailed description relating to a particular eBook. As you review a description for an eBook, look carefully at its ratings and its written reviews, especially if it's a paid eBook.

LEARNING ABOUT AN eBOOK FROM ITS DESCRIPTION

A typical eBook or audiobook listing includes the book's cover artwork, its title, and the author. An eBook or audiobook's description, however, is divided into several sections. Tap the Details, Reviews, and Related tabs to view all information pertaining to a specific book.

> **NOTE** Using iBook Store to shop for eBooks is similar to using the App Store to acquire apps or using the iTunes Store to acquire TV shows, music, or movies. Each title has a detailed description screen, ratings and reviews, and a sample of the book, which you can download for free into the iBooks app.
>
> Figure 16.7 shows a typical eBook description screen. The title, book cover, and price are displayed near the top, and the Details, Reviews, and Related tabs are displayed below this information.

A Share icon appears at the upper-right corner of an eBook description. Tap it to share details about the eBook description with others. In the Share menu, there is also a Gift button. Tap this to purchase and send the eBook as a gift for someone else. To do this, you need to know her email address

> **TIP** You can preview an eBook or audiobook before paying for it. As you're looking at a book's description, tap the Sample button to download a free sample of that book. The length of the sample varies and is determined by the book's publisher. It is usually between a few pages and a full chapter.

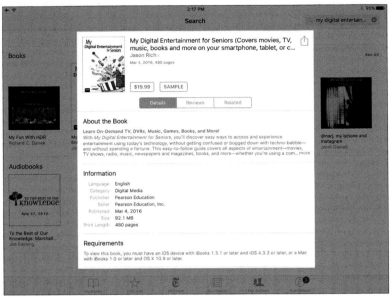

Figure 16.7

Read a detailed description of an eBook before making your purchase and downloading it. The book's Price button and Sample button are also displayed near the top of the description.

Tap the Reviews option to access the iBook Store Ratings chart, which showcases the book's average star-based rating and how many ratings the book has received. You can also see this average star-based rating broken down by how many stars (from one to five) the book has received from your fellow iBook Store customers. Below the star-based ratings are more detailed, text-based reviews written by other iBook Store customers.

PURCHASING AN eBOOK OR AUDIOBOOK

To quickly purchase and download an eBook or audiobook, tap the Price button. When you tap a price button, it changes to a Buy Book button. Tap this button to confirm your purchase decision. You then need to enter your Apple ID password to begin the download process. If your iOS mobile device is equipped with a Touch ID sensor, you can approve your acquisition using a fingerprint by placing your finger on the Touch ID sensor.

If you're downloading a free eBook, the button label is Free rather than Price. Tap Free and then tap the Get Book button.

It typically takes about 30 seconds to download a full-length eBook to your iPhone or iPad, depending on the speed of your Internet connection and the size of the eBook's digital file. (Downloading an audiobook takes a bit longer, due to its larger file size.) As soon as the content is downloaded and ready to read or listen to, the book's front cover artwork is displayed as part of the Library screen in the iBooks app.

CUSTOMIZING YOUR eBOOK READING EXPERIENCE

To begin reading an eBook that's stored in your iPhone or iPad, from the Library screen, tap a book cover thumbnail to open the eBook.

While reading eBooks, you can hold the iPhone or iPad in portrait or landscape mode. Then, as you're reading, tap anywhere on the screen to make the various command icons and buttons appear (see Figure 16.8).

Figure 16.8

A sample eBook page (on an iPad) with the iBooks command icons displayed.

> **✓ TIP** Tap the Library button to automatically bookmark your location in an eBook and return to iBooks' Library (My Books) screen.

Tap the Table of Contents icon to display an interactive table of contents for the eBook you're reading. Then tap any chapter number or chapter title to immediately jump to that location in the book. Or, near the top center of the Table of Contents screen, tap the Bookmarks option to see a list of manually saved bookmarks you have previously set as you were reading that eBook. Tap the Notes tab to review the notes you've manually added to pages as you were reading.

> **✓ TIP** Whenever you tap the Library option while reading an eBook, or press the Home button to return to the device's Home screen, your current location in the book is automatically bookmarked and saved.
>
> At any time, however, you have the option to manually add a virtual bookmark to as many pages in the eBook as you want. Then, by tapping the Table of Contents icon, and then the Bookmarks tab, you can see a complete list of manually placed virtual bookmarks in the eBook, and return to any of those pages quickly.

To exit the Table of Contents screen and return to reading your eBook, tap the Resume option.

Three command icons appear to the right of the eBook title. Tap the AA icon to reveal a pop-up window (see Figure 16.9). It offers a screen brightness slider and a small and large A button, which are used to instantly decrease or increase the font size in the book you're reading.

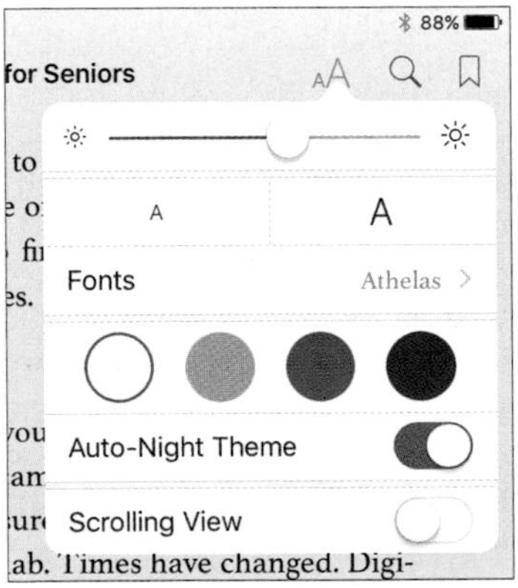

Figure 16.9

Customize the look of each page by choosing a font, font size, and theme, for example.

Tap the Fonts button to change the text font, or tap one of the Themes buttons
to change the theme used to display the text (and the background color) for the
eBook you're reading. Choose the theme that is best suited for the lighting available and is also visually pleasing to you.

> **TIP** If you turn on the virtual switch associated with Auto-Night Theme,
> your iPhone or iPad measures the ambient light in the area where you're reading,
> and then automatically turns on the Night theme if you're reading in a dark or
> dimly lit area.

Tap the Search icon (which is shaped like a magnifying glass) to display a Search
field. Use this feature to locate any keyword or search phrase that appears in the
eBook you're currently reading.

As you're reading, turn the page by swiping your finger from right to left (horizontally) across the screen to move one page forward, or swiping your finger from left
to right to back up one page at a time.

> **TIP** The normal book viewing mode shows each page of the book you're
> reading, as well as icons on the top of the page, and page number information on
> the bottom. The Scrolling View mode, which has a virtual switch to turn it on or off,
> enables you to scroll up or down continuously in an eBook, as opposed to turning
> pages.

> **TIP** To turn the page, you can also tap the right side of the screen to
> advance or the left side of the screen to go back. However, if you have the Both
> Margins Advance option activated (which you can do in Settings), tapping either
> margin advances to the next page.

Displayed at the bottom of the screen is the page number in the eBook you're
currently reading, as well as the total number of pages in the eBook. The number
of pages remaining in the current chapter is displayed to the right of the page
number.

🔍 MORE INFO   As you're reading an eBook, hold your finger on a single word to see a selection of available reading tools: Copy, Define, Highlight, Note, Search, and Share.

Use your finger to move the blue dots on either side of the word to expand the selected text to a phrase, sentence, paragraph, or entire page, for example.

Tap the Define tab to look up the definition of a selected word. (Internet access is required to use this feature.)

Tap the Highlight tab to highlight the selected text. You can choose the color of your highlights, or you can underline the selected text by tapping the yellow circle icon that's above the word. Tap the white circle (with a red line through it) to remove highlights, or tap the Note icon to create a new note.

When you tap the Highlight option, you're given the option to choose a highlight color (shown in Figure 16.10). The last highlight color you selected determines the color of the sticky note that appears when you tap the Note option. This enables you to easily color-code your highlights and/or notes.

If you tap the Note tab on an iPad, a virtual sticky note appears on your device's screen, along with the virtual keyboard. Type notes to yourself about what you're reading. When you're finished typing, tap anywhere on the screen outside the sticky note box.

When you're using an iPhone and you tap the Note tab, the sentence related to the selected word is displayed. Below it, you can type text using the virtual keyboard. Tap Done to save the note.

On both the iPhone and iPad, a sticky note icon appears in the margin of the eBook. You can later tap this icon to read your notes or annotations.

Tap the Search tab to enter any word or phrase and find it in the eBook. A search window appears below the Search field. References to each occurrence of your keyword or search phrase are displayed by chapter and page number. Tap a reference to jump to that point in the book.

Sticky Note Icon
(Tap to Open Note)

Note Being Composed

Highlighted Text

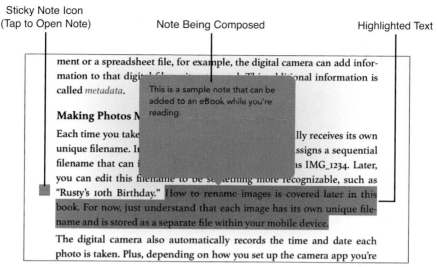

ment or a spreadsheet file, for example, the digital camera can add information to that digital file. This additional information is
called *metadata*.

This is a sample note that can be added to an eBook while you're reading.

Making Photos M

Each time you take ... lly receives its own
unique filename. I ... ssigns a sequential
filename that can i ... as IMG_1234. Later,
you can edit this filename to be something more recognizable, such as
"Rusty's 10th Birthday." How to rename images is covered later in this
book. For now, just understand that each image has its own unique filename and is stored as a separate file within your mobile device.

The digital camera also automatically records the time and date each
photo is taken. Plus, depending on how you set up the camera app you're

Figure 16.10

*It's possible to highlight text as you're reading and/or add a virtual sticky note to the margin of a
page that contains your typed notes.*

ALTERNATIVE METHODS FOR READING eBOOKS

Although Apple has worked out distribution deals with many major publishers
and authors, the iBook Store does not offer an eBook edition of every book in
publication.

> **☑ TIP** In some cases, eBook titles are available from Amazon.com or Barnes
> & Noble (BN.com) but not from iBook Store. Or if Amazon.com, BN.com, and iBook
> Store offer the same eBook title, the price for that eBook might be lower from one
> of these other online-based booksellers.
>
> So, if you're a price-conscious reader, it pays to shop around for the lowest eBook
> prices. Just because you're using an iPhone or iPad does not mean you must shop
> for eBooks exclusively from iBook Store.

Perhaps you previously owned a Kindle or Nook eBook reader before purchasing
your iPhone or iPad and have already acquired a personal library of eBooks formatted for that device. If you want to access your Kindle or Nook library from your
iPhone or iPad, download the free Kindle or Nook Reading apps from the
App Store.

These apps prompt you for your Amazon or Barnes & Noble account information to sync your purchased content to the app. To purchase new Kindle- or Nook-formatted eBook titles, you must visit Amazon.com or BN.com using Safari or your primary computer. After you make your purchase, your eBooks can be automatically synced to the Kindle or Nook app on your device.

> ## Note If you enjoy audiobooks, Audible.com (which is owned by Amazon) offers the largest selection of audiobook content in the world. Download the free Audible app to listen to audiobooks acquired from Audible.com. Visit www.audible.com to set up an account and then purchase or acquire audiobooks from this service, which is a viable alternative to shopping for audiobooks from iBook Store.

EXPLORING THE REDESIGNED NEWS APP

The News app that comes preinstalled with iOS 10 is a powerful yet easy-to-use information gathering tool.

Apple has teamed up with some of the world's leading newspapers, magazines, and news organizations, as well as bloggers, website operators, online publications, and content providers, to offer a single app that gathers articles together and formats this content into a highly personalized, nicely formatted digital publication that provides only articles, information, and news that covers exactly the topics you're interested in.

Best of all, this personalized digital news feed is updated and available 24/7, and it is completely free. The app takes a few minutes to initially set up, but after this process is completed, the News app gathers content on your behalf from potentially a wide range of sources and presents it to you on your iPhone's or iPad's screen.

> ## iOS10 WHAT'S NEW In addition to free content, the iOS 10 edition of the News app enables users to subscribe to specific publications (for a fee) from within the app to access exclusive and complete content from that publisher. Subscription prices and what's included with a subscription varies by publisher.

The News app works in several ways to customize your news feed. First, you can "subscribe" to specific publications and read selected articles published by those sources for free. In some cases, you need to acquire a paid subscription from the publisher (as an in-app purchase) to view all articles or content available from that publisher.

Second, it's possible to select topics of interest to you and have the News app gather information related to those topics from many different sources. Third, you have the option to choose keywords or phrases and have the app gather articles and news stories that contain those specific search terms.

> **TIP** Daily Briefings are available from some news-oriented publications, such as *The New York Times*. These Daily Briefings are published on a daily basis, and summarize important news events of the day. Daily Briefings are updated once per day for each publication. For example, Daily Briefings associated with *The New York Times* is published daily at 6:00 a.m. (EST). It's possible to subscribe, for free, to any available Daily Briefings, from publications or news sources supporting this feature.

The News app works with iCloud, so after you set up the app once to personalize your news feed, the content the app collects syncs across all your iOS mobile devices and Macs automatically. (Your Mac must have macOS Sierra installed to utilize the News app.)

> **WHAT'S NEW** Each time you launch the News app and tap the For You icon, the date and local temperature is displayed at the top of the screen, followed by headings that allow you to access Top Stores, Trending Stories, and breaking news related to topics you've expressed interest about. Then, as you continue scrolling downward, the news topics you've expressed interest in are sorted by topic.

> **TIP** The News app requires Internet access to collect articles and content. However, you can manually select articles to be saved for offline viewing at your convenience.
>
> To save an article, tap the Save (bookmark-shaped) icon in the top-right corner of the screen as you're reading an article (shown in Figure 16.11 on an iPad). On the iPhone, the icons are displayed along the bottom of the screen.
>
> When you want to access your saved articles, launch the News app and tap the Saved icon. A listing of your saved articles is displayed. Tap an article's listing to read it, or swipe from right to left across the listing and then tap the Delete button to delete it.

Save (Bookmark) Icon

Figure 16.11

Tap the Save icon associated with specific articles you want to store on your iPhone or iPad for later review. Then tap the Saved icon to access those articles.

CUSTOMIZING THE NEWS APP

Launch the News app from the Home screen, and then invest a few minutes customizing the app. From the Welcome to News screen, tap the Get Started option.

From the Pick Your Favorites screen, scroll through the displayed list of news organizations, newspapers, magazines, websites, and content providers and choose those you're interested in by tapping their respective thumbnails. Choose at least one of the displayed options, which include CNN, ESPN, *The New York Times*, and *The Wall Street Journal*.

Tap the Continue option. Based on your initial selections, the For You screen is formatted with content of interest to you. However, using the Favorites, Explore, and Search tools built in to the app, it's possible to further customize the content you are presented with on an ongoing basis.

(iOS 10) WHAT'S NEW Get alerted of breaking news stories by adjusting the Notifications options related to the News app. One way to do this is from within the News app, tap the Favorites icon, and then tap the bell-shaped Notifications option.

From the Notifications window (see Figure 16.12), turn on the virtual switches associated with specific channels (publishers) the app is following on your behalf. To be alerted of important (general) news, turn on the virtual switches associated with News Editors' Picks and/or News Top Stories.

To determine how these notifications will be presented to you, launch Settings, tap the Notifications option, and then tap the News option. Turn on the virtual switch associated with Allow Notifications, and then determine the form those notifications will take (such as audible alerts, and/or onscreen Banners or Alerts).

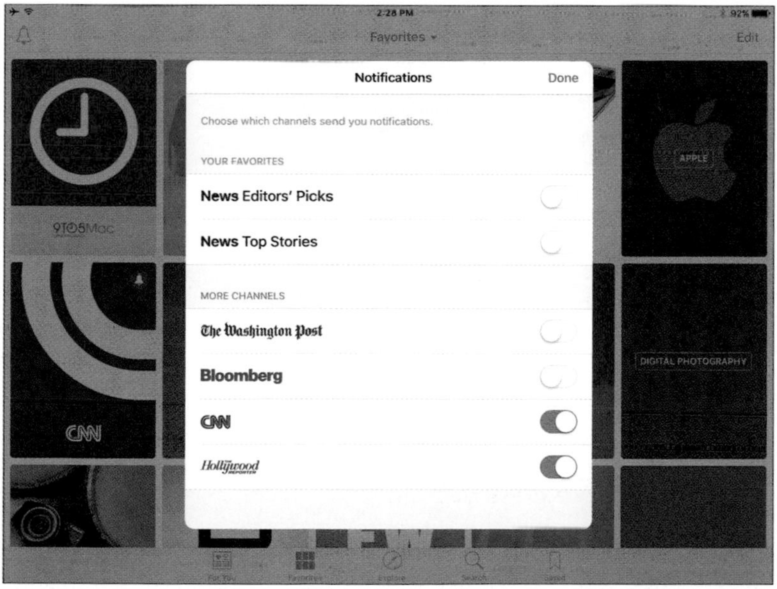

Figure 16.12

Receive an audible alert and notification on your iPhone or iPad when breaking news articles are published.

NAVIGATING AROUND THE NEWS APP

Along the bottom of the News app screen on both the iPhone and iPad are five command icons (shown in Figure 16.13). Here's a summary of what each tool is used for:

■ **For You**—Tap this icon to read your personalized digital publication (news feed) that's continuously updated with content of direct interest to you. Articles are collected in real time from a wide range of online-based sources and content providers.

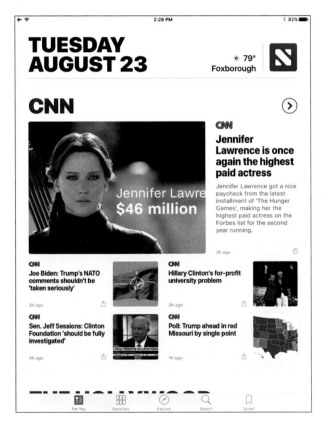

Figure 16.13

Use these command icons to navigate around the News app.

■ **Favorites**—View and edit the collection of sources and content providers that you selected for the News app to follow on your behalf.

■ **Explore**—Based on specific topics and content categories, discover new sources and content providers that you're interested in having the News app follow for you. New sources and content providers are continuously being added, as are specific topics available in each main content category. Tap the + icon for a source listing to add it to your For You feed.

- **Search**—In the Search field, enter a topic, subject matter, keyword, name, company name, industry, hobby, area of interest, or anything else you want the News app to gather articles about on your behalf.

- **Saved**—As you read specific articles in the For You news feed, if there's an article you want to save for later reference, tap the bookmark-shaped Save icon associated with it to save that article for offline viewing.

NOTE Using your iPhone's or iPad's Internet connection, the News app gathers content on a continuous basis and displays only the most current information. As newer content becomes available, older content disappears from your news feed, unless you manually save specific articles.

TIP To further customize the News app, launch Settings, tap the News option, and then manually adjust options related to Location, Notifications, and the app's capability to refresh content in the background. Here you also determine whether the app uses a cellular data connection (when available) to access the Internet (as opposed to using a Wi-Fi Internet connection). Turn on the Show Story Previews option so you can preview an article from the For You newsfeed before taking the time to open it.

WHAT'S NEW From the Home screen, if your iPhone has 3D Touch capabilities, press and hold your finger on the News app's icon to quickly see a breaking news headline or quickly launch the News app and open the For You newsfeed.

READING ARTICLES THAT CATER TO YOUR INTERESTS

After setting up the News app, launch it whenever you have time to browse or read the collected articles in your news feed. To do this, tap the For You icon. All the articles collected for you by the app are displayed on a single screen, using a digital newspaper-style format.

Each article listing in your feed includes a headline, cover photo (when applicable), the first sentence or two from each article, the source of each article, and when it was published (shown in Figure 16.14).

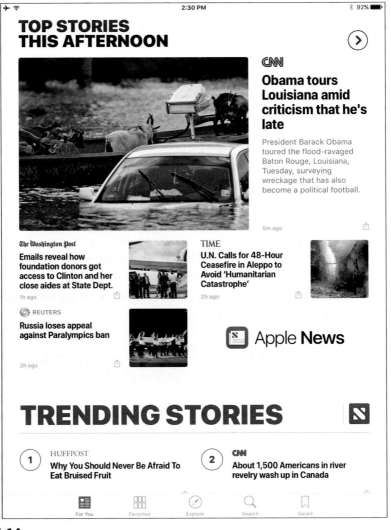

Figure 16.14

Your news feed (shown here on the iPad) is populated with article listings that the News app collects for you. Tap any article listing to read it.

To read an article in its entirety, simply tap its preview listing. Otherwise, keep scrolling down to view all the articles in your current news feed. Keep in mind, your

news feed gets updated continuously as new content is published. The articles
toward the top of your news feed are the most current.

> ☑ **TIP** To view, add to, or modify your collection of Favorite topics and con-
> tent sources, tap the Favorites icon. If you want to delete a source (so the News
> app stops following it for you), tap the Edit option, and then tap the X displayed in
> the thumbnail for the source you want to remove.

EXPANDING YOUR COLLECTION OF SOURCES AND CONTENT PROVIDERS

At any time, to discover new sources and content providers that the News app can
follow on your behalf or to add new topics of interest, tap the Explore icon and
then scroll through the list of publications and content providers that are sorted
by topic, such as News, Politics, Arts & Entertainment, Sports, Business, Science &
Technology, Food, Fashion & Design, Travel, and Health and Living. When you tap
one of these categories, dozens—and in some cases hundreds—of sources and
content providers are listed that you can choose from.

When you come across one or more sources that you want the News app to begin
following, tap the + icon associated with its listing.

> ☑ **TIP** To find articles, content, or news stories based on a specific keyword
> or phrase, tap the Search icon and in the Search field type the word or phrase that
> relates to what you're looking for.
>
> From the listing of search results, tap the Add (+) icons associated with the ones
> of interest. Search results are sorted into sections labeled Top Hit, Topics, and
> Channels.
>
> After selecting any of the search results for the News app to follow, tap the Done
> option. Now, when you tap the For You icon, your news feed is updated with con-
> tent from the added sources.

By using the tools offered by the News app and investing a few minutes per day
to read the articles and content it collects, you can easily stay informed on general
news, company or industry-related news, or any topics whatsoever you're interested in.

> **Note** A *topic* is content about a specific topic or subject matter that you're interest in, regardless of the publisher. A *channel* is content offered by a specific publisher or content producer, such as *The New York Times*, CNN, or 9to5Mac, for example.

The News app focuses only on topics you deem relevant to your personal or professional life and presents the information in a format that makes it efficient to go through quickly, using one centralized app that's available when and where you need it.

> **TIP** When you're reading an article in the News app, tap the Share icon associated with the article to share that article with others, or add it to your Safari Reading List for offline viewing later.

SUBSCRIBING TO DIGITAL EDITIONS OF NEWSPAPERS AND MAGAZINES

Instead of using the News app to read select content from newspaper and magazine publishers, you can acquire the proprietary app for that publication (from the App Store). Then you can purchase complete single issues or a subscription to that publication to download and read all content from the digital edition of the publication.

When visiting the App Store, in the Search field, enter the name of any newspaper, magazine, or digital publication to find, download, and install the proprietary app available for it.

Figure 16.15 shows the app listing for *The Times of London* newspaper. After downloading and installing the free app, from within that app, use in-app purchases to acquire individual issues or a paid subscription.

> **TIP** The Texture app allows you to pay a flat monthly fee for unlimited access to current and past digital issues of more than 150 popular, consumer-oriented, and special interest magazines.

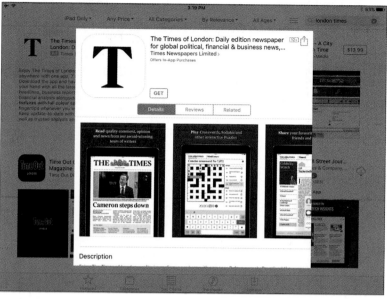

Figure 16.15

Download the proprietary app for your favorite newspaper or magazine, and then load that publication's content from the app to read each issue.

17

USE THE HOME APP TO REMOTELY CONTROL YOUR HOME

As the evolution of Apple's iOS operating system continues, over the years iPhone and iPad users have seen preinstalled apps come and go. The newest app to be added to iOS 10's collection of preinstalled apps is called Home.

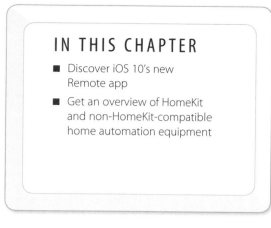 **WHAT'S NEW** This Home app is designed to help iPhone and iPad users manage compatible home automation equipment that's been installed in their home.

The ability to manage and control specialized equipment—referred to as *smart devices*—within the home (using a iPhone or iPad) has been around for several years. Some of the more readily available types of home automation

equipment that is currently available from a growing selection of third-party companies includes

- Ceiling fans and air conditioners
- Digital video recorders (such as a TiVo Bolt) and cable boxes that connect to an HD television set
- Door locks, deadbolts, and video doorbells
- Home security cameras, door and window sensors, and alarms
- In-home baby and pet monitors
- LED light bulbs and lighting fixtures (shown in Figure 17.1)

Figure 17.1

The Philips Hue lighting system (www.meethue.com) utilizes color-selectable LED light bulbs and has its own proprietary app, but it is also HomeKit compatible.

- Remote controlled window shades/blinds
- Remote garage door openers
- Smart electrical outlets
- Smoke alarms and carbon monoxide detectors
- Thermostats

> **NOTE** A selection of "smart appliances" for the kitchen and laundry room, as well as hot water heaters, are also compatible with the iPhone and iPad. They're available from an ever-expanding lineup of well-known major appliance manufacturers.

Each of these smart devices requires a propriety app to be installed on an iPhone or iPad to control the equipment wirelessly (remotely) via the mobile device.

> **TIP** Smart appliances enable you to remotely to turn on or off an appliance or light, unlock your front door for a guest, or see and hear what's happening in any room of your home while sitting on your couch or while you're anywhere in the world. They also enable you to preprogram schedules or routines, so the lights or the temperature in your home can be automatically adjusted on a preset schedule or when you leave your home.

In-home Wi-Fi, and in some cases the use of the iOS mobile device's Bluetooth capabilities and/or a cellular Internet connection, are also required. As a result, smart devices can be controlled from your iPhone or iPad while you're at home or from anywhere in the world, as long as the mobile device has Internet access.

> **TIP** Thanks to increased competition and improved technology, the cost to incorporate home automation equipment into your home is dropping quickly, and you can install most of the equipment yourself, even if you have little or no technical expertise.
>
> Some of this equipment, like LED lighting or a smart thermostat, will also save you money over time on your utility bills. Plus, depending on the type of equipment you use, financial incentives or rebates from local public utility companies may be offered when you install a smart appliance or thermostat in your home.
>
> Meanwhile, by installing smart home security equipment where you live, your homeowners/renters insurance may offer ongoing discounts or other financial incentives related to your annual premium.

"HOMEKIT" COMPATIBILITY

In recent years, Apple introduced a series of app development tools, called HomeKit, that enable companies that create products for the home to fully utilize the technologies that are built in to the iPhone and iPad. The Home app enables iOS mobile device users to remotely control and manage HomeKit-compatible equipment from a single app, plus take advantage of Siri to use verbal commands to control the compatible equipment.

There are hundreds of products designed for use within the home that can be controlled using an iPhone or iPad, but not all of them utilize HomeKit or are compatible with the Home app. For those products, you need a proprietary app to control or manage that equipment from your smartphone or tablet.

> ⌕ **MORE INFO**   For a frequently updated list of HomeKit-compatible equipment that works with the Home app running on an iPhone or iPad, visit https://support.apple.com/en-us/HT204903.

> 🗒 **NOTE**   Home automation equipment, some of which is compatible with HomeKit and the Home app, is available from hardware store chains like Home Depot (www.homedepot.com/b/Electrical-Smart-Home/N-5yc1vZc1jw) and Lowe's (www.lowes.com/l/smart-home.html); consumer electronics stores, including Best Buy (www.bestbuy.com); as well as online (from Amazon.com, and the individual equipment manufacturers).

> 🗒 **TIP**   Some home automation equipment states "Works with iPhone and iPad" on its packaging. In this case, you need a proprietary app to manage or control that equipment from your mobile device.
>
> Only equipment that clearly states that it's HomeKit-compatible will work with the Home app. Look for the "Works with Apple HomeKit" label (shown in Figure 17.2) on the product packaging. Visit www.apple.com/ios/homekit for more information.

Figure 17.2
Look for this Works with Apple HomeKit logo to discover home automation equipment that's compatible with the Home app.

GETTING ACQUAINTED WITH THE HOME APP

The new Home app is useful only if you have HomeKit-compatible home automation equipment installed in your home. Once compatible equipment is set up and working with the proprietary app that was designed for use with that equipment, the Home app automatically works with that smart equipment as well.

You don't have to do any additional setup for the equipment to also work with Siri, which means you can issue voice commands to your iPhone, iPad, or Apple Watch to control that equipment. For example, if you have the Philips Hue lighting system installed, it's possible to activate Siri and say, "Turn on living room lights," "Dim dining room lights," or "Turn hallway lights blue," for example.

> **iOS 10 WHAT'S NEW** The Home app enables you to organize your smart devices on the iPhone's or iPad's screen, making your most frequently used equipment the most readily accessible from the Favorites section of the app. Plus, the equipment you designate as your Top Favorites automatically becomes accessible from Control Center as well.

The first time you launch the app, the Welcome Home screen appears (shown in Figure 17.3 on an IPhone). Tap the Get Started button to begin using the app.

Figure 17.3

The Welcome Home screen of the Home app.

Next, allow the Home app to access your location by tapping the Allow button. From the **My Home** screen, if the app has not already located the smart equipment you have installed in your home, tap the Add Accessory button and follow the onscreen prompts.

Assuming you already have HomeKit-compatible smart equipment set up and working in your home, the Home app automatically loads pertinent information about that equipment into the app.

 NOTE   Each piece of HomeKit-compatible equipment that works with the Home app is referred to as an "accessory."

From the Favorite Accessories screen, select your Favorite Accessories. In this example, the Phillips Hue lighting system has been set up, and Hue light bulbs have been placed in existing lighting fixtures throughout the home. The Home app sorts these iPhone/iPad controllable lights by room.

After choosing your Favorite accessories (which should be the ones you use the most often), tap Next. Because the Philips Hue lighting system enables users to create colorful lighting scenes, the next screen allows users of the Home app to select their favorite scenes for each room. If you're using other types of HomeKit equipment, the initial setup screens will offer different options.

The main screen of the Home app (shown in Figure 17.4) is a centralized control center for all of your HomeKit-compatible equipment.

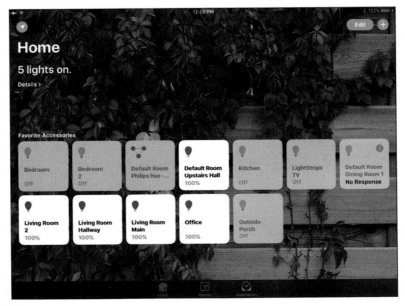

Figure 17.4

Control all of your smart devices from the Home screen in the Home app.

Along the bottom of the screen are three command icons, labeled Home (refer to Figure 17.4), Rooms, and Automation.

> **✓ TIP** To edit what options are displayed on the main Home app's screen, tap the Edit button. To add accessories to work with the app, tap the Add (+) icon.

Tap the Rooms command icon to control HomeKit-compatible equipment on a room-by-room basis. Tap the Edit option to customize this screen, or tap the Add (+) icon to add more HomeKit accessories to each room.

Based on your current location or a time of day, you can "program" each piece of HomeKit-compatible equipment to perform a specific task. For example, when you leave home, lights can automatically be turned off and the thermostat can readjust the temperature. Or at a specific time, lights can come on and the temperature can readjust.

> **(iOS 10) WHAT'S NEW** In addition to controlling HomeKit-compatible equipment from the Home app, Siri, or the proprietary app designed for each smart device, it's also possible to utilize your Apple TV (4th generation) and use it as a control center for your home. This too can be set up from the Home app.

After you've done the initial setup of the Home app so each onscreen button corresponds to a specific piece of smart equipment, or there's a preprogrammed task for that equipment, you can control any HomeKit-compatible device using the app's simple touchscreen interface.

> **✓ TIP** To customize the wallpaper in the Home app, launch the app, tap the Home command icon, and then tap the Location icon. From the menu screen, tap the Take Photo option or Choose from Existing option to select the digital image you want to display in the app (for decorative purposes only).

ALLOWING GUESTS TO CONTROL SMART EQUIPMENT IN YOUR HOME

When you have guests staying in your home who are iPhone or iPad users, you can give them temporary control over your HomeKit-compatible equipment via the

Home app. To do this, launch the Home app, tap the Home command icon, tap the Location icon (in the top-left corner of the screen), and then tap the Invite option.

In the To field, enter the email address of the person you want to give access to, and then tap the Send Invite option. The recipient will receive a notification and must accept the invitation from within their version of the Home app.

Once accepted, the guest can use the Home app on his iPhone or iPad to control the compatible smart devices in your home. When the guest leaves, you can revoke the permission. To do this, from the Home app, again tap the Home icon, tap the Location icon, and then below the People heading tap the guest's name or email address. Next, tap the Remove Person option.

> **TIP** If you have a primary home and a vacation home, the same Home app can control smart devices in both locations. To set up a second home, tap the Home command icon, tap the Location icon, and then tap the Add Home option. Follow the onscreen prompts to link the app with the smart home equipment located in the secondary home.

SOME FINAL THOUGHTS

During the past few years, the technology built in to the latest iPhone and iPad models has progressed incredibly fast and has introduced us to entirely new ways to communicate, stay informed, collect and utilize information, organize our lives, and become more productive. By combining this technology with the powerful iOS operating system, which integrates with the collection of apps that come preinstalled with all iPhone and iPad models, we can do amazing things with these iOS mobile devices as soon as they're turned on for the very first time.

Yet, when you start installing third-party apps to your smartphone and/or tablet, and simultaneously use it to access to the Internet, what's now possible can literally be life changing.

In addition to helping you automate and manage equipment in your home, the same iPhone or iPad can link with your vehicle to help you navigate, safely communicate with others, or stay entertained while you're driving, while also alerting you of maintenance or repair issues that need to be dealt with.

Plus, you now can use your iPhone or iPad to help monitor and improve your health and well-being. For example, you can sync an iOS device with specialized medical, health, and/or fitness-related equipment so you can better manage personal medical conditions, your fitness and daily activity, your diet and nutrition, and even monitor and improve your sleeping patterns.

> **✓ TIP**   The power and capabilities of your iPhone can be expanded upon even more when you use it with the Apple Watch.

Now that you understand how to use your iPhone and/or iPad, as well as the majority of the apps that come preinstalled with iOS 10, begin exploring some of the cutting-edge ways you can use this technology to improve your everyday personal and professional life. Focus on how you can best utilize third-party apps, based on your needs, lifestyle, and work habits, and discover how optional technologies can be used with your iPhone and/or iPad to greatly expand their capabilities.

Just when you think you've mastered your current iPhone and iPad running iOS 10, you can be sure that Apple will introduce new and more advanced iPhone and iPad models, as well as updated versions of the iOS, that will make today's technology soon seem antiquated. So stay tuned for more exciting iPhone- and iPad-related advancement in the months and years to come!

Index